SOCIAL WELFARE AND SOCIAL WORK

About the Author

Dr. Debotosh Sinha (*b.* 1962) did his Master's degree in Social Work specialising in Family and Child Welfare from Tata Institute of Social Sciences, Mumbai followed by M.Phil and Ph.D. degrees from Delhi School of Social Work, University of Delhi and Visva-Bharati University respectively. He also completed PGD in Personnel Management and Industrial Relations from Bharatia Vidya Bhawan, Delhi. Currently, he is serving as Associate Professor in the Department of Social Work, Visva-Bharati, Santiniketan.

He has authored two books titled *Aspects of Industry and Occupational Social Work* and *Problems and Prospects of Child Rights and Welfare in Our Society.* He has presented papers in a number of national and international seminars besides the publication of same in journals of repute with contribution of conducting several sponsored research projects.

He visited a number of countries (London, Italy, Finland, Sweden, Norway, South Africa, Scotland, China, Singapore, Hong Kong, Bangladesh, Manchester, South Korea, etc.) on several occasions for various academic programmes.

Social Welfare and Social Work

Selected Essays

Debotosh Sinha

CONCEPT PUBLISHING COMPANY PVT. LTD.
NEW DELHI-110 059

ISBN-13 : 978-81-8069-814-9

First Published 2012

Published and Printed by

Concept
Since 1974

Concept Publishing Company Pvt. Ltd.
A/15-16, Commercial Block, Mohan Garden
New Delhi-110059 (India)
T: 25351460, 25351794, *F*: 091-11-25357109
E: publishing@conceptpub.com, W: www.conceptpub.com
Editorial Office: H-13, Bali Nagar, New Delhi-110 015, India.

Cataloging in Publication Data--*Courtesy:* D.K. Agencies (P) Ltd. <docinfo@dkagencies.com>

Sinha, Debotosh.
Social welfare and social work : selected essays / Debotosh Sinha.
p. cm.
Includes bibliographical references and index.
ISBN 9788180698149

1. Social service. 2. Social service—India. 3. Women—Services for. 4.Women—Services for—India. 5. Children—Services for. 6. Children—Services for—India. I. Title.

DDC 361.32 23

Dedicated to

My Revered Parents, Beloved Wife and Son

Preface

The purpose of this book is to stimulate a constructive and creative discussion among students, faculty, and practitioners about the future of various emerging social issues. One requisite for such a discussion is a multifaceted analysis of national and global changes currently underway, and the mission and roles of social work in this changing context. Another is a candid consideration of a different possible future. Considering these assumptions, the author has been encouraged to be proactive and raise alternative possibilities. At the same time, he has made an attempt to keep it in mind that what may seem ludicrous and improbable today may soon come to be everyday part of our lives in this unpredictable world. In the light of the above, all the essays are original and lucidly explained.

The book has five parts i.e. from PART-A to PART-E and includes 28 chapters on multifarious issues on social welfare and social work.

PART-A (Family, Genetics and Health) consists of five chapters of which Chapter-1 and Chapter-3 focus on concept of genetics, components of genetics, importance of genetic screening and other relevant and diversified issues centring around it, including genetic counselling and special emphasis is given on the implications for social work practice in this emerging issue and how genetic counselling could be effective in the prevention and treatment of various genetically dreadful diseases with special reference to Thalassaemia. Chapter-2 is basically talking about Amniocentesis (Sex-Determination Test) and its misuse along with other genetic diagnostic technology which are considered to be the blessings of medical science for mankind especially in the field of gynaecology and obstetric science. Here, of course, the relevance of social work has been highlighted pronouncedly. In connection with the Chapter-2,

Chapter-5 brings about the phenomena of infertility affecting millions of women, causes and impact of infertility in the society and how social work professionals could be of help to them in coping with this stressful situation. Chapter-4 warns us about the disease 'Alzheimer' which is quite prevalent today among the elderly people and how miserable are its consequences. A vivid description of the nature, type, causes, prevention, prognosis and treatment of the diseases has also been given in this chapter.

There are six chapters under PART-B (International Perspectives) and all are from international scenario and the author's own experience during his visit to those countries from time to time. Chapter-6, Chapter-7 and Chapter-8 throw light on the family planning scenario, Childcare and health care in Swedish Community respectively. Chapter-9 focuses on Finnish Social Protection System. On the other hand, it is based on the author's long-term association with two universities in Bangladesh. During his visits to Bangladesh on account of academic exchange and research activities he observed and saw how government and non-government organizations in Bangladesh are working collaboratively for disadvantaged groups of people for their livelihood rights in terms of socio-economic emancipation and this episode has been reflected in Chapter-10. Chapter-11 is also almost on the same track, trying to highlight the agricultural activities of small farmers in Bangladesh and the credit programmes extended to them by non-governmental organizations to improvise their activities.

PART-C (Women and Children) also contains five chapters. Chapter-12 is a reflection of a micro-study done by the author on awareness about reproductive health of women among the Santal (indigenous community) population. It was an exploratory study and small samples were adopted and out of the samples the author made an attempt to know their perception towards reproductive health which is a prime agenda in the health sector of Government of India. Chapter-13 guides us in the manner that credit and capital are basic requisites to increase agricultural production. Women and men farmers need short-term credit to buy improved seeds, fertilizers, insecticides and herbicides and to hire farm labourers to work in the fields and help with post-harvest operations. They need long-term credit to invest in more efficient technologies—irrigation, labour-saving tools and implements and transport—and to set up new enterprises if conditions are favourable. Yet, throughout the developing world and even in cases where they are acting as heads of their household, women are denied full legal status that would grant those loans. This limited and often complete lack of access to rural financial services hampers women's efforts to improve or expand their farm activities so as to earn cash income. Under the given canopy a study on the access to credit by women and use of formal and informal credit institutions by them was conducted.

Child health is an important component in the health sector reform of India because of high infant and maternal mortality rate. So, what are the present scenario as well as various other associated dimensions and how social workers can present themselves as an important agent in encountering the child health problems and its improvement in near future have been discussed in Chapter-14. Chapter-15 speaks about juvenile delinquents, causes and their problems along with the legal aspects of juvenile justice system to protect them as well as current enactment and government policies and programmes *vis-à-vis* the role of NGOs in this direction. Chapter-16 illustrates the situation of child labour in tobacco industry in Bharatpur-II, Block of Murshidabad District of West Bengal. After adopting necessary methodology, the author came out with some crucial findings which all have been elaborated on in the chapter.

PART-D (Ageing) is covering three chapters. Chapter-17 and Chapter-18 together have tried to bring them into the mainstream by addressing the issues like problems the elderly population often face (economic, social etc.), how to make their life more dignified by resolving the concomitant and inevitable problems in older age and the atrocity and torture they face in the society in the name of elderly abuse. Chapter-19 describes the problems and constraints the older workers face in industries. In all the three chapters the significance of social work intervention to deal with elderly population in different situations has been the cornerstone of the discussion.

PART-E (General Issues) has taken into account nine chapters. Chapter-20 and Chapter-21 focus on two important social problems—alcoholism and absenteeism. Here, the author has put an endeavour to see the conceptual paradigm, causes, and consequences and lastly how social workers can play a pivotal role in dealing with these two issues. Chapter-22 and Chapter-23 give us a view of conflict management and faculty development strategies for social work teachers. EAP (Employee Assistance Programme) is a vital organ of corporate social responsibility in the context of today's personnel management. What it is and how it functions have been discussed in Chapter-24. NREGA (National Rural Employment Guarantee Act), a phenomenal effort by the Government of India for socio-economic emancipation of poor people by ascertaining 100 days job per family in a year. So, the chapter-25 makes an attempt to see how far the NREGA scheme has been effective and fulfilling the objectives framed by the policy-makers and implementers. The author came to certain conclusive remarks after analyzing both qualitative and quantitative data. On the other hand, Chapter-26 talks about the situational analysis of urban street vendors in the Birbhum District of West Bengal. An attempt has been made in Chapter-27 regarding mission, vision and objectives of Ramakrishna Mission, a renowned faith based non-governmental organization working for the people over fifty years with much emphasis on building up an enlightened community through education and youth empowerment. Chapter-28 argues that because of increasing globalization and interdependence, effective international social work in the next century must be collaborative, rather than dominated by the models developed by affluent, industrialized nations. Four advantages have been mentioned for infusing a greater emphasis on internationalism in the social work profession: (1) greater understanding of alternative economic, political, and social welfare systems; (2) enhanced appreciation for diverse culture; (3) exposure to comparative options for addressing economic and social issues; and (4) increased possibilities for innovation and change in practice and education.

Debotosh Sinha

Acknowledgements

First and foremost, I would like to place on record my spontaneous and profound sense of gratitude towards my guiding teachers, late Prof. P.L. Govil of Delhi University and Dr. G.C. Khan, Retired Professor of Department of Social Work, Visva-Bharati. I always hold both of them in high esteem in terms of academic pursuits and professional growth and development. Prof. Khan has always motivated me to write a book compiling a number of important papers published in various journals from time to time right from my academic carrier and the publication work. This book is an outcome of such a continuous flow of inspiration. It has indeed been a momentous experience to complete this book under his erudite guidance and suggestions. It would be a piece of injustice on my part if I do not recall the encouragement and support from all the faculty members of my department as well as non-teaching staff.

I recall with great pleasure how my wife and little son were always beside me right through the venture and gave their best moral support whenever I was going slack. This book would not have been in its final shape without the blessings of my revered parents.

My sincere thanks and utmost gratitude to all the library staff (Visva-Bharati as well as outside and specially University of Glasgow Library) I met during the progress of the book who tolerated my erratic borrowing habits and extended their helping hands as and when required.

My gratitude to Emeritus Professor Mono Chakrabarty of University of Glasgow for his invaluable suggestions and guidance at the appropriate place and time.

I cannot afford to forget the contribution of Professor Abhijit Sen from the Department of English, Visva-Bharati, who often helped me with the literary part of this book. I am also grateful to Sri Raja Ghosh, Sri Bratin Biswas, Dr. Atin Biswas and Shakt Dhar Sahoo for their sound technical expertise regarding computation of data and other computer related activities. Sometimes, their scholarly guidance and growth producing criticism were also invaluable, highly appreciated and incorporated according to the relevance of the book.

Last but not the least, my profuse thanks are due to all those people including my beloved students who participated and helped me in writing the book in various capacities.

Debotosh Sinha

Contents

PART C

WOMEN AND CHILDREN

PART D

AGEING

PART E

GENERAL ISSUES

PART A

FAMILY, GENETICS AND HEALTH

1

Genetic Counselling

Answer to Thalassaemia and Other Genetic Disorders

Introduction

Thalassaemia is an inherited blood disorder which was uncommon a few decades ago has now become a common disorder in India. This is because of the general ignorance about the disorder, which has caused it to spread slowly and incipiently over the years to assume menacing dimensions today. When individuals, especially babies, are affected their families are faced with lifelong burden and social stigma.

If a child gets one normal gene from one parent and an abnormal one from the other, it is **heterozygous**. It carries the trait and may not suffer very much except in time of strain. But when it inherits two identical abnormal genes, it is **homozygous** and, therefore, Thalassaemia represents a series of conditions that result in reduced haemoglobin in the blood and anaemia, the most common being Cooley's anaemia (Brennan, 1990). Children with the disorder appear normal at birth, but soon become listless, prone to infection and grow slowly (Wymelenberg, 2003).

Thalassaemia shortens the life of the red blood cells (RBCs) from the normal 120 days to 60-70 days. When RBCs break up rapidly, the iron content increases in the blood. To offset the shortage of RBCs, repeated transfusions become necessary. But the new blood also breaks up and there is a further increase in the iron content. Iron gets deposited in the spleen and the liver becomes enlarged. The iron deposits in the heart muscles affect its proper functioning and the deposit of iron in or near the spinal cord may even result in paralysis of the limbs. Progressive anaemia also makes the victim increasingly listless, resistance is affected and the victim becomes susceptible to all kinds of diseases.

Medical science categorises thalassaemia in **three types** depending on the severity of manifestation.

- **Thalassaemia major,** where the patient is anaemic with enlargement of liver and spleen and life expectancy is shortened to below 10 years.
- **Thalassaemia minor** is a mild degree of anaemia which persists from early life. The patient is asymptomatic and lives a normal life.
- **Thalassaemia inter media,** which is clinically milder and the patient is sustained even on the haemoglobin content of 6.7 gm/dl.

Thalassaemic genes are hugely prevalent in Mediterranean countries like Cyprus, Greece and Italy. An epidemiological survey in the Cypriot population showed that 1 in 7 Cypriots was a carrier of thalassaemia.

According to Lahiri (2005), a thalassaemic child is born every hour in India. The disorder is more prevalent in Indian states like Punjab, Maharashtra, Rajasthan, Gujrat, West Bengal, Assam, and Manipur. About 11-13 per cent of the population in West Bengal are carriers of this disorder. The all-India figures for the same are 8-9 per cent.

Treatment of Thalassaemia

It is an expensive and prolonged affair without regular and proper treatment, death is certain. Blood transfusion is the main resource to ensure that the haemoglobin count is maintained at above 10 gm, for every 100 cc of blood (the normal level is 14.5). Normally, a patient who requires at least two blood transfusions in a month has to incur an expenditure of Rs. 4,000.

If the blood is available free, it still comes to Rs. 2,000. This is not the end of expenses. A post-transfusion subcutaneous injection, **Despheral**, is a must. It acts as a chelating agent, flushing out the extra iron deposited in the body after fresh blood is pumped in. Sometimes, 10-12 of these injections are required at a stretch. **Kefler tablets**, an accepted substitute, are prescribed according to the age and weight of a patient. In some places in India, as well as abroad, it has been possible to cure thalassaemia through a **bone marrow transplantation**, but the cost is exorbitantly high. **Splenectomy** (cutting of the spleen) is another line of treatment by which a patient can survive up to 10-15 years. Another type of treatment is the **Iron Chelation Therapy** (that is flushing out the excess iron from the bloodstream of the patient over a period of time). This is very painful, not to mention expensive, for a patient.

Genetic engineering is a fabulous landmark in the field of molecular biology. **Gene therapy** is an application of genetic engineering which is used in treating thalassaemia today. The abnormal beta globin gene of the **Deoxy Ribonucleic Acid (DNA)** in the chromosome (responsible for thalassaemia) is replaced by a normal and healthy beta globin gene by using the gene therapy method. Of course, it is a very complicated process but efforts have been on to make it simple, affordable and less expensive.

The growing foetus receives blood and nutrient supply from the mother's placenta through the umbilical cord. If the stem cells in the umbilical cord blood, which is the precursor of new RBC can be injected into a thalassaemic patient, the condition of the patient improves. This method of treatment can refrain a patient from taking blood transfusions for at least five to six years. In addition to that, iron chelation can also be avoided for a longer period of time.

Children of carrier parents run a 75 per cent risk of infection and the first step towards arresting this ailment is believed to lie in preventing two persons with this disorder from marrying. Knowledge of the genetic configuration of a couple can prevent the birth of children with such disorders. This is why genetic counselling is so important to deal with such problems and to create awareness about the disorder. This needs an integrated approach comprising doctors, nurses and other professionals, if required.

Apart from thalassaemia, there are numerous genetic disorders like Tay-Sachs, Sickle Cell Anaemia, Down's Syndrome, Klinefelter Syndrome, Phenylketonuria, and so on, for which there are no medicines. The number of children born with genetic disorders is increasing and newer disorders are being detected thanks to the phenomenal progress made by the medical science. A patient suffering from a genetic disorder suffers from and causes tremendous mental pressure to his/her family. Here, genetic counselling can prevent the occurrence of these untreatable disorders and also help the doctors and family members to cope with the situation.

Implications for social work

The study of social work provides knowledge, understanding and skills for change and development. The methods and fields of social work are quite diverse. Social workers intervene to help individuals, families, groups or whole communities and at the same time contribute to policy development, programme management or research into various social issues and the services designed to ameliorate them.

The fields in which social services are rendered are gradually expanding. There is an increasing demand for running such services, as the non-availability of trained social workers affects the quality of the services delivered. This is true in the case of health care and especially so in the field of genetic engineering.

As clinicians, social workers walk right into the heart of the pain unlike any other health care team members. Social workers are challenged to work in a setting where their presence is admittedly needed, often beyond expectation. The role of social workers in the health care system in India has become all the more important with the unabated spread of the killer disorder thalassaemia and other genetic disorders along with the usefulness of reproductive technology.

It is high time for medical experts, social workers, policy-makers and NGOs to expand and develop this area for the benefit of the people who are affected by genetic disorders. This might give them some directions with a positive spirit and strong vigour.

Concept of genetic counselling

The most widely used definition of genetic counselling is, appropriately, a communication process which deals with the human problems associated with the occurrence, or risk of occurrence of a genetic disorder in a family (Wymelenberg, 2003). This process involves an attempt by one or more appropriately trained persons to help the individual or family to (Green, 2007):

- comprehend the medical facts, including the diagnosis and the probable course of the disorder, and its management (as available);
- appreciate the way hereditary contributes to the disorder, and the risk of its recurrence in specified relatives;
- understand the options available for subsequent family planning;
- choose the course of action which seems, to them, to be most appropriate in view of the risk, their family goals, and their ethical and religious standards, and to act in accordance with these decisions; and
- make the best possible adjustment to the disorder in an affected family member and/or to the risk or recurrence of that disorder.

Since Kowle's study on the 'in-born errors of metabolism' in 1985, the body of knowledge about human genetics has expanded tremendously. Increasingly, information appears in magazines, newspapers and on television linking conditions such as heart disease, cancer, addictive disorders, and mental health problems to genetic factors. The catalogue of genetic diseases includes more than 300 observed defects of the haemoglobin molecule alone. The prospect of genetic engineering in the ability to replace or repair defective genes is one of the most exciting interventions of the future. For others, genetic engineering causes concern about the moral and ethical implications of this technology.

Counsellors and other helping professionals have, and will, continue to have a major role to play in developing ways of translating this knowledge and technology into methods of helping people understand and cope with their specific problems. It is here that the importance of genetic counselling lies in the present day context. Against the background of this conceptual paradigm, the important objectives of genetic counselling would be to:

- establish a warm and effective relationship with the client.
- suggest alternatives at all levels.
- educate the client about the hereditary and medical facts regarding the genetic disorder(s) including diagnosis, treatment and prevention.
- correct false notions and cultural taboos.
- prepare the couple at risk for prenatal diagnosis.
- provide the client/couple with emotional, social and economic support as far as is possible.
- linkages between the community and medical services.
- encourage community participation in supporting affected individuals and in preventive educational activities.
- provide marriage counselling services.

Who can be a genetic counsellor?

As early as in 1969, the ideal genetic counsellor was defined as that professional who assumed the obligations of learning the general workings of heredity, organized the pertinent source of information for a genetic problem, exercised the art of giving that information properly, and helped to develop a programme of action for families to follow. Whatever his/her professional title, a genetic counsellor was one who took on the above mentioned obligations (Wymelenberg, 2003).

The functional characterization of a genetic counsellor has passed through a number of phases. To begin with, there were medical geneticists, pediatricians, and a certain type of psychiatrists. As time passed, and the work of the genetic clinic proliferated along with new knowledge, more of the counselling service component began to be offered by social workers, psychologists (all of whom learned what they needed to know about genetic diseases informally) and, increasingly, by specially trained professionals who had pursued graduate level curricula in some of the Western countries leading to the position of Genetic Associate.

Qualities and skills of a counsellor

The qualities of a genetic counsellor are much the same as those of a counsellor of any other discipline. He/She would possess as many of the qualities mentioned below for effectively offering counselling services:

I. The counsellor should maintain high standards of personal conduct in the capacity or identity of a counsellor.
II. The counsellor should regard his/her service obligation as primary.
III. Respect, fairness and courtesy for all with whom he/she comes in contact with.
IV. The counsellor should act in accordance with the highest standards of professional integrity.
V. The counsellor should adhere to commitments made to the employing organization(s).
VI. The counsellor should take responsibility for identifying, developing, and fully utilizing his/her knowledge for professional practice.
VII. The counsellor should respect the privacy of clients and hold in confidence all information obtained in the course of counselling.

VIII. A good understanding about human psychology.
IX. The ability to communicate properly and meaningfully (attentive listening is also very important).
X. The counsellors strive to become and remain proficient in professional practice and the performance of professional functions.

Skills

Five important skills are required:

- information gathering and assessment,
- the development and use of the professional self,
- practice activities with individuals and families,
- evaluation, and
- follow-up.

The above discussion can be best conceptualized from the Figure 1.1. The counselling process usually begins with a feeling of concern about something. The concern arises because a need is not met. After thinking about the situation in a particular way (a process called assessment) some action is taken. This

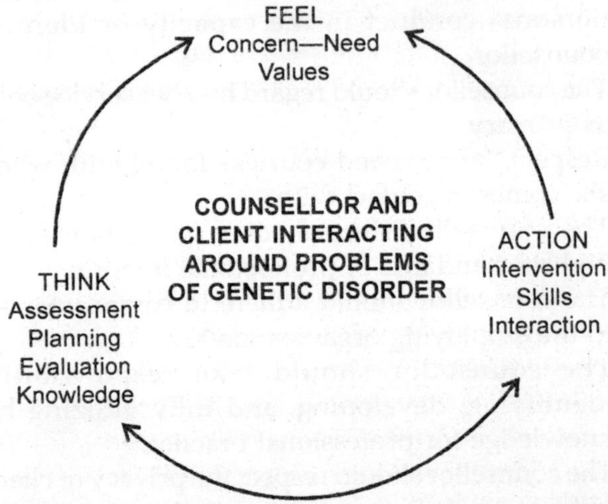

Fig. 1.1 : The Counselling Process: A Feeling, Thinking, Acting, Endeavour

response—feeling, thinking, acting—is cyclical in nature. As the counsellor and client think and act together, new feelings of concern arise and new needs become apparent. As they act, they think about what is happening and gain new insights into the situation. The counsellor's knowledge about human development, human diversity, and the social system theory is used in thinking about the situation.

The role of a counsellor

Counsellors play and will continue to play, a major role in helping people understand and cope with their specific genetic problems (Hamilton and Noble, 1983). Rauch (1988) provides insights into why it is important for counsellors to be knowledgeable about genetic disorders and the influence of genes on development and behaviour. It is because counsellors:

(a) use family and individual histories to evaluate client situations within the framework of a bio-psychosocial model.
(b) provide service to individuals and families affected by disabilities and chronic conditions that often have contributing genetic factors or origins.
(c) must be able to provide accurate information and make referrals to appropriate genetic services for clients who have genetic concerns.

Genetic counselling has medical and psychological aspects. Medical specialists or genetic counsellors provide clients with information about the disorder—the way in which heredity contributes risks of recurrence, and reproductive or treatment options. Such specialist counsellors also help their clients to choose a course of action appropriate to them. Counsellors focus on the psychological aspects of a client, both as members of genetic centre teams and community-based practitioners (Golden, Davis and Heavy, 1981; Hall and Young, 2004).

Genetic counsellors can assess social service needs, make appropriate referrals, and act as case managers. By helping individuals and families to cope with the demands posed by genetic disorders, genetic counsellors also offer crisis intervention during the exacerbation of disorders and if needed, during the terminal stage of life to the bereaved. Counsellors are in a position to identify changing counselling needs and genetic counselling should not be considered a one-time event because changes in the field of human genetics occur so rapidly.

The discovery that genetic liability and single-gene inheritance are factors in some psychiatric disorders has led to genetic counselling in psychiatry (Crowe, 1978; Stancer and Wagner, 2005). In some Western countries, genetic counselling is regularly provided to patients and their families at community mental health centres (Rauch, 1988).

The general public is learning about human genetics through the media. As clients and potential clients become more knowledgeable, they will raise genetic issues with counsellors. Clinical genetic services are proliferating and the use of such services is also increasing as both the public and members of the helping profession become more aware of recent developments.

The policy of deinstitutionalization is maintaining many developmentally delayed or otherwise disabled people in the community. Such individuals come to the attention of genetic counsellors and bring with them their own genetic concerns as well as those of their families. Further, the increased life expectancy of children with genetic disorders is generating a demand for flexible, community-based social services appropriate for different stages of the life cycle, including adulthood. The main concern of genetic counsellors should be that children, youth and adults with disorders should lead as normal a life as possible within the constraints of their conditions.

As Schild (2008) notes, genetic diagnoses touch on intimate, deeply personal areas of life—sexuality, decisions to conceive, and decisions to terminate pregnancy for genetic reasons. A genetic diagnosis also may reveal family secrets such as adultery. Although genetic counsellors can apply genetic skills, genetically affected individuals and families confront unique adaptive demands. Counsellors need to be familiar with specific disorders and their burdens, be able to empathies with their psychological and familial effects, be competent in assessing service needs, and be skilled in making what may be emotionally charged referrals, including referrals to genetic centres. Specific ways in which genetic counsellors can assist clients and their families are by:

(a) helping break down the problem into manageable units.
(b) maintaining the person-environment fit.
(c) providing appropriate support service as the situation demands such as financial assistance, medical equipment and care, and special educational programmes.
(d) keeping abreast of modern changes.
(e) assisting in developing a healthy self-concept.
(f) facilitating the communication and decision-making process.
(g) clarifying and reinforcing medical information provided by other health professionals.
(h) mobilizing the family into meaningful activities such as participation in a support group.

Future promises

Genetic counselling should not be restricted only in dealing with the problem of thalassaemia. Genetic counselling can join hands with reproductive technology and other genetic dis-configuaration in human beings. The threat of HIV/AIDS that the thalassaemic patients face; should genetic counselling be regulated; what are the best possible genetic services that could be made available to the common people, are some of the issues to be briefly addressed as future challenges for the genetic counsellors.

Advances in reproductive technology

The phenomenal development of genetic diagnostic technology such as amniocentesis, foetoscopy, chorionic villuses tests, foetal blood testing and ultrasonography, especially for the pre-natal detection of various genetic disorders, combined with the revolution and stupendous progress in new assisted reproductive technologies such as artificial insemination, in-vitro and in-utero-fertilization, micro manipulation (Srinivasan, 2005), sperm and egg banks (Habibulla, 1994), surrogacy (Halbrook, 1990), and so on, and the availability of techniques (biochemical tests) for detection could extend the services of genetic counsellors in the coming years.

Counsellors must work towards helping society to cope with the problems and opportunities created by the advances in reproductive technology. As reported, that the changing reproductive process offers at once opportunities for liberation and for enslavement. The genesis and revelation of reproductive technology and its biomedical power to determine, manage and control reproduction, has piloted medical sciences across a Rubicon for which there is no return ticket. Genetic counsellors must take a leadership role and approach these challenges on the levels of service and policy.

At the service level, accepting diagnosis of infertility; assistance in explaining feelings about alternatives such as artificial insemination (to date, 400-500 babies have born by this method in India), surrogacy, and many other genetic disorders need access to skilled counselling. Due to the complexities, as well as the growing need for services, counsellors need to be trained in assisted reproductive technology (Reild, 1977). An attempt can be made to develop such courses with special emphasis on the ethical concerns raised by the new techniques. Research relating to this area also needs to be done (Richardson, 2004).

Genetic counsellors are in a good position to learn about the effect of assisted reproductive technologies on families and to contribute, through observation and research, to knowledge in this area. Perhaps, most importantly, genetic counsellors must use knowledge to meet the needs of humanity by helping to develop and formulate a more enlightened public policy concerning the problems and prospects of these new reproductive techniques:

- Identify newborns affected with genetic diseases.
- Providing continuing education to allied health professionals.
- Provide public information on a continuing basis.
- Provide continuing education in genetics to physicians in private practice.
- Cooperative linkages must exist between screening programmes and medical centres.
- Screening must be incorporated into a general programme of prevention and remediation that is primarily service and not research-oriented.
- Priority must be given to conditions of highest incidence and/or greatest severity, which are preventable or treatable.
- A state programme must be reviewed not less than every two years to take into account the advances in medical knowledge and to ensure full public representation and protection.

Should genetic counselling be regulated?

The steady increase in the demand for the services to genetic counsellors has stimulated some discussion on whether genetic counselling should be regulated. If yes, an obvious option would be to develop a system of licensing. Many doctors, geneticists and medical scientists are of the view that it is premature to consider licensing of genetic counsellors for the following reasons:

- The extent and type of responsibilities which should be included in a position with such a title (genetic counsellor) are not yet clearly defined to be regulated or licensed.
- The appropriate training for such a speciality can only be specified when the position is clarified.

- It is not clear whether the organized health care system wishes to expand resources related to this type of service; there is no point in licensing unless there is a demonstrated need for the services to be provided.
- It is not clear whether these persons will function as independent professionals or only in positions subordinate to physicians.

On the other hand, irrespective of the above arguments and on the basis of the foregoing discussion, we feel that the practice of genetic counselling must be legalized. To sum up, enacting a legislation to make the appointment of genetic counsellors mandatory, establishing specialized clinical genetic services, and introducing a degree in genetic counselling in universities (as has already been done in countries like Canada and the United States of America), will give a new dimension to human genetics and the handling of many problems related to it.

Genetic services

Genetic services are not possible without genetic screening. The latter can be defined as the systematic search for persons with a particular genotype in a defined population, and serves as an important adjunct of modern preventive medicine. Such screening has the potential to lessen the devastating impact of genetic disorders. The usual purpose is to identify individuals whose genotype places them or their children at risk of a genetic disease. Research findings by Gilchrist (1998) have revealed that improper and technically unsound genetic screening proves to be futile for productive genetic services. So, counsellors must be very careful about the following events:

- The government should have a *'State Plan for Genetic Services'*.
- Failure to disclose the results of screening.
- Unauthorized disclosure of screening results to persons other than the screened.

- Medical malpractices, that is, professional negligence, including incorrect diagnosis.
- The approach to control of thalassaemia as recommended by the World Health Organization includes: community education, screening for carriers and foetal diagnosis. This should be followed as a policy matter.
- Failure to obtain informed consent to the screening procedure. The entire purpose of the *'doctrine of informed consent'* is to permit the individual to make up his/her own mind regarding a proposed course of action. No matter how irrational the decision of an individual is. It must always be the individual's decision and not the counsellor's.
- Two types of confidentiality problems could arise in the genetic screening situation. The first one relates to the disclosure by a physician of specific information about a particular individual to a third person. The second one involves dissemination of statistical information for research purposes which incidently reveals the identity of and confidential information about a person tested. Caution should, of course, be taken in the revolution of any data for statistical or scientific purposes to assure that the identities of those tested are concealed.

Conclusion

The above discussion indicates that the profession of genetic counselling has a unique role to play in dealing with all sorts of genetic disorders. Any genetic disorder is always surrounded by two aspects—**social** and **medical**. While doctors are trained to deal with problems only from a clinical point of view, the counsellors are trained in social diagnosis. Since genetics and the environments are directly interrelated (Rauch, 2008), the medical profession must join hands with counsellors especially in dealing with the challenges of human genetics and providing the right types of services. The services are as follows:

- Pre-marital and pre-natal counselling.
- Generating consciousness about common genetic disorders, including thalassaemia, and how to cope with the resulting situations in an accepted manner.
- Awareness programmes and eliciting community participation with the help of lectures, exhibitions, leaflets, poster presentations, and so on.
- Coordination and strengthening of existing thalassaemic foundations all-over the country.
- Approach rural areas seriously and sensitively.
- Setting up of more centres with genetic counsellors for blood investigation for carrier status.
- Before marriage a special blood test of the prospective bride and groom must be done to detect whether any one of them are carriers of the thalassaemic gene.
- Monitoring community programmes, which should include annual monitoring of thalassaemia birth rate; assessment of foetal diagnosis; recordings of the counselled couples; interviewing parents of affected children; and determining the number of individuals requesting carrier testing and number of couples at risk, in order to evaluate community education and carrier screening.
- Counselling should also be given to family members who could be involved in counselling, as they are responsible for making decisions regarding treatment and prevention.

SUGGESTED READINGS

1. Brennan, J.R. (1990); *Pattern of Human Heredity*, Prentice Hall.
2. Crowe, R. (1978); "Is Genetic Counselling Appropriate for Psychiatric Illness?" In J.P. Brady and H.L. Brodie (Eds.), *Controversy in Psychiatry*, Philadelphia: WB Saunders, pp. 763-775.
3. Gilchrist, H. (1998); *Genetic Screening and Counselling: The Legal and Ethical Issues*, New York: Macmillan Company.
4. Golden, D., Davis, J.G. and Heavy, L. (1981); "The Contribution of Long-Term Psychosocial Services to the Genetic Counselling Process". In S.R. Applewhite, D.L. Busheck and D.S. Borgaonkar

(Eds.), *Genetic Screening and Counselling: A Multidisciplinary Perspective*, Springfield: Charles C. Thomas, pp. 123-130.

5. Green, R.R. (2007); *Human Behaviour Theory and Social Work Practice*, New York: Aldine De Gruyter.
6. Habibulla, M. (1994); Human Egg on Sale, *Nexus*, December-January.
7. Halbrook, S.M. (1990); "Adoption, Infertility and New Reproductive Technologies: Problems and Prospects for Social Work and Welfare Policy", *Social Work*, 35 (4), pp. 333-337.
8. Hall, W.T. and Young, C. L. [Eds.] (2004); *Proceedings of Public Health Social Work Programme on Genetic Disorders: Social Service Interventions*, Pittsburgh.
9. Hamilton, A.K. and Noble, D.N. (1983); "Assisting Families through Genetic Counselling"; *Social Casework*, 64 (1), 18-25.
10. Lahiri, A. (2005); Deadly Inheritance, *The Statesman*, November 4, Kolkata.
11. Kowles, R.V. (1985); *Genetics, Society and Decisions*, Columbus: Charles E. Merrill.
12. Rauch, J.B. (1988); "Social Work and Genetic Revolution: Genetic Services"; *Social Work*, 33 (5), pp.389-439.
13. Reild, W.J. (1977); "Social Work for Social Problem"; *Social Work*, 32 (6), pp. 425-428.
14. Richardson, J.W. (2004); "The Role of a Psychiatric Consultant to an Artificial Insemination by Donor Programme", *Psychiatric Annals*, 17 (2), pp. 101-105.
15. Schild, S. (2008); "Social Work Intervention with Genetic Problems". In W.T. Hall and C.L. Young (Eds.), *Proceedings of Public Health Social Work Programme on Genetic Disorders*. Social Service Interventions, Pittsburgh, pp. 33-39.
16. Srinivasan, S. (2005); Hi-tech Baby, *Nexus*, December.
17. Stancer, H.C. and Wagner, D.N. (2005); "Genetic Counselling: Its Need in Psychiatry and the Direction it Gives for Future Research", *Canadian Journal of Psychiatry*, 29, pp. 289-294.
18. Wymelenberg, S. (2003); *Science and Babies*, Washington, DC: National Academic Press.

2

Sex-Determination and Sex Pre-Selection Test

Abuse of Genetic Diagnostic Technology

Producing a child in an infertile mother's womb; when to have a child and when not to have a child; determining whether the child to be born is a boy or girl; determining the position of the child in the mother's womb; whether the child has any genetic disorder or not, are all made known to us by virtue of the astounding progress in genetic diagnostic technology and biochemical tests. Various techniques of sex determination and sex pre-selection have been discovered during last twenty years under the phenomenal development of genetic diagnostic technology such as fetoscopy, chorionic villus biopsy, foetal blood sampling, ultrasonography, especially for the prenatal detection of various disorders, combined with the revolution in new assisted reproductive technologies such as artificial insemination, micro-manipulation, in-vitro and in-utero fertilization, sperm and egg banks (Habibulla, M., 1994), surrogacy and so on, and the availability of techniques for detecting already known genetic disorders and the most popular one, **AMNIOCENTESIS**, are increasingly becoming household names in India.

The number of girl children under six years of age has markedly fallen down in comparison to the last decade 945 : 1000 in 1991 to the present ratio of 927 : 1000 in 2005, that is for every 1,000 male children, there are only 945 and 927 female children respectively. Studies also show that for every 1000 foetus aborted, 995 were females (*The Statesman*, 2005). In the general population, the ratio was 933 : 1000 in 1991 and 927 : 1000 in 2001, that is, for every 1000 males there are only 933 and 927 females respectively.

For every 100 men, 105 women should be born. Accordingly there should be 512 million women in India but there are only 489 million women, that is, 23 million women are missing. The most important reason for this is the killing of female foetus by ill-directed and derogatory application of diagnostic technologies. It is estimated that 20 lakh female foetus are being killed every year in India, which is really an alarming figure in the context of the very existence of the female population. So it is a reflection of the fact that the female child is not accepted by our society and, as a result, it has devastating impact on the status of women. It is also been reported that the popularity of sex determination tests is mostly prevalent in the Northern, North-Eastern and Western parts of India.

Sex selection, also known as gender selection, has attracted great interest and controversy over the years. Gender selection has been associated with a number of ethical, moral and legal issues, sex selection may be performed for medical reasons to avoid sex-linked diseases such as Hemophilia, Huntington's Chorea, Thalassaemia, Down Syndrome, Klenfenter Syndrome, Duchenne's Muscular Dystrophy, and is acceptable in many countries of the world. However, gender selection for family balancing purposes is a very controversial issue. Should a couple be free to choose the sex of their child? For some the answer is "yes" because it is a fundamental right, while for others it is a threat to society. First let us understand in brief the technical details of the technique called amniocentesis. Later on we will discuss the controversial aspect along with other concommitant issues circumscribing the phenomena of sex selection.

Amniocentesis

Amniocentesis, a scientific technique that is supposed to be used mainly to detect genetic deformities. The test is conducted after completion of 16 weeks of pregnancy by the removal of amniotic fluid of the expectant mother, in order to gain information about the foetus. The test has become very popular in India for detection of the sex of a fetus. After separating foetus cell from the amniotic fluid, a chromosomal analysis is conducted on it. This test helps in detecting several genetic disorders like mongolism, hemophilia, Down's Syndrome and other types of genetic abnormalities. In some cases, a sex determination test is required to identify sex specific deformities such as hemophilia and retarded muscular growth which mainly affects male children.

Limitation of amniocentesis

The test can give 95-97 per cent accurate results. Thus it is not totally reliable. It has been noted by the doctors that the tests do affect the foetus adversely in one per cent of the total number of cases. Thus, the tests may lead to spontaneous abortions or premature delivery, dislocation of hips, respiratory complications and needle puncture marks on the baby.

As mentioned earlier, the tests are conducted after completion of sixteen weeks of pregnancy and within a week the findings are available. In our country, the facility of amniocentesis is available only in the cities and towns, hence, patients from villages and small towns get the results by post; that takes one more week. By the time they decide to abort the foetus; it is over 18 weeks of pregnancy. Abortion at such a late stage is quite harmful for the mother.

Popularity of the test

Female foeticide reinforces a girl's current subordinate opposition. To pick up a male is to declare that males are more valuable and females less so, which in turn perpetuates the preference (Bennett, 2005).

The amniocentesis test became popular in the last fifteen years though it was conducted in the government hospitals on an experimental basis. Now, this test is conducted in private clinics, private hospitals and government hospitals mainly for sex determination and thereafter extermination of female foetus through abortion. This devaluation of female child through the process of amniocentesis is so popular which reflects in the following paragraph:

"Even as the doctor at the ultra-sound scan diagnostic center adjusts the scanner to zero on the right spot on the women's abdomen, she asks 'KYA HAI'. She can't wait to know the sex of the foetus. Minutes later she gets a report reading 'one healthy foetus' or 'one small foetus' or 'twins'. But the reply to her KYA HAI is given orally and at an exorbitant cost. She pays and leaves the clinic either smiling or sulking. The smiling woman does not go home and throw a party. Rather, she heads for the next ultra-sound center to be doubly sure that she is, indeed, going to be the mother of a son. The approach is equally business-like at nursing homes that offer a package of a set test, a mid trimester abortion, and conception of a guranteed male baby. The patients do not beat around the bush and the doctors do not waste time dissuading them. The woman simply given a date and time, and the list of things to bring with them" (*The Week*, 1993, p. 41).

In a study undertaken by the Government of Maharashtra, where it was observed that at least 50,000 amniocentesis tests for sex determination were conducted annually in Mumbai alone. If it was found female foetus, the next step was the termination of pregnancy (Anjali, 1987). It was stated by Daswani, Britto (2007) and Bajpai (1997) that in 1995 in Mumbai alone, 40,000 female foetuses were aborted. It was reported by them that in one hospital, out of 8,000 abortions, 7,999 were female. Ramanamma and Bambawale (1998) studied the records of three hospitals in Pune, they found that in one of the hospitals, 700 women sought sex determination. Out of 450 women who were informed that they would have a daughter, 95.5 per cent underwent an abortion. However, all 250 women (100 per cent) who were informed that they were carrying a male foetus, carried on with the pregnancy even though in some cases they were warned of a possibility of a genetic disorder. Shah and Taneja (2006) also had observed that in their study out of 300 respondents (150 males and 150 females) in

Delhi regarding sex determination tests, 60 per cent had a highly negative opinion but, disturbingly, 38 per cent had either a positive or somewhat negative opinion.

Unfortunately, even male geneticists seem to have no qualms about abetting female foeticide. Wertz and Fletcher (1995) surveyed the attitudes of 71 medical geneticists in four developing countries (Brazil, Greece, India and Turkey) and 611 geneticists in 15 developed countries. They found that 52 per cent of geneticists in India (the highest percentage amongst the developing countries) would perform prenatal diagnosis to select a male foetus for a couple with four daughters and no sons. Though India was not the only country in the survey with a strong preference for sons, it was the only country using prenatal diagnosis for this purpose. The doctors who said that they would perform prenatal diagnosis for sex selection argued that by aborting female foetuses they would be preventing the suffering and early deaths of unwanted girls. Female foeticide reinforces a girl's current subordinate position. "To pick a male is to declare that males are more valuable and female less so, which in turn perpetuates the preference" (Bennett, 2005). Based on their survey of six hospitals and clinics in Mumbai, a research team at the Women's Aid Centre, Mumbai estimated that 10 women per day underwent the test in 1988.

Abraham and Shukla (2008) said that many hospitals conduct sex determination test. Their handout declares the test as 'human and beneficial'. The hospitals have outpatient facilities and there is such a great rush for the test that one has to book one month in advance. In our country the cost of getting these tests done in between Rs. 200 and Rs. 500 which is very much affordable for anybody who wants to undergo these tests. A survey of several places in metropolitan cities in India (Ghadially, 1991) showed that many women had undergone the test and after knowing that the sex of foetus was female had undergone abortion in the eighteenth or nineteenth week of pregnancy. Their argument was it is better to spend Rs. 200 or even more, than give birth to a female baby and spend thousands of rupees for her marriage when she grows up.

The popularity of these tests has attracted young workers of Larsen and Toubro (Ghadially, 1991), a multinational engineering industry too. As a result, the medical bills showing the amount spent on the tests were submitted by the workers for their reimbursement by the company. The Welfare Department was astonished to find that these workers were treating sex determination test very casually. They organized a two-day seminar in which doctors, social workers, representatives of women's organizations as well as Family Planning Association were invited. One doctor with a flourishing business of sex determination tests stated in the seminar that, " ....from Cape Comorin to Kashmir people ring him up at all hours of the day to find out about the test. So much so that his six years old son has learnt how to ask the relevant questions on the phone like "Is the pregnancy 16 weeks old?" etc. (Abraham, 1994).

A micro research was conducted in 1990 in Bijnor district of Uttar Pradesh. They observed that people in the district still consider birth of a daughter as a loss of prestige. In Delhi, the All India Institute of Medical Sciences started conducting sample survey of amniocentesis in 1997 to find out foetal abnormalities. They were flooded with request for abortion. As soon as the parents were told that the foetus was a girl, they started making arrangements for abortion (Chhachhi and Satyamala, 2008).

A sociological research in Punjab selected in its sample 50 per cent men and 50 per cent women as respondents for their questionnaire on opinions of men and women regarding sex determination tests. All of them knew about the test and found it useful (Singh and Jain, 1998). Punjab was the first to start commercial use of this test way back in 1979. It was the advertisement in newspapers regarding New Bhandari Anti-Natal Sex Determination Clinic in Amritsar that activated the press and the women groups to denounce it equivocally.

Controversy and debate around sex determination tests

Amniocentesis is a topic for interesting discussion from various spheres in terms of its manifestation. What can be the long-term implications if amniocentesis continues? Will it not aggravate the already disturbed sex-ratio? There has been continuous decline in female/male sex-ratio between 1901 and 2001. Between 1971 and 1981 there is a slight increase, but it still continues to be adverse for women. As mentioned earlier, for every 100 men, 105 women should be born. Accordingly, there should be 512 million women in India, but there are only 489 million women, that is 23 million women are missing.

Much of these caused by female infanticide, foeticide and lack of care and nutrition for women and girls. Women are still considered and treated as lesser mortal of society; as a result they face physical, emotional and sexual abuse throughout their lives. What shocked everyone from academic to activists, was that between 1978 and 1983 around 78,000 female fetuses were aborted after sex determination tests in our country (*The Times of India*, June 1992). So it clearly shows that female population is at the low ebb which signifies the denial of female existence and in turn denotes the poor acceptance status of women in the society.

Sycophants of population control advocates this test because they think the government can achieve Net Reproduction Rate (NRR) of one, i.e. replacement of a mother by only one daughter, with the help of sex determination test. According to them, if there are less number of women, there will be less growth of runway population. The government and private medical practitioners justify sex determination test as a measure of population control. Women have always been at the receiving end of all family planning policies. Harmful effects of pregnancy test, contraceptive pills, anti-pregnancy injections, camps for mass sterilization of women with its unhygienic atmosphere are always overlooked by the enthusiasts of family planning policy. Ninety-nine per cent of population control research is conducted on women without any consideration to the harmful effects of research to the women concerned. Advocates of population control with continue cashing on socio-cultural values that treat the birth of a daughter as a great calamity and perpetuate modern methods of massacre of female foetuses on a massive scale.

If supply of women reduces, there demand as well as status will enhance (Seth, 1989). Scarcity of women will increase their value (Bardhan, 2007). According to this logic women won't be easily replaceable commodities. But how the economists forget the socio-cultural milieu in which women have to live. The society that treats women as mere sex objects will not treat women in a more human way if they are scarce in supply, on the contrary, there will be increased incidences of rape, abduction and forced polyandry. In Madhya Pradesh, Harayana, Rajasthan and Punjab among certain communities, the sex-ratio is extremely adverse for women. There a wife is shared by a set of brothers and sometimes even by patrilateral parallel cousins (Dube, 1983). To think that it is better to kill female foetus than give birth to unwanted female child, is very fatalistic. By this logic it is better to kill the poor people or Third World masses rather than let them suffer from poverty and deprivation.

Another argument is that in cases where women have one or more daughters, they should be allowed to have amniocentesis done so that they can plan a balanced family by having a son. Instead of going on producing female children in the hope of getting a male child, it is better for the family's and country's welfare that they abort the female foetus and have small and balanced family with daughters and sons. The concept of balanced family is also a sexist bias. Would couples with one or more sons undergo amniocentesis to get rid of female foetus and to have a daughter for balancing their family? What is the cost of having a balanced family? How many abortions during 16 to 18 weeks can a woman bear without jeopardizing her health? These are some of the critical and debatable issues and concerns which always generate discussions among the people from various disciplines and categories, and common people as well across the globe.

Some of the advocates of banning of sex determination tests may justify this on the reasoning that women themselves do not want to abort daughters, but they are forced to do so by their husbands and in-laws and since the tests reveal the sex of the child there will be coercion on women to go for abortion. These women are socially conditioned to accept that unless they produce one or more male children there is no social worth attached to them (Rapp, 1996). They can be harassed, taunted, even deserted by their husbands and in-laws if they fail to do so. Thus their "Choices" depend on the fear of the society (Devasia and Devasia, 2007). It is true that feminists all-over the world have always demanded the right of women to control their own bodies/fertility and choose whether or not to have a child or children and have facility for free, legal and safer abortions. While understanding these issues in Indian context the scenario is not at all bright in this "male-preference" and "male-dominated" society.

There is also the view that the foetus acquires life or is visible only after a certain period, so before that point of time abortion is justified. There is no universally accepted medical or legal definition of life nor of the period when the foetus can be said to be viable, but in many countries a judgment is implicitly embodied in the law. Thus the Supreme Court of the US decided in 1973 that abortion should be freely available during the first two trimesters of pregnancy. If the foetus as less than 28 weeks old, though attempts are being made to alter the limit. In Britain abortion is freely permissible. In Indian law, abortion is a criminal offence at any stage except in special circumstances under the Medical Termination of Pregnancy Act in 1971.

Amitai Etzioni, a famous sociologist, holds a very different view. In "Genetic Fix" (1973) he examines the consequences of sex control as mass practice—in the US this would probably result in a surplus of boys, at a conservative estimate of 9.5 out of 1000. This surplus, he argues, will have undesirable social consequences such as a rise in crime, and he therefore concludes that this is an area where individual free choice may not be desirable. Vimal Balasubrahamanyam (1992) argues that "breeding male", i.e. aborting female fetuses is the only method of population control that will work in the Third World.

Popularity of sex pre-selection tests can be more dangerous than that of sex-determination tests because the former does not involve ethical issues related to abortion. So, even anti-abortionists can use this method. Dr. Ronald Erikson (1990) who has his chain of clinics conducting sex-pre-selection tests in 46 countries of Europe, America, Asia, and Latin America announces in his handout: "Out of 263 couples who approached him, 248 selected boys and 15 selected girls". This shows that male preference is not limited to a Third World Country like India, but that it is universal. In Erickson's method, no abortion or apparent violence is involved; still it can lead to violent social disaster if one thinks of its consequences in a long-term. Through social consequences of sex selection as well as sex determination tests, the reality shatters the myth of neutrality of linking science and technology with socio-economic and cultural realities. Class, race and sex biases of the ruling elites have crossed all boundaries of human dignity. After 39 years of revolution and socialist reconstruction, sex determination test for female extermination have gained ground after government adoption of a one-child family policy. Chinese couples as well as Indian willy-nilly accept a system of one-child family but it would be a matter of great satisfaction if the child is male. Thus shows how adaptive the system of patriarchy and male supremacy. It can establish and strengthen its roots in all kinds of social structure, pre-capitalist, capitalist and even socialist by making savage use of science. This ethos of patriarchy has to be challenged consistently (Patel, 1984).

Promising future directions to combat with the problem of sex-determination tests

The problem of women as victims of crime and the apathy of society must be highlighted by every conscientious citizen of this land of *Dharma*. Most of the unnatural deaths of women are traceable to the misfortune of their sex and weaker biology. It has been observed that a woman is killed or she is forced to suicide as mainly because of masculine possessiveness and pleasure seeking. She dies of forced and secret abortions necessitated by illicit insemination. The unwed mother, the kidnapped underworld girl, the beggar by day and panderer by night, these foci of crime and to the traditional wife beating by drunken husbands, the destitution of mothers; dowry sale of young girls, such as like other situation make up the entire gamut of sex criminology.

The process of growing up female in the patriarchal, patrilocal milieu of Indian society has received inadequate attention from all quarters. The many subtleties and complexities of the process have been missed out. What does it mean to a girl? At what age does a girl become conscious of the constraints under which she will have to live, of the differential value accorded to male and female children and of the justification behind it ? When and how does she learn the contents of the rules appropriate to her? These are the questions which invariably hit out at the roots of the malaise afflicting the Indian society.

Under this background, the authors would like to focus here how to prevent the inhuman cruelty accorded to girls even before they come out of their mother's womb. To retaliate such an issue any integrated approach consisting of doctors, social workers, government organisations (GO) and non-governmental organizations (NGOs) must be called for. It is not wise to distinguish them from each other. All of them have to execute their roles and responsibilities equivocally.

Public awareness and a consciousness-raising campaign can only bring positive result by changing social values/ attitudes towards women. The campaign should evolve newer forms to highlight the social issues and its various aspects. Some of the effective form for campaign will be the parent-daughter *jatra,* march of school-going girls with flowers, sit-in (*dharna*) by prominent parents having only daughters, and so on. A consistent campaign against the notorious activities of money minded doctors and antipathy of the government towards increasing female foeticide, a Women Forum at all India level should be formed. Doctors, social workers, NGO personnel, women activists, should actively discuss the issue at the social level. Through their talks on public forum, media coverage, poster campaign, exhibition, film, publication, they can try to convey the social implication of the tests. Because they should know that mere reforms in legal or medical fields will not themselves do away with this ever growing phenomenon of female foeticide.

To enhance social literacy of public, they should organize pickets in front of hospitals conducting such tests, and posters condemning the tests should be distributed. The posters should demand that:

1. Mass media should refuse to publish advertisement for sex-determination tests.
2. The government must publish the fact that a woman is not responsible for the birth of a girl.
3. The tests have good amount of side effect on the general health of the women.

A woman gives only X chromosome whereas a man may give an X or Y chromosome which is responsible for the sex of the baby. If a man's Y chromosome unites with woman's X chromosome, a boy is born and if man's X chromosome unites with woman's X chromosome, a girl is born. Hence women should not be blamed for the birth of a girl child. Doctors, social workers and others should highlight that sex-determination tests violate Article 14 and Article 15 of the Constitution of India that guarantees that there will be no discrimination against women.

The state of Maharashtra is the first in the country to ban pre-natal sex-determination test (Maharashtra Regulation of Pre-Natal Sex-Determination Act, 1988). The Maharashtra Act has allowed pre-natal tests on the following grounds:

- Chromosomal abnormalities.
- Genetic metabolic disease.
- Sex-linked genetic disease.
- Haemoglobiopathies.
- Congenital abnormalities.
- Any other abnormalities or diseases as may be declared by the appropriate authority.

Legislative exercises would become redundant if a similar legislation is not immediately enacted by the Union Government to stop the misuse of sex-determination tests across the country. There is a need to introduce certain changes in the Medical Termination of Pregnancy Act, 1971, which would legally lay down the conditions under which amniocentesis can be carried out.

More research on the prevalence of sex-determination tests need to be done. So far we have micro studies on the subject. Women's Studies Departments in colleges and universities, sociologists and social workers must give special attention to this problem as they can help in the process of change by working at policy levels and also by imparting knowledge to younger generation through the educational system.

As these tests are very popular in Gujarat, Madhya Pradesh, U.P. and other states as literature and research findings suggest, it becomes necessary to launch a nationwide campaign against the abuse of sex-determination and sex-pre-selection tests. Researchers should start collection of data to get a realistic picture of the popularity of such tests, the class background of pregnant women going for these tests, the various points and counter-points raised with regards to the efficacy of such tests. In a society where systematic neglect and discrimination against daughters and "son-preference" attitude are so deep rooted and where the very survival of women at stake, these issues need to be taken up in their socio-cultural, economic and political context. What we also need to do is cultural alternatives through strong mass media contesting the myths associated with sons and daughters, giving more teeth to the anti-dowry laws, promoting positive images of women as self-sufficient, special support structure for promotion of education and employment of women and placing these in the matrix of the women's liberation movement against every form of oppression, exploitation, ill-treatment and injustice. The fountains of this putrid trend cannot be discovered nor the turbid streams suppressed without these measures and above all, through a painstaking study of the social syndromes existing in our society.

All doctors should be honest and loyal to their profession. They should not be allured under any circumstances to go for sex-determination tests. If any doctor is found to be guilty, he or she must be punished to the extent that his or her registration should be cancelled. In this case ICMR (Indian Council of Medical Research) must be strengthened, integrated, unbiased and apolitical and in the process ICMR must uphold this noble medical profession in the true sense of the term.

Apart from these measures other promising future interventions that social workers, doctors and others can take up are:

(a) approach rural areas seriously and sensitively as rural people suffer from a host of problems such as:
  (i) superstition and fatalistic attitude,
  (ii) preference for male child,
  (iii) A wait and watch attitude.

(b) more publicity at all levels about the blessed aspects of genetic diagnostic technologies.

(c) to disseminate knowledge about family life education and its invaluable importance.

(d) knowledge about population policy, family planning and reproductive health need to be imparted to both male and female population of the society at all levels from time to time.

(e) genetic counselling which can be practiced very effectively and must intervene in the following areas (D. Sinha and S. Ghosh, 1998):
  (i) genetic counselling is essential in aiding parents in making the decision about amniocentesis. This should be a formal counselling session, not merely a brief discussion in doctor's chamber, the risks and benefits must be spelled out in detail.
  (ii) to establish a warm and effective relationship with the clients.
  (iii) to correct false notions and cultural taboos.
  (iv) marriage counselling is also a very important thrust area to be taken care of.
  (v) to prepare the clients for pre-natal diagnosis for detection of any genetic disorder.
  (vi) to make the patients aware of the pros and cons of amniocentesis.

(vii) to educate the clients about the hereditary and medical facts regarding the genetic disorder(s) including diagnosis, treatment and prevention.

(viii) to provide emotional and social support as far as possible to the clients.

(ix) to suggest alternatives at all levels.

Conclusion

A nation cannot progress without the progress of science and technology. So, technological advancement should not be criticized but what matters most is its manifestation and beneficial application. Undoubtedly, amniocentesis is a phenomenal development in the medical science which can detect a number of genetic disorders in the foetus in a womb and in turn prevent the mother to give birth of a unhealthy child. But when this amniocentesis is used merely for detection of sex of a child it is then disastrous and abuse of science and technology. So, it is a question of attitude of the people and how they would like to perceive the sex-determination tests is a great concern. Unless we rectify our tradition bound attitude towards women, there is no point in blaming the process and the doctors who are involved in the process.

SUGGESTED READINGS

1. Abrahan, A. and Shukla, S. (2008); *Sex-Determination Tests*, Bombay, Women's Centre.
2. Anjali (1987) "Prejudice against girls: abuse of scientific discovery"; *Social Welfare*, 34 (9), December.
3. Bennett, N. G. (Ed), (2005); *Sex-Selection of Children*, New York, Academic Press.
4. Bajpai, S. (1997); "The lesser sex", *The Indian Express*, October 28, p. 1.
5. Bardhan, P. (2007); "Little Girls and Death in India", *Economic and Political Weekly* (*EPW*); September 4, pp. 1448-50.
6. Balasubrahmanyan, Vimal (1982); "Women, Medicine and Male Utopia", *EPW*, October 23, 1982.
7. Chhachhi, A. and Satyamala (2008); "Sex-Determination Tests: a technology which will eliminate women"; *Medico Friend Circle Bulletin*, 1995, pp. 3-5.

8. Daswani, M. and Britto, G.A. (2007); *Women and Health: A Critical Review of Available Information in India*; Foundation for Research in Community Health (mimeo).
9. Dube, L. (1983), "Amniocentesis: The Delete Continues", *EPW*; June 11, pp. 1933-34.
10. Devasia, L. and Devasia, V.V, (2007); *Girl child in India*, Ashis Publishing House, New Delhi.
11. Erikson, Ronald (1991); *Women in Indian Society*; Sage Publication, New Delhi, pp. 181-183.
12. Ghadially, Rehena (1991); *Women in Indian Society*, Sage Publication, New Delhi.
13. *The Week* (1993) ; August 1, p. 41.
14. *The Times of India*, 1983, "Two Pune Women Allegedly Raped", April 2.
15. Habibulla, M., "Human egg on sale", *Nexus*, December 1994-January 1995.
16. Jeffery, Roger and Jeffery, Patricia (1983); "Female Infanticide and Amniocentesis", *EPW*, Vol. XVIII; April 16-23; No. 16-17.
17. Kumar, Dharma (1983); "Male Utopias of Nightmares", *EPW*, Vol. XVIII; No. 3, January 15.
18. Patel, V. (1984); "Amniocentesis: Misuse of Modern Technology", *Socialist Health Review*; 1.2. pp. 69-71.
19. Rapp. R. (1996); "The Ethic of Choice", Background paper for National Workshop on Women, Health and Reproductive Rights, Bombay, December.
20. Ramanamma, A. and Bambawale, U. (1998); "The mania for sons: an analysis of social values in South Asia", *Social Science and Medicine*, 14B (3), 107-10.
21. Singh, G. and Jain, S. (1989); "Opinions of men and women regarding Amniocentesis", Ludhiana; Punjab Agricultural University, College of Home Science.
22. *The Statesman*, July 23, 2005.
23. Sinha, D. and Ghosh, S. (1998); "Problems and prospects of genetic counselling in the medical profession", *The Journal of Family Welfare*; Vol. 44, No. 4, December 1998.
24. Shah, A. and Taneja, S. (2006); "What do males and females of Delhi think about female foeticide", *The Indian Journal of Social Science*, 5(1), January-March, pp. 81-92.
25. Seth, S. (1989); "Place of prenatal sex-determination", paper presented at the Larsen and Toubro seminar, Bombay, September.
26. Vishwanath, L.S. (1983); "Misadventures of Amniocentesis", *EPW*, Vol. XVIII, No. 11; March 12.
27. Wertz, D.C. and Fletcher, J.C. (1995); "Prenatal diagnosis and sex-selection in 19 nations", *Social Science and Medicine*, 37(11); pp. 1359-66.

3

Genetics and Social Work
An Emerging Area of Practice

In 1917 itself, Mary Richmond understood the value of a family genetic history in dealing with individual or family related problems.

> He must aim to get at facts of heredity…The pertinent data would cover the condition of health and cause of death of parents, grandparents, brothers and sisters, uncles and aunts. The items should be especially clear and detailed whenever, in any of these relatives, there seems to be a question of consanguineous marriage, miscarriages, or tuberculosis, alcoholism, mental disorder, nervousness, epilepsy, cancer, deformities or abnormalities, or of any exceptional ability. (p.187)

Genetics is the study of heredity (Brennan, 1985). It is the process of asking and answering questions about the characteristics and continuity of life. Heredity affects each of us on many levels, as individuals, as members of families, and as members of the larger community (Kowles, 1985).

Newman and Newman (1987) describe two types of heredity—(1) It encompasses those attributes people all share as members of the human species. These include things as abstract as "the readiness to learn and the inclination to participate in social interaction". (2) This type of heredity speaks about those characteristics or traits such as hair colour or blood type that are passed through a specific gene pool from one generation to another. These are the things that distinguish us as individuals and link us to our parents and grandparents.

The body of knowledge about human genetics has expanded tremendously. Increasingly, information appears in magazines, newspapers, and on television linking conditions such as heart diseases, diabetes, hypertension, cancer, addictive disorders, dementia, Alzheimer's disease, and various forms of mental health problems to genetic factors. The prospect of genetic engineering, the ability to replace or repair defective genes, leaves some excitedly anticipating future interventions. For others, genetic engineering causes concern about the moral and ethical implications of this technology.

Social workers have, and will continue to have, a major role in developing ways of translating this knowledge and technology into methods of helping people understand and cope with their specific problems. Rauch (1992) had tried to explain why social workers should be aware of genetic disorders and their process of dealing with such problems.

1. In the framework of a bio-psychosocial model, social workers use family and individual histories to evaluate client situations.
2. Social workers must be able to provide accurate information and make referrals to appropriate genetic services for their clients with genetic concerns.
3. Social workers provide services to persons and families affected by disabilities and chronic conditions that often have contributing genetic factors or origins.

Genetics and environment

Many abnormalities and developmental characteristics are influenced by polygenes. The severity or level of malfunction will vary from individual to individual. These conditions can be classified as multifactorial because they are influenced by multiplicity of factors both genetic and environment. There may be a threshold at which the cumulative effect of the associated genes will cause the abnormality to appear as the phenotype or physical characteristics. On the other hand, environmental factors such as nutritional status, exposure to stress, and general health of the individual can exert significant influence on the severity of the presentation.

Some conditions are described as having a genetic predisposition, and are even more susceptible to environmental influence. Environmental factors can either promote or prevent the expression of diseases such as hypertension, diabetes, heart disease and some forms of cancer.

From this we can come to the conclusion that "People differ". This is so because each person has undergone a complex series of transactions between a unique set of genes and a unique sequence of environment. When considering genetics and environment and their contributions to human differences, two important assumptions are worth highlighting (Smith, 1999)—(1) the interactive model assumes genetics and environment are inseparable, and (2) the additive model assumes the components can each be identified and separately analyzed for its contribution.

Genetics and genetic disorders

Better understanding of the etiology, causes, risks of inheritance, course, prognosis, and treatment of genetic disorders now is available to people with genetic concerns. A network of specialized genetic services which are easily accessible are prevalent throughout India as well as across the globe. Because of the astounding progress in the area of technology and information; client's genetic questions now can be answered more fully and accurately than previously was possible. This important new resource is enhancing traditional area of social work practice. In addition, the meaning of the term "**genetic disorder**" is broadening, the number and proportion of clients with genetic concerns is expanding, and new practice sites are emerging.

The study of genetic processes includes the causes of hereditary, similarities and differences among humans, the ways in which they are transmitted from generation to generation, and those factors, both internal and external, that affect gene action and outcome. There are two dimensions of genetics (Rauch, 1992). **(1) medical genetics**—it is concerned with the etiology, prevention, diagnosis, and treatment of genetic disorders. **(2) behavioural genetics**—it examines genetic contributors to variations of conduct that range from innate temperament to major psychiatric disorders.

There are four types of genetic disorders generally found in the literature of medical sciences and genetic engineering (Nagle, 1984; Riccardi, 1977; Schild and Black, 1984; Singer, 1985; Sinha, 1999; Green, 2001).

(a) Single gene inheritance
(b) Multifactorial inheritance
(c) Chromosome aberrations
(d) Exposure to harmful environmental agents

It is also worthwhile to discuss briefly **genetic screening** because when we talk about any genetic disorder and specific services for a particular disorder it mostly depends on proper genetic screening.

Genetic screening can be defined as the systematic search for persons with a particular genotype (genetic information in each cell) in a defined population, and serves as an important adjunct of modern preventive medicine (Sinha, 1999). The clinical purposes of genetic screening are to determine whether a person needs remedial or preventive health care and to obtain information for use in reproductive decision-making. Four types of genetic screening are available.

Carrier screening detects the presence of genes or abnormal **chromosomes** (genes, the basic units of inheritance, are packaged in units called chromosomes) might be harmful to potential offspring. Most often carrier screening is offered on a voluntary basis to persons of reproductive age who plan to have children and who meet criteria for risk of carrying a deleterious gene.

Prenatal screening detects the possible presence of a genetic disorder in a fetus. Elevated level of **alpha-fetoprotein** (AFP, which is a prerequisite for pre-natal care) in the blood of pregnant woman is the signal for birth defects and need for additional evaluation, prevention and treatment. Sonography, which is a means of visualizing the fetus, also is used in prenatal screening.

Neonatal screening identifies the possible presence of serious genetic diseases shortly after birth, even if the baby is asymptomatic. If the results are positive, diagnostic evaluation and treatment can be initiated expeditiously. Newborn screening has had major success.

Presymptomatic screening promotes health by enabling individuals to take preventive action. For example, the person who is predisposed genetically to alcoholism can abstain from drinking. In other cases, presymptomatic screening facilitates accurate diagnosis and appropriate treatment when symptom appear.

Genetic Counselling

Genetic counselling is having both medical and psychosocial aspects. Social workers with genetic counselling as a special field of practice provide clients with information about the disorder—the way in which heredity contributes, risks of recurrence, and treatment option.

Social workers involved in genetic counselling can assess social service needs, make appropriate referrals, and act as case managers. By providing individual, family, and group counselling, social workers can enable individuals and families to cope with the demands posed by genetic disorders. Social workers also offer crisis intervention during disorders and, if needed, during the treatment stages of life and to the bereaved (Rauch, 1992).

Because of their long-term involvement, community-based social workers are in a position to identify when genetic service provision needs change. For example, social workers may learn that the information provided initially was not absorbed and that reiteration may be necessary. Children with genetic disorders may wonder about their fertility or the chances that a child of theirs would inherit the condition. Also, changing knowledge and technology may outdate earlier information. Particularly because changes in the field of human genetics occur so rapidly, genetic counselling should not be considered a one time event. Social workers will need to know how, and when, to refer different members of genetically affected families to genetic centres as their needs change.

Implications for social work practice

A person may be viewed as a bio-psychosocial system who, from birth, is a member of a family and an extended family and who subsequently becomes a member of friendship, educational, recreational, religious, and cultural groups, and civic associations (Northern, 1988). Genetic disorders that impair cognitive or motor development result in chronic illness or any form of dysfunction will have a detrimental effect on the individual's ability to take on the roles and responsibilities necessary to participate as an effective member of these groups. All of these factors increase the probability that social work intervention will be needed, and that the family will be brought to the attention of social work services for assistance.

Social worker's involvement with people who have genetic concerns and with the provision of genetic services are likely getting momentum at a rapid space as mentioned earlier. The general public is learning about human genetics through the media; as clients and potential clients become more knowledgeable, they will raise genetic issues with social workers. Clinical genetic services are proliferating, and the use of those services is increasing as both the public and members of the helping professions become more aware of recent developments. In addition, both the number and size of speciality clinics have increased as more effective treatments have developed and life expectancy has increased. Because these facilities may not have adequate social work staff or may be located far from client's homes, they may refer clients to community agencies for counselling, support services, and case management.

Social work in the ecological perspective focuses on transactions between human beings and their environments.

The ecological perspective emphasizes the biological concept of adaptation or the active efforts of the species to achieve **goodness-of-fit** with its environment over evolutionary time. How individuals "**survive, develop, and achieve reproductive success**" within their environments is also encompassed in goodness-of-fit (Germain, 2000). For social workers to understand its implications in the field of genetics and to help people having genetic disorders must work on the basis of following assumptions which show the relationship among genetics, social work, environment and development; of which environment and development are the core of social work practice (Green, 2001).

- Human beings carry within them chemically encoded information that makes each a member of the human species and each a unique individual.
- Genetic disorders can interfere with an individual's ability to fulfil his or her roles in society.
- Genetic information is encompassed in the bio-psychosocial model; social workers use to evaluate client situations.
- Many genetic conditions are a result of a multiplicity of factors both genetic and environmental.
- People differ because each person has undergone a complex series of transactions between a unique set of genes and a unique sequence of environments.
- Environmental factors can either promote or prevent the expression of some diseases.
- Some conditions have a genetic predisposition and are more susceptible to enenvironmental influences.
- Some genetic disorders are found more frequently in certain ethnic groups or among persons who have origins from specific geographic regions.
- Genetic disorders may stress a family's ability to cope.
- Social workers have a major role in translating genetic knowledge and technology into methods of helping people that are congruent with the client's cultural stance and value base.

- Interventions in genetic counselling are aimed at enhancing the adaptive capacities and strengthening coping mechanisms of client families.

The policy of deinstitutionalization is maintaining many developmentally delayed or otherwise handicapped people in the community. Such individuals come to the attention of social workers and bring genetic concerns and concerns of their families. The increased life expectancy for children with genetic disorders is generating demand for flexible, community-based social services appropriate for different stages of the life cycle, including adulthood. The value that impaired children, youth, and adults should live as normally as possible within the constraints of their conditions is bringing these individuals into schools and other mainstream institutions.

As Shield (1977) noted, social workers use generic knowledge and skills to work with chronically ill or disabled people and their families. However, a genetic diagnosis is distinctive; the condition generally is "permanent, chronic, familial, complex, labelling and threatening". Genetic diagnosis touch on intimate, deeply personal areas of life: sexuality, decision to conceive, and decision to terminate pregnancy for genetic reasons. A genetic diagnosis also may reveal family secrets, such as incest or adultery.

Although social workers can apply generic skills, generally affected individuals and families confront unique adaptive demands involved practitioners need to be familiar with specific disorders and their burdens, able to empathize with their psychological and familial effects, competent in assessing service needs, and skilled in making what may be emotionally charged referrals, including referrals to genetic centres (Avers, 1999).

The specific requirements of social work practice that involves genetics are changing as illustrated by adoption. The acknowledged right of adoptees to know about their biological background and possible genetic risks to themselves or their own children makes genetic histories an important part of the adoption records. Predisposition to alcohol and other agents through pre-natal screening, miscarriage, stillbirth and birth defects which all indicate the importance of preventive intervention by the social workers.

The harmful effects of prenatal exposure to certain environmental agents raises the question of fetal abuse (Abel, 1984; Chambers, 1986; Bonavoglia, 1987). If legislatures or the courts decide that prenatal abuse is possible, social workers will need to be prepared to refer to protective services, which, in turn, will need to accept this new responsibility. Health and reproductive problems associated with exposure to environmental toxics in workplace and communities have advocacy implications for occupational social workers (Elkington, 1999).

Evidence of genetic substance to some behavioural dysfunctions suggests that formal genetic evaluation may become an accepted part of assessment and treatment planning. If clients have had genetic counselling, social workers will need to assess whether faulty comprehension of the information, life-cycle changes, or new developments in genetic knowledge or technology warrant additional genetic evaluation and counselling. When clients raise genetic concerns, social workers will need to provide accurate information, know the limits of their knowledge and skills, obtain consultation, and refer appropriately (Black, 2000).

The definition of "**appropriate referral**" is having different significance. For example, the discovery that genetic liability and single-gene inheritance are factors in some psychiatric disorders has led to genetic counselling in psychiatry (Hamovit, 1998). In many parts of the world genetic counselling is regularly provided to patients and their families at community mental health centres. As this capability becomes more widely known, social workers in various fields will be obligated to ensure that client's psychiatric genetic questions are answered by the results of competent evaluation and counselling (Nyhan, W., 1999).

To be very precise social workers can be very effective in helping clients really existing coping mechanisms or build new ones to deal with the situation. The following list provides specific ways the social worker can assist the client or family having genetic problems. This also in turn shows the implications for social work practice in the area of genetic concerns.

(a) Help client break down the problem into manageable units.
(b) Mobilize the family into meaningful activity such as participating in a support group.
(c) Clarify and reinforce medical information provided by other health professionals.
(d) Assist the client and the family in developing a healthy self-concept.
(e) Facilitate communication and decision making within the family.
(f) Link families up with appropriate support services such as financial assistance, medical equipment and care, and special education programmes.

Social workers in all fields need to be aware of existing genetic counselling services in their community, be able to identify those clients with genetic service needs, and make appropriate referrals when necessary.

Conclusion

Problems of genetic disorders are increasing rapidly. On the other hand, phenomenal development in the medical sciences are trying to treat some of these problems. Families who are affected by these disorders are undergoing tremendous mental agony and the top of that many people are not aware of the proper genetic services available which can minimize their problems. Some of the treatments are also very expensive. Advances in human genetics knowledge and the proliferation of genetic services are transforming the ways in which these concerns can be addressed. Developments in human genetics are broadening the definition of genetic disorders, increasing the number of social work clients with genetic concerns, and adding to the requisites of social work practice. So at this juncture the profession of social work must confront the challenge.

SUGGESTED READINGS

1. Black, R.B. (2000); "Genetics and adoption: A challenge for social work". In M. Dinnerman (Ed.), *Social work in a turbulent world*. Silver Spring, MD: National Association of Social Workers.
2. Rauch, B. Julia. (1992), "Social Work and the Genetic Revolution: Genetic Services", *Social Work*; Vol. 33, No. 5, September-October.
3. Schild, S. (1977); Social work interventions with genetic problems. In W.T. Hall and C.L. Young (eds), *Proceedings*: *Genetic Disorders*: *Social Service Interventions*. University of Pittsburgh., Public Health Social Work Programme.
4. Richmond, M. (1917); *Social Diagnosis*. New York, Russell Sage Foundation.
5. Kowles, R.V. (1985); *Genetics, Society and Decisions*, Columbus, OH: Charles E. Merrill.
6. Brennan, J.R. (1985); *Pattern of Human Heredity*. Princeton, NJ: Prentice Hall.
7. Newman, B., Newman, P.R. (1987); *Development Through Life*: *A Psycho-Social Approach*; Homewood, IL: Dorsey Press.
8. Nagle, J.J. (1984); *Heredity and Human Affairs* (3rd ed); St. Louis, MO: Times Miror/Mosby College.
9. Singer, S. (1985); *Human genetics*: *An introduction to the principles of heredity* (2nd ed.). New York: W.H. Freeman.
10. Riccardi, V.M. (1977); *The genetic approach to human disease*; New York: Oxford University Press.
11. Schild, S. and Black, R.B. (1984); *Social work and genetics*: *A guide for practice*. New York: Haworth Press.
12. Sinha, D. (1999); "Problems and prospects of genetic counselling in the medical profession"; *Journal of Family Welfare*, Vol. 44, No. 4. December.
13. Green, R. (2001); *Human Behaviour Theory and Social Work Practice;* Aldine De Gruyter, New York.
14. Elkington, J. (1987); *The poisoned womb*. New York: Penguin Paperbacks.
15. Chambers, M. (1986, November 16). "Are fetal rights equal to infants?" *New York Times*, p. C2.
16. Bonavoglia, A. (1987); *Reproductive rights*: *The ordeal of Pamela Rae Stewart*. Ms, 16, 92f.

17. Abel, E.L. (1984); Fetal alcohol syndrome: A case of prenatal abuse? In E.L. Abel (ed.); *Fetal alcohol syndrome and fetal alcohol effects* (pp. 213-217), New York: Plenum.
18. Smith, N.W. (1999) "Heredity and environment revisited", *The Psychological Record*; 35, 173-176.
19. Avers, C. (1999); *Genetics* (2nd ed.). Boston: Willard Grant.
20. Hamovit, J. (1998): Genetics, genetic counselling and psychiatric disorders. In J.B Rauch (Ed.), *Educating for practice in a changing world* (pp. 91-100). Baltimore, MD: University of Maryland, School of Social Work and Community Planning.
21. Northern, H. (1988); *Social Work with Groups*, 2nd ed. New York: Columbia University Press.
22. Nyhan, W. (1999); *The Heridity Factor*, New York: Grosset and Dunlop.
23. Germain, C.B. (2000); "Human Development in Contemporary Environments", *Social Service Review*; pp. 565-580.

4

Combating Alzheimer's Disease
Immediate Concerns and Implications for Social Workers

A case study has been discussed below before we go on to the text of the chapter for right and proper understanding of the problem of Alzheimer and time and phases where social workers could come out very useful in dealing with such cases.

Emma Brown is a well-dressed, white female who looks younger than her 80 years. She is generally alert, but frequently confused. She sometimes exhibits agitation and suspiciousness, but is generally pleasant and cooperative. Immediate family lives nearby and includes her sister and her niece. A stepdaughter and two stepsons, who live 90 miles away, write, and send gifts, but do not visit. Mrs. Brown was admitted to Riley's in the spring, following hospitalization for a broken clavicle, which she suffered in a motor vehicle accident. She was *en route* to visit her sister who was in the hospital following a stroke. Following extensive testing, Mrs. Brown was diagnosed with **Alzheimer's disease**. Her history reflects that she had an active, healthy life. A couple of surgeries were performed. She smoked for 15 years, but stopped smoking many years ago. Her alcohol intake is very minimal. She was treated for anemia and resulting peptic disease four years ago. There is no evidence of hypertension or cardiovascular or central nervous system impairment. A detailed social history revealed that memory loss predated the car accident. In the

(*contd.*)

(*contd.*)

fall before her admission to the hospital, she relocated to an apartment complex for the elderly because of forgetfulness and mild confusion. She felt the move would help her cope and provide additional security. However, she soon became unable to find her sister's home or other familiar places. Instead of helping, the move seemed to exacerbate her memory impairment.

Mrs. Brown was discharged from the hospital at the same time that her sister Mary was released for post-stroke recuperation. They were placed together at hospital's minimal care unit. Her sister recovered well and returned back home but Mrs. Brown remained confused and began to wander, particularly at night. She spoke frequently of having to go home, and her wandering seemed to focus around this theme. During her night wandering, Emma supposedly began to fall. The staff would find her sitting on the floor unable to tell them what had happened. Her sister and niece felt Emma's problems were a result of the difficulty of being alone in the hospital. Later on Emma was relocated to her sister's home. Unfortunately, this change did not alter the wandering or the forgetfulness. Mrs. Brown's behaviour became quite disruptive and unmanageable for her sister. She rummaged through drawers and closets, searching for mysterious, lost items. Her sister's frustration was heightened when she began to hoard and scatter clothes as well. Emma was readmitted to hospital once again.

The initial evaluation upon readmission to hospital revealed symptoms consistent with the early stages of Alzheimer's disease. Although the family had been given the diagnosis, little information had been provided and few attempts had been made to discuss with them her poor prognosis and the inevitable progressive decline. Emma was alert and ambulatory, with some insight intact, and was able to hide her cognitive impairments through a social façade. In fact, she experienced marked confusion, time and spatial disorientation, frequent periods of anxiety and agitation, and occasional paranoia regarding the staff.

(*contd.*)

(*contd.*)

Activity staff reported inconsistent participation levels, largely due to her inability to remember when and where activities took place. She exhibited increased wandering and agitation at night, a condition commonly referred to as sundowning. She suffered occasional night time incontinence.

Different assessment scales were introduced to understand the extent of the problem. Mrs. Brown scored lowest in the areas of orientation and recall, and scored average in registration, attention, and calculation. Mild depression was also observed. The areas of concern noted were feelings of disappointment, punishment, self-blame level of irritation, decision making, appearance, and interest in sex. An evaluation of her performance on activities of daily living revealed independence in all but bathing, dressing and continence. Difficulty in these areas stemmed from the need for assistance in focusing her activities, making decisions, remembering instructions and other relevant facts surrounding the activity.

Because of Emma's verbal accessibility and her reasonably high MMS (Mini Mental State), she was assessed as a good candidate for social work intervention. Generally, these were designed to alleviate the behavioural problems associated with the early stages of Alzheimer's disease, and the specific problems noted in ADL (Activities of Daily Living) activities.

[Schwaber Toba and Kerson and Associates; "*Social Work in Health Settings: Practices in context*"; 2007; Haworth Press, New York.]

In discussing mental health, it is important to keep in mind that some older adults experience problems of mental health that continues from earlier life stages. Among psychologists studying ageing, most of the interest centres on mental health problems that are especially among older adults or whose onset of the disease/problem is commonly found in later life.

Dementia is such a most common pathology in late life and a term used to describe a number of physical disorders of the brain arising from different causes. They all have in common a decline in mental function, especially memory. Dementia interferes with daily activities and social relationships. Dementia is usually progressive, irreversible and ultimately fatal. Alzheimer's disease is the most common type of dementia, accounting for approximately 50 per cent of all cases. Also common is vascular dementia in which part of the brain dies off because of blood supply failure to the brain. Vascular dementia accounts for a further 20 per cent of all cases. A further 20 per cent of cases are caused by the changes of Alzheimer's disease and vascular dementia together. Here, in this chapter, we will be concentrating only on **Alzheimer's disease.**

Current status of the elderly

We have started living in the Age of ageing but it is only the dawn of that age. From 12 million in 1901, we rose to be 20 million in 1951 and there are now nearly 77 million older persons in India today (Desai and Raju, 2000). About 11 per cent of elderly are above 80 years and by 2025, 25 per cent of the world's population will be above 80 years.

At a moderate estimate, there are likely to be 177 million older people in India by 2025 (United Nations Projections, 1998). This in itself is no cause for alarm. However, the country is totally unprepared to handle the human problems associated with such a situation. There is no comprehensive national policy for elderly care. Old age pensions are meagre and not all elderly are eligible for it.

The National Sample Survey Organization's data shows that 4.5 per cent of elderly males and 6.7 per cent of elderly females in India were physically immobile (NSS, 1991). Nearly 45 per cent of rural and 44.8 per cent urban elderly suffer from seven major chronic diseases. A recent study of urban and rural elderly in Bangalore found 60 per cent of the older people to be suffering from long-term illnesses. More than a fourth (28.2%) of women aged over 60 years needed help in managing activities of daily living. Many rural women who require care complained that they did not get such help. Also, if the elderly woman is a widow, which is the case with 55 per cent of the elderly women today, it is not a pleasant situation (*Employment News*, 2000: 12-18 August).

More than half (about 50-55%) of the rural elderly have problems in vision and mobility—the two things that are essential for a person to be active and independent (Prakash, 1997). About 90 per cent of older persons today are from the unorganized sector, which means that these people have no regular source of income, provident fund or gratuity, no medical insurance or any kind of social security, after formally or informally retiring from active earning.

Ageing has important implications, both at the macro and micro levels. While at the micro level, it affects individuals and their families; at the macro level it affects the entire nation. With about 33 per cent of the elderly living just below the poverty line and another 33 per cent just above it, but belonging to lower income group, the financial situation of about 66 per cent of the older persons today is fragile. This relates to serious livelihood insecurities caused by factors including growing incidence of prolonged old age ailments, disabilities, dysfunctions, lack of opportunities in gainful activities and no or little familial support.

What is Alzheimer's disease

In 1906, a German neurologist, **Dr. Alois Alzheimer**, described changes in the brain tissue of a woman who had died of what was thought to be an unusual mental illness. These changes are now recognized as the characteristic abnormal changes in the brain of a person affected by Alzheimer's disease.

Webster's Dictionary defines Alzheimer's disease: 'A condition of deteriorated mentality that is characterized by marked decline from the individual's former intellectual level'. The definition closely states that Alzheimer's disease is a decline from a previously high level of intellectual performance. Thus mental retardation from birth which is also characterized by poor intellectual performance is not included within the purview of Alzheimer's disease.

The American Psychiatric Association has given a more medical definition for Alzheimer's disease as follows : 'A decline in cognitive, intellectual and memory functions due to disease processes affecting the central nervous system.' They have also observed in this disorder that brain cells gradually degenerate and deposits of an abnormal protein (**beta amyloid**) build up in the brain. As a result, the brain tissue shrinks, and there is a progressive loss of mental capabilities which is severe enough to interfere with a patient's ability to function in daily life.

People with Alzheimer's disease gradually lose their sense of time and place (Mega and Cummings, 1996). A major symptom is that they forget things they have just said or done, although their memory for past events may, for a time, remain clear. As the disease progresses, people become unaware of their condition although they may still experience distress. They find it increasingly difficult and then impossible to perform even the simplest everyday tasks, including washing, eating and dressing. They may become uncommunicative and inconsistent, sometimes with severe behavioural problems (Phillips, 1995). Eventually, most need 24-hour care either at home or in a nursing home. The disease may go on for many years (5 to 10 years) or more (Allen, 1992). The most susceptible age for this disease is over 65 years. There are stages and phases of Alzheimer's disease (Gruetzner,1992; Volicer and Hurley, 1995) depending upon the severity of the problem. Death usually occurs from an infection or stroke.

Memory loss in Alzheimer's disease is not like normal forgetfulness. Many people especially as they get older, find that their memory is not as good as it used to be. A person who is ordinarily forgetful can still remember details associated with the thing(s) they have forgotten. For example, they may briefly forget their next door neighbour's name but they still know that the person they are talking to is their neighbour. People with Alzheimer's disease forget not only details but also the entire context. They may also have some other problems, such as changes in behaviour and loss of ability to do everyday tasks.

What causes Alzheimer's

Alois Alzheimer's discovery generated great interest at the time, but the disease that carried his name soon came to be regarded as a medical oddity. Why? For many years, the diagnosis appeared to apply only to a very small group of patients under the age of 60. That soon changed, thanks in part to the widespread use of vaccines and antibiotics, which extended the life span. By the 1960s, the number of cases of so called senile dementia had increased to the point that neurologists finally made the connection in most cases, Alzheimer's disease and senile dementia were one and the same.

Alzheimer's researchers, gathered from around the globe for the **Joint World Alzheimer's Congress 2000** in Washington described their progress in finding genes that put people at risk for this disease. They presented evidence that factors put elevated the risk of people getting Alzheimer's disease: for instance, a high fat diets. The researchers also discussed the first clinical trials of compounds that target, what many believe, the cause of Alzheimer's disease—a sticky protein known as beta amyloid. After the discovery of beta amyloid, a research team, to their great surprise, discovered that beta amyloid was a fragment of a much larger protein, which came to be known as the **amyloid-precursor protein** or APP for short. Later, two more early-onset Alzheimer's genes were found, **presenilin-1** and **presenilin-2**. Both genes were dominant—a child who received just one gene from either parent would inevitably get the disease (Corey-Bloom and Folstein, 2004). One more gene, the **APOE4** was found, which could contribute to the development of more than 60 per cent of all late-onset Alzheimer's disease. But unlike the APP and presenilins, the APOE4 is a susceptible gene that is, people who carry this gene do not necessarily develop Alzheimer's disease. Even if they do, their brains appear to be more riddled with plaques and tangles than the brains of Alzheimer's patients who carry the APP or the presenilins.

Researcher at Mount Sinai School of Medicine in New York City (Alice Park, 2000) are concentrating on a protein known as **COX2**, which they have seen rises steeply in the brains of patients in the very stages of the disease. Cells produce COX2 in response to injury, observes Mount Sinai molecular psychiatrist Giulio Pasinetti, who believe it may be COX2 and not beta-amyloid that induces the inflammatory characteristics of the disease.

Researchers have been kept on experimenting to find out some other causes of this disease and in the process they have observed the following factors which are to a great extent responsible for Alzheimer's disease:

1. HIV, the virus which leads to AIDS, can be a cause of Alzheimer's disease. The virus has been found in the brain of people with HIV as early as two days after initial infection. This condition is usually referred to as **AIDS dementia complex (ADC)**.
2. **Fronto-temporal dementias** are also a cause of Alzheimer's disease. It occurs usually in a person in their fifties or sixties. The frontal lobe of the brain is particularly affected. It involves a progressive decline in a person's mental abilities over a number of years. Damage to brain cells is more localized and usually begins in the frontal lobe part of the brain.
3. People who drink too much **alcohol** do seem to be at risk of developing problems with their memory. Some have a specific problem of loss of short-term memory which develops because of vitamin B1 deficiency. Others develop a wider range of problems that resemble Alzheimer's disease.
4. Vascular disease occurs where blood vessels and the supply of oxygen is at risk. If oxygen supply fails in the brain, brain cells are likely to die leading to a series of mini strokes and possible **vascular dementia.**
5. Dementia with **Lewy bodies** is the third most common cause of dementia and may occur in up to 20 per cent of cases. It is caused by the degeneration and death of nerve cells in the brain.

Millions of dollars have been spent and thousands of medical scientists across the globe have been experimenting in the laboratory to find whether there is any relationship between genetic pre-disposition and Alzheimer's disease. Some success has been achieved. So far three genetic defects have been identified in patients of Alzheimer's disease: one defect on chromosome 14, one defect on chromosome 19, and one on chromosome 21. It is possible that there may be other genetic defects which will be identified in patients with Alzheimer's disease. The genetic defects manifest themselves by aggregation of multiple cases of Alzheimer's disease within families, but the extent of the problem is yet to be ascertained.

Alzheimer's disease is not infectious and is not linked to the person's use of his or her brain or stress. It is not linked to gender, social class, ethnic group or geographic location. Alzheimer's disease is more common among older people but younger people can also be affected.

So, it is still a very controversial issue among the researchers in genetics, bio-chemistry, medical sciences and other related disciplines that what exactly causes the disease. No definite findings have been made so far.

Stages of Alzheimer's disease

Early stage

At this stage the disease can often be overlooked and incorrectly diagnosed as "old age". Because onset is gradual, it is difficult to identify exactly when Alzheimer's disease begins. The person may:

- show difficulties with language;
- experience significant memory loss and especially short-term memory;
- be disoriented in time;
- becomes lost in familiar places;
- display difficulties in making decision;
- lack initiative and motivation;
- show signs of depression and aggression;
- show a loss of interest in hobbies and activities.

Middle stage

The problem associated with Alzheimer's disease become more evident, with the person having increasing difficulty coping with day-to-day activities. He/She:

- may become very forgetful—especially of recent events and people's names;
- can no longer manage to live alone without problems;
- is unable to cook, clean or shop;
- may become extremely dependent;
- needs help with dressing;
- needs assistance with personal hygiene, i.e. toileting, bathing and washing;
- has increased difficulty with speech, sometimes wandering and get lost;
- show various behavioural abnormalities, such as unprovoked aggression;
- may experience hallucinations.

Last stage

At this stage the person with Alzheimer's disease is totally dependent and inactive. Memory problems are very serious and the affected person becomes increasingly disabled physically. He/She

(a) cannot recognize family;
(b) bedridden;
(c) unable to remember anything or process new information;
(d) unable to control bladder and bowel function.

Symptoms and disease progression

Alzheimer's disease is uncommon in younger people but becomes more common with age. It can affect people as young as 30 but this is very rare. Up to the age of 65, this disease develops in only one person in 100. Over the age of 65, the chances rise to around 5 in every 100 people. Over the age of 80, this figure rises to 20 in every 100 people. Alzheimer's disease affects each person in a different way. Its impact depends largely on what the person was like before the disease, for example his or her personality, physical condition and lifestyle.

The symptoms of Alzheimer's disease can be best understood in the context of the three stages of its development—early, middle and late. Not all persons with Alzheimer's disease will display all the symptoms mentioned above and they vary from individual to individual. The stages serve as a guide to the progress of the disease, to help caregivers be aware of potential problems and plan future needs. No one person will experience the progress of the disease in exactly the same way as another.

Some of these symptoms may appear in any of the stages. For example, a behaviour listed in the middle stage or late stage may occur in the early stage. Also caregivers should be aware of that in all stages, short, lucid periods can occur.

Extent of the problem of Alzheimer's disease in India

Alzheimer's disease in India is called 'Sathaya Gaya' which means 'turned 60'. Another name for it is 'Satar-batar' which translates to 'turned 70'. These words refer to altered behaviour and loss of memory in the older age groups.

Early changes in cognition which characterize Alzheimer's disease are not enough to convince a family to bring a patient to a doctor. This is dismissed as "age-factor". Even if such a patient is taken to a doctor who has limited experience with this type of disease, will rarely make specific diagnosis. Thus most hospital-based data does not have any significant number of cases of Alzheimer's disease. Lack of awareness about the manifestation of Alzheimer's disease and lack of knowledge on how to care for such patients leads to their inappropriate care. It is not uncommon for a patient to be reprimanded for urinating in the middle of the room and being scolded to 'teach him how to behave'.

As the disease progresses, morbidity rapidly rises because of lack of understanding of the manifestations of the disease amongst caregivers. Thus, conditions such as bronchial pneumonia, hip fractures and other accidents are very common amongst these patients particularly in rural areas leading to early mortality. This high case fatality ratio with high mortality early in the disease leads to poor survivorship amongst cases.

Although Alzheimer's disease can occur at any stage, it is more common with increasing age, very rare in the age group 40-50. In fact the rate of occurrence of the disease increases exponentially with age group 60-65, and in the age group over 80 it is very common. A WHO epidemiological study conducted at Chennai in urban and rural areas; three per cent of the elderly above the age of 65 years are affected by the disease. In population above 80 years, the prevalence of Alzheimer's disease is 15-25 per cent (Kaplon, Sadock and Grebb, 1994). Some researchers also believe that almost 50 per cent of the people over 80 will get Alzheimer's disease in India. Alzheimer's disease is likely to become a major health concern in India because of the rising elderly population.

Diagnosis, prognosis and treatment

There is no simple test to make a diagnosis. Diagnosis of Alzheimer's disease is made by taking a careful history of the person's problem from a close relative or friend, together with an examination of the person's physical and mental status (some physical investigations may be necessary). It is important to exclude other conditions or illness that cause memory loss. Early diagnosis helps the caregivers to know what to expect and deal with the disease. A diagnosis is the first step towards planning for the future.

Doctor typically conduct a battery of tests, which can include blood counts, chest X-rays and tests of thyroid function. American Academy of Neurology (Zarit, 2000) has issued a new set of guidelines that emphasizes the importance of taking CAT scans or magnetic resonance images of the brain. These are particularly good at revealing structural problems caused by ministrokes, blood clots, tumors etc. Treatment, of course, will depend on what the doctor finds. But one does not know what to expect or what treatment will be used until one knows what he or she is dealing with (Gorman, 2000).

There is no specific approved treatment for Alzheimer's disease which can cure the illness. There are a few drugs which have been approved in several developed countries. However, these help only a minority of patients in temporarily improving their memory function and do not cure the disease. Many other drugs are under clinical trial in many parts of the world.

In India, Ayurvedic physicians have used various products for centuries in the treatment of memory disorders. *Brahmi* and *Ashwagandha* are well known ingredients of many Ayurvedic medications. However, none of these preparations have been scientifically tested for their efficacy.

One symptom of Alzheimer's is decreased level of **acetylcholine,** an important chemical that transmits signal between brain cells. Presently reported (July, 2000) by U.S. based Janssen Pharmaceutical and its Belgium affiliate, Janseen Research Foundation along with Britain's Shire Pharmaceutical Group, gained the European Union's approval to market a type of drug which help boosts acetycholine level in Alzheimer's patients and improved their memory and language skills.

Scientists have also opined recently that elevated cholesterol level may contribute not only to heart disease but to Alzheimer's disease as well. So, cholesterol lowering drugs, nerve growth factors, antioxidants, estrogen replacement in post-menopausal women—the verdict on the capacity of such substances to protect against Alzheimer's disease is not yet in but it is coming.

Apart from medical treatment, however, a great deal can be done to help the person with Alzheimer's disease, and ease the burden on one—the **caregiver**. As the disease progresses, the person affected may eventually require 24-hour nursing care. While at first one may be able to look after the person, it will become harder for him or her to cope, so be prepared to accept help from support groups and associations. Social workers as a member of the support group can play an important role to deal with Alzheimer's patients.

We will try to conceptualize broadly the role of social workers as members of the caregiver/support groups. We will make an attempt to categorize the specific assignments of the caregivers in the management of the problem of Alzheimer's disease and also the emotional stress and strains the caregivers have to go through in the process of helping the Alzheimer's patients.

Role of social workers

In all health care settings, social workers have provided a holistic perspective on problems and situations, highlighting the social antecedents and consequences of illness and the need to deal with the larger picture along with the immediate concern. At the level of the individual's acute chronic illness, a social worker's focus is on the patient's physical, psychological, and environmental health needs.

The recognition of the importance of health care for the total well-being of the individual and the ability of social workers to make unique contributions to patient care have resulted in health social work becoming the largest field of social work practice. According to a 1987 NASW (National Association for Social Workers) Membership Survey, about half of NASW members work in the health care field (Dhoper, 1997). The emergence of social work roles and responsibilities and the development of appropriate knowledge and skills have been partly the result of an evolutionary process and partly the profession's reaction to the changing situation and needs of the health care system (Lundberg, 1995).

Social workers must take a careful history to determine whether the Alzheimer's disease has occurred slowly and insidiously rather than suddenly. A second task is to stabilize the person to rule out anxiety and depression as causes and to determine whether relocation is a cause for symptoms. Next, referral to a physician, preferably a geriatrician, is essential to rule out obvious causes for an insidious process, such as a nutritional deficiency, overmedications and drug interaction.

Social workers can play a major role too in providing counselling and supporting services to the Alzheimer's affected persons and their family members. To do so, the following are the essential ingredients which social workers should always remember while dealing with Alzheimer's patients:

- to establish a warm and effective relationship with the client.
- to correct false notion and cultural taboos.
- to liaison between the patient and family members.
- to provide the patient with emotional, social and economic support if needed, as far as possible.
- to suggest alternatives at all levels.
- to educate the family members of the patient about the medical facts of the disease, its diagnosis, treatment and prevention.
- a good understanding about human psychology as well as gerentological issues and perspectives.
- the social workers should respect the privacy of patients and hold in confidence all information, if required, for the benefit of patients.
- development of alternative listening and meaningful communication.

Living with and caring for a person with dementia

Maintaining dignity

The person with Alzheimer's disease is an individual with feelings—treat them with respect and dignity.

Avoiding confrontation

Any type of conflict causes unnecessary stress on caregiver and the person with Alzheimer's disease. Due to the nature of the illness, people with Alzheimer's disease will inevitably forget or deny they have done something wrong or will behave badly. It is important that one does not forget that this is a problem caused by the illness. One should avoid drawing attention to failures and maintain a calm composure.

Keeping active

Some planned activities can enhance a person's sense of dignity and self-worth by giving purpose and meaning to life, as well as maintaining their existing physical and mental capabilities.

Taking daily walks with the Alzheimer's patient will keep him fit also provide plenty of stimulation for conversation. Physical activity may also help a person to sleep better at night.

Improving safety

As the disease progresses, loss of physical coordination and memory, increases the chance of injury, so one should be very careful in making home as safe as possible.

Simplifying tasks

Try to make things simple for the person with Alzheimer's disease. Don't offer too many choices, as this may confuse and upset them. For example, in the early stages of the disease, they may be able to dress themselves. But, as the disease progresses, the caregiver will need to guide them and, eventually clothe them.

Supporting independence

The person with Alzheimer's disease should be encouraged to remain independent for as long as possible. This helps maintain their self-respect and decreases caregiver's burden.

Establishing routines

Daily routine activity decreases the decisions the caregivers need to make and can provide security for the person with the problem. Keeping a routine can also help prompt the person into remembering what they are meant to be doing, bringing order and structure to confused daily life. Although a routine can be helpful, keep things as normal as possible. As much as the changing condition will allow, try to treat the person as one did before the disease.

Communicating

Communication becomes increasingly difficult as the disease progresses. Some of the important aspects which the caregivers must remember and practice while communicating with the patient :

- speak clearly, slowly, face to face and at eye level.
- show love and warmth through hugs.
- caregivers should be aware of their body language.
- pay attention to the patient's body language.
- to find out what combination of words, guidance and demonstration is needed to communicate with the patient effectively.
- make sure that the caregivers have the patient's attention before speaking.

Memory aids

One of the main problems with Alzheimer's patient is the failure of short-term memory. This means that people can forget what has just happened to them. For example, they may forget that they have just eaten and ask for lunch again.

A useful way of helping such person is to create personalized "memory joggers" such as massage boards, handy lists and instruction sheets. For example:

- keep familiar objects in their usual places, where they can be easily found.
- make sure watches and clocks show the correct time.
- indicate to day's date on any calendars.
- put up a message board in a prominent place and establish a habit of using it.
- make a list of the day's activities and put it in a place where it can be easily found.
- if a person with Alzheimer's disease has to be left alone while the caregiver goes out, leave a clear note saying where the caregiver has gone out and when is supposed to come back. Try to establish a regular pattern so that this absence is part of a routine.

Daycare

If caregivers are unable to look after someone with Alzheimer's disease all the time, for example during the day when he or she has to work, he or she may consider using daycare centres. These provide care facilities when he or she need time to themselves.

Respite care

Respite care means having someone look after the person with Alzheimer's disease, where caregivers need a break from the responsibility of caring. It is important that one is able to get rest as a caregiver. One will not be able to look after someone with the problem if one is not fit oneself—this means having time-off. So respite care can give some time to the caregivers.

The personal and emotional stress of caregivers

Alzheimer's disease not only affects the person with the problem, it affects the entire family. The greatest burden is placed on the caregivers. The personal and emotional stress of caring for a person with Alzheimer's disease are enormous and one need to plan ways of coping with the disease for the future. Understanding caregiver's emotions will help him or her successfully cope with the person's problems as well as one's own. Caregivers are important persons in the life of the person with Alzheimer's disease. Without the caregivers, the person would be lost. This is why it is essential that the caregivers should take care of themselves. The followings are very crucial psychological issues which the caregivers should always keep in their mind and act accordingly while dealing with the Alzheimer's patients:

- grief
- guilt
- anger
- loneliness

- embarrassment
- family support
- sharing problems
- taking time out
- know their limits
- not blaming oneself
- seeking and taking advice.

Conclusion

Till medical scientists are not in a position to develop an adequate treatment for Alzheimer's disease, caregivers/social workers will have to content with taking care of their patients. Their care is similar to caring of children. Recently, the mega event "World Alzheimer's Congress " was held in Washington DC on July 9-18, 2000 (*Dementia News*, 2000) where role of social workers along with other professionals with affected families was much discussed and reiterated in dealing with Alzheimer's patients. It was also focused that goals and interventions of caregivers should be eclectic. It includes from crisis intervention (with family), basic problem solving, behavioural techniques, the principle of successive approximation or reinforcing successive steps to the final desired behaviour, issues and perspectives with regard to Alzheimer's disease. The importance of caregivers along with social work intervention could be prioritized in the policy for older people as well as in the health policy operating in India and other parts of the world; or a new policy could be framed for effective management of this disease.

SUGGESTED READINGS

1. Allen, J.E. (1992), *When memory fails; Helping the Alzheimer's and Dementia Patient*, New York: John Wiley and Sons.
2. *Dementia News*; Issue No. 12: November 2000.
3. Gorman, Christine (2000) ; "The New Science of Alzheimer's", *Time*, July.
4. Gruetzher, H. (1992), *Alzheimer's: A Caregiver's Guide and Sourcebook*, New York, John Wiley and Sons.

5. Nerson, T.S. (1998); "Maternal and Child Health"; in T.S. Kerson and Associates, *Social Work in Health Settings: Practice in Context.* (pp. 215-230), New York: Hawarth.
6. Horvath, T.B., and Davis, K.L. (1990); "Central nervous system disorders in aging", in E.L. Schneider and J.W. Rowe, eds., *Handbook of the Biology of Aging.* 3rd ed., pp. 306-329. New York: Academic Press.
7. Lundberg, G.D. (1995); "How to approach universal access to basic medical care without our government doing it". *Journal of the American Medical Association*, 27.3 (3).
8. Mega, M.S., Cummings, J.L., Fiorello, T. (1996); "The spectrum of behavoiural changes in Alzheimer's disease", *Neurology*, 46 (1), pp. 130-135.
9. Mayer, C.H. (1984); "The perils and promises of the health practice domain", *Social Work in Health Care;* 10 (2), pp. 1-11.
10. Park, Alice, (2000); "The New Science of Alzheimer's", *Time.*
11. Philips, G. (1995), "Assessment and management of the dementing patients"; *Journal of Mental Health*, 4 (2), pp. 165-175.
12. Volicer, L. and Hurby, A. (1995); "Protecting self-determination of dementia patients", *Journal of the American Geriatric Society*", 43(8), pp. 935-938.
13. Dhooper, S.S. (1997); Social Work in Health Care in the 21st *Century;* London: Sage Publication.
14. Zarit, S.H. and Orr, N.K. (2000); *The hidden victims of Alzheimer's disease: families under stress*, New York: University Press.
15. Kaplan, H.I. and Sadock, B.J. and Grebb, J.A.1994 Dementia. *Synopsis of Psychiatry*, (345-357), Baltimore: Williams and Wilkins.
16. Desai, Murli and Raju Siva; *Gerentological social work in India*, 2000, New Delhi: B.R. Publishing Corporation.
17. Prakash, I.J., (1997); *Functional competence and well-being of elderly—Indian Data.* Report submitted to Help Age India, New Delhi.

5

Infertility, Adoption and Reproductive Technologies

Challenges before the Social Work Profession

Infertility is the inability to conceive after at least one year of unprotected intercourse or the inability to carry a pregnancy to a live birth. Infertility has become a growing social issue and is affecting a large section of women groups across the globe. This phenomenon of infertility has encouraged the increasing commercialization of children through non-traditional adoption practices as well as through the proliferation of reproductive technologies.

While there has been an increase in infertility attributed to such factors as environmental toxicity and delayed childbearing, the supply of healthy babies available for adoption has simultaneously diminished. The decrease is due to the legislation of abortion, the widespread birth control measures, and the fact that many single women keep babies rather than surrender them for adoption.

The author begins with a discussion of infertility and considers some aspects of adoption, the traditional solutions to fertility. Some historical, technical, ethical, psychological, and social aspects of artificial insemination, along with newer developments of surrogacy, such as in-vitro fertilization and frozen embryos, are also discussed.

Recommendations are suggested for meeting the service needs of people who have problems associated with infertility.

Lastly, the author would like to gloss over the important roles, which can be played by the social workers in the millennium to deal with such problems.

Infertility, the inability to conceive after at least one year of unprotected intercourse or the inability to carry a pregnancy to a live birth, affects one in every six couples of the childbearing age in the United States (Barbara, 2009). The same problem is growing phenomenally in India. The number of years mentioned in the above definition has dwindled in recent times, from five to two to one. Thus the definition conflates inability to conceive with difficulty in conceiving quickly. This routes a large number of women into unnecessary, experimental and costly medical treatment all the sooner. It is very difficult to come out with any particular cause of infertility in the medical sciences. There could be multiple causes among which problems in the reproductive organs, gynecological deficiencies, late marriage, excessive stress and strains, unsatisfied sexual intercourse, use of contraceptives are worth mentioning. Another perception also exists among the medical professionals regarding infertility; environmental pollution and sexually transmitted diseases (**STDs**), as well as medically-induced infertility such as pelvic inflammatory disease (**PID**) caused by IUDs (**Intra-uterine devices**).

The media portrayal of infertility and the infertile is deceptively simple and homogeneous. Those undergoing **IVF** (In-vitro fertilization), for example, are portrayed as forever infertile. Yet a large percentage has had children in a present or a previous relationship. Many women undergo IVF because their husbands are infertile. This is probably one of the only examples in medical practice where a proxy is treated, i.e. another undergoes procedures in place of the actual person who has the problem. Percentages vary, but it has been estimated that 11-35 per cent of women on IVF programmes are there because of male partners' problems. Male-factor infertility is as common as female factor, yet often the male partner is not tested in infertility assessments, or only after the women has undergone extensive and exhaustive evaluation. Women testify that many gynecologists never order analysis of their husbands' sperm. And frequently, men will not undergo the tests, viewing them as offensive to their virility. Because women undergo the IVF procedures, many men are spread the embarrassment of having their infertility known.

Infertile couples often have had difficulties in gaining the emotional support they need during the painful months and years of diagnosis and treatment. In a predominantly fertile world, there are constant reminders of their inability to bear children, and friends and relatives can be awkward or insensitive in their efforts to be helpful. Medical professionals are more aware of the medical aspect of infertility and pay very little attention to the psychosocial dimension of the problem. As a result of their feelings of emotional isolation, infertile individuals often seek support of infertile acquaintances or support groups, or they become involved in therapy when their infertility becomes particularly painful.

Because society does not perceive infertile couples as having experienced a tangible loss, there is little legitimation to the mourning and grief that many of these couples experience. Fortunately, helping professionals are becoming increasingly sensitive to the need of infertile persons to grieve the very real loss of the child they are unable to conceive or give birth to.

However, once a pregnancy has been achieved and the initial feelings of joy and hopefulness have subsided, many previously infertile couples experience an unanticipated series of concerns in addition to the usual adjustments to pregnancy. The psychosocial needs of infertile couples as a result of the inability to conceive, of miscarriage, of ectopic pregnancy or of still birth have been surveyed, but there is still a paucity of literature detailing yet another are of infertility in which social work intervention could be immensely valuable.

Problems of Infertility

Approximately 50 per cent of the infertile couples eventually achieve conception; the goal of having children is at least temporarily suspended for these individuals, causing enormous stress (Costello and Taylor, 1999). Because people grow up thinking that conception and giving birth are matters of choice, they experience infertility as an unanticipated crisis and usually react with shock to the discovery of their condition (Shapiro, 2006). Couples who suspect that they have a fertility problem become preoccupied with conception and their fantasies and delay activities reflect this (Kraft *et al.*, 1989). They often suffer depression with each onset of menstruation as hopes for pregnancy are dashed once again. Thus, the quest for fertility becomes an obsession. Many people who want a family and are threatened with the reality of being unable to conceive feel desperate and will go to great lengths to become parents.

Here the author feels the importance of research along with the necessity for social workers to take a leadership role in helping society both to understand ethical issues related to and to develop enlightened public policy on infertility, adoption, and the new reproductive technologies.

Adoption—The Traditional Solution to Infertility

The traditional option for people who have difficulty with conception has been adoption. Historically, adoption took place on an informal basis within the extended family or community. For example, if a rich person wanted to adopt an heir, this could be handled through individual legislation. With the changing time and space the process of adoption started finding its legal basis in India as well as across the globe.

In India, an adoption is as old as the Hindu law itself. When it becomes necessary to sever parental ties irrevocably, adoption enables children to be brought in other families with the same rights and obligations as those existing between children and natural parents. The origin of custom of adoption is lost in antiquity, and may well have been no more than the natural desire for a son as an object of affection, a protection in old age, and to continue the family lineage to fulfil obligation towards a forefather and to secure an heir to inherit the property. But on account of Brahminical influence, among all classes, which have come under its way, a special religious significance came to be attached to the son. He is necessary for the spiritual salvation of the parental soul. The adoption of girls was not permitted.

The perception started changing with the changing socio-cultural scenario and there was a felt need to legalize adoption in India. A Bill known as **Adoption Bill** was introduced in Parliament in 1970 with the object of providing a uniform code of procedures for the adoption of children, in order to promote the best interest of the child and legally providing a child to the childless couples. It was also reinforced in the Bill that there would be no gender discrimination in case of adoption. In accordance with the ***Directive Principles of the Constitution of India*** under *Article 39*, it has been the endeavour of the Government to make special provisions through legislation, programmes and approaches to ensure that the tender age of children is not abused and that even those living under extremely difficult circumstances are given facilities to develop in a healthy manner and in conditions of freedom and dignity. The **National Policy for Children** (1974), the enactment of the **Juvenile Justice Act** (1986), ratification of the **United Nations Convention on the Rights of the Child** (1992) and the **National Action Plan for Children** (2005) attempted at ensuring that childhood is protected against exploitation and against moral and material abandonment.

India has the second largest population in the world and it is estimated that there are over 32 million destitute children in our country. While some of them are eking out a miserable and endangered existence, struggling for survival on the street, at stations or as child labour, a large number are in orphanages and institutions, which are run either by the Government or NGOs. Every child has a right to love, to be loved and to grow up in an atmosphere of moral and material security. However, well run an institution may be, it cannot give the child the individual care which is so essential to its full development. Here is the importance of adoption due to the problem of infertility.

Though adoption has been an old practice in India, the Legislature though is fit to codify the law. There are *three* Acts dealing with this subject, viz. **Hindu Adoption and Maintenance Act** (1956), **Guardians and Wards Act** (1890) and **Juvenile Justice Act** (1986). As it was mentioned earlier that an Adoption Bill was introduced in 1970 but soon withdrawn following opposition from a section of Muslims. In 1982, the Government sought to bring an adoption law which excluded Muslims. This was allowed to lapse. Till date, the comprehensive **Adoption of Children Bill**, which enables couples to adopt orphan and abandoned children, has failed to see the light of the day. The *Supreme Court* of India has also issued directions in relation to the processing of cases under these Acts particularly with reference to taking of Indian children under guardianship by foreigners living in different countries who are eventually permitted to adopt those children under the local laws of their own country. There has been great concern for the welfare of children at the international level, which resulted in the **Declaration of the Rights of the Child** adopted by the General Assembly of the United Nations on 20th November, 1989.

A **Central Adoption Resource Agency (CARA)** was set up in June 1990 under the Ministry of Welfare to monitor issues related to intra-country and inter-country adoption. Along with this **Voluntary Coordinating Agencies (VCA)** and **Coordinating Voluntary Adoption Resource Agency (CVARA)** are also marching ahead for the support of adoption. However, despite the proliferation of methods to procure children, the demand continued to exceed the supply of babies. This factor, along with various scientific developments, caused people to pursue vigorously new reproductive technologies (Holbrook, 1990).

Reproductive Technologies

In the last two decades the use of reproductive technologies (RTs) has become an inevitable and often indispensable part of women's lives. On the other hand, the increased knowledge and availability of a wide range of RT options has redefined 'traditional' notions of conception and procreation. On the other hand, the introduction of each new device or technique has served to renew a growing flux in the way reproductive choice is understood. The right to bodily integrity—defined as the inalienable right of women to have control and autonomy over their bodies—has been central in the feminist understanding of choice. Women's bodies, in particular her reproductive functions, are increasingly being subjected to techno-medical interventions to satisfy non-medical aspirations with regard to conception and procreation. The case of sex selection and sex selective abortion is a classic example of both the non-medical use of RTs and of the misappropriation of the definitions of reproductive choice.

Women's health and rights activists have often emphasized the need to define reproductive rights and choice in gendered terms so that its fulfilment is not only dependent on the availability of technical choice and information. It is indeed important to argue that RTs cannot be viewed as a magic bullet that will help alleviate women's reproductive 'burdens'. When this is done with little or no effort to change the often oppressive arrangements for reproduction, the result can be a reinforcement of gender based inequality. This misappropriation of prenatal obstetric diagnosis and abortion, by families and the medical community alike, to systematically eliminate female fetuses is one example. The introduction of hormonal and other provider-controlled contraceptives has also been the site of controversy. Besides questions concerning the safety of these methods, the government's efforts to achieve its demographic goals by using women as the vehicles for population control, while disregarding their safety and well-being, has been vehemently criticized.

The phenomenal development of genetic diagnostic technology such as *amniocentesis, fetoscopy, chorionic villus tests, foetal blood testing, and ultrasonography*, especially for the parental detection of various disorders, combined with the revolution in new assisted reproductive technologies such as *artificial insemination, in-vitro and in-utero fertilization, micro-manipulation, sperm and egg banks, surrogacy* and so on, and the availability and accessibility of techniques challenge the confrontation between the infertility and conception (Sinha, 1998).

Artificial Insemination

It is also called artificial insemination by donor (AID). This procedure, in which a doctor injects into the genital tract of the woman, semen from a donor. This procedure is most often used when the husband is infertile but the wife can conceive. Recently, single woman who want children have also used this process. Success rate is almost 80 per cent by this method but many attempts may be necessary before conception (Noble, 2007). The practice of artificial insemination took its shape in the United States. This procedure was kept relatively secret because of its ethical concerns. It was also found in the literature that soldiers before going off to war used to freeze their sperm so they would be able to sire a child if they were incapacitated or killed. During that period freezing and thawing of sperm was relatively inadequate but due to scientific revolution and phenomenal progress in the medical sciences this process of artificial insemination has become more scientific and easily accessible to the childless couples. Glycerol based preservative that would keep the sperm intact during freezing and thawing was used (Robinson and Pizer, 2005).

Many ethical questions are cropping up nowadays which are highly debatable regarding the acceptability of this process:

- Children conceived *via* this process are never told about this method;
- Doctors, generally don't want the parents to share this experience with their children to keep husband's infertility secret;
- If children come to know the incapacity of their father to produce a child, it will create a devastating psychological impact;
- Children are deprived of the basic facts about their origins, an enormous violation of human rights;

- Children are also unable to know the biological information about the father if the donation was made through a sperm bank.

Surrogacy

When insemination is the adoption of sperm; surrogacy is the adoption of egg *via* 'rental' of a womb. The surrogate mother donates her egg and bears the child for another couple, making her the biological mother. Surrogacy is used when the wife is unable to conceive or unable to carry a pregnancy to term. Her husband's sperm is used to artificially inseminate the surrogate mother.

If we have a glimpse over the pages of history it has been observed that the concept of surrogacy has occurred throughout the ages. As Field (1988) pointed out, in the Bible when 'Sarah, Racheal, and Leah were infertile, they gave their handmaids—Hager, Bilhah, and Zilpah—to have babies for their husbands' (Genesis 16:1-4, 15; 30; 1-10). Over the years people who could not have children persuaded friends, relatives, or strangers to carry babies for them. Then, in the mid-1970s, contract surrogacy emerged. As scientific techniques have become more sophisticated, new options have become available. For example, if a wife has viable eggs but is unable to carry a pregnancy, her cycle can be synchronized with that of the surrogate mother, after which doctors can retrieve her eggs, fertilize them with her husband's sperm, and then implant the embryo into the surrogate. In this case, the surrogate mother becomes the gestational but not the biological mother.

The most critical question, which needs to be addressed today when surrogacy is a method of reproduction under reproductive technologies—who is the mother of the child/ the woman who gives birth to the child? Or the woman married to the child's father?

In-Vitro Fertilization

In-vitro fertilization refers to a process by which doctors stimulates a woman's ovaries with medication, removes several eggs in a surgical procedure called *laparoscopy*, and fertilize them in a Petri dish. The resulting embryos are then implanted into the womb. This technique became a reality in 1978 when Louise Brown was born after years of work by Dr. Robert Edwards and Dr. Patrick Steptoe in Oldham, England. In 1979, Howard and Georgeanna Joes brought in-vitro fertilization to the United States and set up a clinic at the *East Virginia Medical School* (Perloe and Christie, 1987). There are some antagonistic views prevailing against this method, i.e. life created outside the womb upset the natural process of conception and denies God's intent.

Frozen Embryos

This addresses a major problem created by in-vitro fertilization; when several eggs are fertilized in the lab and then implanted. Sometimes, this creates multiple pregnancies and the life of the mother is jeopardized. By freezing embryos doctors can implant fewer at a time but what should be done with the leftover after pregnancy occurs. The process of using new reproductive technology to produce children has created embryonic orphans (Rothman, 2008). There is no enactment as such in any part of the globe regarding frozen embryos. A ***Biomedical Ethics Board*** could be established to look into some of these issues and to deal with such a situation.

Reproductive Technologies—An Ethical Dilemma

All reproductive technologies and arrangements are a political issue. They are an indication of the power or lack of power that women have over their bodies. And they are an indication of the degree to which access to the female body has become as normative in the reproductive realm as it has been in the sexual realm. The image of women as reproductive objects, as the image as sexual objects, is fast becoming a reality. Portrayed as medical miracles by the media, we must ask why these medical miracles require that women adapt to painful and deliberating intervention.

Why are women channelled, at such a cost to their bodies and to themselves, into reproducing children for themselves and for others? Or, as is the case in many developing countries, why are women routed into not reproducing by state mandate or incentive programmes that promote more risky and harmful methods such as **Norplant, Depo-Provera** and the vaccines? In many countries, why is it that women who want safe and adequate contraception have difficulty obtaining it when religion and the state combine to legislate women's reproductive options? Why do these techniques reinforce the biomedical view that a woman's reproductive system is pathological and requires an enormous amount of intervention?

Under the cover of a new science of reproduction, is the female body being fashioned into the biological laboratory of the future? These are some of the questions which are very difficult to answer and here lies the dilemmas of accepting reproductive technologies which have become a much debated issue across the globe.

Towards the Future

Social work profession must take up challenges to cope up with the problems of infertility and its allied dimensions with the problems and opportunities of reproductive technologies. As reported by Lee and Morgan (1989) "The changing reproductive processes offer at once opportunities for liberation and for enslavement. The genesis and revelation of reproductive technology and its proper biomedically to determine, manage, and control reproduction, has piloted medical science across a Rubicon for which there is no return ticket" (p. 2). Social workers can operate both at the service and policy level.

At the service level, people who are suffering from infertility problems need many types of assistance—(a) appropriate medical treatment; (b) counselling with regard to painful aspects of medical problems; (c) assistance in explaining about alternatives such as in-vitro fertilization or artificial insemination, and help in coping with the failures and successes of these attempts; (d) anxiety reduction; (e) information seeking; (f) open communication; (g) decision making (Shapiro, 1986). Those considering adoption need services to help them evaluate their readiness, learn about the process, decide upon the types of adoption, deal with legal aspect, sort out finances, and so on. Similarly, people considering surrogacy and pregnant women contemplating the surrender of their children for adoption need access to many services, including skilled counselling with regard to the option available, reliable legal advice, and medical help. Adoptees or offspring created by new reproductive technologies (especially those struggling with issues regarding their natural, biological, or adoptive parents) and biological parents (who may have surrendered their children long ago, given them up in surrogacy arrangements, or donated sperm to sperm banks) need access to counselling.

Two perspectives that can be used by the social workers when they counsel infertile couples:

- **(a) crisis theory**
- **(b) process of grief and bereavement** (Martin Seligman, 1990)

In development and life cycle literature, a crisis is viewed as turning point that offers the opportunity for regression or for growth. Expectable crises in the life cycle of the family traditionally are organized around events that relate to child-parent interaction and/or husband-wife relationship. Infertility is an unanticipated crisis. It is neither expected, nor have most couples developed coping mechanisms to respond to the narcissistic hurt that accompanies the fruitless effort to conceive and bear a child. A couple may be considered to be in crisis to the extent that their usual coping mechanisms are inadequate to respond to the impact of infertility on their marriage. Lydia Rapoport (1962) emphasizes that a crisis situation creates a problem that is perceived as a threat, a loss, or a challenge. These components all may be present, usually at different times, as a couple struggles with their shock enter into a period of **mourning**. The therapeutic value of mourning has long been recognized by helping professionals who have assisted clients to cope with death, with terminally ill family members, and with the birth of a handicapped child. Most recent literature has highlighted the importance of mourning in achieving a healthy resolution of the impact of fertility (Barbara, 2009).

The social workers can play a crucial role as a source of emotional support, as a facilitator, and as a provider of concrete information in facilitating a healthy resolution of the infertile client's problems. If both husband and wife are involved in counselling, it is important for the social worker to be sensitive to the different paces at which they acknowledge and work through their feelings about the impact of infertility on their lives and on their marriage.

Because of the abundance of complexities in the issues of infertility, adoption and reproductive technologies, social workers need to be trained in these areas. Schools of social work should develop courses to train social workers and other professionals and paraprofessionals (lawyers, doctors, nurses, psychologists and psychiatrists) to deal with such problems, with special emphasis on the ethical concerns raised by the new reproductive technologies. Miall (2007) pointed out that extreme technological innovation encourages a system of values that devalues involuntary childlessness. If an attempt could be made regarding certification of licensing of people providing guidance in these fields then it could improve services and make it easier for the public to find reliable professionals. Prolific research work must come forward to take up such research activities and come out with relevant findings which would add new knowledge to the practice (Richardson, 2003).

The social work profession also needs to take up leadership in making the needed services available to all. It is worth mentioning here that infertility, adoption and access to reproductive technologies are sometimes very expensive, beyond the affordability of many people who are downtrodden, disadvantaged and are victims of utter poverty. This even becomes worse when the infant mortality of a country is estimated to be alarming. To quote Frank and Vogel (2007), "While the health care system allows the wealthy to conjure up babies out of Petri dishes, the same system affords little care to poor infants who have been conceived without medical intervention" (p.125). Perhaps social workers should use some of the problems and opportunities caused by the new reproductive technologies not only to work towards resolving new issues but also to highlight and point the way towards ameliorating existing injustice.

Social work professionals, through the mechanism of counselling can learn about the effects of infertility, adoption practices, and the new reproductive technologies on families and to contribute, through observation and research, to knowledge in these areas. Perhaps most importantly, social workers must use knowledge, experience, and commitment to meet the needs of humanity by helping to develop and to formulate a more enlightened public policy concerning the problems of infertility and the new reproductive technologies.

SUGGESTED READINGS

1. Barbara Eck Menning (2009); *Infertility: A Guide for the Childless Couples,* Englewood Cliffs, NJ: Prentice-Hall.
2. Costello, C.G., and Taylor, P.J. (1999); "Adjustment to Infertility"; *Journal of Abnormal Psychology*, 96, 108-116.
3. Field, M.A. (1988); *Surrogate Motherhood,* Cambridge, MA: Harvard University Press.
4. Frank and Vogel (2007); *The baby makers,* New York: Carroll and Graf.
5. Holbrook, S.M. (1990); "Adoption, Infertility and the New Reproductive Technologies"; *Social Work;* July, Vol. 35, No. 4; 289-384.
6. Kraft, A.D., Palombo, J. Mitchell, D. (1989); "The psychological dimensions of infertility"; *American Journal of Orthopsychiatry*, 50, 618-627.
7. Lydia Rapoport (1962); "The State of Crisis: Some Theoretical Considerations"; *Social Service Review*, 36, June; pp. 211-217.
8. Lee, R. and Morgan, D. (1989); "Is birth important?" In R. Lee and D. Morgan (Eds.), *Birthrights* (pp. 1-16). London, England: Routledge and Kegan Paul.

9. M. Seligman. (1990); *Helplessness: On Depression, Development and Death;* San Francisco: W.H. Freeman.
10. Miall, C.E (2007); "Reproductive Technology vs. the stigma of involuntary childlessness"; *Social Casework,* 70; pp. 43-50.
11. Noble, E. (2007); *Having your baby by donor insemination,* Boston: Houghton Miffin.
12. Perloe, M. and Christie, L.G. (1987); *Miracle babies;* New York: Penguin Books.
13. Richardson, J.W. (2003); "The role of a psychiatric consultant to an artificial insemination by donor programme"; *Psychiatric Annals,* 17 (2), pp. 101-105.
14. Robinson, S. and Pizer, H.F. (2005); *Having a baby without a man;* New York; Simon and Schuster.
15. Rothman, B.K. (2008); *Recreating motherhood;* New York: W.W. Norton.
16. Shapiro, C.H. (1986); "The impact of infertility on the marital relationship"; *Social Casework;* 63, pp. 387-393.
17. Shapiro, C.H. (2006); *Infertility and pregnancy loss;* San Francisco: Jossey-Bass.
18. Sinha, D. (1998); "Problems and prospects of genetic counselling in the medical profession"; *Journal of Family Welfare;* Vol. 44, No. 4.

PART B

INTERNATIONAL PERSPECTIVES

6

Family Planning Perspectives in Swedish Community

Attitudes in Swedish society towards sexuality have changed radically over the last hundred years. Women's reproductive health has improved, as has the ability of women and men to plan their families. Important social reforms behind this development are sex education in schools, public education on sexuality and gender issues, legislation on abortion, sterilization and contraception, ante-natal care and family planning services integrated into the public health system.

In contrast to other countries, population statistics in Sweden are based on register information. Since 1686, Sweden has had a unique church—record system for the recording of all individual demographic changes at parish level. Closely linked to these registers is a continuously updated register of the Swedish population. Compilation of census data and vital statistics based on these registers started in 1749. Since then, an uninterrupted series of demographic data has been available for a period of nearly 250 years, reflecting the transformation of the country from an agrarian subsistence economy into a modern post-industrial society. Life expectancy in Sweden is nowadays one of the highest in the world.

The past

In 1750, Sweden had a population of 1.8 million. One hundred years later the population had doubled in size to 3.5 million, and by 1930 it had reached 6.1 million. Sweden's demographic development has on the whole been similar to that of most of today's industrialized nations. A period of high mortality and high fertility has given way to a period of low fertility and low mortality. This development is called the demographic transition.

The first phase up to around 1810 was a period of high fertility and high mortality. Both fertility and mortality fluctuated greatly from year to year due to epidemics, famine and war. Population growth during this period averaged just over 0.6 per cent. During the period 1810-1870, the death rate then began to decline, due in part to rising agricultural output and medical advances. The heavy fluctuations in mortality from year to year are now a thing of the past.

Social control over sexuality and childbearing was strict. In the 19th century, women gave birth to many children and mortality and morbidity in relation to childbirth were high. Although termination of pregnancy was a crime, many women resorted to illicit abortions, risking their health and life.

In the early 1900s, Sweden experienced a demographic transition and the total fertility rate dropped from four children per woman at the turn of the century to less than two in the 1930s. A law from 1910 banned public information on the sales of contraceptives, and the available means of birth control were traditional methods such as coitus interruptus, lengthy breast feeding and periods of abstinence. There were also a considerable number of illegal abortions. Some information on condoms and diaphragms was spread by population educators and activists and by the non-governmental organization, the ***Swedish Association For Sex Education,*** founded in 1934. Table 6.1 shows the changes in the population of Sweden from 1931 to 2008 and its dramatic decline.

In the 1930s, partly as a reaction to the declining birth rate, a number of social reforms were introduced. These included universal ante-natal and child health care. The ban on contraceptives was lifted and family planning services were offered under the aegis of the public health service.

Sex education was introduced into state schools as early as 1942, and in 1954 it became a compulsory subject in the school curriculum. Initially it focused on biological facts, protection against unwanted pregnancies and venereal diseases; sexual relations were condoned only within marriage.

Table 6.1 : Population dynamics—1931-2008

Year	*Births*	*Deaths*	*National Population Increase*	*Net Immigration*	*Population Increase*
1931-40	14.5	11.7	2.8	0.6	3.4
1941-50	18.5	10.4	8.1	2.0	10.1
1951-60	14.7	9.7	5.0	1.5	6.5
1961-70	14.8	9.9	4.9	3.0	7.9
1971-80	12.6	10.7	1.9	1.1	2.9
1981-90	12.3	11.1	1.2	2.1	3.2
1991-01	14.4	3.3	2.9	2.9	0.8
2001-10	14.2	3.3	2.3	2.3	0.3

The absolute ban on abortions was lifted in 1938 by a law permitting abortion on medical, humanitarian and eugenic grounds. Amendments in 1946 and in 1963 included socio-medical distress and diagnosed foetal disorders as indicators for legal abortion. Abortion could be obtained after the consent of two doctors, specialists in psychiatry and gynecology, and/or after the approval of the *National Board of Health and Welfare*.

In the period 1930-1960, between 3,000 and 6,000 legal abortions were estimated at 15,000-20,000. Legal abortions were chiefly granted to women with somatic or mental illnesses or women who had many children, while applications from young and single women were regularly refused. As a result, illegally induced abortions were particularly common among young women, causing injuries, infections, infertility and even deaths. Consent to abortion was sometimes given on condition that the woman was sterilized at the same time. Not until the early 1960s was the practice stopped.

With the economic growth in the 1960s, social attitudes towards sexuality and reproduction also changed. It became increasingly common for young people to live together without marriage and these informal unions were fairly soon generally accepted. Gender issues were under debate and new, effective contraceptives, however, were expensive and not easy to obtain, and abortion law was still strictly applied. Women who could afford it went abroad (to Poland) or paid privately to get an abortion, while many women, teenagers in particular, still resorted to illegal procedures. Women's groups, NGOs, activists and female politicians argued for the women's right to decide on abortion, and doctors and health workers protested against women having to endanger their health with unsafe abortions.

In 1965, a governmental commission was appointed to prepare a liberalizing of the law, and meanwhile, the law was being applied more liberally. Legal abortions increased, replacing the previous practice of back-street abortions, especially among young women. The number of annual legal abortions rose from 16,000 in 1970 to 30,600 in 1974, the same year that a new Abortion Act was approved by Parliament.

In the 1970s, several reforms were implemented to protect reproductive rights and improve gender equality. The national policy in relation to reproductive health and rights includes: legislation on abortion, contraceptives and sterilization; provision of contraceptive services within the public health system; a comprehensive health education programme on sexuality, fertility and gender issues.

Under the 1974 Abortion Act, a woman has the right to an abortion up to the end of the 18th week of pregnancy. After that limit, permission must be obtained from the National Board of Health and Welfare, which can approve an abortion in certain circumstances. The upper limit for an abortion is determined by the foetus ability to survive ex utero. According to the Board's present practice, abortions are not allowed after the end of the 22nd week. Abortion must be carried out at a general hospital by a qualified medical doctor. The right to an abortion extends to Swedish citizens and foreign women who have been resident in the country for at least three months. Women from abroad must apply to the National Board of Health and Welfare for permission, and have to pay the full price for the operation.

The *Abortion Act, 1974* was combined with a law making contraceptive services free of charge and subsidizing the price of contraceptives. In addition, a number of preventive activities were launched. Governmental fund was provided for a long-term health education programme aimed at preventing unwanted pregnancies. State grants were allocated to women's groups and youth and immigrant organizations for information on sexuality and contraception. As part of the programme, contraceptive services were expanded throughout the country. Midwives working in ante-natal care were trained to provide contraception services, thus making modern methods easily accessible at local health centres all-over the country, including school health units and youth clinics.

The idea behind these preventive efforts was to prevent unwanted pregnancies by means of contraception, using abortion only as a last resort. In legalizing abortion, society also had an obligation to make contraceptives equally accessible.

According to the 1976 *Sterilization Act*, sterilization as a means of birth control is permitted for men and women over the age of 25. The only condition is that the individual has received counselling and understands the nature and consequences of the operation. In the age group 18-24, sterilization is only permitted on genetic or (for women) medical grounds. Sterilization is not allowed under the age of 18 for any reason. The Act also prohibits any authority, representative of society, guardian or other person from putting pressure on an individual to be sterilized. About, 7,000 sterilizations are performed every year in Sweden (data available till 2001), of which three-quarters are on women. Most people who practice contraception rely on reversible methods, while less than 10 per cent have chosen sterilization.

In addition, sex education in schools and popular education on sexuality and co-habitation were essential components of the national programme to prevent unwanted pregnancies. The curriculum for sex education in schools was reformed and developed in the 1970s. Teacher training was improved. Education on sexuality, reproduction and contraception was to be given in different steps and adapted to the age and developmental stage of the pupils. Biological, social, emotional and ethical aspects of sexuality were integrated into school subjects such as biology, religion and social science.

The prevention programme included the training of educators and health education on sexuality, fertility and gender through many channels such as the health care and social services, the leisure sector, the Church and non-governmental organizations. The goal was to disseminate information and reach the public through the professionals. Abortion was put in a broader context of sexuality and human relations, and the underlying message was that of the child's right to be wanted.

Experience gained from the health education programme of the 1970s have proved important in efforts to prevent sexually transmitted diseases (STD), including HIV/AIDS. The aim is to give information on risks and ways of transmission, while maintaining a positive and responsible attitude to sexuality.

In early 1980s, a governmental sub-committee was appointed to evaluate the 1974 Abortion Act and the associated prevention programme. The committee established that the overall abortion rate has not increased since the liberalization. Abortions are now performed at an early stage of pregnancy, causing less physical and psychological strain for the women. Furthermore, all illegal abortions have ceased. As a result, maternal mortality in Sweden fell to the present low level of less than five deaths per 1,00,000 live births.

Many of the preventive activities were directed towards teenagers. One of the lasting effects of the health education programme was a more open, relaxed social attitude towards teenage sexuality. In addition, a general decline in teenage fertility occurred from 1975 up to 1985. After a moderate increase in the abortion rate among teenagers in the late 1980s, the abortion and birth rates are now being declining.

Present scenario

During the economic depression of the 1930s, unemployment was high and the birth rate very low. Population growth fell to just 0.3 per cent. The prospect of a decline in population made population growth a political issue. Steps were taken towards constructing a national family policy aimed at improving the situation for women and helping them to combine work and family life. These steps were largely inspired by Gunnar Myrdal's book on the population crisis in Sweden which appeared in 1935.

The birth rate started to rise again after the mid-1930s. In fact the fertility increase started before any of the ideas promoted by the Myrdal were put into practice. In the mid-1940s fertility reached 2.6 children per woman compared to the low point of 1.7 in 1935. Fertility increased over the subsequent decades and remained at 2.2 to 2.5 until the mid-1960s.

After the introduction of modern contraceptives in the mid-1960s fertility started to decline, much in line with similar developments in other countries. By the end of the 1970s, the birth rate in Sweden had declined to a level of 1.6 children per woman, but then the pattern reversed. It started to rise rapidly in an almost unique development which attracted attention, not least abroad. In 1990, the birth rate reached a level of 2.1, which was one of the highest in the whole of Western Europe.

This pattern shattered many theories about what influences fertility. Sweden is known as a country with an unusually high female labour-force participation rate, extensive non-marital cohabitation and relatively high divorce/separation rates, all of which are commonly believed to reduce rates of child bearing. Immediately after 1990, however, Swedish fertility plummeted in another unique movement, and had fallen to 1.5 children per woman in 2000. This is the lowest birth rate in Sweden ever—although still above the European average. No other Western country has demonstrated such a roller-coaster fertility pattern in recent decades.

Young men and women nowadays often live together for several years without intending to start a family. They want to complete their education and find a job before they have their children. Modern contraception is widely used both for limiting the number of children and for timing childbearing, mainly to postpone the first child. In 1965, the mean age for first birth was 23, and 20 years later it was 26.

Around 70 per cent of all sexually active couples use contraception. One-quarter of these practices; one of the three most common methods—the PILL, CONDOMS and IUD, while the remaining one-quarter relies on methods such as COITUS INTERRUPTUS, SAFE PERIODS, DIAPHRAGM or STERILIZATION. The pill and condoms are the chief methods before childbearing period, while IUD is the most common among those who have completed their family size.

Contraceptive services are easily accessible and free of charge in the health services. Oral contraceptives, injectables or emergency hormonal contraceptives must be prescribed by a physician or a midwife, and like other prescribed drugs, they are subsidized. Condoms and spermicides are bought by the users at market price.

The annual number of abortions over the past twenty years has been between 30,000 and 35,000, and the abortion rate for women of fertile age around 20 per thousand. The percentage of abortion in relation to all known pregnancies has fluctuated between 20 and 25 per cent. Given the present fertility and abortion rates, a Swedish woman will on an average have two children and 0.6 abortions during her reproductive life. Over the years there have been some changes in the different age groups. Marked is the fertility decline in the age group 15 to 19. The highest fertility is in women between 20 and 30, and the comparatively high abortion rate in this age-span reflects the increasing tendency to postpone childbearing.

A woman who considers an abortion is offered contact with a social worker if so she wishes. The aim of the counselling is to help the woman to reach a decision and give her support, regardless of whether she decides to terminate or to proceed with the pregnancy.

Abortions after the 18th week, which need the consent of the National Board of Health and Welfare, constituted 0.48 per cent of all abortions or 155 cases in 1996. Most of these abortions are carried out after foetal diagnosis of hereditary disease or chromosomal disorder. Almost 93 per cent of all abortions were performed before the 12th week of pregnancy. Vacuum aspiration on an outpatient basis used to be the main method for early abortions. Since 1992, a drug-induced method has been available. Up to the 8th week of pregnancy, the woman can choose between vacuum aspiration and the medical procedure. In 1996, 17 per cent of early abortions were drug-induced, with variations from 50 per cent in some areas to 5 per cent in others.

Future promises

Contained within the comprehensive document known as the Programme of Action, the main message in Sweden for improving individual well-being comprises two elements: to provide contraceptive methods within broader reproductive health services, and to advance women's equality in education, health, and economic opportunities.

Within the 'fertility reduction' paradigm, these two elements are consonant with the determinants of unwanted and wanted child-bearing. While fertility has declined under conditions of lack of sound knowledge in reproductive health and extreme gender disparities, the provision of contraceptive services within the context of reproductive health can be expected to reduce unwanted fertility, and movement towards gender equality can be expected to create conditions favourable for smaller families.

The relationships between a population policy, a family planning programme, and reproductive health are to be examined in different dimensions. The first scenario is to retain the narrow interpretation of population policy as fertility reduction through family planning programmes. The second is to equate population policy with a reproductive health policy, and the third is to expand the scope of family planning programmes to incorporate all reproductive health services.

They emphasize to recognize that the delivery of reproductive health services cannot become the sole responsibility of family planning programmes. Reproductive health advocates will have to work with both family planning and health departments to ensure that a complete package of reproductive health services is delivered.

One way to accomplish this goal is to advocate that those reproductive health services that interact directly with the reduction of unwanted child-bearing are paid for and delivered through family planning programmes, while other aspects of reproductive health become the responsibility of health programmes. In this case the purpose of family planning programmes would have to be revised from the reduction of total fertility to the reduction of unwanted child-bearing in a healthful manner.

They need to define the goal of a fertility-reduction policy and of a population policy explicitly in terms of improvements in individual well-being through a reduction in fertility and population growth. This would mean that we take a public stand against those government activities oriented to reducing fertility that are not consistent with the overall objective of improving individual well-being. Above all, it is needed to advocate publicly for these changes in policy making, programme implementation, and evaluation. They also feel that they should give much attention to the qualitative issues of people's lives than they give to the quantitative issues of population size and the growth rate. They feel to think of population issues as one aspect of a social reform movement for improving individual well-being, and to establish stronger ties with other social reform movements, including but not limited to the feminist movement, only then they will be able to provide a more comprehensive population policy in their country.

So family planning programmes and population control in Swedish community is quite appreciating. They are very much aware of the importance and the intricacies of family planning programmes both in urban and country side.

SUGGESTED READINGS

1. *Childcare in Sweden*—Ministry of Social Affairs and Health, Stockholm; 2006.
2. OECD (2007); Employment Outlook.
3. OECD (2008); Economic Surveys, Sweden.
4. *Swedish Family Planning* (a mimeo), 2001; Ministry of Health, Sweden.

(OECD—Organization for Economic Cooperation and Development)

7

Childcare in Sweden

Prelude to Swedish childcare

Swedish childcare has twin objectives—(1) to make it possible for parents to combine parenthood with employment or studies and, (2) to support and encourage children's development and learning and help them grow up under conditions that are conducive to their well-being.

This dual purpose approach was officially laid down in the early 1970s with the launching of a large-scale development programme for Swedish childcare. Along with the parental insurance and child benefit systems, childcare has been one of the mainstays of Swedish family welfare policy while at the same time having an explicit educational orientation. In recent years, the educational policy aspects have become increasingly important and in July 2007 responsibility for public childcare has been transferred from the Ministry of Health and Social Affairs to the Ministry of Education and Science.

From crèches to daycare centres

The roots of the Swedish childcare system can be traced back to the second half of the 19th century. The first infant crèche was opened in 1854 for the children of single mothers obliged to work for a living. Work shelters, which appeared at roughly the same time, took in school children from poor families and sought to instill in them the values of duty and diligence as well as teaching them some rudimentary handicrafts. Both the crèche and the work shelter were social institutions usually run by private citizens or by charities. They were soon joined by the kindergarten, based on the ideas of German educator Friedrich Frobel. Kindergartens had a purely educational purpose and were attended mainly by the children of well-to-do families where the mothers did not go out to work.

During the 1930s and 1940s, attitudes towards the private or charitable character of crèches and work shelters changed. The public authorities, it was felt, should assume greater responsibility for the care and training of young children, and the stigma of poverty should be removed. In the mid-1940s, government grants were introduced for both work shelters and infant crèches. A growing number of local authorities took over responsibility for these activities. The crèches were renamed day nurseries or daycare centres and the work shelters became leisure-time centres. The number of children at these centres however was still fairly modest—they were mainly to be found in the cities—whereas attendance at kindergartens or play-schools was more widespread.

In the 1960s, demand for childcare provision increased. Female labour was in demand and calls for a major expansion of childcare facilities intensified. In 1968, the government of the day appointed special commission, the National Commission on Childcare, instructing it to the present proposals as to how a childcare system that met social, educational and supervisory needs might be developed in Sweden.

The 1968, National Commission decisively influenced the future direction of Swedish childcare. Its report formulated vital pedagogical principles and ideas that made a considerable impact and still survive today. Among other things, it laid the foundations for the Swedish pre-school model-daycare centres and play-schools were to be combined in a pre-school system that would serve the interests of children as well as allowing parents to work or study. The report condemned the outdated view that supervision was something you offered the poor while educational activities were for the stimulation of better-off children. Care and education were to be merged in a completely new way. As a result of the Commission's report, all six-year-olds were given the right to free education. Children in hospital and immigrant children were also to be entitled to municipal childcare. Further, the report raised the question of school-age daycare and proposed rapid development of the country's leisure-time centres.

Despite rapid progress in the 1970s and early 1980s local authorities were unable to expand facilities to such an extent that the waiting list for places disappeared. As a result, the Swedish Parliament decided in 1985 that all children from the age of 18 months and up until school age were to have access by 1991, at the latest, to a pre-school place either at a daycare centre, in a part-time pre-school group or at an open pre-school centre. The birth rate increased rapidly, however, as did the number of mothers in gainful employment, and the target was not achieved. Legislation was therefore tightened in 2007, when local authorities became duty bound to provide a childcare without undue delay for all children requiring it.

This rule together with the high birthrate in Sweden led to the creation of a record number of new childcare openings in the mid-1990s. Waiting lists disappeared and today the number of places largely conforms to needs. Public childcare has become an integral part of the Swedish welfare state and of most families' everyday lives.

A highly developed childcare system has been a precondition for the changes in family patterns and gender roles that have been taking place since the 1970 and the same thrust continues till to date. The proportion of women in the labour force has steadily approached that of men, and most children in Sweden today grow up with parents who share responsibility for supporting the family.

For almost three decades, childcare has been a matter by priority in Swedish public life. Reforms in this field have received widespread support in parliament and this has allowed successive governments to pursue the policies originally drawn up in the early 1970s. The aim has been to provide quality childcare, with full access for those needing places, run principally by local authorities and financed out of the public pursue. The main incentives have been consideration for the well-being of the upcoming generation and a desire for greater equality between the sexes.

Content and pedagogical principles

The Swedish childcare is based on overall view of the child's development and learning needs combining care, fostering and teaching. Proper care is seen as a prerequisite if the child is to feel happy and content, which in turn is a prerequisite for its ability to absorb knowledge and to progress in life. Ensuring the well-being of a child also has an educational effect. When children are to eat or rest, or when an adult helps them sort out conflicts with other children, they learn about themselves as well as about others and about life in general. Children learn all the time and with all their senses.

The importance of play for a child's development and learning is emphasized both in pre-school pedagogical programmes and in school age childcare, and is included nowadays in the national curriculum for compulsory schools. Playing games helps the children to understand the world around it, to develop its imagination and creative powers and to learn to cooperate with others.

Another characteristics feature of Swedish childcare is a high degree of parent-staff cooperation. A setting-in-period, which may last for up to two weeks in the case of the youngest children, provides the basis for this cooperation and it is further developed in day-to-day contacts. Parents are given an opportunity to know their children and how they behave with others which in turn how it helps in the process of socialization.

Pedagogical activities are based on the children's individual capabilities and are linked to what the child has already experienced and learned. Children are encouraged to engage in their own activities and discover things for themselves, for instance in theme work. By working of a particular theme for a lengthy period and examining it in a variety of ways, the child can introduce new knowledge into a meaningful context.

The socialization and development of children takes place in groups. Consequently, the group has an important pedagogical function in childcare, and both the individual child and the group are focal points in pedagogical programmes.

Children who need special supports have special rights in the childcare system. These children are entitled to a place at a pre-school or leisure time centre irrespective of how their parents are occupied. This group is not closely defined—it may include disabled children or children with more diffuse problems such as difficulties concentrating or psychosocial predicaments. An express principle is that these children's needs are primarily to be met in regular childcare and not by singling them out for special treatment.

Many children in Sweden today have roots in some other culture. Childcare has to a large extent become a multicultural meeting-place. Supporting children's dual cultural affiliations and their chances of actively developing bilingual skills is one of the explicitly stated objectives of childcare in Sweden. To help with this, special mother tongue teachers provide tuition to children whose mother tongue is not Swedish. Some 15 per cent such children at pre-school or family daycare homes receive mother-tongue tuition.

Childcare today—forms and scale

Public childcare is extended to children aged 1-12. Children who have yet to start school can attend pre-school activities, while school children have access to school-age childcare. In Sweden, compulsory school begins at the age of seven but almost all six-year-old attend voluntary pre-school classes. This means in principle that pre-school care encompasses children aged 1-5 and school-age childcare those aged 6-12.

Under the **Education Act**, pre-schooling is provided at pre-schools, in family daycare homes and at open pre-schools while school-age childcare is provided at leisure-time centres, in family daycare homes and at open leisure-time centres.

The pre-school cares for children during their time; their parents are away working or studying, and also takes in children with special needs of their own. Pre-schools are open all year round and daily opening times are varied to fit in with parents' working hours. Children are registered and the parents pay a fee which in most areas linked to the family's income and/or the child's total hours of attendance. Children are generally divided into groups of between 15 and 20. As a rule, three employees from pre-school teachers and daycare attendants are allocated to each group. The average pre-school comprises three such groups.

Family daycare involves municipal child-minders providing care in their own home. The children are registered and opening hours are varied to fit in with parents' working hours. Family daycare is an alternative to pre-school in particular for children who for one reason or another need to be in smaller groups or who live far from the nearest pre-school. This alternative is more common in rural areas and in small towns than in metropolitan areas. The number of children in family daycare has steadily declined since the late 1990s. Today, some 12 per cent of all children aged 1-5 receive this form of care. Family daycare is sometimes provided for school children outside school hours as well.

Open pre-schools are a supplement to regular pre-school for the children of parents who are at home during the day. They may also serve as a supplement to family daycare. Together with their parents or municipal child-minders, children are invited to take part in a pedagogical group programme. In some housing areas, open pre-schools have an explicitly social function and collaborate with public bodies like the social welfare services and the maternity care and child health care services. The children are not registered and nor are they required to attend regularly. Most open pre-schools are free of charge.

Leisure-time centres provide care for children whose parents are in gainful employment or studying during the time the child is not at school, i.e. morning, afternoon and during holidays. Most of the children as registered fall in the age group of 6-9 years. The centres are open all year round and daily opening hours are varied to fit in with parents' working hours. Children are registered and as in the case of pre-school and family daycare, parents pay a fee which in most areas is linked to the family's income and/or the child's total hours of attendance.

Leisure-time centres are intended as supplemented to schooling and are supposed to help children in their development and provide them with meaningful recreation. Policy-makers have declared their intention to bring schools and leisure-time centres closer together and today most leisure-time centres collaborate with schools in the area to a greater or lesser degree.

Leisure-time centres are the form of public childcare that has increased most rapidly during the period 1990-2008. Open leisure-time activities are described in the Education Act as an alternative to leisure-time centres and family daycare for children aged 10-12. Such facilities however are not very widespread. About three quarters of the country's local authorities lack open activities directed at this age group.

Local authorities provide grants for non-municipal childcare, i.e. undertakings run by a principal other than the local authority. The sum paid for each child may not differ unduly from the cost per child in a corresponding municipal undertaking. About 13 per cent of all children registered with pre-schools attend a pre-school operating under non-municipal auspices. The most common form is the parent cooperative.

Today the overwhelming majority of children in Sweden receive childcare in one form or another. The expansion of facilities in this sector has meant that the number of children in pre-schools, leisure-time centres and family daycare homes—which all offer full-daycare—increased more than tenfold from 61,000 to 7,21,000 between 1999 to 2009. Today, almost 75 per cent of all children aged 1-5 and 60 per cent of all school children aged 6-9 are registered. Virtually all local authorities are now fulfilling their obligations under the Education Act to provide childcare at a pre-school, at a leisure-time centre or in a family daycare home without undue delay.

Thus childcare needs have more or less been met for the children of parents working or studying. The children of the unemployed however are largely without childcare provision. About 40 per cent of local authorities have adopted rules whereby a pre-school child forfeits its place in the childcare system when a parent becomes unemployed, and only one local authority in four makes childcare available to children with a jobless parent. In the case of children with a parent who is staying at home to look after a younger sibling, the rules are even more restrictive.

Staff

Childcare staff are well trained. There are four categories of staff—who are mainly responsible for childcare system—**pre-school teachers, leisure-time pedagogues, daycare attendants and child-minders in family daycare.**

Pre-school teachers and **leisure-time pedagogues** undergo a three-year pedagogical training programme at university focusing on teaching methods, development psychology, family sociology and creative activity. As a rule, **daycare attendants** have upper-secondary qualifications while municipal **child-minders** have often attended training courses organized by the local authority itself.

Over half of all pre-school employees have university degrees in pre-school education while just over 40 per cent of staff are daycare attendants. At leisure-time centres some 70 per cent have degrees in recreational or leisure education or in some other kind of teacher's training, while 20 per cent are daycare attendants. About five per cent of pre-school employees are men.

Division of responsibility

During the 1990s, the division of responsibility between central and local government has altered. Governance by rule has been replaced by a more target-oriented and result-oriented system. This means that Central Government now outlines the overall goals for childcare while the local authorities are responsible for implementing them. Central Government contributes financially through grants to the local authorities. Nowadays, these government grants are disbursed across the board.

During the period when childcare in Sweden was expanding, Central Government control was firmer. To ensure consistently high quality, the National Board of Health and

Welfare, which was the supervisory authority at the time, issued recommendations and guidelines on such things as premises, staff training, frequency of staff and the size of children's groups. Earmarked government grants are now used to stimulate the expansion of facilities and also to control the orientation of childcare.

Today, the National Agency for Education is the central supervisory authority for both childcare and schooling. Its tasks include ensuring fulfilment of the national goals for childcare by means of follow-ups, evaluation, development, research and supervisory work, and in general supporting the advancement of the childcare sector.

Legislation

On 1st January 1998, the regulations governing childcare were transferred from the **Social Service Act** to the **Education Act**. Presently, also, the childcare in Swedish community is governed by the same Act. The Education Act defines pre-school care and school-age care and in what forms they operate. It also affirms the obligation of the local authorities to provide pre-schooling and school age children for children between the ages of one and twelve to the requisite extent in order for parents to work or study. Childcare is to be provided 'without much delay', i.e. normally within three or four months of the parents having applied for a place, and as close to the child's home as possible. Special regard is to be taken of the parents' own wishes.

The local authorities have a particular responsibility for children who for physical, mental or other reasons need special support for their development. Under the law, these children are to be offered places in a municipal pre-school or leisure-time centre if their needs cannot be met in any other way. Local authorities are also required to try and find out which children in this category are in need of such support and seek to ensure that they make use of the places allocated.

The law also specifies requirements for the quality of the care provided. Employees are to be so trained or experienced that they can satisfy the children's needs as regards both care and stimulating pedagogical activities. Children's groups are to be suitably mixed and of appropriate size and premises are to be well suited to the purpose in hand. The activities provided are to be based on the individual needs of each child, and children in need of special support are to be provided with care appropriate to their needs.

The bulk of present legislations in the childcare sector have been prescribed stricter compliance with the local authorities' obligations than previous laws had done. One of the reasons for tightening up the laws was that Central Government's opportunities for influencing developments declined when its earmarked grants for childcare were replaced by general-purpose grants.

Part of lifelong learning process

On 1st January, 1998, the childcare regulations were transferred to the **Education Act**. At the same time, a new school form was introduced, the pre-school class. The responsibility of the local authorities to offer all children 525 hours of free pre-schooling from the autumn term of the year they turn six was replaced by an obligation to find children a place in a pre-school class. Pre-school classes and the compulsory school are to work closely with each other. Two separate educational traditions—that of the pre-school and that of the school meet and in doing so give rise to new ideas about learning and forms of working. The pre-school classes also help children to start school on an equal footing. Pre-school classes are voluntary but are attended by virtually all six-year-old who have not begun attending compulsory school.

In July 1996, the Ministry of Education took over responsibility for childcare from the Ministry for Social Affairs, and childcare activities have thus acquired more of an educational policy orientation. The aim is to bring childcare and schooling closer together and encourage a joint pedagogical approach to the learning and development of children and young people. All pedagogical activities for children and young people are part of a lifelong learning process and should be viewed as a whole.

As part of the process of integrating childcare and schooling, two new national curricula have been produced. Pre-schools have been given a curriculum of their own and the curriculum for compulsory schools has been reviewed and adapted so as to encompass pre-schools and also to some extent leisure-time centres. The curricula are on the whole similarly constructed. They interconnect and are based on the same attitude towards the way in which children and young people learn and develop. These two curricula along with the curriculum for voluntary forms of schooling cover the first twenty years of life in the Swedish educational system.

Pre-school curriculum

Since August 2007, pre-schools have had their own national curriculum. Like the compulsory school curriculum it takes the form of a government decree and compliance is therefore mandatory. The curriculum specifies the overall goals and orientation of pre-schools in Sweden but does not state how the goals are to be achieved. It is up to those working in pre-schools. The goals cover the following areas:

- norms and values
- development and learning
- children's own influence
- cooperation between pre-school and home
- interaction with the pre-school class, compulsory school and the leisure-time centre.

The guidelines are addressed partly to all those working in pre-schools and partly to the individual work team, i.e. the pre-school teachers and daycare attendants working together in the same children's group. An important part of the curriculum deals with basic values. The same fundamental values are to permeate both pre-school and compulsory school. They involve care and consideration towards others—solidarity, gender equality and tolerance.

The pre-school curriculum proceeds from the assumption that the child is competent and is constantly seeking to improve its understanding of life around it. The task of the pre-school is to utilize this thirst for knowledge and lay the foundations of a lifelong learning process.

Pre-school for all

Nowadays, pre-school is seen as the first step in the educational system and an important part of a child's development and learning. The Government considers therefore that all children should be entitled to a pre-school place and that is up to parents to decide whether they want their children to attend pre-school or not. Today, the right to a place is dependent on how the parents are occupied—local authorities are only required to provide childcare for children whose parents are either working or studying or in cases where the child has its own care needs.

The Government has announced in the year 2008 that a universal, non-fee-paying pre-school has been in operation. The first stage has involved giving all four- and-five-year-old the right to three hours of pre-schooling a day free of charge. Furthermore, children aged one to five years whose parents are seeking employment have been entitled to attend pre-school for at least three hours a day.

Table 7.1 : Proportion of children in different age groups registered in Swedish childcare in percentage, 2008

Age of child	*Pre-school/leisure- -time centre*	*Family daycare*	*Total*
1	34%	8	42
2	60%	13	73
3	64%	13	77
4	69%	13	82
5	73%	12	85
1-5	61%	12	73
6-9	56%	4	60
10-12	7%	0	7

[Pre-school is for children aged 1-5, leisure-time centres are for children aged 6-12 and family daycare is for children aged 1-12]

Table 7.2 : Proportion of children in different types of Swedish pre-school and leisure-time centres in percentage, 2008

	Pre-school	*Leisure-time centre*
Municipal	87	95
Non-municipal:	13	5
Parent cooperatives	7	2
Company-run facilities	3	1
Association-run facilities	2	2
Staff cooperatives	1	0
Total	**100**	**100**

The Government has also noted the significance of childcare fees. In many local authorities the fees are determined by parental income and by the number of hours of childcare needed. This means that the economic gain for the family from a rise in income can be small and this can erode the inclination of parents (chiefly mothers) to increase their working hours or return to work after being unemployed. In order to tackle these marginal effects, the Government's proposal for a universal pre-school system has been combined with recommendations for a ceiling for childcare fees which will apply to all local authorities.

SUGGESTED READINGS

1. *Childcare in Sweden*—Ministry of Social Affairs and Health, Stockholm; 2006.
2. OECD (2007); *Employment Outlook.*
3. OECD (2008); *Economic Surveys,* Sweden.
   (OECD—Organization for Economic Cooperation and Development)

8

Scenario of Health Care in Swedish Community

Good health and equal access to health services for everyone are the goals of the Swedish health care system

A fundamental principle of the health care system is that it is a public sector responsibility to provide and finance best health care services for the entire population. Responsibility for these services rests primarily with the county councils, which levy taxes to raise the financial resources required and also operate almost all the services provided. Thus it is mainly local, in 21 geographical areas, who are responsible for health services in Sweden. Two characteristics of Swedish health care system are worth mentioning—(a) **decentralization** and (b) **democratic principles.**

A glimpse of health situation

- By international standards, health in Sweden is relatively good.
- Infant mortality is low, at 4.1 deaths per 1,000 in the first year of life.
- Cardiovascular diseases especially **CAD (Coronary Artery Diseases)** and **PAD (Peripheral Artery Diseases)** are very common among all the diseases prevalent. However, deaths attributed to these diseases diminished substantially during 2003-2005 because of

high level of health awareness among the people and this has resulted into an increased average life expectancy.

- For men average life expectancy is 76.5 years and for women 81.5 years.
- Over a long period of time, mortality from injuries, alcohol-related diseases and suicide has also declined.
- More than one-third of all Swedish residents say that they suffer some form of allergy or over-sensitivity.
- Overweight among individuals and children is quite rampant due to intake of high fat contained food.
- The number of elderly people has risen substantially with the greatest rise in the age group 80 years and older due to phenomenal development of medical sciences. Sweden is seen as having the world's oldest population, with 18 per cent aged 65 or over.

The health services

The primary level is the level of the health care system to which people shall be able to turn all their health problems. The primary care sector has the aim of improving the general health of the people and treats diseases and injuries that do not require hospitalization. This sector employs many different professional categories—physicians, nurses, auxiliary nurses, midwives and physiotherapists. Their work has been organized in health centres, which has facilitated teamwork. During recent years there has been a structural change in the work of the doctors in primary care—today everyone may choose a doctor who has qualified as a general practitioner as their own family doctor.

In addition to local health centres and family doctor, surgeries, primary care is also provided by private doctors and physiotherapists; at district nurse clinics; and at clinics for child and maternity health care. At the children's clinics, vaccinations, health check-ups and consultations as well as certain types of treatment are provided free of charge to all children under school age. At the maternity clinics, there are both midwives and doctors. These clinics are visited by expectant mothers for regular check-ups, which are free of charge during the entire pregnancy. The district nurses give medical treatment as well as advice and support, both at their clinics and when visiting patients in their homes. Industrial health services and school health services are also available to specific groups.

By adapting housing, using technical aids, and providing medical services and nursing in the homes of patients, it is both possible and easier for elderly and disabled people to stay in their own homes. People in hospitals for long-term care, in nursing homes and those living in service apartments have access to nursing services 24 hours a day. Great importance is attached to making these places as much like as home as possible. All facilities a person enjoys at home, all the nursing homes extend those facilities at the best of their level for the patients so that they recover as soon as possible.

For conditions that require hospital treatment, medial services are provided at county level and regional level. County medical services are available at some 80 central county hospitals and district county hospitals. Here, somatic care is provided in a number of specialist fields, partly as inpatient care and partly at clinics (outpatient care). The county medical services also include psychiatric care, which is provided to an increasing extent in outpatient forms. The regional medical system is operated at nine regional hospitals, which have a greater range of specialist and sub-specialist fields than at county level, for example neurosurgery, thorasic surgery, plastic surgery and highly specialized laboratories.

In Sweden, a relatively large proportion of the resources available for medical services have traditionally been allocated to the provision of care and treatment at hospitals. This can be seen, for example, in the low number of visits per person and year to doctors in the primary care services. The number of general practitioners is also low in relation to the total number of doctors (approximately 30%).

The number of days of short-term care per person and year has decreased during the last few years for all age groups.

In long-term care, too, the number of inpatient days has decreased per person per year in most age groups. Extensive changes have been made in the area of psychiatric care during the last ten years. People with mentally challenged have, to a great extent, left institutional care and now live in the community. At the same time as reductions have been made in inpatient care, more outpatient care have been established.

The changes that have taken place in inpatient care must be seen in relation to the deliberate emphasis given to various forms of outpatient care. An increasing proportion of visits to doctors are made outside the hospitals and the nature of these visits has also changed. An increasing amount of treatment is given and operations performed without the patient needing to be taken into hospital. The introduction of day surgery, for example, can illustrate the changes that are taking place. The deliberate emphasis on outpatient forms of care also means that visits to medical staff other than doctors is changed.

Management and planning

In Swedish society there are three political and administrative levels—**central government, county council** and **local authority.** All these levels have important roles in the welfare system and are represented by directly elected political bodies that have the right to finance their activities by levying taxes and fees.

One important role for central government is to lay down basic principles for the health services through laws and ordinances. The most important of these is the **Health and Medical Services Act of 1982,** which lays down that the people shall be offered health and medical services of good quality which shall be provided on equal terms and be easily accessible to all. The services provided shall be based on respect for the patient's integrity and his right to make his own decisions. They should, also, as far as possible, be organized and performed in consultation with the patient.

Other laws regulate the obligations and responsibility of personnel, professional confidentiality, patients, records and the qualifications required by personnel to practice in the health professions. Today central government is more interested in the results and performance of the services rather than how they are organized. It is chiefly by means of systems for follow-up and evaluation that central government can exercise control over the health services.

The ***Ministry of Health and Social Affairs*** is responsible for developments in areas such as health care, social insurance and social issues. The Ministry draws up terms of reference for government commissions, drafts proposals for parliament on new legislation, and prepares other government regulations.

The ***National Board of Health and Welfare*** is the government's central advisory and supervisory agency in the field of health services, health protection and social services. The key task of this agency is to follow-up and evaluate the services provided to see whether they correspond with the goals laid down by central government.

Another important government agency (**Swedish Council of Technology Assessment in Health Care, SBU**) which is also very important and engaged in evaluation work regarding the proper and just utilization of all resources. The SBU shall contribute towards the efficient utilization of the resources allocated to the health services by evaluating both new and established methods from medical, social and ethical perspectives. Reviews of current knowledge in the field and syntheses of existing scientific material are produced with the aid of experts. Information on the SBU's findings is then disseminated to central and local government officials and medical staff to provide basic data for decision-making purposes.

Under the ***Health and Medical Services Act,*** the county councils are responsible for providing health services and for striving to achieve a good standard of health in the population. One local authority also has the same responsibilities as the county councils where health care is concerned. In addition to health services, the county councils are responsible for certain issues related to education, culture, public transport and regional development. County councils elections are held at the same time as parliamentary elections—every fourth year. The county councils decide on the allocation of resources to the health services and are responsible for the overall planning of the services offered. It is also the county councils which own and run the hospitals, health centres and other institutions, even if these institutions are supplemented by those of private organizations which, in most cases, have contracts with the county councils.

The total domination of the county councils in the provision of health services enables them to make decisions on structural issues in the health services. During recent years considerable changes have taken place in this area, particularly the reduction in the number of beds but also where other hospital activities are concerned, such as casualty wards open 24 hours a day. The reduction in the number of beds has been achieved by increasing in productivity generated by new medical technology, shrinking financial resources, and incentives resulting from the development of financial management system.

One significant change introduced by the county councils in recent years is the freedom for patients to choose where and by whom they wish to be given medical attention. Patients can choose the health centres and/or family doctor and even which hospital they wish to attend. If a patient wishes to receive medical care at a hospital outside the county council in which he or she resides, a referral may be required. A patient does not usually need a referral to obtain specialist hospital care—he/she can go directly to the hospital without going *via* the primary services. The primary level therefore does not always have a referral function; the way in which the county councils can influence patients' decisions about which part of the health care system to approach first is to differentiate consultation fees.

Where highly specialized care is concerned, and, to a certain extent, research and the training of doctors, the county councils cooperate with other bodies—government or private. This collaboration is based on agreements between the county councils in the region, for example, on the prices that shall be charged for highly specialized care. The county councils also collaborate at national level through the ***Federation of County Councils***.

One example of the management of the health services is the introduction of a care guarantee for patients which has been in force since 1992. This guarantee was the result of an agreement concluded at national level by the ***Ministry of Health and Social Affairs*** and the ***Federation of County Councils*** to reduce the waiting time for certain forms of treatment for which there were long queues. The nature of the agreement has changed, and it is now chiefly concerned with accessibility for patients. The primary care services shall offer help the same day that the patient contacts them, with a medical consultation within eight days. Where necessary, the patient shall be able to see a specialist within three months or within one month if his or her medical condition has not been clearly diagnosed. The aim of these new criteria for accessibility is to reinforce the position of the patient *vis-à-vis* the care services. This aim is to be further emphasized by the extension of the care guarantee to patients with severe chronic illness, such as diabetes, who will be ensured an agreed standard of care.

The local authorities also have their own area of responsibility in the field of health services. In 1992, the responsibility for, among other things, nursing homes was transferred to the local authorities from the county councils. At the same time, the local authorities also assumed the obligation to pay for patients who had been treated in a hospital and who were obliged to remain in hospital since the local authority could not offer a suitable place in, for example, a nursing home. A similar change in responsibility came into force in 1995 and still continuing, that concerning the living arrangements, employment and support for those suffering from long-term mental illness.

Pharmaceutical preparations

Before a medicine may be sold in Sweden, it must be registered at the ***Medical Products Agency***, which is a government authority responsible for the control of pharmaceutical preparations. The activities of this authority are regulated in a new law governing medical products that has been adapted to European Union regulations. The number of registered pharmaceutical preparations is approximately 4,800. The prices of pharmaceuticals are set by means of negotiations between the central government and pharmaceutical companies.

The responsibility for financing the pharmaceutical subsidy previously rested with the central government, but from 1998 it was taken over by the county councils, which have traditionally borne most costs of health services in Sweden. The financing is based on annual negotiations between the ***Federation of County Councils*** and the ***Central Government.***

The ***National Corporation of Swedish Pharmacies,*** in which the state is the majority shareholder, has the sole and exclusive right to retail medicines, both to the general public and to hospitals. The pharmaceutical companies have insurance coverage that provides compensation to patients who are harmed by a medicine.

Dental care

The county councils are responsible for ensuring that all children and young people up to the age of 19 years receive free dental care. Here the emphasis is placed on preventive care. The dental health of this group has improved considerably since the 1970s and continues to improve steadily. Adults received an economic subsidy from the national dental insurance system for basic dental care. The pricing of dental care has been deregulated, which means that providers set their own fees for each form of treatment. There is also an option to sign two-year agreements on the provision of basic dental care at a fixed price. For certain more extensive dental procedures, there is a special high-cost protection system, aimed at limiting patient's outlays. Approximately, half of the dentists work in the national dental service, which is run by the county councils; the others are private dentists. The county councils are responsible for ensuring that sufficient specialist dental care is available to meet the needs of both children and adults.

Training and research in the health care system

Doctors are trained at various universities and colleges. The training programmes are linked to the operations of the university hospitals and other relevant parts of the health services, for example the primary health services. To become a registered doctor, a student must successfully complete a study programme of five and a half years and an 18-month pre-registration period as a house officer. On registration a doctor is authorized to practice medicine, but almost all doctors continue their studies in order to qualify as a specialist after five years' service in one of the 62 recognized specialist fields of study offered by the medical colleges. Every year some 900 students complete medical training programmes. The study programme for nurses lasts three years and is available at some 50 colleges of nursing which produces some, 4,000 nurses each year.

Swedish medical research has a prominent international position in many fields. It is characterized by strong links between basic research and clinical research and by the integration of research and development into the health services, particularly at the university hospitals. Medical research is mostly financed by government funds, but the county councils also provide resources for clinical research that is closely connected to patient care. The strong position occupied by medical research in Sweden is demonstrated by the fact that about 30 per cent of university research spending goes to the medical field.

Quality and safety

During the 1990s, quality-oriented development work has gained a stronger position in the Swedish health services. The aim of this work is to generate value-added for the people the services are intended for—patients, their relatives and the public in general—and to improve the health care system's ability to meet their needs.

Important target areas are the availability and client focus of health services and the degree to which they are knowledge-based. Special agreements between the ***Central Government*** and the ***Federation of County Councils*** have established that this is a desirable orientation for the development efforts that are underway in the Swedish health care system.

In 1994, the National Board of Health and Welfare issued a set of regulations on quality issues, which it reworked in 1997 and is still constantly running with a high degree of achievement. These regulations state that all heath services in Sweden should include a system for continuous quality improvement. One expression of this increased activity is that since 1996 there has been a Swedish instrument for analyzing the ability of the health services to achieve systematic quality improvement, known as **QUL**. Developed by the ***Federation of County Councils***, this instrument is linked to the ***Swedish Health Services Quality Award***, presented annually to an organization that, after an evaluation procedure, can be considered to provide a model for the Swedish health care system.

The Swedish health services have access to another invaluable asset: the clinical improvement efforts represented by some 50 national health care quality registers, each containing data on health care outcomes and treatment measures in an equal number of illness categories. These registers serve as a knowledge base for continuous improvement efforts.

To build-up a broader knowledge base in the health care system, evidence-based diagnostic and treatment guidelines are being developed at the national level for such major categories of chronic illness as diabetes, stroke and **CAD**.

If, in connection with medical care or treatment, a patient suffers a serious injury or illness, or is exposed to the risk of injury or illness, the institutions providing the care or treatment is obliged to report this fact to the ***National Board of Health and Welfare***. Where faults or negligence are attributable to members of staff, the matter can be referred to the ***National Medical Disciplinary Board***, a government authority whose organization is somewhat similar to that of a court. A patient or a relative of a patient can directly approach the Board if he or she considers that health service staff members have acted incorrectly. The Board can decide on disciplinary measures (warning or admonition) or remove the person from the professional register.

The Board does not deal with the matter of financial compensation for a patient who has suffered an injury. There is a patient's insurance scheme which covers such claims. Till now, the county councils and other institutions providing health care services have voluntarily assumed responsibility to grant financial compensation to patients who have suffered injuries during treatment. A patient who has been injured, infected or has met with an accident in connection with an examination or treatment can be compensated, regardless of whether it is the responsibility of the medical services or not.

Current issues

Responsibility for subsiding pharmaceuticals was transferred in 1998 from the central government to the county councils. The background was sharply raising pharmaceutical costs over a period of years, but so far the reform has not slowed these cost increases to the extent desired. Meanwhile now, expensive drugs are being introduced, leading to a intensive discussion of prioritization—pharmaceuticals are, after all, financed from the total county council budgets for health services and thus compete with other forms of treatment. Letting patients pay a larger share of drugs costs or eliminating all subsidies on drugs mostly related to lifestyles are examples of measures under discussion.

Throughout the 1990s, the position of patients has gradually become stronger. This includes expanded options for choosing care providers (hospitals, local health centres, doctors, surgeons etc.) and maximum waiting time for visits and treatment. Another aspect is stronger, patient's influence in health services, for example improved and individually tailored information on patient's health condition and treatment alternatives, as well as greater opportunities to influence the choice of treatment.

The hottest topic, however, is the issue of overall health care resources. The financial resources of the Swedish health services have been shrinking throughout 1990s. Altogether, this represents cost reductions of nearly 10 per cent in real terms. Meanwhile health care needs have risen, due to both demographic trends and medical progress. There are two opposing viewpoints on this issue. One says that there is still room to meet growing health care needs by means of continued efficiency-raising measures. The other side argues that further cost reductions are not possible without severe consequences, both for patients and for employees in the health care system.

Table 8.1 : Distribution of public health care costs, 2009

Somatic short-term care	60%
Geriatric care	4%
Psychiatric care	12%
Primary care	17%
Dental care	4%
Other	2%

Table 8.2 : Employees in the county council health services (selected professional categories, 2009)

Doctors	23,000
Nurses	70,000
Auxiliary nurses	64,000
Physiotherapists	5,000
Occupational therapists	4,000

SUGGESTED READINGS

1. *Organization of the Swedish Health Services, 2009;* published by the Swedish Institute.
2. OECD (2008); *Economic Surveys,* Sweden.
(OECD—Organization for Economic Cooperation and Development)

9

Finnish Social Protection System and Its Operation

There are three important components of Finnish social protection system which are as follows: (a) preventive social and health politics; (b) social and health care services; (c) social insurance.

The basic thrust of social protection system centring around two dimensions:

- Securing livelihood through comprehensive basic security and the income related benefits that guarantee the possibility to maintain a reasonable standard of living in different situations of risk.
- To provide comprehensive social as well as health services.

The social protection system is the result of measures that have taken decades to implement. It is characterized by universability of benefits. As in other Nordic states, social protection is based mostly on residence in the country. The social protection system has guaranteed coherence, fairness and equality in society. Almost all households receive some kind of cash benefits and health services from time to time.

A strong principle of equality is included in the social protection system. The vigorous development of the daycare system for small children has enabled women to participate widely in working life. In Finland about 80 per cent of mothers of young children participate in working life. All children under school age (7 years) have the right to municipal daycare or, alternatively, the families can receive financial support for private daycare or taking care of their children at home.

Preventive action is a central part of social protection in Finland. Its aim is to forestall a range of risks and problems, in part so that the use of more expensive services and forms of assistance can be minimized. People are encouraged to look after their health and cut their use of tobacco and alcohol. The main areas of preventive action are environmental health care, effective primary health care, occupational health care, maternity and child welfare services and prevention of social exclusion.

The State and the municipalities are responsible for organizing the social and health care services in Finland. Municipalities are responsible for arranging services either alone or together with other municipalities. Most municipalities have less than 10,000 inhabitants. The financial responsibility for services is divided between the State and the municipality. Municipalities are entitled to levy local taxes. The proportion of fees collected from the clients is relatively small, and municipal services are subsidized by the State.

Some of the social protection systems which are presently prevailing and vibrantly making a gesture are synoptically discussed below.

Cash benefits: Cash benefits are always income transfers in the form of money. They account for about two-thirds of social protection expenditure. The share went up during the recession as unemployment security expenditure went up, but it has fallen since. The financing of cash benefits varies according to the type of benefit. The aim of reforms is to finance the basic income security with tax revenue, while employment-related benefits will be financed with contributions from employers and the insured.

Unemployment security: The number of recipients of earnings related and basic daily unemployment allowance fell in 1998. The improved employment situation has not reduced the number of recipients of labour market support, because they are chiefly long-term employed or young people.

In 1997, the so-called training guarantee system was introduced as a way of supporting the training of the long-term unemployed. The second stage of this system entered into force on August 1, 1998. The aim is to support self-motivated vocational training and general studies by the unemployed. In 1998, daily allowances were raised. Presently, the number of unemployed youth has been reduced quite considerably but of course, employment is not a smooth flow in the Finnish society as it is expected.

Family benefits: The aim of the child allowance system is to even out the costs to families of bringing up children. No changes or index rises are made to the child allowance payments or parental allowances. The fall in the birth rate caused a decrease in the number of recipients of both child benefit and parental allowances.

Health insurance: The number of recipients of daily sickness allowance increased as the employment situation improved. The number of deductible items for medicines refunded by health insurance continued to rise, if only slightly. The insurance refund cover for preventive dental care is expanded to new age groups. Expensive medicines without established treatment practices are kept outside the sphere of health insurance.

Pension security: The changes in working life in recent years are reflected in the employment pension system. As of the beginning of 1998, all employment relationships, even short ones, contributed towards employees' pensions. Pension, contributions are healthy and paid on monthly basis. The age limit for a part-time pension has been reduced temporarily to 56, in order to bring about a reduction in full-time pensions. The aim is to help people cope with their work and remain in working life for longer.

Social and health care services: The strategic areas of emphasis in social and health care services in 2000 were to increase the efficiency of services and care procedures and to increase efficiency in steering and monitoring of municipal services. At the end of 2007, Parliament approved a reform of control systems for social and health care services. The former national plan for social and health care has been replaced by a target and action programme approved for four-year periods and an annual separate decision on the resources of municipal social and health services. The change entered into force on January 2008.

Minimum security: The Act on Social Assistance entered into force on March 1, 1998. The new Act being together is the existing legislation of social assistance. At the same time, the own risk of recipients of this benefit has been increased. In connection with the reform, the level of unemployment security and housing allowance has also been raised. As a consequence of the reform, the number of recipients of social assistance has gone down and the grounds for granting the benefit have been standardized.

Services for the elderly: An expansion of the holiday entitlement of family cares has improved the position of elderly group. Community services have been reinforced through creating new local operating models in cooperation between different professional groups.

The transfer to a service structure based mainly on non-residential care has meant that the municipalities have reduced the number of places in old people's homes, replacing them with service housing. The limit for reductions in institutional care places seems to have been reached already. There are considerable differences between municipalities in this respect. Home help services have been targeted at those persons in greatest need, bringing about a reduction in the number of recipients. Services become increasingly oriented towards individual clients. According to comparison of European Community Member States, care for the elderly in Finland is still of a high quality.

Services for the disabled: The Finnish Government has put lot of emphasis on services for the disabled and in this regard more housing services, home help services, family care, daytime activities as well as support and guidance for families have been the cornerstones for improving the conditions of disabled.

Care for small children: The system for care of small children was reformed in 1997 as part of a project to eliminate incentives traps. The share of private daycare was still small compared with municipal daycare. At the end of 2000, 12,800 children under school age received daycare with the help of private childcare allowance. There were an estimated 2,18,000 children in municipal daycare. The costs for municipal daycare in 2000 were an estimated **FIM** (earlier currency before euro) 40,000 per child for the year.

In 2008, 64 per cent of all children under 6 were in municipal daycare and receiving the pre-school teaching given there. In addition, some 6-year olds received pre-school teaching in private daycare centre or in the school system.

Health care services: Health care expenditure went up slightly in 2000. The total expenditure for health care in Finland was nevertheless below the OECD (Organization for Economic Cooperation and Development) average. Finland's expenditure in 2000 was estimated at 7.2 per cent of GDP. According to a comparative study of European Members States in 2005, 86 per cent of Finns were satisfied with health care services. Finland's health care services also received a good rating in the recent OECD study.

There are big differences between different operating units as regards the resources of primary health care, the availability of services and care procedures. The personal doctor system has continuously expanded in primary health care. This has speeded up access to health centre services and improved the continuity of care. As technology develops, the emphasis in primary health care has shifted towards outpatient care. At hospitals, the average length of stay has continually become shorter. The change in service structure has shifted responsibility for care and a considerable part of primary health care to social service institutions and services.

Preventive social and health policy: The aim of preventive social and health care policy is to create healthy and socially secure environments for both work and living, to promote healthy lifestyles and support collective responsibility.

The areas of emphasis in preventive work are to promote the health and welfare of children and young people, to maintain and improve the health, fitness and quality of life of the population, to prevent exclusion, to develop preventive policy on intoxicant abuse, and to promote a healthy and safe environment in general.

Alcohol use among young people has become increasingly common. The number of teenage pregnancies has remained fairly stable. The favourable trend in dietary habits amongst the population at large continued. The differences between population groups nevertheless seem to remain unchanged or to even be increasing. Thanks to effective preventive action, the HIV virus has not spread in Finland to the same extent as in other European countries. Increased alcohol consumption has caused an increase in problems of abuse and the costs for related care.

New solutions to the debt problems of households are sought through measures such as '**social credit**'. Testing of this system began during the year under review. The fall in the numbers of homeless people came to a standstill in 2008. The increased number of homeless people is a reflection of the pressures of the housing market in the bigger cities.

Working conditions, occupational safety and health and labour protection: The aim of occupational safety and health is to reduce the health risks associated with working conditions. In 1998, insurance companies and the State Treasury received about 1,40,000 applications for compensation for occupational accidents and disease.

The accident rate has gone down steadily since the early 1980s. The accident rate for 1998 is still estimated top have been higher than that for 1997. The reason is the rapid economic growth and the increased employment rate. Fatal occupational accidents have been cut by half in 2007. The situation concerning occupational disease is also better than a decade ago.

The labour protection districts are in charge of regional occupational safety and health development, monitoring and customer services. The main objective of the labour protection districts is to strengthen the occupational safety and health work in individual workplaces and to assess risks associated with exposure to chemicals. Particular attention has been given to workplaces with over 20 employees. The demand for customer services amounted to about 1,40,000 customer contacts in 2006. Forty seven per cent (47%) of the performance targets have been achieved.

Other activities in the social affairs and health sector: The institutions and agencies under the Ministry of Social Affairs and Health can be divided into research and development institutions on the one hand and permit and monitoring authorities dealing mostly with administrative matters on the other. At the end of 2006 under review, about 3,31,000 people worked in these administrative units in these sectors, including the Ministry itself. Performance targets were set for each institution and agency in the sector, and these were laid out in the management by result agreements between the Ministry and the Unit.

Slot Machine Association: The administrative sector of the Ministry of Social Affairs and Health includes the Slot Machine Association. It is the only body in Finland licensed to engage in slot machine, lottery and gaming operations. The profit of the Slot Machine Association is distributed through the State budget to promote health and social welfare.

According to the opinion surveys, the Finnish social protection system has widespread public support. The main challenges of the coming years are:

1. Weakening dependency ratio,
2. The ageing population,
3. The high level of long-term unemployment, and
4. Social exclusion and securing sustainable financing.

Due to the structural reforms of the pension system and because of curbs on public spending and the improved employment situation, financing the system is now on a more firm base than in the period of recession of the early 1990s. Funding to provide pension security for the 'baby boom generation' will demand moderate growth in the economy and a lower unemployment rate than at the present. In tune with the very essence of protection system and future promises, the **seven strategic goals** of the social affairs and health sector for the year 2020 as envisioned by the Finnish government are:

- Supporting employees to maintain the capacity to work and to continue the working life.
- Reducing poverty and social exclusion.
- Guaranteeing the level and functioning of social and health services.
- Strengthening activating elements of social protection.
- Ensuring sustainable financing of social protection.
- Strengthening equality between sexes both in working and family life.
- Continuing the ongoing reforms of social protection.

The European Union (EU) is increasingly becoming the environment in which social and health care policy operates. The creation of Euro has generated discussion about the financing of social protection. The entry into force of the Amsterdam Treaty has reinforced the social dimension at the EU level. Challenges shared by the entire Union include unemployment, the prevention of exclusion, an ageing population and how to maintain its working capacity

SUGGESTED READINGS

1. *The Finnish Social Protection System and its Operation*—Ministry of Social Affairs and Health, Helsinki; 2008.
2. *Trends in Social Protection in Finland* (2000-2008); Ministry of Social Affairs and Health; 2008.
3. OECD (1997): *Employment Outlook,* Finland
4. OECD (1998): *Economic Surveys,* Finland.

(OECD—Organization for Economic Cooperation and Development).

10

Government and Non-Governmental Organizations

A Collaborative Approach for Socio-Economic Emancipation of Disadvantaged People in Bangladesh

Introduction

There has been a significant growth of NGOs and their programmes in Bangladesh over the last two decades. Their relationship with Government Organizations has undergone a perceptible change in the last two decades. The relationship is still evolving. It is a fact that NGOs are working at the back and front and sometimes at the breast, of movement agencies. But in the operational sense in some cases the NGOs are supplementing the work of government agencies, sometimes they are competing with government agencies and in some cases they are working in isolation with obscure target groups. These NGO activities have of course created a new development climate in rural and urban communities which is mixed with appreciation and criticism. The crucial role of NGOs *vis-à-vis* Governments efforts to improve the condition of the poor and the disadvantaged has been debated since independence. In the absence of a clear NGO policy of the government, this chapter makes an effort to explore the role of the government in the promotion of the NGO sector in Bangladesh. Although government documents and government appointed committee reports reflect the need for increased NGO participation in government sponsored development efforts. Only a few concrete steps have been taken in this direction. There is an ever increasing realization about the importance of a continuous dialogue between different levels of bureaucracy and the NGO sector to develop confidence and accept each other as equal partners for the development of the poor, deprived and disadvantaged. This is also the objective of this particular chapter to analyze the present relationship for the greater interest of economic emancipation.

Bangladesh is among the bottom few out of the 43 least developed economies of the world in terms of per capita income. About 115 million people—a large proportion of them are hungry, impoverished and suffering from illiteracy, lack of health care, malnutrition and poor housing. Population growth is high at 4.17 per cent in Bangladesh and its density (about 800 per sq.km) among the world's highest. Most of the poor live in villages but a substantial number of them live in city slums and for them it is a fight for survival. Infant mortality is about 100 per thousand live births. It is a recognized fact that a country like Bangladesh is best with thousands of problems. To overcome these problems it is not possible for GO to minimize the problem with its limited resources. Here lies the question of rationality of NGO interventions towards development activities. The term used to describe the NGO-GO relationship is highly sensitive and also require some clarification. The use of complementarity is questioned by some NGO staff because it suggests a subordinate role for NGOs. Collaboration has often been preferred as a more equal description of joint activity, but carried with it negative political associations. Many NGOs, therefore, wish to be seen as catalysts for development, without necessarily taking permanent role in the process. The idea that NGOs should engage in substitution for government services without attempting long-term improvement in efficiency, is not role sought by most NGOs. How can the NGOs collaborate with the Government while relating their basic attitudes? Can NGOs function in isolation of the Government? To what extent can

NGOs perform their role effectively if they link up with government policies and programmes. There is a need for an on-going dialogue between NGOs and Government. This will create opportunities for both the parties to meet, interact, work together and build-up mutual confidence for the common cause. An environment is to be created for the Government and the NGOs to accept each other as equal actor in the development process which will prepare them to listen, learn and act on a mutually agreed path.

Emergence of NGOs in Bangladesh

Voluntarism undertaken by individuals or groups intending to serve and benefit the people have been in vogue for centuries in Bangladesh, drawing energy and inspiration from humanitarian, social and cultural values. With changing social structure and consequent changes in beliefs, practices and social relations, the concept of voluntarism has marked a radical swing along a direction that involves professionalism, invites specialization and invoke formal organizational and management structure which can be seen in non-governmental organizations (NGOs) operating in Bangladesh today. Recognizing the need for development for alleviating endemic poverty in the country, NGOs began to shift their emphasis from relief to socio-economic development and to pursue initially rather haphazard programmes aiming at health care, family planning, income generation and self-reliance for the disadvantaged and the poor. As poverty continued to deepen and encompass enormous number of people, more foreign NGOs came to work in this country and, at the same time, the numbers of local NGOs grew fast.

Classification of NGOs working in Bangladesh

Given the diversity and plurality of development of NGOs, it is somewhat difficult to classify them into distinctive types. One could differentiate these NGOs on the basis of ideology and approach as:

- **Welfare-oriented**
- **Development service-oriented**
- **Empowerment process-oriented**

They could also be categorized on the basis of spatial coverage and sources of funds such as local NGOs which operate in only a few villages in an upazilla or a union, receiving funds from local sources or from national or international NGOs. National NGOs which operate in several geographical locations covering a number of districts, mostly receiving funds, and international NGOs which operate in several geographical locations, having their headquarters based outside the country and being operated by expatriates.

Kinds of 'NGO' activities in Bangladesh

The majority of people in Bangladesh are poor without having regular income and productive assets and resources. Consequently, they are subjected to exploitation and social injustice, and are mostly deprived of their due share of the public sector development resources provided by the government. NGOs have concentrated all their efforts targeting the rural and urban poor on mobilizing them to develop their own organizations for alleviating their poverty. One of the major contributions of NGOs in development has been in building organizations of the poor through social structural analysis. NGOs make the poor aware of the causes of their poverty, dependence and domination and put emphasis in the critical needs to assimilate together. NGOs set different criteria for enrolment of the organizations. The intention was to ensure that the enrolment was limited to only those persons for whom the organizations had been formed. Criteria (Hussain, 2008) for enrolment of members usually related to:

1. Age
2. Gender
3. Landholding size
4. Occupation

5. Income
6. Asset

The sectors in which NGOs have provided inputs and services encompass agriculture, livestock and poultry, horticulture, sericulture, bee-keeping, nursery development, irrigation and water management, and such non-farm activities as handicrafts, weaving, local transports etc. In agriculture, NGOs have introduced new crops like soyabeans, which appears to have a bright prospect in the country. Besides, they have also introduced agricultural practices without using chemical fertilizers and insecticides which NGOs term as organic agriculture. Through the use of green manures and compost fertilizers, NGOs meet the need for soil nutrients which are otherwise met by traditional chemical fertilizers. Instead of using insecticides, they have introduced the system of biological pest control through diverse cropping. Hussain (2008) has made an attempt to categorize such NGO activities as follows:

1. Organizing the rural poor through conscientization,
2. Mass education for eradication of illiteracy,
3. Credit traders and skill training,
4. Income-generation activities and employment,
5. Health, nutrition and family planning,
6. Development of physical infrastructure, and
7. Research and publication.

Comparative advantages of NGO

NGOs provide one of the most creative dimensions in development in Bangladesh. This creativity is due to the relative small-scale size of NGOs which made them more efficient and effective in dealing with their beneficiaries. Bureaucracy is less and the gap between planning and implementation is minimal (Lewis, 2005). The NGOs have successfully devised and demonstrated several alternative development concepts, approaches and strategies. The target group approach innovated by them has been incorporated in the mainstream development too. The concepts and approaches introduced by them such as sustainability, participation, human development, conscientization, empowerment etc. have been widely accepted. As is well known, NGOs can play an effective role in the following areas:

- NGOs can easily identify the group who are really poor as they work at the grassroots; they can also monitor poverty and specific needs of the poor in different regions of the country.
- Creation and testing of new ideas, methods, programmes and strategies of poverty alleviation through social experimentation and their replication; this can be shared by other partners of development including the government organizations.
- NGOs can act as a pressure group for establishing the right of the poor.
- Conscientization and awareness building among the poor is an important area of work where the NGOs have vast experience.
- They can tap the resources and reach it to the poor such as credit, technology etc.

Some studies (Maudud, 2001; Quasem, 2006; Rahman, 2007) have identified the following factors responsible for relative success of the NGOs:

- NGOs usually organize the poor with similar socio-economic background and make them more conscious of their potentials.
- They have complemented credit programmes with conscientization and training.
- NGO credit programmes have been blended with appropriate technology.
- They have intimate knowledge of local conditions and the capacity to reach the intended target groups with cost-effectiveness.

- NGOs have a great financial and administrative flexibility.
- NGOs believe that the poor are bankable if properly organized; they may, therefore, be supplied with collateral free credit.
- NGOs are not required to routinely support the decisions and programmes of the government, they may differ, resistant against governments moves if they so decide.

Criticism of NGOs

The Task Force on Bangladesh Development Strategies for the 1990s while reviewing the management of the development process observed that although NGOs have made significant contributions to national development, they are not free from weaknesses. However, in most cases, such criticisms are perhaps due to misunderstanding and a lack of proper information-flow. The shortcomings so identified are summarized below.

Some NGOs do not prefer organizational structure and management system on the ground that such structures usually emulate an elitist and bureaucratic approach which stifles creative initiatives. NGOs need to have an effective organizational structure and systematic management standard accompanied by professionalism and accountability mechanism to operate effectively with strategic planning capacities and capture public confidence. NGOs without such management system under an effective governing board are bound to suffer management lapses leading to failures, even disintegration.

Not only that there are NGOs which tend to undertake programmes which are determined by and dovetailed to the critical needs of the target beneficiaries and thus can defeat the ultimate programme objectives. In consequence, their competence is questioned projecting a negative image of the NGO sector as a whole.

NGOs are generally found individualistic and often egoistic and as such prevent them from taking a coordinated and planned action programmes aiming at effective distribution of available resources—human, material, and ideas. The sooner is the approach abandoned, the better would be the climate for collaboration leading to more effective realization of the ultimate objective of poverty alleviation and human development.

In order to effectively combat poverty there is a need for embarking micro-scale interventions and to that respect, a building among the NGOs, the government of the country and the donor agencies is a must. But no concrete initiative has emerged from the NGOs to this end fearing that they might loose their independence, flexibility, responsiveness and innovativeness.

When funding flow is discontinued due to policy changes of the donor's own government, the donor-resource dependent NGOs face a big problem and that impedes their service delivery system which in turn affects the target group. Added to this vulnerability, these NGOs are exposed to the dictates of the concern donors. No effort has yet been made to critically address and strategically plan palpable solution to such problems.

Even after two decades of operation at the grassroots, NGOs in general (with the exception of some) have failed to document their insights and experiences for the benefit of others as well as for themselves to redirect their programmes and priorities based on the documented experience.

NGOs are also often criticized as clandestinely supporting certain political groups, as having religious motive, as serving the global interest of donor countries, as remunerating richly their employees and so on.

GO-NGO cooperation—some examples

Government has been characterized by the NGOs as being incompetent, corrupt and without motive. NGOs have been seen by the government as unaccountable, amateurish, subversive and drawing away funds which could be used in a more constructive manner. NGOs have also been viewed as being the instruments of the donors, maintaining a level for continuing external agenda. From an initial phase of mutual distrust and misgivings, government agencies and the NGOs are now increasingly collaborating together. Grameen Bank (GB), a successful NGO which started its experiment at Jorba, Chittagong in 1976 is very well known for its achievement in the field of poverty alleviation and developing grassroots organization. Till now, GB borrowed fund from Bangladesh Bank (BB) at available bank rate which is an example of GO (BB) and NGO (GB) collaboration in rural development.

Similar examples can be found from a number of other NGO experiments such as NGOs and banks collaborative programmes like **Small Farmer Development Project (SFDP), Productive Employment Project (PEP), Small Holders Livestock Development Project (SLDP), Rural Poor Cooperative Project (RPCP), Rural Women Employment Creation Project (RWECP)** etc.

In the area of GO-NGOs collaboration for socio-economic development of disadvantaged people there are some research studies done by relevant scholars from time to time (Abdul, 1996; Elahi, 2005; Roy 2008). All these studies show that there are four collaborative factors involved in the study area, i.e. in terms of households—marginal or small farmers groups, market partners of the groups and the supporting elements like *Bangladesh Bank (BB), Rangpur-Dinajpur Rural Services* and some other NGOs and *Department of Agricultural Extension* (GO).

The study also suggests that through collaborative approach, the self-help capacity of the farmers should be more strengthened. Hasanulla (1999) in a study found that in GO-NGO collaboration what is currently desirable is to have a symbolic functional relationship, which may be formal or informal, institutional or behavioural. The study shows that the collaboration between GO and NGO is taking place at two stages, i.e. at policy level and at implementation level. Bangladesh experience provides examples of both single and double-tier GO-NGO cooperation. This cooperation involves a series of activities ranging from planning, exchanging of ideas, and designing of projects to sharing of responsibilities to execution of projects. In other words, GOs and NGOs apart from implementing their own routine programmes are working for facilitation of each other programmes. In the process of implementing these programmes, the participating actors have transcended from the role of facilitator to performer and paved the way of improving their respective role from assistance to collaboration and subsequently to partnership.

Siddiqui and Mustafa (1992) in a study found that the NGOs are highly flexible in taking up new challenges and they are in a close contact with beneficiaries through participatory approach. The study suggests that to emerge as a significant sector in national development, more cooperation, sharing of resources, ideas and personnel are indispensable for GOs and NGOs. There is a tendency in some GO quarters to view NGOs as parties and the NGOs feel their role to be that of a *Partner* working in the area where they have comparative advantages. The NGOs are to complement and supplement GO efforts and they are to see their roles as beginning with participation in policy formulation till implementation and evaluation.

In another study Nanda (2003) found that the *National Bank for Agriculture and Rural Development* (NABARD) in India introduced a pilot project for linking 500 SHGs (Self-Help-Groups) with banks in 1992 after in-depth discussions with the Reserve Bank of India, the commercial banks and the NGO. The study also shows that the results of GO-NGO collaborative projects ensure larger participation of women in savings and credit management; membership of the SHGs comes mostly from the poorest section; demand for credit is frequent and even the very poor are able to save. The study concludes that this collaborative project should be expanded in more areas considering the quality of credit, peoples' participation and self-help grassroots institution.

Where the partnership can work

Although a large number of NGOs and quite a few government agencies are involved in poverty alleviation programmes, there is almost no or very little coordination among them resulting in duplication, overlapping and absence of concerted efforts at reaching the goal. With better and regular coordination, GO and NGO could be more productive and fruitful. Government programmes relating to training, motivation, functional and vocational education, conscientization, market promotion, family planning, health, water management and sanitation and various aspects of agriculture and rural development may involve experienced and tested NGOs to supplement and complement the government efforts. The NGO Bureau should play a more effective role identifying the NGOs specializing in poverty alleviation programmes and linking them up with other agencies and publishing reports on their activities. NGOs have to realize that government is certainly the main channel and instrument of rural human development and that they should be striving for breakthroughs, however small, in its much faster rural development plans. And government has to recognize that there is much that can be learned from the experience of the NGOs and that by placing some confidence in their versatility and flexibility and dedication to the cause of the poor, the resultant sharing can be of great benefit to both. There are, therefore, a number of constructive roles which could form the basis for effective partnership between NGOs and GOs.

Delivery partnership

Joint NGO-GO activity (with respect for mutual priorities) is selected such as the targeted delivery of scare inputs. Ideally, this will also include in the training of government personnel. This functional compatibility may however have only a limited period of success before more serious structural contradictions begin to raise new issues.

Technology innovation and dissemination

NGOs can test and adapt technologies developed by government agencies, and can also provide innovations for possible replication by the public sector. Mechanisms are also needed for NGOs to communicate their research priorities to government institutions, based on participatory needs assessment of target groups.

Training

In seeking to avoid the 'substitutional model' of NGO-GO relationships by NGOs can be deployed at both senior and junior staff level in order to create sustainable improvements in government performance, improved levels of participation, motivation and creative thinking amongst government staff.

Policy inputs

In order to influence government projects from the outset, NGOs can provide inputs, using their specific knowledge and perspectives, to the policy process. This is the true test of the measure of respect afforded to NGOs by governments.

Mobilization and advocacy

The NGOs mobilize and motivate target groups to lobby for better government facilities and services, legal rights and entitlements, accountability of local government staff and need-based extension support etc. For example, the Unadilla has a wide range of services which it is supposed to provide.

Conclusion

It is now recognized that NGOs have made useful contributions in the field of socio-economic development, health care and family planning activities. The NGOs are playing a significant role in the national development of Bangladesh. An umbrella forum at the national level comprising representatives from all relevant organizations for monitoring the poverty alleviation programmes should be created. The NGO Bureau can play pivotal role identifying the NGOs specializing in poverty alleviation programmes and linking them up with other agencies and publishing reports on their activities. NGOs are giving thrust for the alleviation of poverty when poverty alleviation is one of the prior objectives of the government too. So instead of working parallelly and individually, coordinated and united efforts are necessary for alleviating poverty and to achieve the objectives of socio-economic development.

SUGGESTED READINGS

1. Hasanulla, A. (1999); *Social Development in Bangladesh*; Dhaka University Press, Dhaka.
2. Nanda, K. (2003); *GO-NGO Interface* (Mimeo); Centre for Policy Dialogue, Dhaka.
3. Hussain, Abdul, Hye (2008); *Below the line: Rural Poverty in Bangladesh*; Dhaka University Press Limited.
4. David, J. Lewis (2005); "NGOs in Agricultural Technology and the State in Bangladesh"; *Journal of Social Studies*, No. 65, July.
5. Siddique, R. and Mustafa, H. (1992); *Rural Development—Some Concerns;* (monograph); Dhaka University Press Limited.
6. Maudud, Ahmed (2001); *Democracy and the Challenge of Development—A Study of Politics and Military Interventions in Bangladesh*: Dhaka University Press Limited, Dhaka.
7. Elahi, K.Q. (2005); "Reducing Small Farmer Vulnerability to Impoverishment in Bangladesh: An Action Programme"; Proceeding of the Rural Development in Bangladesh Workshop.
8. Roy, Mihir (2008); "A unique kind of collaboration to promote rural upliftment"; *The Daily Independent*, (March 22nd).
9. Rahman, A. (2007); "Rural Development from Below: Lesson Learned from Grameen Bank Experience in Bangladesh"; paper presented in the International Seminar on Rural Development in Bangladesh.
10. Rahman, A. (1996); *NGO Relation with Government* (mimeo); Dhaka University Press, Dhaka.
11. Quasem, Md. Abdul (2006); "Financial return of irrigation equipment to owners and users: The case of shallow tubewells in Bangladesh (1981-1991"; *Journal of Social Studies*, No. 70.

11

Small Farmer Credit Programme in Bangladesh

Success of NGO Approach

Introduction

Bangladesh is a country of villages with about 80 per cent of the rural population and about 57 per cent of them live below the poverty line. This poor section of the people is hard to reach (Maudud, 2000). Agriculture is the main economy of rural Bangladesh and it is also along with its branches of animal husbandry, forestry, fisheries and horticulture are the largest segment of Bangladesh economy. About 56 per cent of the total income is derived from agriculture and about 76 per cent of the total foreign exchange earnings is contributed by agriculture. Besides, agriculture provides food and supplies raw materials for the industries. So, the prosperity of Bangladesh is vitally linked with the progress of its agriculture.

Small farmers lead the agriculture of rural Bangladesh. They constitute the majority of rural farm households. Small farmers are highly productive especially when they have access to improved inputs, e.g. modern varieties. They are also found to be the better users of agricultural inputs and have higher propensities to invest in agriculture compared to other farmer groups. Because of their large number and high level of productive capacity, they have considerable potential to increase agricultural production and to contribute to economic growth. Moreover, improvement in the economic condition of small farmers is essential to alleviate rural poverty and prevent further rural immerserization as they are under constant danger of becoming landless. A number of constraints, e.g. limited access to land, credit, irrigation and other inputs, employment, unfavourable market situation due to limited staying power preclude majority of small farmers from contributing to economic growth commensurate with their potentials. To improve the situation, credit can play critically important role as it increases the effective demand of small farmers for other inputs necessary for increased agricultural productivity. With respect to distribution of credit to the extent of coverage of small farmers by existing credit institutions and projects are still limited. There has been no extensive programme operating specifically for meeting the credit needs of small farmers. As a consequence, the majority of small farmers remain outside the institutional credit distribution system. There is an urgent need to develop a specific programme to cater to the credit needs of small farmers as a separate target group.

Who are small farmers ?

Small farmers are defined as rural households owning and operating land between 0.05 to 2.41 acres and whose major occupation is farming. The characteristics of small farmers in rural Bangladesh could be pointed out as following:

(a) Small farmers are disadvantaged and low income farming population who is concerned with agriculture, livestock, agro-forestry and aquatic production.
(b) They are mostly tenants, informal tenants (e.g. share-croppers) and small owner-croppers.
(c) Farming (cropping, fishing, and livestock raising) constitutes the main occupation of the household and provides the major source of income for the families of small farmers.
(d) They lack effective shares of economic and political power in their villages (Elahi, 1996).

Importance of small farmer credit

Bangladesh is a land of farmer, agriculture provides the basic sources of livelihood to about 85 per cent of total population. About three-fourth of the total workers are engaged in agriculture and allied agricultural sectors. Bangladesh agriculture is characterized by small sized farm, most of which do not produce enough food for the family, and are indebted. The average size of land is 2.2 acres, and 70 per cent farms had below 2.5 acres (Bangladesh Rural Development Board, 2000). The existing technology is still traditional although 25 per cent of cultivated land is irrigated, and per acre application of nutrient fertilizer is 25 kgs (BRDB, 2000). The land is cultivated by bullock power and its productivity is very low. The production in agriculture is highly dependent on weather. The future of agriculture in Bangladesh is predominantly dependent on poor and small farmers and landless workers. So the development policies related to agriculture should be directed towards development of appropriate technologies and raise the capabilities of those small farmers and their co-workers who try to make efficient use of all resources. These in turn would lead to higher agricultural productivity (Quasem, 1999).

Inadequate infrastructure, capital shortage, low yields, traditional practices and frequent natural calamities characterize the agricultural economy of Bangladesh. Small farmers hold a strategic position in that situation. They have considerable potential for augmenting agricultural production and contribution to economic growth in Bangladesh. They are highly productive, efficient and invest proportionately more of their capital in agriculture. In spite of these qualities, small farmers are among the more vulnerable groups to impoverishment in Bangladesh. One of the perennial problems faced by the small farmers is the private money lending system practiced in rural Bangladesh. Before the modern system of banking was introduced—and particularly provisions for agricultural loans earmarked for farmers was developed a private money lending system (called a mohajoni system) was in operation. Farmers used to borrow from the lenders at a high rate of interest (sometimes as much as 80 or 100 per cent per annum). And in the process the small farmers were subjected to extortion and exploitation by the lenders who are generally influential people in the area. This system sent to the subjugation of the farmer at the hands of the moneylenders, who would not only seize crop but the land itself if the farmer could not pay back the loan on time. Accordingly, for generations of families of small farmers have been ruined, becoming landless and homeless (Maudud, 2000).

There are multifarious causes and reasons for such vulnerability among small farmer groups in Bangladesh. The main problem of rural small farmer of Bangladesh is poverty, which is caused by unemployment, is also the root of other problems and it is a vicious cycle. It is recognized that so long unemployment continues, poverty also continues. (Quasem, 1999). In that case, credit plays a significant role in breaking the chain of poverty by creating employment. It also plays a catalytic role in giving accesses to an important means of production and in asset creation. Supervised credit system is very effective to make rural people active, to grow their potentialities and in the long-term for achieving self-reliance.

Government intervention towards credit

Government intervention in credit system for meeting small farmer's demand in rural Bangladesh is hardly new. Banks and cooperative societies in past few years have promoted efforts towards strengthening the organized credit market. Government and semi-government organizations have been making credit available for various kinds of rural economic activities. But the truth is that even in such context and development, organized rural credit sector could not substantially reduce the role still being played by the unorganized counterpart. Total institutional credit given to agriculture has increased by about twelve folds between 1991-92 and 2001-2002. In this period, the institutional credit had risen from Tk. 381 million to Tk. 5034 million. Institutional credit in Bangladesh started to rise sharply from 1976-77 with the launching of the Special Credit Scheme (of Tk. 1000 million per year). Most of the institutional credit has been disbursed in the form of short-term loans to purchase inputs like seeds and fertilizers. Medium-term loans have also been to purchase agricultural implements and draft animals as well as to arrange for irrigation. It is interesting to note that tea has received, on an average, 30 per cent of total institutional credit to agriculture. The *Bangladesh Krishi Bank* (*BKB*) is the major institutional source of agriculture; currently it supplies about two-thirds of such credit. The other major source of institutional credit is the nationalized commercial banking system.

Table 11.1 : Access to Non-Institutional Credit Sources

Land Ownership Group (acres)	*Non-Institutional Credit*			*Average loan (institutional and non-institutional per house-hold in the group)*
	% of loanee households	*Avarage credit per loanee household*	*Average loan per household (Tk) in the group*	
Landless and functionally landless (up to 0.49)	15.9 (8.5)	4806	762 (329)	1303
Marginal (0.50-1.49)	22.4 (13.3)	5308	1191 (690)	2821
Small (1.50-2.49)	17.6 (13.2)	9206	1624 (1328)	3140
Medium (2.50-4.99)	13.0 (6.2)	9537	1241 (860)	4104
Large (5.00+)	9.7 (3.6)	18175	1173 (695)	7887
All groups	16.6 (9.5)	6426	1074 (606)	2606

Source: Analysis of Poverty Trends Project, BARD (2008), 62 Village-Survey (Bangladesh Academy for Rural Development).

The volume of agricultural credit available from institutional sources has been less than the total credit

Table 11.2 : Pattern of Distribution of Credit Advances amongst Different Land Owning Groups

Land Ownership Group (acres)	*% of households*	*Distribution of institutional credit*	*Non-Institutional Credit Sources*						*All sources (institutional+ non-institutional)*
			Professional money-lenders	*Rich land-lords*	*Traders/ shop-keepers*	*Friends/ relatives*	*Total non-institutional credit sources*	*Total non institutional credit sources (excluding friends and relatives)*	
Landless and functionally landless (up to 0.49)	48.8	17.3	39.2	19.2	49.9	45.2	34.9	26.5	24.4
Marginal (0.50-2.49)	21.4	22.8	19.6	29.5	25.3	22.6	23.7	24.6	23.3
Small (1.50-2.49)	11.1	11.0	17.5	41.8	1.5	7.0	16.7	24.3	13.4
Medium (2.50-4.99)	11.9	22.2	21.1	6.6	23.3	9.7	13.7	16.9	18.6
Large (5.00+)	6.8	26.7	2.6	2.9	-	15.5	11.0	7.7	20.3
All groups	100.0	100.0	100.0	100.0	100.0	100.0	100.0	100.0	100.0

Source: Analysis of Poverty Trends Project, BARD (2008), 62 villages—Survey.

requirements of the farmers. Institutional credit in real terms increased by less than one per cent annually from 1972 until the mid-1980s when agricultural production was growing at a faster rate. Since then, however, non-institutional credit has been increasing rapidly. Results of various surveys show that over 80 per cent of the total credit requirements of agriculture are still met from non-institutional sources; the rates of interest charged on such loans are quite exorbitant (often exceeding 100 per cent).

The traditional banking system has excluded the poor from the umbrella of their credit operations on the ground that it is extremely risky to lend to them because they do not have any collateral and their capacity to repay is low. Because of the stiff terms and conditions for obtaining bank loans, which obviously favour the large land owning farmers, the bargaders and small land-owners still largely depend on this informal sector for borrowings and credit farmers access to loans from BKB and other commercial banks is limited due to many factors. First, their loans are given on the basis of land-ownership and collateral, which the small farmers cannot provide. Secondly, official procedures are cumbersome and time consuming for such farmers. Finally, the small farmers are not welcome in the banks because they require small loans and come from lower—social strata (Rehman, 2008). Even small farmers can not avail of the special credit facilities, because they do not know how to fill in the forms and they are unable to prepare the necessary production plans. They cannot approach the manager of the typical commercial bank. The iron-gate, the guard with a gun and the glass house where the manager sits, all these are alien to the small farmers' simple culture. Together they create a sense of fear among small farmers. Furthermore, the manager and the staff are not trained to deal with small farmers and small loans. Traditional banking approaches are therefore incompatible with small farmer development.

An important feature of the present institutional mechanism of agricultural credit disbursement is the low coverage for the small farmers who constitute about 50 per cent of the rural households. At present nearly 85 per cent of the small farmers have no access to institutional sources of credit.

Table 11.3 : Poverty Indices by Organizations

Organization	Incidence of moderate poverty (%)		Incidence of extreme poverty (%)		Severity of poverty	Rate of reduction of moderate poverty per year among programme participant (%)
	Programme participant	Programme non-participant	Programme participant	Programme non-participant	Programme participant	
Grameen Bank	62	72	19	17	Less severe	4
BRAC (Bangladesh Rural Advancement Committee)	70	67	14	16	—	1
BRDB (Bangladesh Rural Development Board)	64	67	—	—	Less severe	6

Source: Targeted Credit Programmes and Rural Poverty in Bangladesh (2008); BARD.

Moreover, small farmers obtain small amount as well as a low percentage of loans compared to medium and large farmers on a per acre basis. But the repayment performance of small farmers is better than that of large farmers (Krishok Somaybay Samiti, 2000). It has also been established that a negative relationship has been found between farm size and repayment behaviour (Krishok Somaybay Samiti, 2000). The repayment performance of small farmers is much better than the repayment of medium and large farmers. The poor are not unproductive. Truly, they are the most productive segment of the population. But unfortunately, the better of segment of the population through economic, social, and political manipulations usurps fruits of their labour. All these manipulations find their strength in their control over financial resources. If the control over financial resources can be loosened, the poor can, at the very best, begin to enjoy some fruits of their labour, begin to expand their economic base, live with dignity and look forward to build better for themselves. In spite of governments' relentless effort it is observed that the small farmers are not getting credit according to their demand and needs. However, most small farmer credit programmes have failed in achieving their objectives. This had lead to an increasing realization that even though such programmes do have a role to play within a comprehensive development success depends much on the initial distribution of resources (and other related issues) within the recipient society. A number of obstacles that have been identified are stated below:

(1) There exist an unholy alliance between the urban interests and the rural elite that act against the rural poor in availing institutionalized facilities.
(2) Even though the new technology is scale neutral (except in the case of the provision of irrigation) and is profitable, it also requires a much deeper financial involvement by the farmer. So long as the main basis of economic poverty based on unequal ownership of land, an equitable access to the resources on the part of the small farmers is unlikely.
(3) Low interest rates act as a disincentive for the supplying agencies (e.g. the commercial banks).
(4) Due to lack of investment opportunity for the poor, their demand for credit is low.
(5) If borrowing cost are included, the effective interest rates on institutional credit are relatively higher for the small farmers and poor. Thus their demand for it is low (Islam, Parkinson and Adams, 2007).

As a consequence , small farmers are unable to contribute to agricultural development in proportion to their potential. The existing rural credit institutions and programmes, in most cases has proved ineffective in removing the constraints on small farmer development because they lack many characteristics which small farmers credit programmes require, such as collateral free loan, simple lending procedure, target group approach, supervised credit, formation of appropriate groups etc. (Planning Commission, 2000).

NGO approach towards credit

Limited access to government owned institutional credit source make the land-poor groups dependent on alternative source of credit. Credit programmes of NGOs offer such an alternative but only a limited sense. The NGOs have provided a dynamic service to the rural people of Bangladesh by trying many alternative methods of providing them with financial services. The innovative credit delivery systems and human resource development activities of these NGOs for the assetless poor, has proven the replicability and sustainability of the approaches. NGOs efforts indicate that with appropriate encouragement and moderate support, they cannot only expand programmes but continue to innovate for wider participation of the poor in the development process. And in this aspect NGOs experience is, if lending is made to the groups who have reached an institutionally developed stage, under close supervision ensuring their personal stake in the scheme, and if such lending is followed by borrowers' training, technical assistance and the provision of marketing facilities the neglected poor can be transformed into effective tools of development (Graham, 1997).

The Grameen Bank (GB) and some NGOs have shown that the rural poor are indeed, creditworthy, and that given credit systems appropriate to their unique needs, institutional credit could be very useful in poverty alleviation. They have also shown an ability to reach women among the rural poor. The GB and such NGOs have been able to reach the target group, deliver credit at the door of the poor without collateral, inculcate a habit of saving, enforce repayment schedule, reduce rates of loans overdue and increase loan recovery rates, exert favourable impacts on the income of the poor and facilitate asset formation. However, the coverage of small farmers by the GB and NGOs is limited. Moreover, these institutions only serve the rural people who have no or little (less than 0.5 acres) land. A few impact studies have so far been done on the poverty alleviation programmes by NGOs. In recent years, this branch of study has received increasing attention of policy-makers, researchers, development economists, social scientists and donors. At different times government organizations and individual researchers have tried to estimate and analyze the poverty alleviating impact of various programmatic interventions.

All these studies have been carried out under a three-year joint programme of BIDS (Bangladesh Institute of Development Studies) and the World Bank. The BIDS/World Bank project, based on a sample household survey in 87 randomly selected villages where GB, BRAC and BRDB credit programme are going on among the rural poor. Among the 87 villages, GB had been operating in 28 villages, BRAC (Bangladesh Rural Advancement Committee) in 40 villages, and BRDB (Bangladesh Rural Development Board) in 19 villages for at least three years before the survey period (1998-99). The survey results of the projects reveal that the various programmes have indeed contributed to alleviating poverty of its beneficiaries, but that the results vary at wage levels in the surveyed villages, since wage earnings tend to be a major source of income for the hard core poor. It has been found from the study that on an average daily wage were Tk.5.00 higher in the GB targeted villages than the control villages without a GB programme. In contrast, the BRAC targeted villages showed no real change compared to the control villages. The BRDB's villages targeted under RD-12 (Rural Development-12) programme again indicated a higher average daily wage than in the non-targeted villages. This evidence may of course derive from the specifics of the modes underlying the study which itself may not have satisfactorily captured the dynamics of wage determination in the selected villages. Nor may it has been sensitive to the distinctive properties of the nature of the respective credit programmes or the characteristics of their target group. The available evidence does suggest some improvement in wage rates at least in the GB villages, which indicate that the GB programme may generate external economies, which go beyond the targeted household and impact on the community.

Do NGOs have a comparative advantage?

Despite the attention currently being given to NGOs by donors and government, there are significant gaps in the field of NGO evaluation. This is partly a result of the practical considerations of limited resources, a lack of effective recording systems by NGOs themselves, transient NGOs presence in many areas, and the difficulties of attributing causality by those providing external funding. It is extremely difficult to secure accurate comparable figures on both NGOs and government costs. Government costs can sometimes appear low, but may be higher in real terms on account of the subsidies provided in the form of bribe taken by government employees on inadequate salaries.

There are also important ideological issues surrounding the concepts of empowerment and social development, which are difficult to measure in terms of evaluative indicators. They may reflect subjective changes in the quality of life, shifting community values and self-realization. Conventional cost benefit analysis can therefore provide little insight into the social aspects to NGO programmes, which may include (for example) mobilizing poor men and women to demand better services from government, increasing their confidence to take collective action for securing better wages or access to common property resources, raising the awareness of peoples rights under the law and the democratizing of decision making and increased accountability within the community. Despite the lack of methodology for assessment and the conceptual difficulties of comparing qualitative difference, there seems little doubt that egos have made a name for themselves in the successful pursuit of a number of tasks, at least by comparison with government agencies. The recent BIDS (Bangladesh Institute of Development Studies) study, already quoted, provided evidence to show that whatever the cost, NGOs are better at reaching low-income people. NGOs, therefore, have a comparative advantage over most government agencies which is derived from (a) the quality of the relationships they can create and (b) the way in which they can structure their organizations.

The Grameen Bank experience

By the above discussion we have experienced that Government and other commercial bank has proven their inefficiency in disbursement of rural credit because of their stiff and cumbersome rules and regulations. And in this respect, some NGOs are playing successful role in this area. For example, we will discuss Grameen Bank's experience in this regard. The Grameen Bank is one of the most prestigious institutions to have come out from a Bangladeshi environment. Although established sometime in the seventies, it is only recently that it has received worldwide acclaim for its capacity to provide credit services to the poor, more particularly poor women, small farmers and assetless. Very little need to be added to what has already been said about this institution whose name has today become a by-word in small-credit financing and in poverty alleviation.

The special features of the Grameen Bank's credit activities are as follows:

1. Loans are provided without any collateral.
2. Peer pressure act as collateral.
3. Repayment of loan in weekly instalment.
4. Mutual accountability among group members.
5. Preparatory training of group members before involving them in loan transactions.
6. Collective managemıent of finance.

Contrary to the conventional banking practice that the lone comes to the bank to receive and repay the loan, the GB is going to its clienteles for both disbursement of loans and collection of repayments. As the clienteles come from a very poor economic background, credit is disbursed in small amounts and the repayments are collected in weekly instalments. In addition, the bank takes the responsibility of giving intensive training to its clienteles in credit discipline. All this mean that the paperwork and the manpower needed for servicing a given loan amount would be substantially higher for GB than that under a normal rural credit programme. So while the recovery of credit is expected to be higher because of close supervision, the cost of servicing the credit is also expected to be high. It is necessary to estimate this cost in order to see the feasibility of operating such a semi-supervised credit programme on a commercial basis and also to advise an interest rate policy for the project.

Table 11.4 : Coverage of Grameen Bank Loan, November 2008

Item	*Sex*	*Cumulative Nos.*	*Cumulative amount disbursed (million taka)*
Number of members	Male	1,20,221 (6%)	3,454.79 (9%)
	Female	18,82,598 (94%)	35300.20 (91%)
	Total	20,02,819 (100%)	38754.90 (100%)
Cumulative number of borrowers for housing loan	Male	28,081 (10%)	418.63 (9.1%)
	Female	2,55,963 (90%)	4108.17 (89.9%)
	Total	2,84,044 (100%)	4526.79 (100%)

Source : Independent Review of Bangladesh's Development (2007/2008).

The Grameen Bank project was started as a bold effort, in defiance of all standard rules of traditional banking. Its aim was to reach banking facilities, without security stipulations to the poor. It would thus give them a chance to save themselves from the clutches of the moneylender. Poor people would be able to choose their own way of earning with bank support. They would be able to form their own small organizational units, inculcate the habit of saving and thus create opportunities for further work. The guiding policy of this project was, the term poor will not mean poor men only but will include both men and women, people will not come to the bank, instead, the bank will go to the people (Yunis, 1998). Bank workers go around in the villages and talk to the villagers informally to explain the rules and procedures of GB. Any person whose family owns less than 0.5 acre of cultivable land, and the value of all the family assets together does not exceed the market value of one acre of medium quality land in the area, is eligible to take loans from the GB for any income generating activity. To get the loan he/she must form a group of five who are like-minded and have similar economic and social group elects its own chairman and secretary. Each group must hold its weekly group meeting in the same village according to their convenient day and time. This congregation is known as a 'centre'.

All the group-chairman in a 'centre' elects a Centre-Chief and a Deputy Centre-Chief from amongst them. Centre-Chief conducts the weekly meetings and is responsible for the observance of all rules prescribed by the bank. Loans are given to the individuals or groups. Although there are lot of interlocking responsibility in distribution but formally only the lone is responsible for his loans and repayment period may be extended for one year, if needed. They are to be paid back in weekly instalments. Repayment rate is over 99 per cent. GB is operating in 1191 villages of Bangladesh. Thus, the Bank has generated self-employment opportunities for women members whom either unemployed earlier thereby increasing the labour force participation rate in the area of its operation. It is difficult to estimate the exact income effect of the programme as the income of Grameen Bank members or female members cannot always be separately estimated from their household income. However, the total cumulative amount of savings in the group fund of all the GB members rose to Tk. 2,982.80 million by the end of November 2002. This indicates a strong positive income effect of their loans. An impact survey done by Mahbub Hossain of Bangladesh Institute of Development Studies in 1998 indicated that the proportion of the population living in moderate poverty was 84 per cent for target-group non-participants in a project village and 80 per cent for the target-group in a control village.

But the same figure for Grameen Bank members was 61 per cent in the target village. The percentage of Grameen Bank members living in extreme poverty was 48, while it was about 78 per cent for its control group counterparts. These figures suggest that the GB has been able to alleviate poverty for its members (Centre for Policy Dialogue, 1999). However, it is unfortunate to note that in spite of this dynamism of the poor in the field of loan utilization, neither the NGOs nor the government financial institutions are giving them adequate loanable funds. The hard core poor are receiving only about 7 per cent of the institutional loans. As for credit fund from the NGOs, a study of 64 NGOs showed that from the beginning of their operation to 2002 November, about 4.5 million loanees got about Taka 30,108 million out of which GB alone covered about 8.42 per cent of the loans advanced and about 46.56 per cent of the loanees.

Towards an accepted model

Among the various government programmes, the credit programmes are very important for small farmer development. Small farmer's access to institutional credit is limited. Non-institutional sources dominate the rural financial market. A variety of features and policies of credit institutions also favour the access of large farmers to credit but limit the access of small farmers. Because of the special characteristics of small farmers, credit disbursement in the conventional sense would not improve small farmers' economic condition. In order to reach the poor more effectively with sufficient credit and other supporting assistance package (i.e. better technology, education and training, healthcare, fair markets and adequate infrastructure etc.); the existing institutional capacities for micro-credit delivery, saving mobilization and business promotion has to be strengthened and new capacities built through increased networking and exchange of experiences at both national and international levels, designing appropriate policies and making provision for better skill and management training for the social entrepreneurs and the micro credit managers.

The legal, administrative, and regulatory rules and regulations must also be changed and re-oriented ensuring greater flow of productive resources to the poor as well as the non-poor potential micro-entrepreneurs. A credit programme should have the following characteristics:

Collateral: Credit should be collateral-free because small farmers may not have tangible assets to provide.

Lending Procedures: Lending procedures should be simple because small farmers are illiterate.

Continuity: The credit programme should be continuous through self-sustained financing.

Small Farmer Development Bias: The institution should not be biased towards small farmer development.

Credit Supervision: Credit should be supervised so that it is utilized in productive enterprises.

Target Group Approach: Credit and co-operative institutions are said to be dominated by large farmers. This infiltration should be stopped by the target-group approach. The GB and some NGOs have demonstrated the utility of the target-group approach.

Group Formation: Small farmers should be organized into small groups of like-minded people. The group approach will be helpful in credit disbursement and realization, and to break-up the existing power structure.

Point of Credit Disbursement and Recovery: Small farmers may not like to come to banks situated in the upazilla headquarters. Thus, credit should be disbursed and recovered in the villages.

Coverage: The programmes should be national rather than area specific.

Conclusion

The role of credit has long been realized to be a significant one and the system is now recognized as an instrument of agricultural development. It is thought to be a key element in bringing about technological change and modernizing agriculture. In the developing world credit has been used as a mechanism for development particularly that associated with increased productivity and the use of purchased inputs.

Generally, it is argued that there is a limited supply of credit in the rural areas and this must be increased in order to help boost the agricultural production. There is no doubt that given access to credit and basic skills training large number of small farmers could become actively and profitably self-employed, contributing substantially to household and per capita incomes. All available evidence indicates that small farmers have shown higher rate of saving and repayment. We actually need a drastic change in incentive structure in agriculture, which will lead to higher income and facilitate active participation of farmers and their importance of credit in technological change in agriculture has been accepted by a large number of studies. It is pointed out that the availability of adequate and timely credit raises liquidity in the hands of the farmers and ensures greater use of purchase inputs. The small farmers, in spite of better use of credit, suffer from lack of credit. Even so, in order to achieve higher production through better use of inputs, the credit distribution system should be oriented to provide a still higher amount of credit to small farmers than what they are getting at present.

SUGGESTED READINGS

1. Maudud, Ahmed (2000), *Democracy and the Challenge of Development: A Study of Politics and Military Interventions in Bangladesh*, Dhaka University Press Limited, Dhaka.
2. Elahi, K.Q. (1996), *Reducing Small Farmer Vulnerability to Impoverishment in Bangladesh: An Action Programme.* Proceeding of the BRDB Workshop.
3. Quasem, Md. Abdul (1999), "Financial Return of Irrigation Equipment to Owners and Users; The Case of Shallow Tubewells in Bangladesh", *Bangladesh faces the future*, Dhaka University Press Limited, Dhaka.
4. *Bangladesh Rural Development Board Study*, 2000.
5. Rehman, Sobhan (ed), *Report of the Task Force on Agricultural Labourer*, 2008.
6. *Bangladesh Planning Commission Report*, 2000.
7. *Krishok Somaybay Samiti Report*, 2000.
8. Graham, D.H. (1997); *A Critique of Traditional Agricultural Credit Projects.* Dhaka University Press Limited, Dhaka.

9. Parkinson, R., (1999); *Bangladesh: The Test Case of Development*, Dhaka University Press Limited, Dhaka.
10. *Independent Review of Bangladesh's Development (1999)*, Centre for Policy Dialogue.
11. Islam, K.; Parkinson, L. and Adam, S. (2007); *Agriculture in Bangladesh;* Centre for Policy Studies, Dhaka.
12. Yunis, M. (1998), *Small Farmers in Bangladesh*, Dhaka University Press Limited, Dhaka.

PART C

WOMEN AND CHILDREN

12

Reproductive Health of Women
With Special Reference to Santal Community

Introduction

India was the first nation in the world to have launched a formal State sponsored **Family Planning Programme** in 1951. In 1976, during emergency, government formulated a Population Policy which became counter-productive because of a clause which permitted states to go for compulsory sterilization. The government was voted out of power in 1977, and the next government changed the term family planning to 'family welfare' and announced another Population Policy which ruled out compulsion. In 1991, the government appointed a Committee on Population headed by Mr. Karunakaran and the committee submitted a report to the National Development Council in 1993 in which it pleaded for a National Population Policy. In 1993, the government appointed Dr. M.S. Swaminathan as Chairman of an Expert group to draft a Population Policy. It submitted the Draft Population Policy in May 1994 and it was tabled in Parliament. From 1994 to 2000, because of unstable politics at the Centre, the Draft Population Policy lay dormant. In 1999, the government asked a Group of Ministers to examine the policy drafted by the Ministry of Health and Family Welfare. In February 2000, the government announced the **National Population Policy, 2000.**

The **Reproductive Health (RH) programme** was launched in India on October 15, 1997, inspired by action plans and approaches emerging out of the International Conference on Population Development in Cairo during 1994 and the Beijing Conference in 1995. RH was incorporated as a major thrust area in the National Population Policy, 2000.

The RH programme lays emphasis on the reorientation of our family planning programmes and addresses the issues relating to fast changing developments in health care and population policies in an integrated, democratic, decentralized and informed choice-based rational way. The programme has taken into account our earlier approaches, e.g., the Clinical Approach, the Community Extension Approach, the Cafeteria Approach and the Camp and Target Oriented Approach. Some of the important dimensions of this programme are integration of services, quality care, gender sensitivity, decentralized decision making, bottom-up planning, target free implementation and felt need-based planning.

The Concept of Reproductive Health

Reproductive health, according to the UN, is a state of complete physical, mental and social well-being and not merely the absence of disease or infirmity, in all matters relating to the reproductive system and to its functions and processes (UN, 1994). This definition falls short of comprehensive perspectives on reproductive health because it provides only a slight modification of the WHO's definition of health. In addition, it is too general and does not focus on essential specific aspects of reproductive health.

Following WHO's definition of reproductive health, GAO Ersheng (1997) wrote "Reproductive health is a term that is much used but frequently ill-defined. Most experts would agree that the three key dimensions are as follows:

(a) People have the ability, the information and the means to bear children and to regulate their fertility safely as they choose.

(b) Women go through pregnancy and childbirth safely and have the best chance of having a healthy child.
(c) People's sexual relationships are not overshadowed by the danger of contracting diseases."

Another author Jejeebhoy (2002) while reviewing the existing definitions of reproductive health, of course, has expanded this concept, but even her synthesized statement falls short of comprehensiveness. She writes, "in short, a reproductive health orientation, drawn from this and other sources, includes:

(1) a satisfying and safe sex life free from the fear of diseases, and free from coercion and violence.
(2) the capability to reproduce and the freedom to decide if, when and how often, to do so, that is, access to both infertility services, on the one hand, and contraceptive services, on the other.
(3) access to safe and affordable abortion facilities.
(4) access to services for the prevention and care of reproductive health problems, both gynaecological and obstetric, in a culturally sensitive manner.
(5) special attention to adolescents whose reproductive health needs have been particularly overlooked.
(6) safe child bearing: access to appropriate health care services that will enable women to go safely through pregnancy and child birth and provide for a healthy infant.
(7) Reproductive choice for women and men, that people have the right to be informed and have access to safe, effective, affordable and acceptable methods of family planning of their choice."

However, while operationalizing any definition of RH, WHO has listed four specific goals of reproductive health, which are the following:

GOAL 1—experience healthy sexual development and maturation and have the capacity for equitable and responsible relationships and sexual fulfilment.

GOAL 2—achieve their desired number of children safely and healthy, when and if they decide to have them.

GOAL 3—avoid illness, disease and disability related to sexuality and reproduction and receive appropriate care when needed.

GOAL 4—be free from violence and other harmful practices related to sexuality and reproduction.

Despite the interest in women's reproductive health in India, information on their reproductive health situation continues to be patchy. As expected, the most comprehensive data are available on one aspect of reproductive health-contraceptive use patterns. In contrast, there is almost no information available on the prevalence of RTIs (Reproductive Track Infections), abortion-related morbidity and infertility (as seen in Table 12. 1). Yet the available evidence accumulated in this table suggest a situation of considerable reproductive health of women in India.

Table 12. 1 : Reproductive Health Situation in India

Safe pregnancy	
Maternal mortality ratio	437
% receiving ante-natal care	63
% skilled attendance at delivery	66
Access to abortion	
No. of approved MTP centres (All India)	9,467
% located in Bihar, M.P., U.P., Rajasthan	16
% of functional centres	Approx. 25
Estimated abortion ratio	18.1
Abortion ratio (community based rural study)	14
Adolescents as abortion seekers (%)	1-10
Unmarried women as abortion seekers (%)	2-30
Contraception and unmet needs	
Contraceptive prevalence rate	45.8
Number of female sterilizations conducted annually	Approx.4 million
Sterilized women as a proportion of all couples using a modern method (%)	70
% couples practicing contraception at parity 1	19
% couples practicing contraception at parity 1, if son (NFHS)	41
Non-terminal method discontinuation rate	High

(*Contd.*)

(**Table 12.1** *contd.*)

Sexually transmitted infections	
Estimated new infections annually (GOI)	40 million
Most widely prevalent infections	Syphilis, Chancroid, Gonorrhoea
Among women	Syphilis
Infections on the rise	Genital herpes Genital warts
Study of two STI clinics	
%monogamous married women (of all women)	43
%HIV+ among monogamous married women	14
%HIV+ among sex worker group	50
Sentinel surveillance findings	
% increase in HIV incidence among STI clinic attendees	Ten-fold
% increase in HIV among antenatal clinic attendees in monogamous unions	Two-fold
% increase among female attendees	10-29

Source: *Women's Reproductive Health in India;* edited by Ramasubban Radhika and Jejeebhoy. J. Shireen, Rawat Publications, New Delhi, 2006, Chapter-1, pp-38-39.

Maternal mortality and Infant mortality

Among the multiple components these two are very important aspects of reproductive health. So the author would like to present some statistical data, which are available till to date to show the present Indian trends in this regard.

India's *maternal mortality* ratio is estimated at 400-500 per 1,00,000 live births—about fifty times higher than that of many industrialized nations and six times as high as that of neighbouring Sri Lanka (UNICEF, 1999). This appears to be an underestimate and a more realistic estimate is probably 555 as estimated by Mari Bhat *et al.* (2000), though higher estimates in the range of 700-900 (Mathai, 1992) have also been made. Even so, using the estimated MMR of 400-500, in the global perspective, it is estimated that India accounted for 19 per cent of all live births worldwide, and for as much as 27 per cent of all deaths.

Table 12. 2 : Infant and Child Mortality by State

Name of the State	Neo-natal mortality	Post-natal mortality	Infant mortality	Child mortality	Under five mortality
	(Probability of dying in the first month of life)	(Difference between infant and neo-natal mortality)	(Probability of dying before the first birth-day)	(Probability of dying between the first and fifth birthday)	(Probability of dying before the fifth birthday)
Assam	50.9	37.8	88.7	58.7	142.2
Bihar	54.8	34.4	89.2	42.0	127.5
Manipur	25.1	17.3	42.4	20.2	61.7
Orissa	64.7	47.4	112.1	21.3	131.0
Uttar Pradesh	59.9	40.0	99.9	46.0	141.3
West Bengal	51.8	23.5	75.3	26.0	99.3
Madhya Pradesh	53.2	32.0	85.2	49.3	130.3
Meghalaya	37.8	26.3	64.2	24.3	86.9
Himachal Pradesh	34.2	21.7	55.8	14.1	69.1
India	48.6	29.9	78.5	33.4	109.3

Source : National Family Health Survey, 2008.

Some latest figures of ***infant and child mortality*** in nine States have been presented in Table 12.2. The table shows that mortality of children under five years of age is the highest in Assam and Uttar Pradesh, followed by Orissa, Madhya Pradesh and Bihar. It is also found that neo-natal mortality rate is the highest in Orissa, followed by Uttar Pradesh, Bihar, West Bengal and Assam.

In terms of ***rural infant mortality*** rate, the picture in Bihar, Madhya Pradesh, Rajasthan and Uttar Pradesh is indeed grim. Madhya Pradesh has the highest rural infant mortality rate (103), higher than in rural Orissa (101).

Objectives of the study

(1) To know the perception of the women about the use of contraceptives.
(2) To know their experience about abortion and infertility.
(3) To see the child-rearing practices among the Santhal women.

(4) To know their idea about HIV/AIDS, STD (Sexually Transmitted Diseases).
(5) To look into the common gynaecological problems including menstruation cycle, the women generally suffer.

Implications of the study

Santal, the third largest scheduled tribe community in India with a population of 5,959,764 (Census, 2001), they are distributed in the states of Bihar, West Bengal, Orissa and Tripura. The largest concentration of the Santal is in Bihar. After that another state in which the Santals are concentrated is West Bengal 2,862,980 (Census of India, 2001).

The Santals have a rich artistic tradition. They observe multifarious ceremonies and perform down the generation different kinds of rituals which are very specific, traditional and culturally bound. Santals are also thickly populated in the Birbhum district of West Bengal. They are scattered in different villages under different Blocks and Gram Panchayats.

The Santal community is developing at a much faster rate in their outlook, intellectual ability, socio-economic condition, educational status (not in the case of females), health consciousness, concern for women etc. The overall literacy rate, of course, was not very satisfactory. This process of change and development may be the manifestation of the continuous government support through various welfare policies and programmes under the welfare measures for scheduled tribe population and ongoing interactional process with the outer world and specially the influence of surrounding enriched cultural environment.

Due to the close affinity and easy accessibility with the villages and the villagers of these Santal dominated community, the researcher had developed an inquisitive mind to see the reproductive health awareness among the Santal women when reproductive health is the call of the day for women development and empowerment are concern. It is also a matter of fact that many research studies are being carried out in the area of RH across the country both at micro and macro level but the study in the area of RH in the tribal community has not been done in that way as it should have been done. The another reason for taking up this micro study is, after exploring the level of awareness and understanding about RH among the Santal women, what could be the constructive interventions for future for making the RH programme more effective and consolidated in the tribal community when upliftment of scheduled tribe is one of the prime objectives of the Government of India.

Methodology

It was a micro study and a very simple methodology was adopted. It was basically a exploratory research design. Exploratory design was taken into consideration to see the respondents' attitude, awareness and study of some of the important qualitative aspects regarding RH. No hypothesis was framed. Only primary data was used for the study. It was tried to make the samples as representative as possible. Respondents were married women and interviewed by a set of questions to know their knowledge, understanding, awareness and attitude towards RH programme. Tabular representation with simple frequency distribution and some charts (bar and pie) for explaining the data and highlighting the major findings were made convenient for us.

Universe

Three small villages, namely Pearson Palli, Bagan Para and Bali Para were adopted for this particular study. Pearson Palli, Bagan Para and Bali Para have 100, 80 and 70 households respectively. Their socio-economic conditions have definitely developed to some extent over the last ten years. Majority of the male population are cultivators and daily wage earners engaged in different types of works right from construction workers to scavengers. Of course, one can find that a couple of them are literate, as well as studying and working in offices. Women population are quite active and working with their husbands in agricultural activities and also engaged in some other activities to economically supplement the family earnings. They are also doing the household work right from bearing, caring and nurturing the child to cooking and other activities. Educational status of the women is very poor.

Sampling

One hundred and fifty married women in the age group (20-30) were taken as respondents for the study from the above mentioned number of households. The factor was kept in mind during the time of selection of respondents that those women who would be selected must have at least one child. The selection of respondents was made randomly and no pre-choice was ever thought off. The interview was carried out according to their convenient time. Two female investigators were employed for the collection of data. This had made the data collection more authentic and we received many important information which would not have been possible if the researcher himself would have asked the questions.

Tools of data collection

The structured interview schedule with both open ended and close ended were prepared. All the questions were framed relevant to the area of the study keeping our objectives in mind. The questions were very simple and specific. Field notebooks were properly maintained.

Major findings

Table 12.3 : Occupation of the respondents

Housewife	40 (N)	26.66 %
Maid servant	40	26.66 %
Daily labour other than agricultural labour	20	13.33 %
Agricultural labour	50	33.33 %
Total	150	100 %

Table 12.3 indicates that out of the total respondents, 50 (33.33%) are engaged in agricultural activities followed by 40 (26.66%), 40 (26.66%), and 20 (13.33%) are housewives, maid-servants and daily labour respectively. Surprisingly none of them are literate except two women (housewives) who could read and write a bit.

Table 12 4 : Users of contraceptives

Husband	110 (N)	73.33%
Wife	35	23.33%
Didn't reply	5	3.3%
Total	150	100%

Researchers have highlighted the importance of birth base family planning demonstrating the demographic fact that women with a young child are the most likely to be pregnant next. The total fertility rate (TFR), which gives the average number of births per woman, is therefore a measure of a woman's well-being as well as an indicator of the control she has over reproductive decisions. India's TFR, estimated at 3.6 children per woman in 2001 was well above the replacement level of 2.0 (Dolly Singh, 2001).

In our study, it has been observed that out of the total women interviewees, 125 (83.3%) women were having two children, either male or female or both followed by 25 (16.6%) women had reported that they were having more than two children. So it was a very encouraging figure and also reflects the well acceptance of family planning programmes.

Official statistics indicate that contraceptive use for the country as a whole increased from practically nil at the beginning of the plan period, to 10 per cent around 1970, to an impressive level of 48 per cent in 2000-01 (Radhika and Jejeebhoy, 2002).

The above trends of the use of contraceptives also support our findings of the study. Table 12.4 shows that 145 (96.6%) couples used contraceptives and only 5 (3.3%) women didn't reply anything and surprisingly these women are having more than two children. Apart from this negligible percentage, the acceptance of contraceptive uses are much prevalent in the Santal community.

The other important dimension of the table is that 110 (73.33%) males use contraceptive whereas only 35 (23.33%) of females use contraceptives. It clearly emphasizes that males are becoming conscious about the RH for their counterpart. So, the use of contraceptives is not only the responsibility of the women, men are also playing a pivotal role in this regard in the Santal community.

Figure 12.1 shows the types of contraceptives used; where 42 per cent, 36 per cent and 22 per cent are users of condoms, pills and copper-T respectively. Other types of contraceptives such as jelly, withdrawal or any other modern methods (hormone injection or intra-muscular injection or tablets which can be taken after the intercourse, but of course within 12 hours) are not known to them.

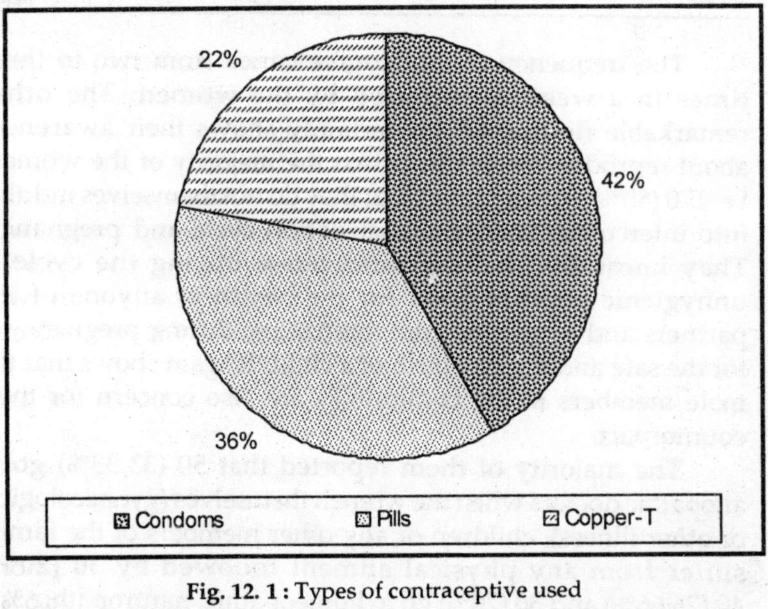

Fig. 12. 1 : Types of contraceptive used

So, condoms users are more and obviously it emphasizes that the male partners are also using contraceptives. So it is not only the women who are only responsible for use of contraceptives. Pills are easily accessible, so many women prefer it and it is much easier to use than copper-T. The important point here is that the women are very particular in taking pills and they know how to maintain the regularity of taking pills.

Regarding permanent methods of family planning Table 12.5 shows that out of the total respondents majority of them (73.33%) didn't go through any such experience only a very few (6.66%) and (20%) had vasectomy and tubectomy operation respectively.

Table 12. 5 : Permanent methods of family planning

Vasectomy	10	6.66%
Tubectomy	30	20%
Not undergone any such experience	110	73.33%
Total	150	100%

The frequency of intercourse varies from two to three times in a week as reported by the women. The other remarkable finding which certainly shows their awareness about reproductive health is that the majority of the women, i.e. 120 (80%) who reported that they do not themselves indulge into intercourse during menstruation cycle and pregnancy. They know that having intercourse during the cycle is unhygienic and not good for the health of anyone of the partners and to refrain from intercourse during pregnancy is for the safe and healthy birth of a child. It again shows that the male members in the community are also concern for their counterpart.

The majority of them reported that 50 (33.33%) go to allopathic doctors when the women themselves (gynaecological or other illness), children or any other members of the family suffer from any physical ailment followed by 30 (20%), 40 (26.66%) and 30 (20%) go to homeopathic, naturopathic and both allopathic and naturopathic (Figure 12.2).

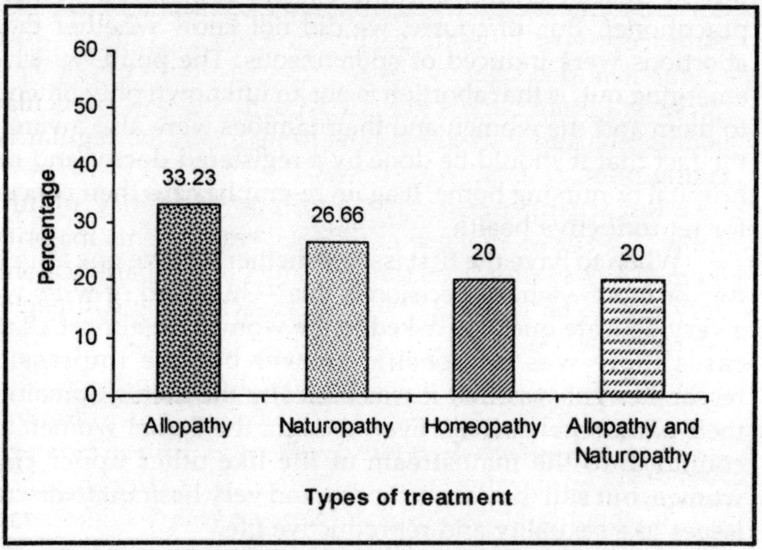

Fig. 12.2 : Types of treatment preferred

Table: 12.6 : Abortions among the women

Yes	10	15%
No	140	93.33%
Total	150	100%

According to WHO estimates, globally 13 per cent of all pregnancy-related deaths (1 in 8) take place due to unsafe abortions, and nearly 90 per cent of unsafe abortions take place in developing countries (WHO, 2000). Most of the evidence in India is based on hospital studies. The data indicate that between 2.5 and 3.0 per cent of hospital maternal deaths can be attributed to abortion related complications. Community-based evidence is limited but generally shows lower levels of mortality than those indicated in hospital studies of the same region (Bhatia, 1999; Nandan and Saxena, 2001).

In our study we observe that in 140 cases (93.33%) there was no abortion and only in 10 cases (15%) women were aborted and it was also reported that the abortion was carried out in nearby nursing home by the registered medical practitioner. But, of course, we did not know whether those abortions were induced or spontaneous. The point, which is emerging out, is that abortion is not an unknown phenomenon to them and the women and their families were also aware of the fact that it should be done by a registered doctor and in a hospital or nursing home. It again re-emphasizes their concern for reproductive health.

When to have the first issue; whether to have one issue or two or more—whose decision is this?—husband or wife; was a very delicate question asked to the women. In almost all the cases there was no specific answer but the impression researcher got was that it was basically the men's domain in their patriarchal society. Even though, the Santal women are coming into the mainstream of life like other upper class women, but still they are orthodox and very hesitant to discuss issues like sexuality and reproductive life.

It was also found that 90 (60%) women had childbirth at home by untrained local women nurses followed by 60 (40%) had delivery at hospital under the supervision of registered gynaecologist (Table 12.7). It definitely reflects that still a good percentage of women in the Santal community are not aware of the anticipated unhealthy consequences of home delivery. Similarly, 50 (33.33%) women didn't get their children properly immunized as it should have been (Table 12.8). Only 100 (66.66%) women got their children immunized. So, the scenario regarding the children immunization is not very appreciating. They also don't have much idea about the peri-natal (from 28 weeks of pregnancy to seven days after delivery), anti-natal (right from conception till delivery), pre-natal (1st week after the delivery) and post-natal care for the newborn babies and even afterwards for their proper growth and development.

Food intake during pregnancy and after the birth and all such other measures, which should be taken by the women, are neither maintained nor they are aware of in most of the cases. It was also reported that 70 per cent women did not get check-up by any gynaecologist during their pregnancy. Breast feeding, of course is quite common (almost in 100% cases) but other aspects of child's health and hygiene are not at all found to be satisfactory.

Table 12.7 : Places of childbirth

Home	90	60%
Hospital	60	40%
Total	150	100%

Table 12.8 : Immunization of children

Yes	100	66.66%
No	50	33.33%
Total	150	100%

Gynaecological and Obstetric Morbidity are also an important area for reproductive health which the researcher wanted to look into.

Reproductive morbidity refers to health problems related to reproductive organs and functions, including and outside of child bearing (Zurayk *et al.*, 2000). It covers both gynaecological and obstetric morbidity as well as related morbidity, such as urinary track infections, anaemia, high blood pressure and obesity. Gynaecological morbidity includes health problems outside pregnancy, like RTIs (Reproductive Track Infections), menstrual problems with intercourse. Obstetric morbidity refers to ill health in relation to pregnancy.

In our study we see that out of the total respondents 127 (85%) had never heared of the term STDs. Only 15.3 per cent women were little aware of these problems. On the other hand, 60 per cent women didn't have any idea about HIV problems. So, it is due to illiteracy, lack of media information, lack of government's effort to make the women more aware of the phenomena

Regarding gynaecological and obstetric problems, they were absolutely in dark. They had no conception at all. Only a couple of them had mentioned that they often suffer from menstruation problems, pain in abdomen and urinary track but for which they hardly visit any recognized medical practitioners.

Conclusions and Recommendations

The study findings reveal that the women in the Santal community (in respect to our study area) are aware in some of the areas of RH which had already been discussed in the major findings but overall awareness are very poor and specially in the aspect of child caring. The factors, which are mainly responsible, are low literacy level, poor economic condition, lack of knowledge about general health. Being the backward classes, they are, of course, trying to develop themselves and women are becoming receptive to the fast changing socio-cultural milieu. If some of the following areas are to be thrust upon the awareness among the women regarding RH would be much more enlightening:

(a) improve the educational standard and specially women education.
(b) improved facilities to promote institutional deliveries.
(c) improved maternity services and health standards.
(d) improved auditing of maternity services provided in the community.
(e) improved facilities for referral services.
(f) use mass media to raise men's awareness of reproductive health.
(g) encouraging fathers to share in the daily responsibilities of parenthood.
(h) educate health providers and the public about the myths and realities of vasectomy.
(i) creating awareness about the menace of STDs and HIV.
(j) NGOs need to be more active and make the women more aware of the RH through their different action plans.
(k) community participation needs to be strengthened.
(l) training of community leaders including the members of Pachayati Raj System.

SUGGESTED READINGS

1. Singh, Dolly, (2001); *Child Rights and Social Wrongs (An Analysis of Contemporary Realities)*, Vol. 1, Kanishka Publishers, Distributors, New Delhi.
2. Radhika, Ramasubban and Shireen J. Jejeebhoy, (2002); *Women's Reproductive Health in India*, Rawat Publications, New Delhi.
3. Census India, 2001.
4. *Employment News;* January, 2001.
5. Zurayk, H., H. Khattb, N. (2000); *Reproductive Health*, Oxford University Press, UK.
6. M. El-Mouelhy and M. Fadle, (2000); "Concepts and measures of reproductive morbidity", *Health Transition Review*, 3, 1GAO Ersheng and Iqbal Shah, 1997, 'Reproductive Health Research: Progress and Policy Implications'. In: *Progress of Social science Research on Reproductive Health*, Shanghai: China Population Publishing House.
7. Mason, Karen, (1974). *Women's Labour Force Participation and Fertility*, Research Triangle Park, N.C. Research Triangle Institute.
8. Mahadevan, K. *et al.* (1989); 'Status of Women and Population in India', In *Women and Population Dynamics*, (ed) K. Mahadevan, New Delhi: Sage Publications.
9. Tuan, K. and Mahadevan, (1993); *Status of Women and Population Dynamics: A Conceptual Model*. Sage Publications, New Delhi.
10. Safilios Rothschild, C. (1982); 'Female Power, Autonomy and Demographic Change in the Third World', In: *Women's Roles and Population Trends in the Third World*, (eds) Richard *et al.* London: Croom Helm.
11. UN Report, (1994); *Population and Development: Programme of Action* adopted at the International Conference on Population and Development, Cairo.
12. World Health Organization Report, 2001, *Gynaecological Implication and Reproductive Health.*
13. UNICEF Report,1999, *Nutritional Status of Children.*
14. Indian Institute of Population Studies Report, 1999, *National Family Health Survey.*
15. *ICMR Bulletin*, 1991, Evaluation of the Quality of Family Welfare Services at the Primary Health Centre Levels.
16. Government of India Bulletin, 2000, *Health Information of India.*
17. UNAIDS, 1995. *Women and AIDS: Agenda for Action.* Document for the International Conference on Women, Beijing.
18. WHO Report (Press Release), 2000, *Unsafe Abortion: Division of Reproductive Health.*

19. Nandan, D. and B. Saxena (2001); 'Maternal morbidity and mortality patterns in Uttar Pradesh'; *Indian Journal of Community Medicine*, 12, 1: 10-15.
20. Bhatia, J.C. (1999); 'Levels and causes of maternal mortality in southern India', *Studies in Family Planning*, 24, 5:310-318.
21. Singh, Meharban and V.K. Paul, (1999); 'Strategies to reduce perinatal and neonatal mortality in India', *Indian Pediatrics* 23, no. 8 (August).
22. Mari Bhat, P.N., K. Navaneetham and S. Irudaya Rajan (2000); 'Maternal mortality in India: estimates from an economic mode', *Population Research Centre*, Dharwad.
23. Mathai, Saramma T. (1992); 'Women and health system' in C. Gopalanand, Suminder Kaur (eds), *Women and Nutrition in India*, New Delhi: Nutrition Foundation in India.

13

Access to Credit by Women in Agribusiness Trade

Empirical Evidence on the Use of Formal and Informal Credit in Rural West Bengal

Both women and men play critical roles in agriculture throughout the world, producing, processing and providing the food we eat. Rural women in particular are responsible for half of the world's food production and produce between 60 and 80 per cent of the food in most developing countries. Yet, despite their contribution to global food security, women farmers are frequently underestimated and overlooked in development strategies.

Rural women are the main producers of the world's staple crops—rice, wheat, and maize—which provide up to 90 per cent of the rural poor's food intake. Women sow, weed, apply fertilizer and pesticides, harvest and thresh the crops. Their contribution to secondary crop production, such as legumes and vegetables, is even greater. Grown mainly in home gardens, these crops provide essential nutrients and are often the only food available during the lean seasons or if the main harvest fails. Woman's specialized knowledge about genetic resources for food and agriculture makes them essential custodians of agro-bio-diversity. In the livestock sector, women feed and milk the larger animals, while raising poultry and small animals such as sheep, goats, rabbits and guinea pigs. Also, once the harvest is in, rural women provide most of the labour for post-harvest activities, taking responsibility for storage, handling, stocking, processing and marketing (Farrington, 2007).

The division of Labour

The division of labour between men and women in crop production varies considerably from region to region and community to community. However, it is usually men who plough the fields and drive draught animals whereas women do the major share of sowing, weeding, applying fertilizer and pesticides, harvesting and threshing.

Similarly, men tend to do the work of large-scale cash cropping, especially when it is highly mechanized, while women take care of household food production and small-scale cultivation of cash crops, requiring low levels of technology. This pattern is particularly pronounced in sub-Saharan Africa, where men and women have customarily farm separate plots. Men tend to grow cash crops and keep the income, while women use their land primarily for subsistence crops to feed their families.

Women make an essential contribution to producing staple crops. In Southeast Asia, for example, it is women who provide up to 90 per cent of the labour for rice cultivation. They do almost all the work of planting and transplanting, fertilizing, weeding, irrigating and harvesting. After the rice has been harvested, they also carry out the post-harvest tasks before the rice can be stored, marketed, cooked or eaten.

Women also play a big role in growing secondary crops, such as legumes and vegetables. In addition to providing essential nutrients, these crops are often the only food available during the lean season between harvests or when the main harvest fails. Home gardens, often tended almost exclusively by women, also claim precious labour-intensive time.

Despite their often complementary roles in agriculture, studies have shown that in almost all societies, women tend to work longer hours than men. The difference in workload is particularly marked for rural women, the world's principal food producers. Women are involved in every stage of food production and, although there is a gender-based division of labour, women do tend to shoulder the larger share. In addition to food production activities, women have the responsibility of preparing and processing the food while fulfilling their fundamental role of nurturing and caring for children and attending to elderly members of the household.

Women's share of the workload is increasing. Lack of employment and other income-generating opportunities in rural areas of sub-Saharan Africa has led to increasing seasonal or permanent emigration of male populations. The ***feminization of agriculture*** is exemplified by a significant rise in the numbers of female-headed households.

The problems facing these female-headed households vary according to their degree of access to production resources. The absence of male labour, however, may force women with an expanded workload to grow less labour intensive—and often less nutritious—crops with a reliance on child labour. This has serious implications both for the family and the human capital of the country. Technological innovations can provide important opportunities to free women's time, boost women's production potential as well as improve their quality of life and that of their families.

The division of labour between genders still remains poorly understood. This is because much of women's work in crop production consists of unpaid labour in fields that produce for the household rather than the market. As a result, women's work goes unrecorded in statistics. Because of this scarcity or—in most cases—sheer lack of available information, there has been little effective recognition of women's labour in agriculture. But gender-disaggregated data is needed to help technicians, planners and policy-makers identify the role differences in food and cash crop production as well as men's and women's different managerial and financial control over the production, storage and marketing of agricultural products.

Significance of credit access in agricultural production

Credit and capital are basic requisites to increase agricultural production. Women and men farmers need short-term credit to buy improved seeds, fertilizers, insecticides and herbicides and to hire farm labourers to work in the fields and help with post-harvest operations. And they need long-term credit to invest in more efficient technologies—irrigation, labour-saving tools and implements and transport—and to set up new enterprises if conditions are favourable. Yet, throughout the developing world and even in cases where they are acting as heads of their household, women are denied full legal status that would grant those loans (Kabeer, 2005). This limited and often complete lack of access to rural financial services hampers women's efforts to improve or expand their farm activities so as to earn cash income.

Although both women and men small farmers have problems acquiring credit in developing countries, the situation facing women is more serious because they lack collateral. As men are the legally recognized landowners, it is they who provide the collateral. When they migrate to towns and cities, leaving women to manage the household farm, the problem is clearly compounded. An analysis of credit schemes in developing countries found that women received less than 10 per cent of the credit awarded to small holders and only one per cent of the total amount of credit directed to agriculture (Kabeer, 2004). Ironically, studies and experience both show that, when women succeed in obtaining credit, they are more reliable than men in their debt repayments.

A number of factors determine the reluctance of banks and credit organizations to lend to women:

- They tend to be inexperienced borrowers—both a cause and a consequence of the problem.
- They usually request small loans.
- They are not normally involved in the development and extension programmes or structures that act as an interface with lending institutions.
- Widespread female illiteracy means that many are often incapable of following application procedures.
- Women's limited participation in male-dominated farmers' associations and cooperatives also reduces the likelihood of their receiving credit when it is allocated.

India remains a underdeveloping country. Some 75 per cent of the population continues to live in rural areas and they depend on agriculture for their livelihood. How the country can transform itself and its agricultural sector to a more modern society remains a critical policy issue. Access to credit for small holders and women is as elsewhere a key ingredient in the promotion of agricultural production and transformation. It forms an essential element of any poverty-oriented strategy for the future development of the financial system. Access to credit affects household welfare through at least two key channels—(a) It alleviates capital constraints on agricultural households. This can significantly improve the ability of poor households to procure needed agricultural inputs, and will also reduce the opportunity costs of capital-intensive assets, encouraging labour-saving technology and raising labour productivity; (b) Credit access increases the risk-bearing capacity of household and altering risk-coping strategies. Households with access to credit may be more willing to pursue promising but risky technologies and will be better able to avoid adopting risk-reducing but inefficient livelihood strategies.

Rural households need credit for a variety of reasons. They need it to meet short-term requirements for working capital and for long-term investment in agriculture and other income-bearing activities. Agricultural and non-agricultural activities in rural areas are typically seasonal and households need credit to smooth out seasonal fluctuations in earnings and expenditure. Rural households, particularly those vulnerable to what appear to others to be minor shocks with respect to income and expenditure, need credit as an insurance against risk. In a society that has no free, compulsory and universal education or health care, and very few general social security programmes; rural households need credit for different types of consumption (Pareek, 1964). These include expenditure on food, housing, health and education. In the Indian context, another important purpose of borrowing is to meet expenses for a variety of social obligations and rituals. If these credit needs of the poor are to be met, rural households need access to credit institutions that provide them a range of financial services, provide credit at reasonable rates of interest and provide loans that are unencumbered by extra-economic provisions and obligations.

Constraints of rural credit markets for small business

Historically, there have been four major problems with respect to providing credit to the Indian countryside: (a) the supply of credit from formal sector has always been inadequate; (b) rural credit markets in India themselves have been very imperfect and fragmented; (c) the distribution of formal credit sector has been always unequal, particularly with respect to region and class, caste and gender; and (d) the major source of credit to rural households has been from informal sector which are usually given at an exorbitant rate of interest. Further, the terms and conditions attached to these loans have given rise to an elaborate structure of coercion—economic and extra-economic—in the countryside.

These factors constitute what may be called the **'problem of rural credit'** (Simanowitz, 2007) has been well recognized in official evaluations and scholarship since the end of the nineteenth century. Given the issues involved, the declared objectives of public policy with regard to rural credit in the post-independence period were, in the words of the Governor of Reserve Bank of India, "to ensure that sufficient and timely credit, at reasonable rates of interest, is made available to as large a segment of the rural population as possible". The policy instruments to achieve these objectives were to be, *first*, the expansion of the institutional structure of formal sector lending institutions; *secondly*, directed lending followed by concessional or subsidized credit. Public policy was thus aimed not only at meeting rural credit needs but also at pushing out the informal sector and the exploitation to which it subjected borrowers. Rural credit policy in India envisaged the provision of a range of credit services including long-term and short-term credit and large-scale and small-scale loans to rural households.

Rural women in agricultural economy

Much of Women's Economic Activity is Not Reflected in Statistics (Rot and Tisdell, 2009). Although most women in India work and contribute to the economy in one form or another, much of their work is not documented or accounted for in official statistics. Women plow fields and harvest crops while working on farms; women weave and make handicrafts while working in household industries; women sell food and gather wood while working in the informal sector. Additionally, women are traditionally responsible for the daily household chores (e.g. cooking, fetching water and looking after children). Although the cultural restrictions women face are changing. Women are still not as men to participate in the formal sector.

In the past, cultural restrictions were the primary impediments to female employment; now, however, the shortage of jobs throughout the country contributes to low female employment as well. The 1991 Indian census divides workers into two categories *'main'* and *'marginal'*. Main workers include people who worked for 6 months or more during the year, while marginal workers include those who worked for a shorter period of time. Detailed data on marginal workers have not been tabulated from the 1991 census, but many of these workers are agricultural labourers. Unpaid farm and family enterprise workers are women account for a small proportion of the Indian labour force, even though the number of female main workers has grown faster in recent years than that of their male counterparts. The 2001 census shows that the number of male main workers increased 23 per cent since the 1991 census while the number of female main workers increased 40 per cent. However, women are still accounted for only 23 per cent (64.3 million) of the total.

Women are a vital part of the Indian economy, constituting one-third of the national labour force and a major contributor to the survival of the family. It is observed that the poorer the family, the greater its dependence on women's income. Despite progress in several key indicators, a gender analysis of most social and economic data demonstrates that women in India continue to be relatively disadvantaged in matters of survival, health, nutrition, literacy and productivity.

Agriculture has been a major sector in the employment of female labour. The majority of women fall within the low-income category, with up to 87 per cent of the female population residing in rural areas. Nationally, a higher proportion of women are unemployed, compared to men. Up to one-third of the rural households in the country are female headed, with up to 60 per cent of them having no male support, and up to 44 per cent of the female headed households being classified as very poor. Approximately 68 per cent of the active female population is engaged in subsistence farming (World Bank Report, 2005). The incidence of poverty is, therefore, higher for such households. There is an implied prevalence of poverty among female-headed households indicated by the fact that at higher level of income, there is a higher proportion of male-headed households, while at lower income level, there are a higher proportion of female-headed households. The economic position of women in West Bengal, therefore, shows a situation of marginalization.

The result of this marginal situation has meant that women's productivity is still low, mainly because of the restricted access to resources and the related constraints. Although majority of women (80%) resides in rural areas. They have limited access to production resources, especially land, improved inputs, market information and credit (World Bank Report, 2007). This has prompted most of them to engage in off-farm activities for additional income. Due to their marginal economic position, women in rural areas have responded to their situation by engaging in supplementary income generating activities, mainly petty trade in agriculture and agricultural commodities. However, their ability to realize increased income is limited by among other things, lack of access to financial resources.

More than 90 per cent of rural women in India are unskilled, restricting them to low-paid occupations. A number of factors perpetuate women's limited job skills. If women have to take training for economic activities they need to leave their village. This is usually a problem for them. Unequal access to education restricts women's abilities to learn skills even functional level of literacy. In terms of skill development, women are impeded by their lack of mobility, low literacy levels and prejudiced attitudes of the society towards women. When some women negotiate with banks and government officials for credit access, other men and women in their community often say *'too forward'* and ostracize them. Government and bank officials have preconceived ideas of what women are capable of and stereotypes of what is considered women's work (Cheston, 2008). Women generally have no control over land and other productive assets, which largely excludes them from access to institutional credit and renders them dependent on high-cost informal sources of credit to secure capital for consumption and/or productive purposes.

Women and small business

Lack of land for farming is perhaps the severest constraint by the rural poor, and one that affects more women than men. In rural areas, there are very few employment opportunities. For those with little or no land, some of IFAD's (International Foundation for Agricultural Development) projects have provided strong support for non-farming activities, such as marketing, processing and other micro enterprises. Self-employment in small-scale businesses presents a constructive option for income generation. In many developing countries, a high percentage of small-scale businesses that cater to local needs are controlled or owned by women. Women's enterprises tend to be relatively small, having informal structures, flexibility, low capital needs, modest educational requirements, high labour intensity and depend on local raw materials. They are also characterized by their dependence on family labour and limited technical and managerial skills. Commonly, these enterprises are not registered, maintain no business records and do not have access to credit from formal credit institutions. Rural women are active participants in retail trade and marketing, particularly where trade is traditional and not highly commercialized. In many parts of Asia, women market foods such as vegetables and other major commodities and in

India and Bangladesh, women account for nearly all local marketing. Through their marketing efforts, women provide valuable links among farmers, intermediaries and consumers. Petty trade often thought of in the past as non-productive, in fact serves to stimulate the production and consumption in the local community. IFAD has successfully facilitated a variety of micro enterprises developments among the rural poor by helping men and women form groups (Deaton, A., 2008).

Formal and Informal credit for small scale business

Access to transfers and credit, whether cash or in kind, is a major source of poverty alleviation in many developing countries around the world. For many households, these public and private loans make-up a substantial portion of their yearly incomes and provide an important means to generate additional income. Women may especially benefit from transfers and credit in countries such as India where they often have few work alternatives.

As such, the formal financial sector is currently one of the principal areas of intervention intended to provide social protection and poverty alleviation for the poor rural women. The intervention has taken the form of formal transfers and improved access to credit and/or subsidization of credit. In addition, the development community is increasingly interested in ways to create an enabling environment for the private sector, including banks, to provide the poor with improved access to financial services. The informal financial sector is also a key source of social protection, especially in areas with limited access to the formal financial sector. In fact, in rural areas of West Bengal, the informal sector is much larger than the formal sector. The informal sector which includes transactions such as loans from relatives, friends, and neighbours may overcome barriers to the formal sector. If this is so, formal programmes designed to increase access to formal financial services may actually prompt reductions in the informal sector.

In this report, we descriptively examine the formal and informal sectors of rural West Bengal, placing a special emphasis on differences between women in agriculture and non-agricultural business. This analysis uses unique empirical data on the credit and transfer behaviours of 300 women. Throughout the analysis, the research focuses on five important questions: (1) how important are the formal and informal sectors?; (2) What are the primary sources of loans within those sectors?; (3) Do women in agriculture and non-agricultural business rely on different sources for finances (e.g., formal *vs.* informal) or different types of finances (e.g., loans); (4) How have the financial sectors evolved during last one decade?; (5) What is the relationship between the formal and informal sectors?. The report is primarily descriptive. However, this research used cross-tabulation analysis to further investigate the relationship between the formal and informal sector credit sources.

Formal credit and transfers may not only alter the allocation of resources within the household, they may also alter the allocation of resources between altruistically liked households. Households that are recipients of formal transfers and credit may transfer some of the benefits by increasing (decreasing) gifts and loans to (from) altruistically linked households, generating possible third-part effects. In the most extreme cases, formal sector programmes could have no income effect on their targeted population if the formal sector fully replaces the informal sector. Even in this extreme of no income effect, programmes may still have important impacts on broader measures of welfare such as women's empowerment. The sign of the relationship between the formal and informal sectors is indeterminate because assets acquired through formal sector programmes may increase the creditworthiness of households and thus lead to improved access to financial services from other sources. As part of a larger project, the final section of this report begins to explore the relationship between the formal and informal sectors.

The single most commonly reported obstacle to investment and entrepreneurship is inadequate access to capital; however, demand constraints may also be a factor underlying restricted access to credit. Prospective rural investors do not lack all access, but loan size and maturity are often limited. Given lack of access to formal credit, the main source of fund is often from the savings and assets of the extended household. Initiative from NGOs and government to promote micro-finance have in some cases made access better, but coverage is still incomplete and often still excludes the poor. Private sector loans remain important as does informal financial services; because domestic savings capacity is often limited.

In the recent past, there has been an increased tendency to fund credit programmes in the small-scale enterprises (SMEs) and various multi-trade based income generation activities to women self-help groups. Such credit programmes largely resemble earlier attempts to assist small farmers through credit in so far as they have similar assumptions, policies and the same type of projected justifications. These efforts have however yielded minimum results especially in reaching the targeted groups, mainly, the time-scale farmers and entrepreneurs. Experience from informal finance has, however, shown that the rural poor, especially women, often have greater access to informal credit facilities compared to formal source.

Through policy mandates women's perspectives should be included in designing and implementing macro-economic and social policies by institutionalizing their participation in such processes. Their contribution to socio-economic development as producers and workers must be recognized in the formal and informal sectors (including home based workers) and appropriate policies relating to employment and to her working conditions should be drawn up (National Policy for the Empowerment of Women, 2001).

Study design

Significance of the study

Considering that women constitute over half of the total population in India. This indicates the level of inadequacy of women's participation in the agribusiness sector. Hence, while official policy recognizes the contribution of women in the process of economic development, not much has been done in terms of policy to raise their potential. When looked at in the light of their limited access to productive resources, women in rural areas need other forms of income generating activities to supplement their meager resources in order to meet their multiple responsibilities.

The importance of women in agriculture and the rural economy in general can be appreciated from the increased roles they have assumed over time, especially at the household level as well as their availability in agriculture sector as cheaper labour. This has mainly resulted from male migration to urban areas leaving women in-charge of agriculture and other rural activities. Women have, therefore, assumed more responsibilities in the rural areas, especially in agriculture and consequently have more to contribute towards agricultural production and other rural activities. Efforts to reach development goals may not be achieved if women and the factors affecting their productivity are not taken into account. Despite this importance of women, policy statements have only recently pointed out the important position of women, and the need to improve their contribution in the country.

The study involved an in-depth and empirical analysis of the credit policies in the rural financial markets affecting the access of women headed small-scale enterprises to financial services from both formal and informal sources in rural West Bengal. It has further paid attention to the factors behind the use of credit from formal and informal sources by rural women engaged in agribusiness trade.

Therefore, the **primary objective** of this study was to investigate and assess the role of the institutional lending policies by formal and informal credit institutions in determining the access to and use of credit facilities by women operated agriculture based small scale enterprises in rural West Bengal.

The **formal sector credit** is the sector in which loan transactions are regulated by legislation and other public policy requirements. The institutions in this sector include commercial banks, cooperative banks and credit societies and other registered financial institutions.

The **informal sector credit** is not regulated by public authorities and the terms and conditions attached to each loan are personalized, and therefore, vary according to the bargaining power of borrowers and lenders in each case.

Objectives of the study

1. Identify the main features of the lending policies by formal and informal credit institutions which determine the access to and use of credit by small-scale enterprises and problems associated as perceived by women entrepreneurs.
2. Analyze the factors, which determine the participation of rural women entrepreneurs in credit markets and their choice of credit sources in West Bengal.
3. Explore the temporary and permanent cost-benefit ratio and internal rate of return through using the formal and informal credit.
4. Enumerate the type of women operated enterprises and its financial sources as well as the changing socio-economic conditions of their families.
5. Draw policy implications for financial services to small-scale enterprises in West Bengal.

Research design

Exploratory research design was followed because the main purpose of such design was to formulate a problem for more precise investigation or to develop some working strategies from an operational point of view. The major emphasis was to explore ideas and insights. This research design was therefore flexible enough to provide opportunity for considering different aspects of the problems of rural women's use of credit from formal and informal sources for different agricultural and non-agricultural trades under study.

Universe of research

The study was conducted in two districts of West Bengal—Birbhum and Murshidabad. It could be ascertained that both the districts were selected for the present study as the reasons given below:

A. Availability of a large number of rural women entrepreneurs involved in different trades.
B. Availability of huge number of rural women involved in agricultural and non-agricultural business.
C. Availability of both types of credit sources—formal and informal.

Therefore, at first stage two blocks, namely Bolpur-Sriniketan and Bharatpur-II of Birbhum and Murshidabad districts were selected purposively because of the convenience of the research team and prior association with the villagers over there. In second stage two gram panchayats, namely Ruppur and Talibpur from Bolpur-Sriniketan and Bharatpur-II block were chosen. Five villages from each gram panchayats, i.e. altogether ten villages were selected for the study.

The following empirical data reflects the socio-economic condition of the villages adopted for carrying out the study. This would only give us a glimpse of the villages at the time of study.

District level demographic information (2001 Census)

Data Parameters	*Districts*	
	Birbhum	*Murshidabad*
Gender Gap (Total)	19.3	13.1
Gender Gap (Rural)	19.8	12.9
No. of Illiterates (Person-Total)	146570	3246031
No. of Illiterates (Person-Rural)	1380634	2936693
No. of Illiterates (Male-Total)	626480	1502276
No. of Illiterates (Male-Rural)	593272	1368397
No. of Illiterates (Female-Total)	833090	1245674
No. of Illiterates (Female-Rural)	787362	1568296

Data Parameters	Districts	
	Birbhum	Murshidabad
No. of Literates (Person-Total)	1553852	2620538
No. of Literates (Person-Rural)	1376368	2197142
No. of Literates (Male-Total)	920153	1502724
No. of Literates (Male-Rural)	820825	1264799
No. of Literates (Female-Total)	633699	1117814
No. of Literates (Female-Rural)	555543	932343
Population Density	663.5	1101.9
Population Density (Rural)	613.3	988.2
Population (Person-Total)	3015422	5866569
Population (Person-Rural)	2757002	5138815
Population (Male-Rural)	1414097	2633196
Population (Female-Rural)	1342905	2500639
SC Population (Person-Total)	889894	703786
SC Population (Male-Rural)	426868	313445
SC Population (Female-Rural)	403832	297284
ST Population (Person-Total)	203127	75953
ST Population (Male-Rural)	99598	37090
ST Population (Female-Rural)	99014	36112
Percentage of Agricultural Workers (Rural-Person)	40	32
Percentage of Agricultural Workers (Rural-Male)	36	38
Percentage of Agricultural Workers (Rural-Female)	19	42
Percentage of Cultivators (Rural-Person)	25	22
Percentage of Cultivators (Rural-Male)	30	26
Percentage of Cultivators (Rural-Female)	11	5
Percentage of Main Workers (Rural-Person)	27	28
Percentage of Main Workers (Rural-Male)	46	46
Percentage of Main Workers (Rural-Female)	8	9
Percentage of Marginal Workers (Rural-Person)	10	6
Percentage of Marginal Workers (Rural-Male)	9	6
Percentage of Marginal Workers (Rural-Female)	12	6
Percentage of Non-Workers (Rural-Person)	62.1	66.5
Percentage of Non-Workers (Rural-Male)	45.5	48.7
Percentage of Non-Workers (Rural-Female)	78.7	85.3
Percentage of Other Workers (Rural-Person)	29	29
Percentage of Other Workers (Rural-Male)	31	30
Percentage of Other Workers (Rural-Female)	23	24
Percentage of Total Workers (Rural-Person)	54	51
Percentage of Total Workers (Rural-Male)	54	51
Percentage of Total Workers (Rural-Female)	49	50
Total Workers (Rural-Person)	104448	1718547
Total Workers (Rural-Male)	771182	1349909
Total Workers (Rural-Female)	273266	368638
Sex Ratio (Rural)	950	950

Block level demographic information (2001 census)

Data Parameters	*District*	
	Birbhum	*Murshidabad*
	Block	
	Bolpur-Sriniketan	*Bharatpur-II*
No. of Illiterates (Person-Total)	86912	82104
No. of Illiterates (Person-Rural)	86912	82104
No. of Illiterates (Male-Total)	37146	37456
No. of Illiterates (Male-Rural)	37146	37456
No. of Illiterates (Female Total)	49766	44648
No. of Illiterates (Female-Rural)	49776	44648
No. of Literates (Person-Total)	91199	68029
No. of Literates (Person-Rural)	91199	68029
No. of Literates (Male-Total)	53737	39257
No. of Literates (Male-Rural)	53737	39257
No. of Literates (Female-Total)	37462	28772
No. of Literates (Female-Rural)	37462	28772
Population (Person-Total)	178111	150133
Population (Person-Rural)	178111	150113
Population (Male-Total)	90883	76713
Population (Male-Rural)	90883	76713
Population (Female-Total)	87228	73420
Population (Female-Rural)	87228	73420
SC Population (Person-Total)	53184	27580
SC Population (Male-Rural)	27334	14158
SC Population (Female-Rural)	25850	13422
ST Population (Person-Total)	31960	155
ST Population (Male-Rural)	15901	84
ST Population (Female-Rural)	16059	71
Percentage of Agricultural Workers (Rural-Person)	43.9	30.8
Percentage of Agricultural Workers (Rural-Male)	38.1	36
Percentage of Agricultural Workers (Rural-Female)	55.9	8
Percentage of Cultivators (Rural-Person)	21	19.9
Percentage of Cultivators (Rural-Male)	26.3	23.4
Percentage of Cultivators (Rural-Female)	10.1	4.9
Percentage of Main Workers (Rural-Person)	31.1	28.4
Percentage of Main Workers (Rural-Male)	48.1	48.5
Percentage of Main Workers (Rural-Female)	13.5	7.4
Percentage of Marginal Workers (Rural-Person)	12.6	4.8
Percentage of Marginal Workers (Rural-Male)	9.8	4.3
Percentage of Marginal Workers (Rural-Female)	15.5	5.2
Percentage of Non-Workers (Rural-Person)	56.3	66.8

Data Parameters	*District*	
	Birbhum	*Murshidabad*
	Block	
	Bolpur-Sriniketan	*Bharatpur-II*
Percentage of Non-Workers (Rural-Male)	42.1	47.2
Percentage of Non-Workers (Rural-Female)	71	87.4
Percentage of Other Workers (Rural-Person)	31.1	41.2
Percentage of Other Workers (Rural-Male)	33.6	36.6
Percentage of Other Workers (Rural-Female)	26.1	61.6
Percentage of Total Workers (Rural-Person)	43.7	33.2
Percentage of Total Workers (Rural-Male)	57.9	52.8
Percentage of Total Workers (Rural-Female)	29	12.6
Total Workers (Rural-Person)	77886	49783
Total Workers (Rural-Male)	52586	40508
Total Workers (Rural-Female)	25300	9275

Gram Panchayat level demographic information (2001 Census)

Data Parameters	*District*	
	Birbhum	*Murshidabad*
	Block	
	Bolpur-Sriniketan	*Bharatpur-II*
	Gram Panchayat (s)	
	Ruppur	*Talibpur*
Total Population	28666	24115
Total Population (Male)	14397	12392
Total Population (Female)	14269	11723
SC Population	7155	1252
SC Population (Male)	3623	673
SC Population (Female)	3632	579
ST Population	5508	0
ST Population (Male)	2722	0
ST Population (Female)	2786	0
Literates (Person)	16274	8876
Literates (Male)	9193	5240
Literates (Female)	7081	3636
Illiterates (Person)	12392	15239
Illiterates (Male)	5204	7152
Illiterates (Female)	7188	8087

Data Parameters	*District*	
	Birbhum	*Murshidabad*
	Block	
	Bolpur-Sriniketan	*Bharatpur-II*
	Gram Panchayat (s)	
	Ruppur	*Talibpur*
Total Worker	12149	8323
Total Worker (Male)	8117	6358
Total Worker (Female)	4032	1965
Percentage of Literates	65.1	44.7
Percentage of Literates (Male)	73.6	51.5
Percentage of Literates (Female)	56.6	37.5
Percentage of Total Workers	42.4	34.5
Percentage of Total Workers (Male)	56.4	51.3
Percentage of Total Workers (Female)	28.3	16.8
Percentage of Main Workers	34.3	30.4
Percentage of Main Workers (Male)	50.8	46.5
Percentage of Main Workers (Female)	17.7	13.5
Percentage of Marginal Workers	8.1	4.1
Percentage of Marginal Workers (Male)	5.6	4.8
Percentage of Marginal Workers (Female)	10.5	3.3
Percentage of Non-Workers	57.6	65.5
Percentage of Non-Workers (Male)	43.6	48.7
Percentage of Non-Workers (Female)	71.7	83.2
Percentage of Cultivators	10.1	13.0
Percentage of Cultivators (Male)	12.5	15.9
Percentage of Cultivators (Female)	5.2	3.6
Percentage of Agricultural Labour	31.5	32.4
Percentage of Agricultural Labour (Male)	25.6	42.0
Percentage of Agricultural Labour (Female)	43.5	1.1
Percentage of Household Industry Workers	3.4	4.9
Percentage of Household Industry Workers (Male)	2.6	3.0
Percentage of Household Industry Workers (Female)	5.0	11.1
Percentage of Other Workers	55.0	49.7
Percentage of Other Workers (Male)	59.3	39.1
Percentage of Other Workers (Female)	46.4	84.1
Sex Ratio	991	946

Village level demographic information (2001 census)

Data Parameters	*District(s)*									
	Birbhum					*Murshidabad*				
	Block (s)									
	Bolpur-Sriniketan					*Bharatpur-II*				
	Gram Panchayat (s)									
	Ruppur					*Talibpur*				
	Study Villages (5)					*Study Villages (5)*				
	Benuria	*Balla-bhpur*	*Goal-para*	*Syam-bati*	*Surul*	*Talib-pur*	*Purbba Gram*	*Hat Pilk-handi*	*Sar-masta-pur*	*Ram-naba-rakhi*
Total Households	565	385	368	571	2362	2388	424	263	1348	199
Total Population	2592	1747	1882	10247	10247	12562	1386	1386	6525	1011
Total Males Population	1308	851	934	5029	5029	6424	710	710	3377	533
Total Females Population	1284	896	948	5218	5218	6138	676	676	3448	178
Total SC Population	558	413	401	2821	2821	982	50	50	59	0
Total Male SC Population	284	199	196	1399	1399	530	28	28	32	0
Total Female SC Population	274	214	205	1422	1422	452	22	22	27	0
Total ST Population	302	753	436	1093	1093	0	0	0	0	0
Total Male ST Population	147	358	205	534	534	0	0	0	0	0
Total Females ST Population	155	395	231	559	559	0	0	0	0	0
Total Literates	1419	943	1113	6290	6290	776	776	665	2075	326
Male Literates	831	528	651	3408	3408	429	429	397	1179	201
Female Literates	588	415	462	2882	2882	347	347	268	896	125
Total Workers	1040	806	762	1001	4186	4931	657	487	1825	306
Male Workers	729	499	542	717	2824	3300	537	384	1737	291
Female Workers	311	307	220	284	1362	1631	120	103	88	15
Total Mail Workers	803	660	762587	980	3680	4485	598	409	1539	214
Male Main Workers	681	463	466	706	2620	3076	532	360	1511	211
Female Main Workers	122	197	121	274	1060	1409	66	49	48	3
Total Cultivators	147	128	106	3	109	370	33	47	510	55
Male Cultivators	140	94	88	3	98	336	28	45	491	55
Female Cultivators	7	34	18	0	11	34	5	2	19	0
Total Agricultural Labour	279	130	84	278	503	860	268	140	883	128
Male Agricultural Labour	213	77	70	152	331	855	267	139	876	128
Female Agri-cultural Labour	66	53	14	126	172	5	1	1	7	0

Data Parameters	District(s)									
	Birbhum					Murshidabad				
	Block (s)									
	Bolpur-Sriniketan					Bharatpur-II				
	Gram Panchayat (s)									
	Ruppur					Talibpur				
	Study Villages (5)					Study Villages (5)				
	Benuria	Ballabhpur	Goalpara	Syambati	Surul	Talibpur	Purbba Gram	Hat Pilkhandi	Sarmastapur	Ramnabarakhi
Total Households Industry Workers	37	11	28	10	149	252	5	16	8	1
Male Households Industry Workers	36	3	24	8	85	139	5	14	8	1
Female Households Industry Workers	1	8	4	2	64	113	0	2	0	0
Total Other Workers	340	391	369	689	2919	3003	292	206	158	30
Male Other Workers	292	284	284	543	2106	1746	232	162	136	27
Female Other Workers	48	102	85	146	813	1257	60	44	22	3
Total Marginal Workers	237	146	175	21	506	446	59	78	266	92
Male Marginal Workers	48	36	76	11	204	224	5	24	226	80
Female Marginal Workers	189	110	99	10	302	222	54	54	40	12
Total Marginal Cultivators	22	21	22	0	34	16	2	6	29	1
Male Marginal Cultivators	14	5	2	0	13	11	2	6	25	0
Female Marginal Cultivators	8	16	20	0	21	5	0	0	4	1
Total Marginal Agricultural Labour	87	95	127	2	147	132	2	12	188	43
Male Marginal Agricultural Labour	14	18	59	0	62	129	2	10	185	43
Female Marginal Agricultural Labour	73	77	68	2	85	3	0		3	0
Total Marginal Households Industry Workers	15	2	7	1	57	103	1	2	17	3
Male Marginal Households Industry Workers	2	1	3	0	9	19	0	2	1	0
Female Marginal Households Industry Workers	13	1	4	1	48	84	1	2	16	3

Data Parameters	District(s)									
	Birbhum					Murshidabad				
	Block (s)									
	Bolpur-Sriniketan					Bharatpur-II				
	Gram Panchayat (s)									
	Ruppur					Talibpur				
	Study Villages (5)					Study Villages (5)				
	Benuria	Ballabhpur	Goalpara	Syambati	Surul	Talibpur	Purbba Gram	Hat Pilkhandi	Sarmastapur	Ramnabarakhi
Total Marginal Other Workers	113	28	19	18	268	195	54	0	32	45
Male Marginal Other Workers	18	12	12	11	120	65	1	58	15	37
Female Marginal Other Workers	95	16	7	7	148	130	53	6	17	8
Total Non-Workers	1552	941	1120	1702	6061	7631	1506	52	4700	705
Male Non-Workers	579	352	392	650	2205	3124	565	899	1649	242
Female Non-Workers	973	589	728	1952	3856	4507	942	326	3060	463
Total Illiterates	1173	804	769	963	3957	7780	1387	721	4450	685
Male Illiterates	477	323	283	386	1621	3550	673	313	2198	332
Female Illiterates	696	481	486	577	2336	4230	714	408	2252	353

Selection of samples and sampling method

Stratified random sampling is a sampling technique where the target population is first divided into a number of homogeneous strata. A simple random sampling of appropriate size is drawn from each stratum in order to make the whole sample. This method ensures that the sample is a representative of the population, when the population consists of units of homogenous characters.

The method of stratified sample was adopted to select the final sample in ten (10) villages from Birbhum and Murshidabad districts. Stratification was done on the basis of type of credit access by the rural women involved in agricultural business. Sample from each stratum had been drawn according to proportional allocation rule without replacement method.

Women entrepreneurs were mainly identified from agricultural as well as non-agricultural business to form a sampling frame after obtaining primary level information regarding existence of such women entrepreneurs in the study area. The respondents for the study were selected after obtaining relevant information about them from concerned gram panchayat offices, rural banks and local level bodies.

Methods of data collection

Both primary and secondary data were collected for the study. Primary data were collected from individual woman entrepreneurs receiving credit from both formal and informal credit institutions as well as who didn't. The formal financial credit institutions were basically—**Local Rural Banks, Nationalized Banks, Post Office Savings Bank**. Apart from banking institutions, **NABARD (National Agricultural Bank for Rural Development)** and **Block and District Level Authorities** were also noteworthy formal credit institutions. The informal financial institutions were consisted of friends, welfare associations, shopkeepers, traders and community based organizations and NGOs. A structured interview schedule was developed for primary data collection. Small-scale women entrepreneurs engaged in farming, wholesale and retail trading as well as primary processing of agricultural products were given priority during the time of selection of samples. Relevant reviews and information had also been collected from website and official documents of formal credit institutions to fulfil the secondary data requirement for the study.

Data processing and analysis

Data was collected through interview schedule and then coded on the code sheet developed for the purpose. Data were also processed with the help of SPSS software. Various tabular and graphical representations were used for meaningful interpretation of the facts and figures.

The major variables of the study

Household and enterprise characteristics

These include main occupation, income, household size, age of the enterprise and saving behaviour of the women.

Main occupation of the respondents

These include selling fruits and vegetables, selling other agricultural goods, farming etc. by the rural women.

Women entrepreneurs characteristics

These include gross weekly income, gross monthly income, distance to the nearest sources, household size, age of the enterprise and proportion of saving part of their income etc.

Access to and the use of formal and informal credit sources

Different sources of credit used by the women traders have been investigated. These have been classified into formal and informal sources. Access and use of credit from these sources have been explained with participation in both formal and informal markets separately.

Amount of credit from formal and informal sources

These include formal and informal credit category, initial capital, operating capital, past credit and current credit etc.

Amount of credit applied for and the amount received from both formal and informal sources

This includes informal lenders. More emphasis has been placed on information about borrower creditworthiness and short-term and small loans as well as flexible arrangements to the borrower who respond by maintaining discipline in order to sustain their access to credit. In the formal credit market the inability to satisfy the existing credit demand and difficulties in loan administration of their investments in screening of applicants and loan monitoring has also been taken into account.

Factors related to participation in credit markets and choice of credit sources

This includes the women traders who have been using informal source of credit more than the formal sources. In this area, an attempt has been made to advance arguments explaining this trend. This has been done in relation to those factors which divide formal and informal financial markets and affect the cost of credit to the borrowers. Enterprise characteristics influence individual's decision to participate in credit markets.

Differences between selected characteristics for credit users and non-users

This includes weekly income, monthly income, value of land owned, value of livestock owned, distance to the nearest credit source, age of the business etc.

Thematic analysis

Household Level Information about Women Entrepreneurs

- The major representation of women entrepreneurs (i.e. 273 in number) out of total 300 respondents were from Hindu community and among them 60.44 per cent belonged to the age group 26-37 years. The percentage of Muslim respondents was insignificantly low. Table 13.1 reflects the same.

Table 13.1 : Religion and Age group

Age	*Religion*				*Total*	*%*
	Hindu	*%*	*Muslim*	*%*		
18-25	50	18.32	2	7.41	52	17.33
26-37	165	60.44	17	62.96	182	60.67
38-47	49	17.95	7	25.93	56	18.67
47>	9	3.30	1	3.70	10	3.33
Total	273	91.00	27	9.00	300	100.00

Table 13.2 : Educational Status and Caste

Caste	*Educational Status and Caste*										*Total*	*%*
	Illiterate	*%*	*Primary*	*%*	*Secondary*	*%*	*Higher Secondary*	*%*	*Graduate*	*%*		
General	24	26.67	55	29.73	7	35.00	2	50.00	1	100.00	89	29.67
SC	45	50.00	110	59.46	11	55.00	2	50.00	-	0.00	168	56.00
ST	21	23.33	20	10.81	2	10.00	-	0.00	-	0.00	43	14.33
Total	90	30.00	185	61.67	20	6.67	4	1.33	1	0.33	300	100.00

- Table 13.2 shows that a considerable number of women entrepreneurs involved in agricultural business from general, SC and ST community were illiterate (30%) and majority of them (61.67%) were not able to access primary education. Barring a few exception, post-primary education and above were very poorly reported. When MDG (Millennium Development Goal) heavily stressed on women education, the study found altogether a different scenario. So, it could be concluded that poor educational status among those women was the leading constraint in decision making and participatory process in agricultural business as well as credit market.
- It was empirically observed that out of the total respondents 279 (93%) women were married. This also gave us an idea that women only after marriage got into the agricultural business and allied activities.

Table 13.3 : Average family income and family category

Family category	*Average family income*								*Total*	*%*
	500-1000	*%*	*1001-2000*	*%*	*2001-3000*	*%*	*3001-4000*	*%*		
APL	0	0.00	62	45.59	38	1000.0	12	85.71	112	37.33
BPL	112	1000.0	74	54.41	0	0.00	2	14.29	188	62.67
Total	112	37.33	136	45.33	38	12.67	14	4.67	300	100.00

- A considerable number of women (i.e. 112) entrepreneurs joined in agricultural business and credit market from below poverty line and their average monthly family income was ranging from Rs. 500 to Rs.1000. It was also found that there were 62 and 74 number of women from above and below poverty line category under the monthly family income range of Rs. 1001 to Rs. 2000.
- The point also to be noted that out of total 300 respondents 112 (General—15; SC—70; ST—27) falls in the income group between Rs. 500-1000. Majority of them, i.e. 136 (General—56; SC—74; ST—6) number of women fall in the income group of Rs. 1001-2000.

Table 13.4: Caste and age group

Age	*Caste and age group*						*Total*	*%*
	General	*%*	*SC*	*%*	*ST*	*%*		
18-25	16	17.98	30	17.86	6	13.95	52	17.33
26-37	48	53.93	109	64.88	25	58.14	182	60.67
38-47	20	22.47	26	15.48	10	23.26	56	18.67
47>	5	5.62	3	1.79	2	4.65	10	3.33
Total	89	29.67	168	56.00	43	14.33	300	100.00

Caste has been taken as an important variable in the study to understand the caste dynamics among the women entrepreneurs with their age categories. The research team intended to see whether Scheduled Caste and Scheduled Tribe community have more scope and space in agricultural business over general category. The result was that out of total respondents 168, 89 and 43 were from SC, General and ST population respectively. The age group 26-37 was most significant and majority of the women belongs to this group (General—48; SC—109; ST—25).

Table 13.5 : Family category and type

Family type	*Family category*				*Total*	*%*
	APL	*%*	*BPL*	*%*		
Joint	36	32.14	78	41.49	114	38.00
Nuclear	76	67.86	110	58.51	186	62.00
Total	112	37.33	188	62.67	300	100.00

Table 13.5 reveals that women entrepreneurs joined in agricultural business were mostly (i.e. 188) from below poverty line representing joint and nuclear family types. On the other hand less than half of them (i.e. 112) were found from above poverty line. The most remarkable finding was that though a majority of women entrepreneurs in agricultural business belonged to nuclear family but they were from below poverty line.

Synoptic analysis

The above description of the tables envisaged that representation of women entrepreneurs in agricultural business was an essence not for their economic benefit but also an effort to consolidate and improve livelihood standard in relation to their socio-economic condition.

- More representation of women entrepreneurs (i.e. 273) out of total 300 respondents were from Hindu community and of which majority were found to be from the age group of 26 to 37 years.
- Majority of women entrepreneurs (168) were from Scheduled Caste community and belonged to the age group between 26-37 years.
- A considerable number of women (279) out of the total were found to be married. So, representation after marriage was pronounced.

- In the caste composition the average family income (i.e. Rs.500-Rs.1000 and Rs. 1001-Rs.2000) was very poor among the Scheduled Caste women entrepreneurs.
- It was a very frightening observation that the women entrepreneurs participated in agricultural business were mostly from BPL family category under the family income range of Rs. 500 to Rs. 1000 and Rs. 1001 to Rs. 2000.
- When Millennium Development Goal (MDG) had stressed on education as a tool of empowerment for rural women, it was found that considerable numbers (i.e. 89, 168, 43) of women out of total 300 entrepreneurs from general, Scheduled Caste and Scheduled Tribe community were illiterate and not able to access to primary education respectively. So, it might be concluded that poor educational status among those women was the leading constraint in decision making and participation process in agricultural business as well as credit market.
- There were 188 and 112 women from BPL and APL category. Out of 188 BPL families, 110 were found to be from nuclear family. So, the trend of the nuclear family shows that fulfilment of economic and livelihood needs of their families, women were also inspired to be involved in agricultural business along with their counterpart for their economic self-reliance as well as improvement of family income.

Perception of Women Entrepreneurs on Formal and Informal Credit Sources

Table 13.6 : Caste and awareness on different formal credit sources

Awareness about	*Caste*			*Total*
different credit sources	*General*	*SC*	*ST*	
Unaware	82	105	39	226
Rural Bank	4	58	4	66
Post Office	3	4	—	7
NABARD	—	1	—	1
Total	89	168	43	300

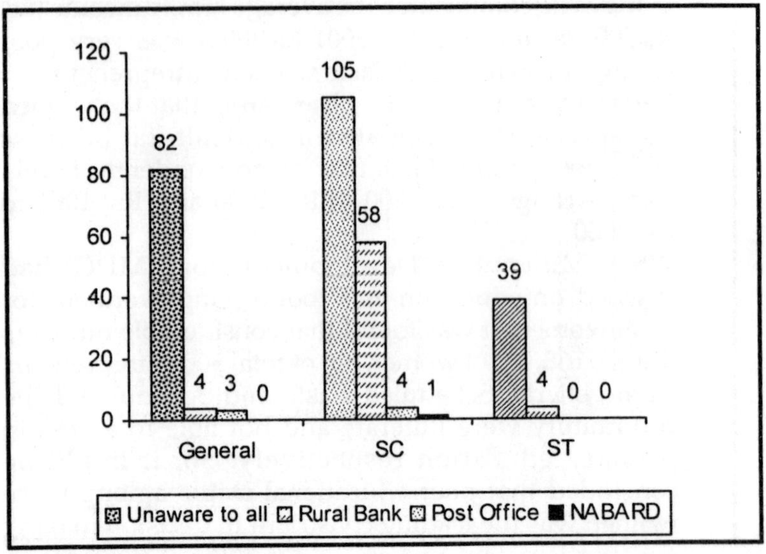

It reveals that the majority of women (226) were completely unaware about formal credit sources/institutions among which 82, 105 and 39 were from General, SC and ST population respectively. A few women (66) out of the total respondents including all three sections were having access to rural bank. Very few heard of post office and NABARD.

Table 13.7 : Caste and awareness on government schemes and entrepreneurship programme

Awareness on government schemes entrepreneurship programmes	*Caste*			*Total*
	General	*SC*	*ST*	
Unaware about government schemes	84	121	41	246
SGSY	5	43	1	49
PMJY	—	2	1	3
Other	—	2	—	2
Total	89	168	43	300

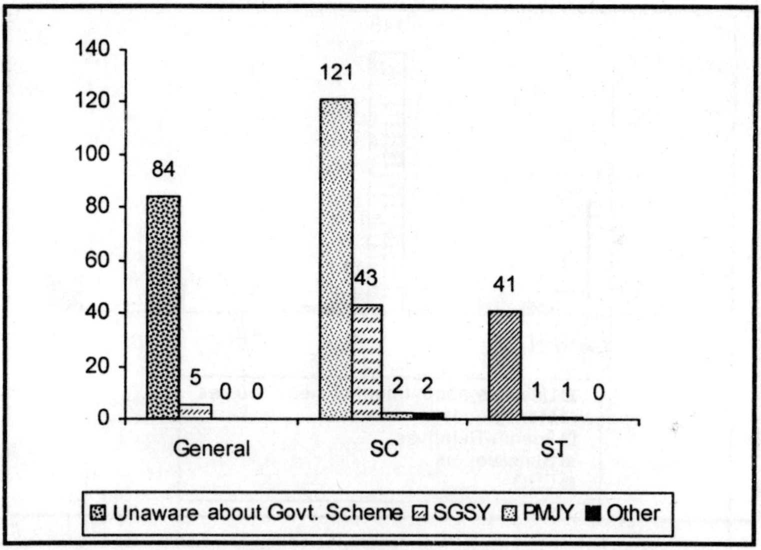

As far as women empowerment is concerned, Central and State Governments have already introduced several schemes and entrepreneurship programmes mainly for the rural women for their economic self-reliance. In this regard Table 13.7 reflects that the majority of the women community (246) was still unaware about any said scheme or programme irrespective of the caste they belong to. Very few women from all the three sections knew some of the programmes very sporadically not concretely.

Table 13.8 : Caste and awareness on different informal credit sources

Informal credit sources	*Caste*			*Total*
	General	*SC*	*ST*	
Unawareness	2	2	—	4
Moneylenders	64	149	16	229
Friends/Relatives	14	11	4	29
Shopkeepers	8	4	1	13
CBO	1	2	22	25
Total	89	168	43	300

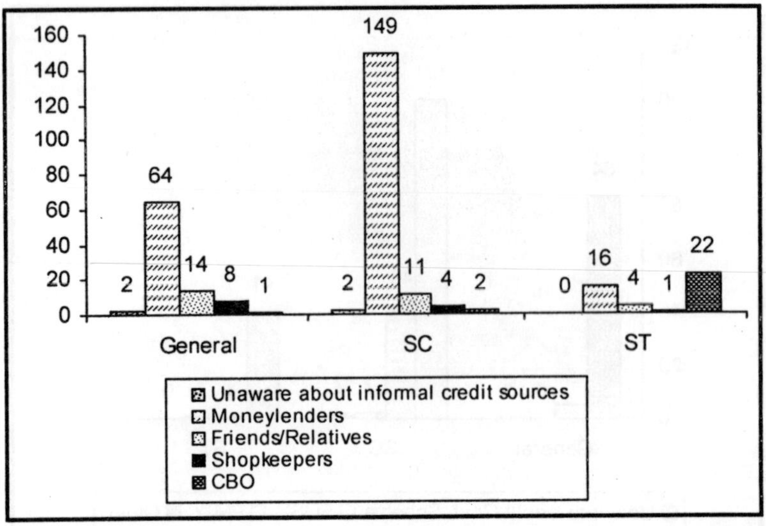

Altogether 229 women entrepreneurs considered moneylenders as the most significant informal credit sources for their agricultural business. Of course, there were some women entrepreneurs who received credit from friends/ relatives, shopkeepers and CBO as informal credit sources as well. This was also evident that majority of women (228) preferred informal credit sources as their first choice against formal credit sources and among which 107, 82 and 39 entrepreneurs were from SC, General and ST community.

Table 13.9 : Reasons for formal credit sources

Reasons	*No. of women*	*Valid Percentage*
More flexible credit policy	17	24
No security deposit	9	13
Low rate of interest	18	25
High rate of subsidy	12	17
Enough time to repay the credit	11	15
Cooperative behaviour of the staff members	2	3
Adequate and easy information available	3	4
Total	72	100

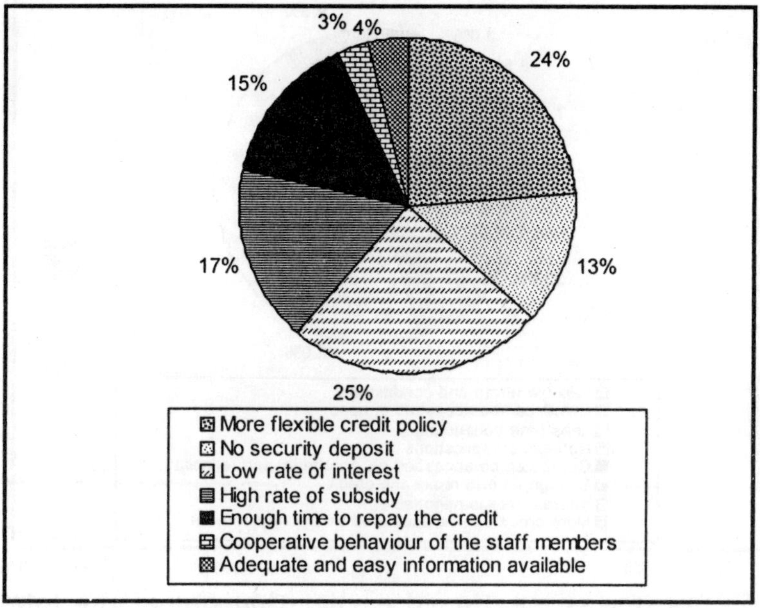

More flexible credit policy, no security deposit, low rate of interest and high rate of subsidy, adequate time for repayment etc. were some of the reasons stated by the women for their preference to formal credit sources. Low rate of interest was the most important because out of 72 women who were inclined to formal credit, among which 18 (25%) were satisfied with the low rate of interest.

Table 13.10 : Reasons for informal credit sources

Reasons	*No of women*	*Percentage*
Flexible terms and conditions	20	9
Credit can be accessed in need	54	24
Less time consuming	50	22
No legal complications	53	23
Credit can be accessed on good faith and reliability	17	7
Enough time to repay the credit	15	6.5
Interest rate is negotiable	7	#
More credit can be accessed as per requirement	12	5.5
Total	228	100%

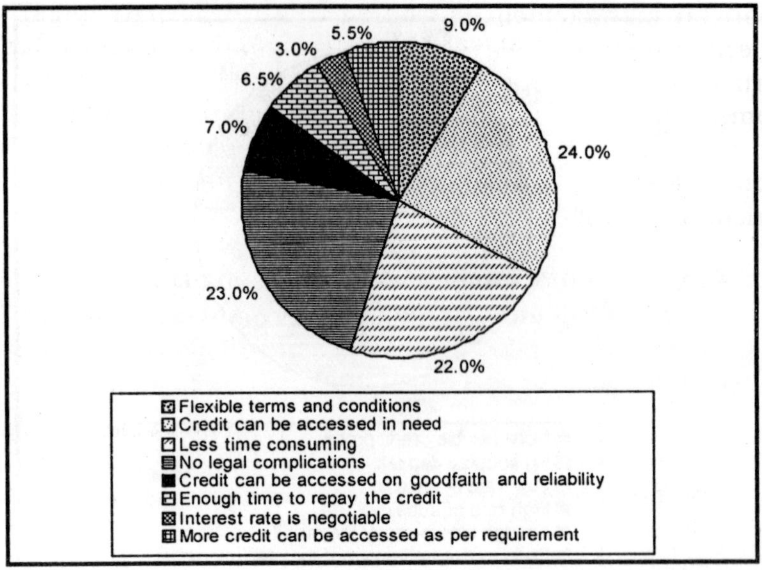

As it was mentioned earlier that out of the total respondents 228 were in favour of informal credit sources. Some of the crucial reasons they explained were—no legal problem, adequate time for repayment, negotiable rate of interest, less time consuming process etc. Again, of course, out of these reasons—accessibility of credit in time (24%), quicker processing (22%) and devoid of legal complexities (23%) were most important as stated by the women entrepreneurs.

Synoptic analysis

Agriculture is becoming progressively feminized. Many rural women engaged in family farms are still reported as economically not active. Nonetheless, even according to Census of India, the proportion of female labour force in agriculture has increased between 1971 and 2001. Although women contribute substantially to agriculture both in terms of labour input and decision making—women's access to land and financial management is limited due to the patrilineal inheritance system. Nevertheless, the rural agriculture is partially dependent on women due to male migration, and women operate most of the land and agricultural business. So, the research team cultivated collateral perceptions of 300 women entrepreneurs regarding credit needs for their agricultural business.

- A large proportion of women entrepreneurs (i.e. 246) were still unaware of government schemes or entrepreneurship programmes in relation to credit promotion for small scale business.
- The most frightening trend was that 229 women entrepreneurs considered local moneylenders as important informal credit source for their agricultural business.
- Comparative preferential trend showed that 228 rural women entrepreneurs intended to lend credit from informal credit sources and remaining 72 women were in favour of formal credit sources.
- The remarkable feature was that 226 women entrepreneurs were not aware of formal credit system.
- Those women entrepreneurs who have strong adherence to informal credit group explicitly pointed out the prime benefits such as no legal formalities, negotiable interest and credit access on business requirement, faith and reliability.
- In case of formal credit system, the women entrepreneurs got the benefits of flexible credit policy, easy interest rate and subsidies, proper and adequate information dissemination and behavioural communication and considerable time for credit repayment.

Preferential Credit Market for Rural Women Operated Agricultural Enterprises

Table 13.11 : Creditable choice of agricultural trade for small scale business

Choice of the respondents	*Frequency*	*Percentage*
Potato and onion	85	28.30
Cauliflower and cabbage	2	.70
Plantation of mustard seeds	3	1.00
Mushroom	2	.70
Green vegetables	57	19.00
Rice and wheat	150	50.00
Sugarcane	1	.30
Total	300	100

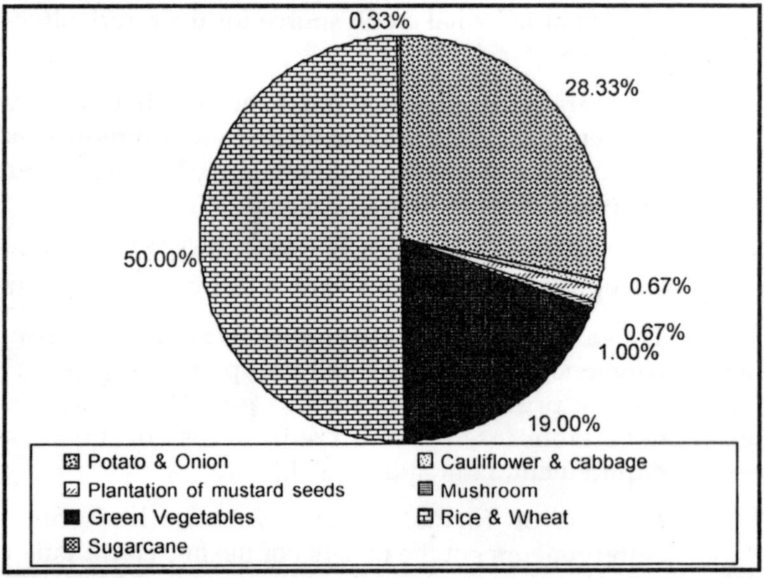

Table 13.11 clearly depicts that the majority of the women entrepreneurs, i.e. 150 perceived rice and wheat as their creditable choice for business. Also a considerable number (i.e. 85 and 57) of women perceived potato and onion as well as green vegetables as their choice for business. Whereas only

a few women members had given their liking for creditable business on cauliflower, cabbage, mustard seeds etc.

The point which is very striking in the parlance of this discussion that an attempt was also made here to verify whether the women entrepreneurs accessed information from government officials on agricultural schemes, availability of credit facility and market analysis for their desired business. The outcome was that 55 per cent didn't approach for information access and remaining 45 per cent approached and among which 42 women got the proper information and the rest were unable to get any sort of idea.

Observation and analysis

The rural financial market is composed of various distinct sub-sectors: a formal segment and various segments of an informal market. In rural West Bengal, formal lenders comprise credit and saving schemes of rural banks or substitute institutions. Formal lenders are institutions regulated by the government and banking system, whereas informal lenders are operating beyond the regulatory framework of the financial system. The informal sector is highly heterogeneous with respect to the type of relationship between borrower and lender, such as social cohesion or the existence of an interlinked transaction. When social cohesion is taken as stratifying criteria, informal credit lenders can be grouped into two segments. The first segment consists of moneylenders, relatives, friends, and to a lesser extent, informal self-help groups that provide the bulk of short-term informal credit. All other informal lenders have a more socially distant relationship with their borrowers, and frequently provide credit linked with transactions in commodity. These three segments of the rural financial market provide credit services that differ from each other with respect to many product characteristics such as average duration and amount of credit, its use, and the interest rates and transaction costs. Economists have long recognized the uniqueness of credit contracts in rural financial markets. This characteristic implies limited substitutability of credit from different market segments and limited competition between the segments. However, as empirical analysis frequently assumes that the formal sector is the cheapest source of credit and that it fulfils the credit demand, whereas the informal sector does not fulfil the credit demand and satisfies any spillover demand at varying interest rates.

Considering the significance of formal and informal credit market for promotion of agricultural business among the rural women entrepreneurs, it is needless to say that they need subsequent schematic and credit based information as well as agricultural extension services to identify creditable and marketable trade for their micro business. Though the present trend has clearly shown that informal sector is still preferable for women because it reached nearly three times as many women as the formal sector.

As it was empirically proved on several occasions that rural women have significant contribution in agricultural production. On the basis of this view, it had found that majority of rural women preferred rice, wheat, potato, onion and other green vegetables as common trade for their agricultural business because of stable seasonal production and market demand. So, rural women always intended to lend credit for these essential agricultural commodities to gain subsequent profit and to play an important role in demand and supply process.

Determinants of Women Entrepreneur's Participation and Choice of Credit Sources for Agricultural Business

Justifying the role of formal credit institutions, the research team tried to explore the types of technical and supportive services received by the women entrepreneurs for their agricultural business. It was found that 48 numbers of women received the required support and of which 29 women (60%) received training regarding the technicalities involved in starting agricultural business (Table 13.12).

Table 13.12: Types of technical and supportive services received from formal credit institutions

Types of technical and supportive services	*No.of respondents*	*Valid Percentage*
Trade based knowledge and technical information	6	13
Training to start preferred agricultural business	29	60
Incessant technical expertise support	5	10
Up-to-date credit market information	7	15
Information and accessibility for market end produces	1	2
Total	48	100

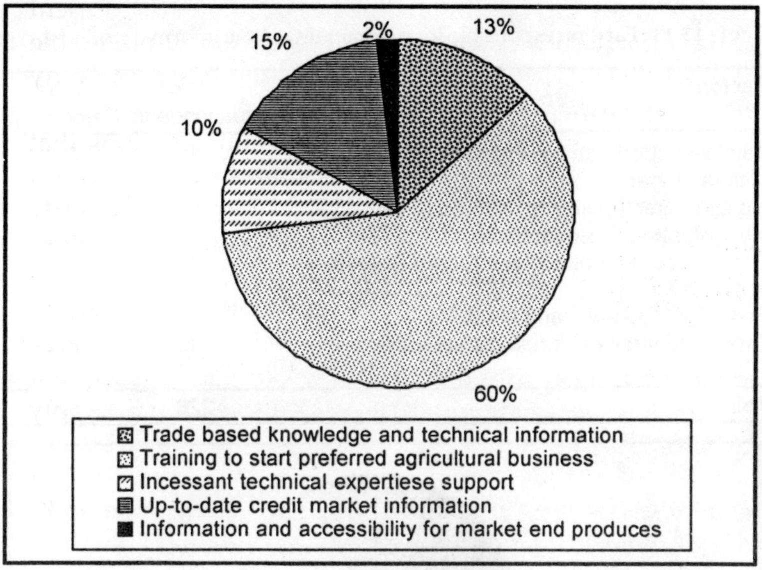

In connection with the earlier discussion, the pie diagram clearly speaks of that 82 per cent women entrepreneurs didn't access any motivational support from formal credit institutions in terms of rural credit meeting or relationship campaign. Whereas only 18 per cent among them availed such facility directly when they approached to formal credit institutions.

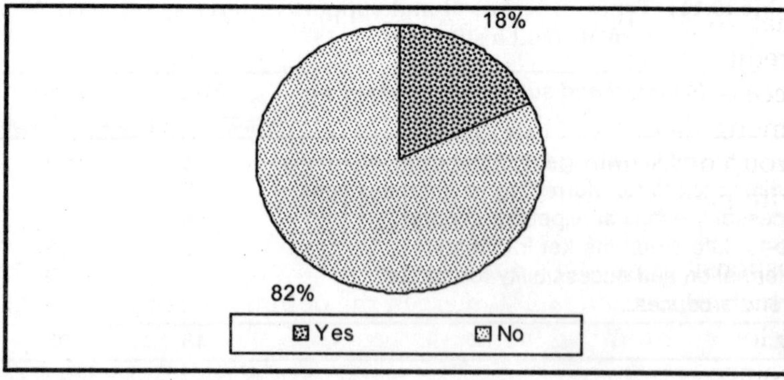

Table 13.13 : Factors responsible for participating in the informal credit market

Factors	*No.of respondents*	*Valid Percentage*
Family support can be accessed at the time of credit	19	8.3
No strict credit policy is followed	66	28.9
Rate of interest is negotiable	41	18.0
Credit environment is much more acceptable by the family	47	20.6
Based on goodfaith and reliability	40	17.5
Credit requirement is fulfilled appropriately as per need	15	6.6
Total	228	100

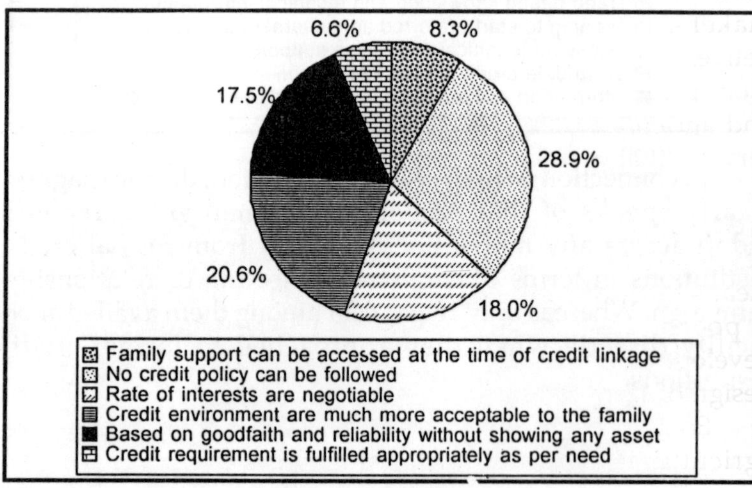

In the process of conducting the study, it was realized that 76 per cent women entrepreneurs were able to operate credit market more flexibly because this section preferred to access credit from informal sources. Whereas, 24 per cent among them were not able to operate smoothly because this group of women had access to credit from formal institutions with plenty of stringent rules and regulations.

Table 13.13 and the pie chart show the different factors responsible for participating in the informal credit market of which 19 women (8.3%) were in the opinion of family support followed by other factors as reported. The majority of the women entrepreneurs (28.9%) were found to be happy because of no such strict credit policy was followed during the disbursement of loan.

Observation

As the FAO (Food and Agricultural Organization) studies demonstrate that while women in most developing countries are the mainstay of agricultural sectors, the farm labour force and food systems (and day-to-day family subsistence), they have been the last to benefit from or in some cases have been negatively affected by prevailing economic growth and development processes. Gender bias and gender blindness persist: farmers are still generally perceived as 'male' by policy-makers, development planners and agricultural service deliverers. For this reason, women find it more difficult than men to gain access to valuable resources such as land, credit and agricultural inputs, technology, extension, training and services that would enhance their production capacity.

Despite the fact that women are the world's principal food producers and providers, they remain 'invisible' partners in development. A lack of available gender disaggregated data means that women's contribution to agriculture in particular is poorly understood and their specific needs ignored in development planning. This extends to matters as basic as the design of farm tools.

So, the above empirical statement has shown the need of agricultural extension programmes for the rural women entrepreneurs who might ensure that information on new technologies, plant varieties and cultural practices would reach to them. However, the result has shown that only 53 women entrepreneurs out of 300 numbers reached to formal credit institutions because still the common practice to direct extension and training services are primarily towards men entrepreneurs. A recent FAO survey showed that female farmers receive only five per cent of all agricultural extension services worldwide and that only 15 per cent of the world's extension agents are women.

Credit and capital are basic requisites to increase agricultural production. Therefore, these women entrepreneurs are needed short-term credit to buy improved seeds, fertilizers, insecticides and herbicides and to hire farm labourers to work in the fields and help with post-harvest operations. Also they need long-term credit to invest in more efficient technologies—irrigation, labour-saving tools and implements and transport—and to set up new enterprises if conditions are favourable. Yet, throughout the study area, and even in cases where they are acting as heads of their household, it has been observed that these women entrepreneurs were denied full legal status that would grant them credit from formal credit sources. This limited—and often complete lack of—access to rural financial services had hampered women's efforts to improve or expand their agricultural business so as to earn cash income.

Although these women entrepreneurs have faced problems in acquiring credit mainly from formal credit institutions, the situation facing women was more serious because they lack collateral. Whereas men were the legally recognized landowners, it was they who provided the collateral. When they migrated to towns and cities, leaving women to manage the household farm, the problem is clearly compounded. A numbe: of factors determined the reluctance of formal credit institutions to lend to those women entrepreneurs:

- They were found as inexperienced borrowers—both a cause and a consequence of the problem;

- They usually requested small credit;
- They were not normally involved in the development and extension programmes or structures that act as an interface with lending institutions;
- As found earlier that illiteracy means that many were often incapable of following application procedures.
- Their limited participation in male-dominated agricultural business and credit market reduced the likelihood of their receiving credit when it had allocated.

Economic Impact of Credit Access on Rural Women Operated Agricultural Business

Table 13.14: Credit supported agricultural enterprise and economic self-reliance

Responses	*Frequency*	*Percentage*
Yes	277	92.3
No	23	7.7
Total	300	100.0

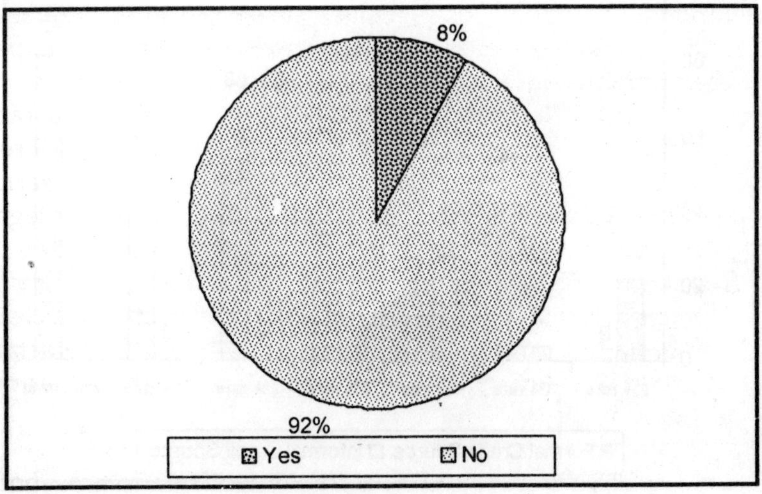

It was empirically proved by the Grameen Bank of Bangladesh that rural women would be socially and economically empowered if viable and feasible credit opportunities rendered to them. In the view of this, it was an attempt to enumerate whether the credit mechanism helped women agricultural enterprises for their economic self-reliance. Table 13.14 projects that 92.3 per cent women asserted that the different credit sources certainly had a huge impact on their socio-economic life contrary to only 7.7 per cent responded negatively. So it can be concluded that credit opportunities are acting as a catalyst towards the empowerment of rural women.

Table 13.15 : Interest rate and formal and informal credit sources

Credit sources	*Fixed rate of interest for accessing credit*							*Total*	*%*
	2%	*3%*	*4%*	*5%*	*6%*	*7%*	*7% >*		
Formal	22	—	22	9	—	—	—	53	17.6%
Informal	—	4	12	21	68	60	82	247	82.4%
Total	22	4	34	30	68	60	82	300	100.0%

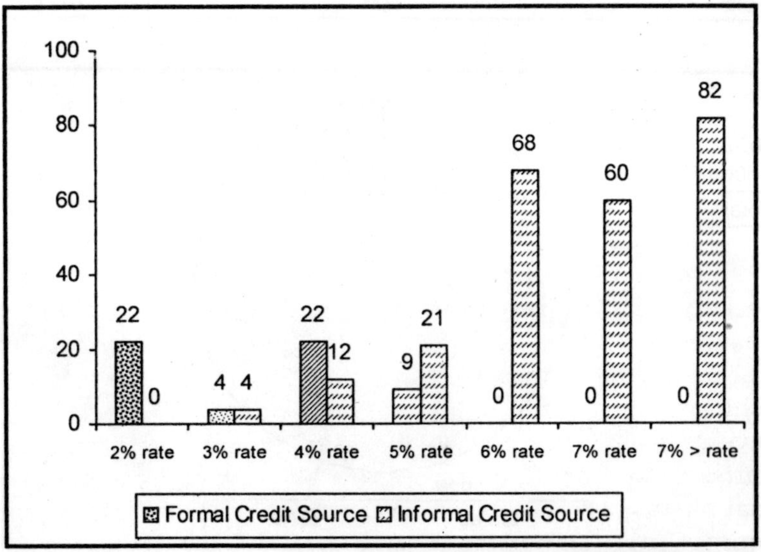

Empirical evidence stated earlier that flexible rate of interest lead to more credit accessibility and consequently more profit in business as well. Considering this fact an enumeration of variations of rate of interest and credit sources have been done. It is clearly mentioned in Table 13.15 that 247 (82.33%) respondents had access to informal credit with a high rate of interest and, i.e. 7 per cent and above. Only 53 (17.67%) availed credit from formal credit institutions with a low rate of interest ranging from 2 per cent to 5 per cent.

On gleaning the facts from the table it is evident that the rate of interest charged by informal credit institutions is much higher than formal credit sources. Due to the dominance of informal sources, there is rampant exploitation of illiterate and ignorant women; and formal credit institutions are unable to break this vicious circle due to their lack of dissemination of information and are not being able to motivate people.

Table 13.16 : Amount of credit and rate of interest

Amount of credit	*Rate of interest*							*Total*
	2%	3%	4%	5%	6%	7%	7%.	
Rs.<5000	44	4	24	43	34	58	81	288
Rs.5000-10000	—	—	—	4	4	2	1	11
Rs.10000-15000	—	—	—	1	—	—	—	1
Total	44	4	24	48	38	60	82	300

Table 13.16 indicates that the majority of the credit seekers (96%) took credit of less than Rs. 5000 and the interest charged varies from 2-7 per cent of which 81 per cent women fall under the category of more than 7 per cent interest rate which is 27.33 per cent of total respondents. The data also reveals that the prevalent rate of interest in the credit market varies from 7 per cent and above. As it is mentioned earlier that the majority of women access credit from informal credit sources, so it can be stated that the rate of interest charged is mostly based on wish of the informal credit sources. The women entrepreneurs are prepared to take credit at any rate

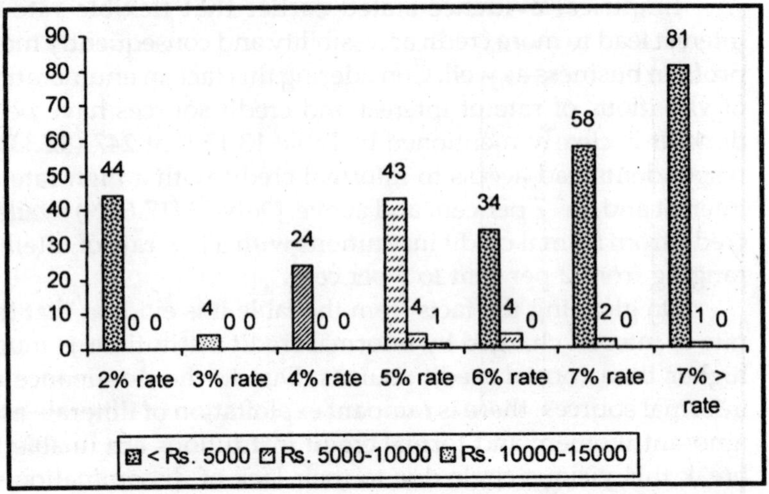

of interest. Due to the prevalence of informal credit sources there is no uniformity in the rate of interest charged.

Table 13.17 : Sources of credit and rate of profit

Sources of credit	*Amount of profit*			*Total*
	Rs.<2000	*Rs.2000-3000*	*Rs.3000-4000*	
Formal	32	11	10	53
Informal	184	44	19	247
Total	216	55	29	300

Before we move on to explain the rate of profit, let us view a couple of important and relevant issues. It was observed that the majority of women (92%) had access credit to rural bank and a very few number took credit from NABARD or Block authorities as far as formal credit sources are concerned. In terms of informal credit 77.3 per cent women took credit from moneylenders followed by 16.6 per cent, 4.5 per cent and 1.6 per cent of women took it from friends/relatives, shopkeepers/traders and NGO/CBO respectively.

In every government headed scheme, subsidized credit facilities are extended to the poorer section in rural areas with

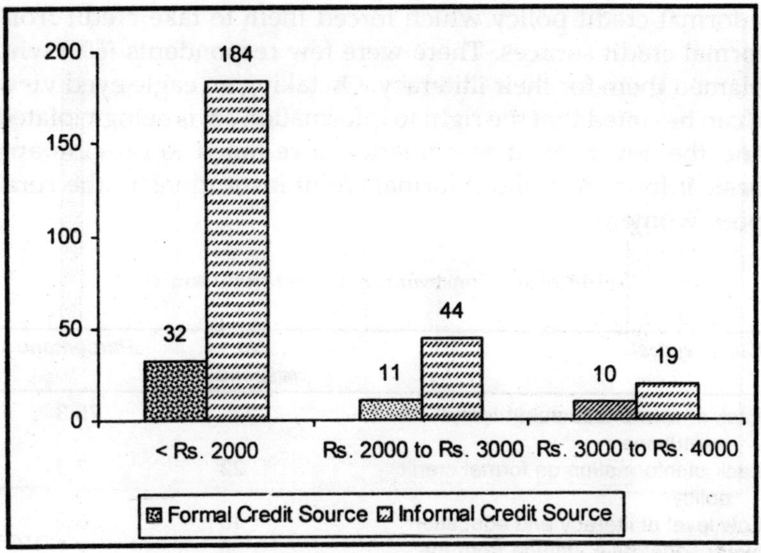

special thrust on empowering the women by providing opportunities for easy access to credit either individually or in group for agricultural business. The business size may be small or big. The point is to see that in spite of subsidized/flexible credit either from formal or informal sources, the amount of profit they get out of the credit facilities rendered to them is not very encouraging. It was realized that out of the total respondents 216 (72%) asserted that they earn a profit (apart from credit amount) less than Rs. 2000. On the other hand 55 women (18.33%) had profit range of Rs. 2000-3000. The maximum profit was derived by only a meagre 29 (9.67%) respondents ranging between Rs. 3000-4000.

Perception of Rural Women Entrepreneurs on Associated Problems in Credit Market

Table 13.18 explores the constraints behind not availing credit from formal credit sources. Out of the total 300 respondents 226 respondents, i.e. 75.3 per cent asserted that they were totally unaware about formal credit institution. Whereas 22 respondents, i.e. 7.3 per cent didn't have any information about informal credit policy which forced them to take credit from formal credit sources. There were few respondents (6%) who blamed them for their illiteracy. On taking an eagle eyed view it can be stated that the right to information act is being violated and the government machineries have failed to provide any basic information about formal credit institutions to the rural poor women.

Table 13.18 : Constraints in formal credit sources

Constraint(s)	*No. of respondents*	*Percentage*
Lack of awareness about formal credit institutions	226	75.3
Lack of information on formal credit policy	22	7.3
Low level of literacy and education	18	6.0
Non-cooperative attitude from the official in formal credit institutions	8	2.7
A sense of hesitance in approaching to formal credit institute	16	5.3
Time consuming process	10	3.3
Total	300	100

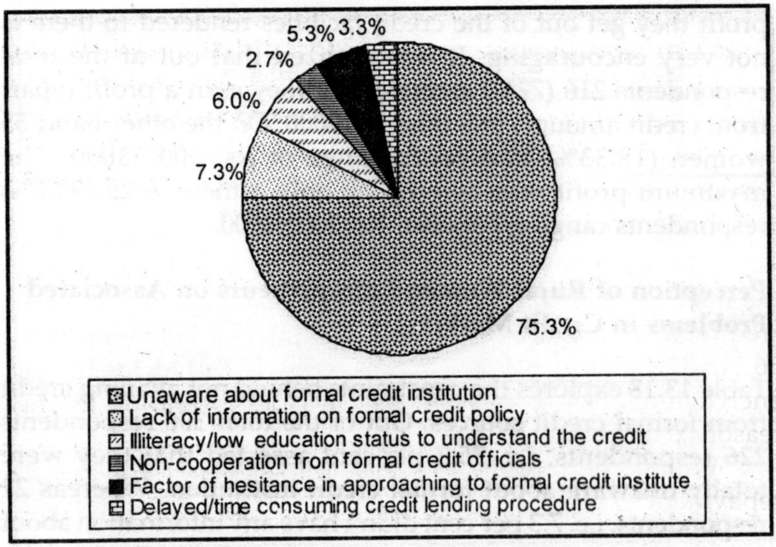

Table 13.19 : Constraints in informal credit sources

Constraint(s)	*No. of respondents*	*Percentage*
No opinion	16	5.3
Need guarantor for credit	20	6.7
Exorbitant rate of interest	82	27.3
Reasonable margin of profit amount paid for repayment	43	14.3
Low level of education	46	15.3
Illegal encroachment of assets or force used	56	18.7
No legal agreement	37	12.3
Total	300	100

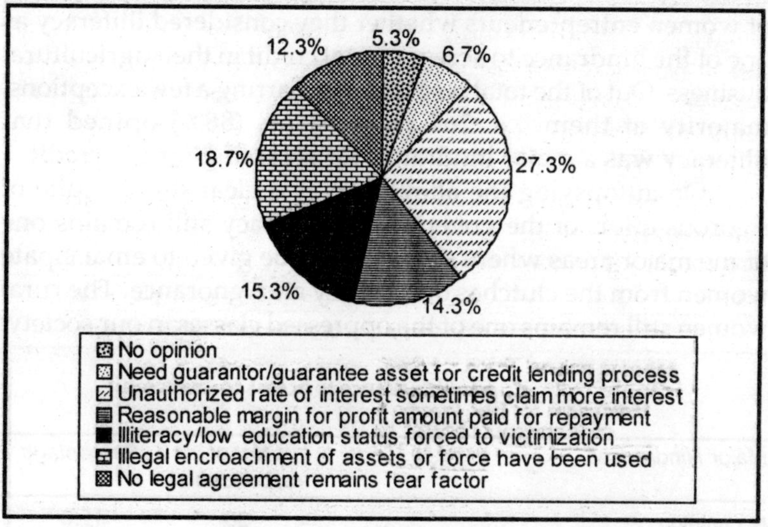

It is clearly mentioned that out of the total 300 respondents 82 (27.3%) of them who consist the majority reported to us that the main impediment for not accessing credit from informal credit sources was unauthorized rate of interest. Following this, 56 (18.7%) and 46 (15.3%) respondents reported for illegal encroachment of assets and low level of education as the reasons/constraints for informal credit.

Women entrepreneurs face quite a lot of problems in repayment of loan in both the cases—formal and informal.

Majority of the women were of the opinion that the time bound credit repayment is the biggest problem they face in the case of formal credit sources. While in the case of informal credit sources—high rate of interest, forceful repayment, and seize of household assets by the moneylenders—are the important issues for women.

Perception of Rural Women Entrepreneurs on Associated Factors in Credit Access

As the national policy of women states that basic literacy and education are essential ingredients for women empowerment. In the light of the above, it was an attempt to seek the opinion of women entrepreneurs whether they considered illiteracy as one of the hindrance to access formal credit in their agricultural business. Out of the total respondents, barring a few exceptions, majority of them, i.e. 264 respondents (88%) opined that illiteracy was a major hindrance for accessing formal credit.

On autopsying the above fact, it is clear that in spite of rigorous effort of the government, illiteracy still remains one of the major areas where stress should be given to emancipate women from the clutches of illiteracy and ignorance. The rural women still remains one of the oppressed classes in our society.

Table 13.20 : Type of hindrance to access formal credit

Major Hindrances	*No. of respondents*	*Percentage*
No opinion	36	12.0
Unable to interact with formal credit institutions	138	46.0
Elements of fear to ask for credit from formal institutions	75	25.0
Formal credit institutions are less interested to give credit	49	16.3
Easy information is not available to understand formal credit system	2	.7
Total	300	100.0

The research team liked to see the multiple opinions of women entrepreneurs on type of hindrances they face to access formal credit. Table 13.20 gives us a very distinctive feature about the various opinions of the women entrepreneurs and among which inability to interact with formal credit institutions and interplay of elements of fear to move forward for accessing credit were the major hindrance as reported by the respondents.

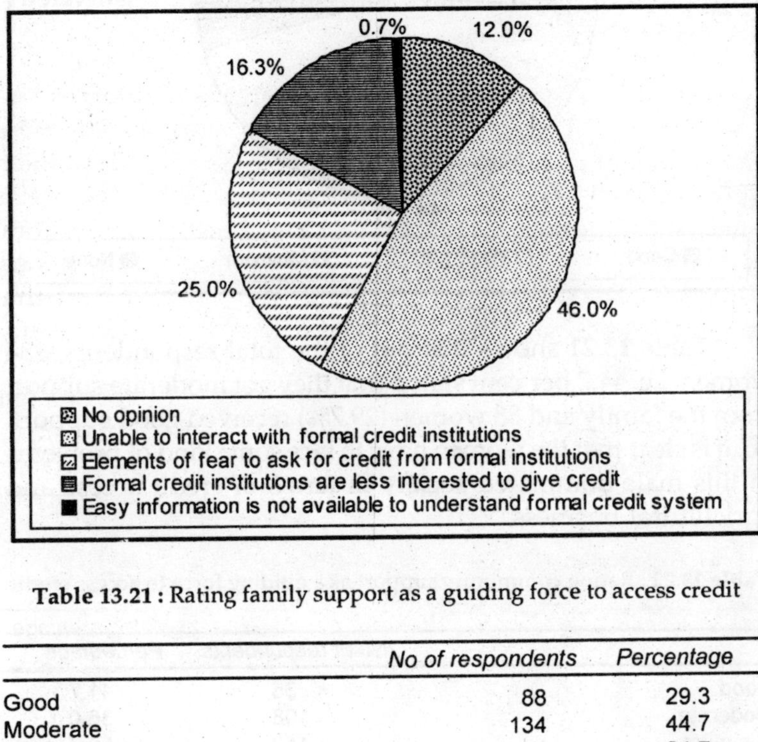

Table 13.21 : Rating family support as a guiding force to access credit

	No of respondents	*Percentage*
Good	88	29.3
Moderate	134	44.7
Minimum	74	24.7
None	4	1.3
Total	300	100

An attempt (Table 13.21) has been made by the research team to rate the family support of the women entrepreneurs as a guiding force to credit access and entering into agricultural business.

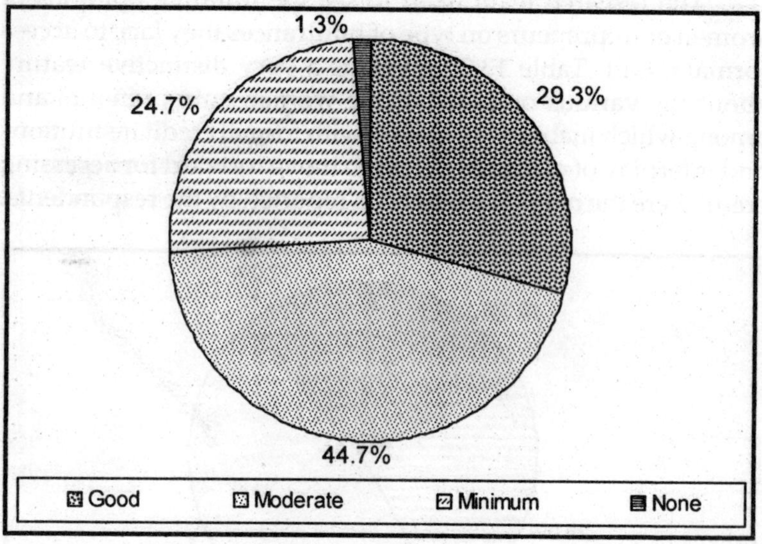

Table 13.21 shows that out of the total respondents, 134 women, i.e. 44.7 per cent stated that they got moderate support from the family and 88 women (29.7%) received good support. So, it is clear that the women have to face some kind of problems in this male-dominated society in terms of credit access and agricultural business.

Table 13.22 : Rating community support as a guiding force to access credit

	No of respondents	*Percentage*
Good	35	11.7
Moderate	108	36.0
Minimum	152	50.7
None	5	1.7
Total	300	100.0

Table 13.22 enumerates the point that the women entrepreneurs do not get adequate support from the community for carrying out their agri-based business. If we take a close look, it is evident that 50.7 per cent women viewed that they got minimum support from the community. Whereas

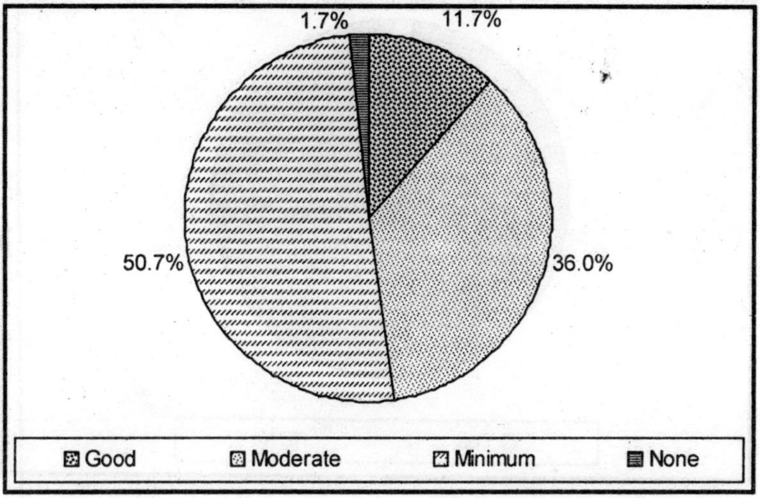

36 per cent of them asserted that they got moderate support and on the other hand only 11.7 per cent reported about good support. Taking all the facts into account it can be stated that the women entrepreneurs have to encounter some problems to start their own agri-based business because of loose community back up.

The important dimension of the study which came out after having discussion with the various women groups that the presence of credit access acts as a tool for women empowerment. But interestingly, 59 women (19.7%) out of our total respondents opined negatively. Due to the availability and access of various credit sources women are able to carry out their agricultural business and through this they gain economic self-reliance and sustainability.

Table 13.23 : Technical expertise and understanding credit policy

	No of respondents	*Percentage*
Yes	294	98.0
No	6	2.0
Total	300	100.0

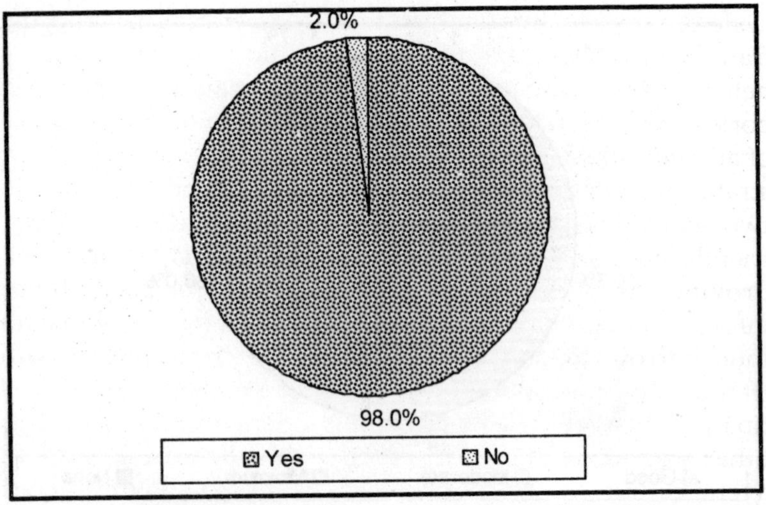

As the national agricultural policy and programmes stated that extension services are available for rural women and farmers group in terms of information, training, off and on field demonstration for improvement of agricultural production and business. Therefore, the research team took the opinion from the women whether technical expertise has anything to do to understand the formal credit policy and associated issues. Out of the total 300 respondents, i.e. 98 per cent (Table 13.23) stated in favour of technical expertise which would really benefit them. The formal credit institutions do not have the adequate infrastructure that would guide the women entrepreneurs for better understanding of the credit policy. If this problem is taken care of the formal credit institutions would enjoy more popularity among the rural women.

Observation

The rural financial market is composed of various distinct subsectors: a formal segment and various segments of an informal market. In rural West Bengal, formal lenders comprise credit and savings schemes by the government and banking system, whereas informal lenders are operating beyond the framework of the financial system. The informal sector is highly heterogeneous with respect to the type of relationship between borrower and lender; such as social cohesion or the existence of an interlinked transaction. When social cohesion is taken as stratifying criteria, informal credit lenders can be grouped into two segments. The first segment is moneylenders, relatives, friends, and, to a lesser extent, informal self-help groups that provide the bulk of short-term informal credit. All other informal lenders have a more socially distant relationship with their borrowers, and frequently provide credit linked with transactions in commodity. These three segments of the rural financial market provide credit services that differ from each other with respect to many product characteristics such as average duration and amount of credit, its use, and the interest rates and transaction costs. Economists have long recognized the uniqueness of credit contracts in rural financial markets. This characteristic implies limited substitutability of credit from different market segments and limited competition between the segments. However, as empirical analysis, frequently assumes that the formal sector is the cheapest source of credit and that it fulfils the credit demand, whereas the informal sector does not fulfil the credit demand and satisfies any spillover demand at varying interest rates.

Considering the significance of formal and informal credit market for promotion of agricultural business among the rural entrepreneurs, it is needless to say that they need subsequent schematic and credit based information as well as agricultural extension services to identify credible and marketable trade for their micro business. Though the present trend analysis has clearly shown that informal sectors were still preferable to women because it reached nearly three times as many women as the formal sector.

As it was empirically proved that rural women have significant contribution in agricultural production. It was also found that majority of rural women preferred rice, wheat, potato, onion, and other green vegetables as common trade for their agricultural business because of stable seasonal production and market demand. So, rural women entrepreneurs always intended to lend credit for these essential agricultural commodities to gain subsequent profit and to play important role in demand and supply process.

SUGGESTED READINGS

1. Farrington, S. (2007); "Welfare and Economic Growth in India (1914-2004)"; *Women Development*, 14 (9): 1151-1160.
2. Kabeer, T. (2005); *Rethinking Globalization—Critical Issues and Policy Choices;* Zed Books, New York.
3. Pareek, L.M.L., (1964); *Development of Microeconomics;* Oxford University Press, Oxford.
4. Simanowitz, P. (2007); "A Model of Accumulation", in *Essays on the Theory of Economic Growth*, Macmillan, London.
5. *World Bank Report*, 2005.
6. *World Bank Report*, 2007.
7. Cheston, L. (2008); *Growth and Development with Special Reference to Developing Countries*, London, Macmillan.
8. Rot, L. and Tisdell, A. (2009); *Nonlinear Effects of Inflation on Economic Growth*; IMF Staff Papers 43, pp. 199-215.
9. Deaton, A. (2008); "Is World Poverty Falling?"; *Finance and Development* 39, 4-7.

14

Child Health Care Services and Social Work Intervention

A Linkage—Indian Scenario

The United Nations declared 1979 as the International Year of the Child (IYC). Dr. Mahler, Director General of WHO in a special message on World Health Day that year, drew attention to the fact that 12 million (mostly in developing countries) of the 125 million children born in 1978, would probably not live to see their first birthday. The majority of the 1220 million children living in the developing countries suffer as a result of malnutrition, infections, poor housing, lack of safe drinking water and sanitation. Dr. Mahler's message concluded with the hope that the activities generated by the IYC and World Health Day would create a socio-political climate of urgency in regard to the needs and problems of today's children and lay the groundwork for continuing and systematic action focusing on the health and well-being of the child.

Since then, allover the world, the perspective on health have undergone a revolutionary change contrary to the old paradigm of economic growth in which health was viewed as an item of consumption, health is now recognized as a critical commodity of investment for development. In the development approach (Narayana, 2004), improvement in health status is viewed primarily as a product of socio-economic development. By definition, development implies improved nutrition, hygienic living and working conditions, fall of crude birth rate and infant mortality rate, conducive ante-natal and post-natal care, family care, family planning and re-productive health, greater awareness of health problems, and wider accessibility to health care services which all have a favourable effect on the health status of the people. Improvement in health status as well as health care are treated as integrated components of the development process. Since health is a product of multivariable production process, impact of state intervention on health status on its overall socio-economic policies (S. Joshi, 1999).

The UNICEF Health Strategy, revised in 1995, continues the emphasis on reduction of child illness and death through such activities as immunization, breastfeeding, improved nutritional practices and sound management of illness. It also places greater stress on the protection of children in the second decade of life and on reproductive health. A sharpened focus on the needs of adolescents aligns UNICEF health policy more closely with the Conventions on the Rights of the Child and recognizes that the health, attitudes and behaviours of teenagers profoundly affect their capacities as adults.

The strategy was revised to better respond to economic, demographic and lifestyle changes affecting families throughout the developing world. The new strategy reflects the reality that, while infant and child mortality rates have fallen dramatically since the 1960s, communicable diseases such as malaria, diarrhoea, pneumonia and measles widespread. In addition, health problems related to increase in poverty, environmental hazards and risky behaviours are growing at alarming rates.

Health indeed is the basic need and a fundamental ingredient of human rights. It is a positive right which can acquire meaningful content only if the state is willing to ensure its implementation. The Constitution of India states in the Directive Principles of State Policy "The State shall regard the raising of the level of nutrition and standard of living of its people and the improvement of public health as among its primary duties" (Article 47).

At this juncture, it is imperative to bring out the significance of our focus on child health. Child health can be the greatest resource of our country. More so for a developing country like India where children form a wide base of population pyramid. In India 17 per cent of the population comprises children under 5 years and another 35 per cent in the range of 5 to 16 years.

But it is not by sheer number alone that the advocates of comprehensive health care for the child population stress their point. The most crucial period in a child's life is the first five years during which about 40 per cent of physical and 80 per cent of mental growth and development occurs.

The foundation of healthy mind and body is laid in childhood. A healthy child, to state a truism, grows into a healthy adult. Only physical, social and mental well-being can provide sufficient energy to allow people to become productive and creative. Health of our children, therefore, is of fundamental value to the nation. However, the issue of child health cannot be understood without knowing the socio-political environment in which they are raised. The roots of ill-health of children are in the social and economic structure of our society and unless these are changed children will continue to be in poor health.

Providing health care to ensure holistic development of 300 million children living in abject poverty and neglect is an enormous and challenging task. A child is exposed to many a type of deprivation right from conception stage. Disparity between the rich and poor, between the rural and urban settings, gender discrimination, variation in geographical locations, illiteracy among parents are all contributing factors in the threat to the well-being of the child. Destitution and exploitation, children of AIDS affected family also pose additional threats to child survival, growth and development.

Child health scenario and services in India

The concern for Indian people for health care and development of children goes back to time immemorial. India had an inbuilt mechanism providing health care for children through joint family system, kinship and other social institutions. In ancient and medieval period voluntary and community efforts provided main sustenance to child health services. There were some enlightened rulers who also in a limited way, promoted child welfare activities with special emphasis on health under their patronage. During the British rule voluntary effort rather than state endeavour was the main provider of child health services.

Prior to independence the social, political and economic status of people of India had degenerated to an extent that hunger and malnutrition was rampant. Primary Health Care was non-existent and a majority of the population was illiterate. The number of health personnel was inadequate. There was only one doctor for 6,000 people, one nurse for 5,000 and one midwife for more than 10,000 population. Infant mortality was high; for every one thousand children born, 162 died before the age of one year, and 40 mothers lost their lives during child birth and postpartum period. Around half of the children died before the age of five years.

To add with, the mortality rate of children under five which is the best indicator of child health of any country continues to be high. True the rate has shown a consistent decline over the years—236 (1960), 177 (1980), 126 (2006), but this decline is still very slow. If we are determined to meet the target of Infant Mortality Rate below 60 by 2011, we need to have 6.5 reduction in the 0-5 year mortality.

The mortality figures also reveal that the female child mortality rate is much higher than the male in all age groups. Out of over 15 million girls born in India every year, only 13 million live till their 15th birthday. The difference in 0-4 mortality between male and female is not so marked in urban areas but the variation is over 25 per cent in rural areas. A feature worth mentioning is the maldistribution of child health care system in India. The total expenditure in health care in cities works out to be Rs.160 per person while in the villages the estimate is only Rs.16.

Post-independence period ushered in a new era in the field of child welfare. The efforts in this field were inspired by various provisions in our Constitution regarding the need for emphasizing and improving child health. To reiterate, the

Constitution of India provides a framework within which the constitutional vision of the rights of the Indian child can be given a concrete shape. The Constitution of India postulates the goal of a Welfare State and envisages child welfare activities as an organized part of national development. Article 39 (prohibition of employment of children) ; Article 45 (provision for free and compulsory education); Article 38 (children should be given opportunities to develop in a healthy manner) have a bearing on the well-being of children.

India has the unfortunate distinction of having nearly 75 million malnourished children below the age of five years, the largest number of malnourished children in the world. Even at birth, one in every three children born in India is of low birth weight: the result of undernourishment in the womb. In the world today, only children in Bangladesh and Nepal are more malnourished than Indian children.

It was also only after independence that the foundation for a comprehensive health care system was laid and the concept of universal outreach of primary health care was evolved. There has been a considerable expansion in the health system in the Five Year Plans right from First Five Year Plan to 10th Five Year Plan. The maternal and child care too received considerable attention in planning and implementation of health services at the national level. The first three Five Year Plans (1951-1966) focused on expansion of maternity and child health services and during the Fourth Plan an intensive family planning programme was integrated with health services. Also the current plan (11th Plan) has also given much emphasis on maternal and child health as well as family planning and reproductive health. The primary health care approach aims at integrating curative, preventive, and rehabilitative services to promote health status of children. The infrastructure facilities and the network of Primary Health Centres (PHCs) set-up during different plan periods is available to a large number of families, both in the rural and urban areas, of the country.

Till today 2007, there are 20,531 PHCs and Subsidiary Health Centres, 1,30,390 sub-centres, and 1,852 community health centres in the country. At the grassroots level, there are 5,98,793 trained Birth Attendants, 4,08,790 Village Health Guides (VHGs), 2,45,405 general housing midwives, 1,32,923 Auxiliary Nurses/Midwives/Health Workers and 1,58,817 Health Visitors. Currently, the doctor population ratio varies from 1 : 820 in the Union Territory of Chandigarh to 1 : 15,631 in Uttar Pradesh. Out of 141.99 million eligible couples around 69.03 million are being protected by family planning measures.

The financial outlays under the health services have been increased over the successive five Year Plans. The total Tenth Plan investment outlay for all heads of development is Rs.1,00,000 crore out of which Rs. 3,392.9 crore is allotted for health, Rs. 3,256.3 crore for Family Welfare and Rs. 6,522.5 crore for Water Supply and Sanitation.

The Independent Commission on Health in India (ICHI) was facilitated by the Voluntary Health Association of India (VHAI) in 1995. The Commission with the help of policy-makers and distinguished personalities from the health and development sector, critically diagnosed the maladies affecting health services in the country and recommended remedial measures.

The ICHI report was very widely distributed and discussed at different fora. Active interaction between the Commission, the Planning Commission, the Prime Minister's office and the Health Ministry followed which culminated in the formation of the National Health Policy in 1999.

The Commission identified the following areas for future attention in the next millennium and among which primary health care and reproduction and child were much emphasized:

- Primary Health Care
- Medical Education
- Indian System of Medicine
- Health Sector Reform
- Reproductive and Child Health
- Private Sector in Health Care and Medical Ethics

National Population Policy, 2002 has also made a number of commitments for the twenty-first century in the area of child health keeping intact the very essence of National Health Policy.

(1) Address the unmet needs for basic reproductive and child health services, supplies and infrastructure.
(2) Reduce infant mortality rate to below 30 per cent per 1000 live births.
(3) Reduce maternal mortality rate to below 100 per 1,00,000 live births.
(4) Full coverage of registration of birth.
(5) Convergence of service delivery at village levels.
(6) Empowering women to improve health and nutrition.
(7) Decentralized planning and programme implementation along with emphasis on community participation.
(8) Integrate (Indian System of Medicine) in the provision of reproductive and child health services and in reaching out to households.
(9) Achieve universal immunization of children against all vaccine preventable diseases.
(10) Achieve 80 per cent institutional deliveries and 100 per cent deliveries by trained persons.

The latest child population in the age group of (0-6) years in India (Census, 2001) is as follows:

	Persons	*Males*	*Females*
Total	150,421,175	77,322,151	73,099,024
Urban	116,828,332	59,963,100	56,865,232
Rural	33,592,843	17,359,051	16,233,792

For the benefit of such a vast child population the National Policy for Children spells out that it shall be the policy of the State to provide adequate services to children both before and after to ensure their full physical, mental and social development. All the children in the country should enjoy optimum condition for their balanced growth.

Universal Immunization Programme (UIP) was started in India in 1985 with the objective of achieving a coverage of at least 85 per cent in respect of infants and 100 in respect of pregnant women. The Government of India had taken up "Pulse Polio Immunization"(PPI) programme as a party to the WHO's resolution of eradication of Poliomelis (Polio), a major crippling childhood diseases by the year 2000 AD. All new borns are sought to be immunized before completion of the first year of their life with BCG (tuberculosis), DPD (Diphtheria, Wooping Cough, Tetanus). Recently, vaccine against Measles, Hepatitis A, B and C, Chicken Pox, Meningitis for all children have been taken up as policy issues.

No one can claim that immunization plus Oral Rehydration Therapy (ORT) equals health for the child. But it is fair to say that progress towards universalizing of these two particular techniques is both a measure and a means of progress towards health for all. ORT is a 100 per cent centrally sponsored scheme with the objective of reducing mortality amongst children below five years of age by promoting ORT. Studies reveal, that 90 per cent of the children suffering from diarrhoea can be managed successfully at home by mothers by administering home-made fluids (combination of water, salt and sugar) available at home at the onset of diarrhoea. Only 10 per cent of the cases need to report to the health facilities and only one per cent out of these requires intravenous fluids. A little over a decade ago, ORT, the low-cost life saving method of preventing and treating dehydration caused by diarrhoeal diseases, was hardly known to the outside world. Today, it is being used by almost 40 per cent of all Indian families and saving about a million lives each year. Despite such phenomenal progress over the last two decades, 3 million succumb to diarrhoeal diseases.

Acute Respiratory Infections (ARI) are among the most common childhood illnesses in India. They continue to be the major cause of death among children under five, where in 1995 more than 1 million children died of pneumonia and a further 1.1 million from ARI compounded by other ailments: ARI/measles, 6,40,000; ARI/pertussis (whooping cough), 2,60,000; ARI/malaria, 1,90,000; and ARI/HIV, 20,000. With as many as eight episodes per child annually, ARI is also a leading cause of sickness and serious disabilities such as deafness. India has taken up a training package to teach health care workers to look into these problems. UNICEF-supported ethnographic studies have found that their own ideas about how to treat illnesses. An understanding of community perceptions is essential to the preparation of effective information and education strategies that can be adopted to a local context. Apart from many other countries, India has also started experimenting it at a large scale.

Social work in health care

In all health care settings, social workers have provided a holistic perspective on problems and situations, highlighting the social antecedents and consequences of illness and the need to deal with the larger picture along with the immediate concern. At the level of the individual's acute or chronic illness, a social worker's focus is on the patient's physical, psychosocial, and environmental health needs. In the second half of the 19th century, social workers were in the forefront of the movement for reform in labour, housing, relief, sanitation, and health care. They were acutely aware of the interdependence of all dimensions of human life. They saw how such social factors as poor housing, neighbourhoods, work conditions, family situations, and diet adversely affected health and how poor health in turn produced a host of social problems. They viewed health as more than the mere absence of illness and considered physical health as necessary for social, psychological, and economic well-being.

The recognition of the importance of health care for the total well-being of the individual and the ability of social workers to make unique contribution to patient care have resulted in health social work becoming the largest field of social work practice. According to a 1987 NASW (National Association for Social Workers) membership survey, half of NASW members work in the health care field (Social Work Speaks, 1994).

The emergence of social work roles and responsibilities and the development of appropriate knowledge and skills have been partly the result of an evolutionary process and partly the profession's reaction to the changing situation and needs of the health care system. Many factors have affected the development and practice of social work. The complexity of health care organizations with a number of variables such as "the organization's perception of social work practice; the resources of the organization; the organizational climate; the competencies of social work practitioners; administrative and interdisciplinary support" (Holosko, 2007) has resulted in the differential use of social work skills. There is also much variation in the nature and functions of various health care organizations even within each health care sector. Here, we look at child health and how social work intervention is effective.

Child health and social work knowledge and skills

In India, the professional training in social work was introduced in mid-thirties of the present century. Ever since almost all Universities have introduced professional training in social work at the Post Graduate and the Under-Graduate level.

The trained social workers have been working successfully in the various fields of social welfare. Child welfare is one of the important fields, where the trained social workers utilize their social work knowledge, skills and techniques in the implementation of family and child welfare in general and child health services in particular.

The trained social worker is armed with the basic knowledge of health and society, skills and techniques of application of various methods of social work in working with individual, group and the community.

Here an attempt has been made to explain how the various methods of social work are being used by the trained social workers in the implementation of child health services.

Social worker as a case worker and counsellor

Social case work as an important method of social work is applied in dealing with the individual in his own environment whenever he has some individual needs to be fulfilled. In this existing Indian socio-economic situation, the intervention of social case work has its own importance in maintaining individual health. The medical and psychiatric social workers, family counsellors and social engineers get in touch with individual families, try to find out their socio-economic and psychological factors that influence the utilization of the available medical care facilities in improving the health condition of their children.

Presently in India, under Integrated Child Development Services Scheme (1975-76) and National Health Programme (1983) many facilities have been provided to the children, e.g. treatment of diseases, supply of medicine, immunization services, etc. free of cost. In this situation professional social worker can play the role of a liaison between available resources and the children. A social worker by using social case work method can help particular children and family in need of these services through professional relationship.

A social worker can also play the role of family counsellor in the crisis situation of the family by dealing with the problem on scientific lines: diagnose the root causes and give socio-scientific solutions to overcome such problems. The best examples of these could be motivating the eligible couples to adopt the family planning methods, imparting knowledge about adverse effect of early marriage or late marriage, ill-effects of repeated pregnancies or abortions, on the health of the mother and child. Under such circumstances, a trained social worker as family counsellor can efficiently and effectively manage client problems by motivating temporary/permanent methods of family planning. Only by means of professional relationship, a client and health worker could be made to share and understand the very personal and intimate issues such as: the use of contraceptives, misconceptions about health, etc.

which are causing hurdles in the effective implementation of mother and child health services.

Social woker as a community liaison and a community organizer

In the twenty-first century, most hospitals and primary health care centres, will be involved in the community. This involvement may take several forms, such as (a) the creation and implementation of new hospital-based and, as well as community-based services that are needed in the community; (b) the coordination of community health and human services; and (c) collaboration with other health and human services agencies. Successful community-oriented programmes are the result of the creativity of social workers. In the next century, the hospital's community service orientation and social work's increased emphasis on the integration of micro and macro modes of practice will converge. No specific delineation should exist between micro and macro social work. Macro issues are just micro issues that have been repeated many times. The potential for social work contribution is endless.

The client and programme-related dealings, as well as other formal and informal contacts within the local professional community, create a network of relationships. Most social workers should also be the members of various coalitions and special interest groups. Hospital-based social workers should build on these existing contacts and relationships to perform functions pertaining to their community liaison and community organizational roles.

They should also recognize and address the barriers to inter-agency collaboration. The first step in addressing the problem is to initiate or renew communication. Various tools aid in accomplishing this. The tool of focus groups is quite common. Another tool is the "organizational mirror". Agencies prepare lists for each other covering strengths and weaknesses as well as an empathy list that states the perceived difficulties of the role of the other (Iles and Auluck, 2008). The next steps are to formulate mutual goals and to plan strategies for working towards those goals.

Social workers should realize that their skills and basic problem-solving expertise not only are good for micro situations but also are invaluable for their community liaison and community organizational work. Social work differs from other health professionals primarily in its acceptance of responsibility to vulnerable people (Caroff, 2007). That responsibility has meant sensitivity and empathy for and an ability to relate to and work with vulnerable populations.

Social workers may visit as a part of community organization the homes of rural/slum dwellers to find out: why are they not making use of the services available next door or within close proximity? Why are they not sending their children for immunization and periodic health check-up? Why is supplementary nutrition food not being used? Why are they ignoring their personal health and hygiene? After obtaining answers for all these questions, the social workers would be in a better position to motivate the client(s) to make use of the facilities available within the vicinity of their own homes. Thus a social worker as a community organizer may bridge the gap between welfare needs and services of the community by coordinating the needs and resources.

Social worker as a group worker

The social group work method could also be used in improving the child health services. For example a woman hesitant to discuss about her very personal health problems or the problems of her children would be encouraged to do so when she is allowed to share her problems with other women, with the similar problem. In the group living, group experience could, thus, be helpful to overcome doubts, resistance and inhibition. Thus, if a group member tells the woman in question that she is ignoring her children's health by lack of intake of nutritious food and lack of care during pre- and post-natal period, she is likely to be more convinced about the need for change in her beliefs and practices, than when the suggestions are made by the health worker at one-to-one relationship.

The group work principles and skills are very much essential in the field of child health services, particularly in health and nutrition education and motivation programmes. Further the social workers can organize and train the women folk in organizing self-help group in helping each other with their problems relating to health and well-being in a given locality/settlement.

The professional social worker can also avail the opportunity to impart knowledge to entire group about new skill or provide useful suggestions which may serve the common needs of the whole group. In the group, the phenomenon of identification also comes into play whereby one member learns from the example set by other members. The group situation provides opportunity for self-evaluation, self-perception, recognition, ventilation of feelings and to accept a new idea in a free atmosphere, as the group members share the feelings of oneness, and common interest. Thus, the phenomenon of group pressure and group contagion may be successfully utilized by the social group worker to achieve the goal of child health services.

Social worker as a collaborator and a consultant

In the twenty-first century, teamwork will be the hallmark of child health care. A more holistic view of the patient and patient problems, the need to relate health care to the patient's quality of life, ethical issues raised by complex medical technology, and the necessity for coexistence among many diverse professionals will highlight the importance of collaboration. Collaboration is the best type of teamwork—working together in a joint venture. Collaborative teamwork requires communication, cooperation, and coordination. The major components of teamwork, can be improved and enhanced. These are facilitated by (a) clear common purpose, goals, and approach; (b) an understanding of the roles, functions, and responsibilities of all members; and (c) continuous team-building efforts directed both at monitoring team development and seeking organizational support.

Social workers as coordinators should remember the following for their effective service delivery system:

(1) Apply the problem-solving approach, which social workers are so well versed in, to teamwork.
(2) Be aware of the barriers to teamwork and consciously work on removing or reducing them.
(3) Work on changing the "bureaucracy of the mind" by becoming non-threatening teachers of other professionals.
(4) Attend to the practical barriers that may be the cause or the effect of a lack of congenial environment for team meetings and deliberations.
(5) Remember that team building is a continuous process and that the relationships among team members must be constantly nurtured.

This section ends with a list of major attributes of teamwork that the **STEAMWORK** model proposed by Maple (1992) is built on :

Sensitivity—being sensitive to the problem-solving process and to each other.

Tolerance—listening for similarities among differences.

Empathy—putting oneself in the place of other.

Acceptance—making efforts to accept others.

Maturity—sitting back and observing one's own behaviour and having a willingness to change.

Wisdom—recognizing that one does not have all the answers, having the willingness to learn, and knowing when to speak and when to be quiet.

Ownership—owing a piece of the picture to complete the process.

Responsibility—accepting that where we are is not always someone else's fault.

Kindness—being kind even when familiarity tends to breed contempt.

Social workers should realize that they already possess in abundance many of these attributes in terms of providing services in the field of child health. Social worker's familiarity with and skills in problem solving can be used in consultation. Problem-solving approaches to consultation have been of great value to people in organizations (Kurpius and Fuqua, 2006). Similarly, their understanding of systems theory can be a definite plus as "whether implicitly or explicitly, current models of organizational consultation are based upon systems theory" (Brown, Pryzwansky, and Scultz, 2005).

Social worker as a discharge planner and resource planner

This point basically tries to emphasize on those group of children who require hospital based health services. Discharge will begin even before a patient comes into the hospital and will continue after he or she has gone back into the community. It will include preadmission planning, discharge planning, post-discharge follow-up, available resource utilization and the expanded definition will also fit into the hospital's efforts to go beyond the provision of illness care and provide wellness and health maintenance services as well. Social worker's current discharge planner role will grow into the role of social health care manager, the provider of psychosocial services aimed at helping patients and families with transition to and from the hospital.

The following points are worth mentioning and must be remembered by the social workers who are closely involved in the field of child health services:

(a) Development of systems that ensure timely and efficient identification of patients who require discharges planning.
(b) Assessment of the psychological, social, environmental, and financial impact of illness on patients and families.
(c) Provision of psychosocial services to patients and families.
(d) Coordination of the contributions of the health care team.
(e) Development and maintenance of liaison with local, state, and federal resources.

(f) Establishment of systems to monitor and evaluate the effectiveness of the discharge planning process.
(g) Identification of services that are not available to meet the post-hospital needs of patients and families with a view to effecting the development of needed resources.

The specific case situations determine the degree of emphasis on any of the above components, and the complexity of discharge plans varies from case to case. The above-named document describes four levels of outcome of discharge planning:

(a) patient and family understanding of the diagnosis, anticipated level of functioning, prescribed treatment, and plan for follow-up.
(b) specialized instructions so that the patient and the family can provide post-hospital care.
(c) coordination of the essential community support system.
(d) relocation of the patient and coordination of support system or transfer to another health care facility.

The above lists highlight only something that social workers do. Social work activity with the patient and family is based on a grasp of the psychosocial context within which illness, hospitalization and discharge occur.

Social worker as a researcher

The social work knowledge would also help in undertaking systematic study to identify the psychosocial problems which may be useful in early diagnosis of the problem and further help the social workers to undertake effective measures to provide the best possible health services. For example, the mothers suffering from anaemia, the children suffering from malnutrition, diarrhoea/dysentery or mental retardation are not taken to a doctor at the earliest, is it because of the ignorance or stigma? Why the mothers do not seek the treatment for their children in rural areas? Is it due to the financial burden? Are they so busy in their household chores and have little extra time to seek remedies for their psychosocial and physical problems? Do the husband/family members take adequate care of the ailments? Are the children—at least the grown up and educated ones—paying due attention not only to their health but to their mother's health and well-being? These and many other questions could be understood and answered by making use of research knowledge. This knowledge may help in devising suitable measures in the successful implementation of mother and child health services in the society.

Role of voluntary organizations

In a democratic society like ours, the role of voluntary organizations becomes crucial for growth and the development of voluntary efforts bear testimony to the fact that each and every citizen bears a responsibility towards social ends. Voluntary organizations have a proven record to share the developmental responsibility of the nation since independence and even before. Since the government has realized its limitations and recognized the role played by voluntary action in outreach and immediate relief to needy, voluntary organizations have an extended responsibility towards community health. While big international organizations are collaborating with governments providing international expertise in planning, management, infrastructure development, transfer of appropriate technology and technical expertise in other nations, training manpower and supply of sophisticated equipment, micro-level small voluntary organizations are doing yeoman's task with poverty-stricken, ignorant and illiterate, tradition bound people at the grassroots level. Though the voluntary sector is miniscule in comparison with the country's population and economy, it nevertheless plays an important role as the conscience-keeper of our society.

The Government shall endeavour that adequate resources are provided for child welfare programmes and appropriate schemes are undertaken. At the same time, voluntary organizations engaged in the field of child health will continue to have the opportunity to develop either on their on or with state assistance in the field of health and social welfare services. India, under the leadership of Nehru was influenced both by the British and Soviet system of socio-economic development had chosen the socialistic pattern of society and accordingly our voluntary organizations are working and should be working along side the government to achieve this goal and thus valuable contribution to the human well-being but only as delivery agents for providing child welfare services. It shall be the endeavour of the State to encourage and strengthen voluntary action, so that State and voluntary efforts complement each other. The resources of voluntary organizations would have to be tapped to the extent possible for promoting and developing child health programmes.

Conclusion

India being a vast country with different socio-cultural environment, no single strategy would be good enough to bring success in the field of child health. Specific strategies, therefore, will have to be evolved keeping in mind the socio-cultural settings. Interventions need to be introduced at an early age. Effective approaches like "child to child" education programme and other innovative ways need to be experimented with. The special problems requiring focus are immunization and family planning, Sexually Transmitted Diseases like AIDS are going to affect and cause a severe damage to society at large in the coming years and requires immediate attention.

While government spending on health and family welfare has been steadily increasing, in absolute terms, the proportion of plan outlay spent on child health care has been declining from plan to plan. The pattern of health expenditure is yet to be geared fully to the concept of primary health care, which remains the main instrument for moving towards health for all. The holistic approach to child health requires integration of services like education, health, nutrition, mobilization of community support etc. Two such programmes already in existence—Integrated Child Development Scheme (ICDS), and Urban Basic Services, have shown some positive results in improving the health situation of the children.

The health facilities and personnel can establish functional linkages with the expanding ICDS infrastructure, the school system, the water and sanitation programme, district centres for disability rehabilitation, nutrition support programmes and so on. This is the common aim of health education. The social demand for health care is linked not only to the ability in terms of time, energy and money to seek it but also to the perception of need through better awareness. Effective use of media for imparting messages built in their day-to-day life can bring about the desired behavioural changes. Using folk media and traditional communication pattern such as puppets, street play etc. are likely to be more effective techniques for imparting health and nutrition education particularly in rural areas due to their familiarity and appeal. The health for all goal presumes several changes primarily a shift from an over-professionalized system to a redefined role for medical personnel, social workers, and common families. There is an unmet need to match skills and resources with requirement. It is clear that child health is more of a socio-political problem and unless we integrate socio-political actions and work towards the social justice much cannot be achieved in the direction. Appropriate strategies, giving recognition to the social workers, worked out to improve the status of women in the community, increase access to health care and health awareness, enhance allocation of funds and rationalization of priorities will result in better child health.

SUGGESTED READINGS

1. Caroff, P. (2007). "Clinical social work: Present role and future challenge". *Social Work in Health Care*, 13 (3), 21-23.
2. Joshi, S. (1999). *Child Survival, Health and Social Work Intervention;* Concept Publishing Company Pvt. Ltd., New Delhi.
3. Narayana, K.V. (2004). *Health and Development;* Rawat Publications, New Delhi.

4. Bajpai, P.K. (1999). *Social Work Perspective on Health*, Rawat Publication, Jaipur.
5. Saxena, Deepak. (2000). "Trends and Determinants of Immunization Coverage in India", *Journal of the Indian Medical Association*, Vol. 90; No. 1, January.
6. Iles, P. and Auluck, R. (2008). "Team building, interagency team development, and social work practice"; *British Journal of Social Work*, 20, 151-164.
7. Kurpius, D.J. and Fuqua, D.R. (2006). "Fundamental issues in defining consultation"; *Journal of Counselling and Development*; 71, 601-606.
8. Maple, M.F. (1992). STEAMWORK: "An effective approach to team building", *Journal of Specialists in Group Work*, 17, 144-150.
9. Holosko, M.J. (2007). Social work practice roles in health care: Daring to be different. In M.J. Holosko and P.A. Taylor (eds), *Social work practice in health care settings*. Toronto: Canadian Scholars' Press.
10. Brown, D., Pryzwansky, W.B. and Schultz, A.C. (2005). *Psychological consultation: Introduction to theory and practice*. Needham Heights, MA: Allyn and Bacon.
11. Dhooper, S.S. (1999). *Social Work in Health Care in the 21st Century*, Sage Publication, UK.
12. UNICEF (1999); *Child Survival and Population Growth*, Oxford University Press, UK.
13. *Child in India—A Statistical Profile*, (2000); National Institute of Public Cooperation and Child Development, New Delhi.

15

Juvenile Justice System

To Ensure Protection for Children in India

Juvenile Justice is an umbrella term used to refer to a novel Jurisprudential approach towards young miscreants through a set of institutions that make a series of interrelated decisions regarding State intervention into children's lives against the backdrop of shared goals. Thus, the juvenile justice system refers to the legal counsel for the child, juvenile detention centres, juvenile correctional facilities and social agencies that take children on placement on order of juvenile court.

Ideally, the juvenile justice system has multiple functions and aims. It is concerned both with protecting society and serving the best interests of the child, while at the same time meeting the child's needs and protecting his rights. It, thus, performs welfare-*cum*-criminal justice functions. In this duality of its roles, the system strives to achieve special social goals, such as the provision of minimum standards of child care and safeguard the Rights of the Child. It functions not only as a vehicle for providing for the special needs of children who commit crime, but also extends a protective umbrella to those vulnerable or endangered to do so under situational compulsions.

The notions about juvenile delinquency held by laymen and some law enforcement officials are faulty and misleading. For onething, they often assume that juvenile crimes are simply under-age criminals, that is, non-adult criminals, or juveniles who engage in offences that constitutes crimes when committed by adults, and are between the age of seven and 16 or 18 years, as prescribed by the law of the land. The maximum age today for juvenile delinquents according to the Juvenile Justice Act of 1986 is 16 years for boys and 18 years for girls, but earlier, according to the Children's Acts, it varied from state to state.

The term "juvenile delinquency or juvenile crime" applies to the violation of criminal code and/or pursuit of certain patterns of behaviour disapproved of for children and young adolescents. Thus, both age and behavioural infractions prohibited in the statutes are important in the concept of juvenile delinquency.

The difference between juvenile and adult crime is made by the conduct involved, the methods employed by the court, the philosophy and methods applied in treatment, and the individuals' status, reputation and civil rights in the community after adjudication.

Evolution of Juvenile Justice System in India

In India, the beginning of special legislation for young offenders was made during the latter half of the 19th century by passing the Reformatory School Act, 1876, which was modified in 1897. The Code of Criminal Procedure passed during this period introduced special procedure for children, specially Section 562, which bought in provision for release of young persons on probation of good conduct. The Report of the Indian Jail Committee, 1919-20, emphasized the need of separate treatment of youthful offenders. Following these recommendations, Madras, Bengal and Bombay enacted Children Acts in 1920, 1922 and 1924 respectively. The main objective of these Acts was to provide for custody, protection and treatment of young offenders and children in need. After Independence, the subject came within the State list and many States undertook to special legislation for children. The Government of India passed the Children Act, 1960 meant for the Union Territories, which was further amended in 1978. It also served as a model on the basis of which many States amended or introduced new legislation for children. The Central Act introduced new features, such as, establishment of Child Welfare Boards for dealing with neglected children. Thus, the broad principle, that children and juveniles below a certain age should not be dealt with by criminal courts and that they should not be sent to prisons was accepted by most of the States.

The experience of two and a half decades of the implementation of the Children Acts suggested to the Government of India that the quality of services under the Children Acts were not up to the mark. It also brought to four basic deficiencies like lack of uniformity in the provision of the Children Acts being implemented by different States; absence of clearly laid down minimum standards for basic needs, living conditions and therapeutic services for children in juvenile correctional institutions; and the non-availability of specialized infrastructure in most of the States. The major problem areas were incomplete geographical coverage, the number of children courts was pretty small, child welfare boards were virtually non-existent, children in certain States were still lodged in jails, and variations in the upper age in defining the child, the content of correctional services were very week, inadequately trained personnel and lack of public participation.

Concept of Juvenile Justice System

Juvenile Justice System is distinct from criminal justice system in all respects. Juvenile Justice System is not only a system of law and justice, which only mistakenly understood by majority of concerned people even within its sub-systems. It is a complete system of justice in terms of the fulfilment of the basic needs and rights of the child. We have been working on a well tested premise that the basic needs of the child are also his basic rights. These rights have been broadly categorized in the UN Convention on the Rights of the Child, 1989 as (i) right to survival, (ii) right to protection, (iii) right to development, and (iv) right to participation.

The Juvenile Justice System in India briefly known as (JJS) has three distinct phases, i.e. a protective and rehabilitative law, a humanistic procedure to deal with the legal institutions and finally, a temperamental attitude of welfare to treat the juvenile delinquents and crimes. This is the triology of the whole system.

Nature and Incidence of Juvenile Crime

Of the total delinquencies committed by the juveniles, hardly 2 per cent come to the notice of the police and the courts. The statistics compiled by the National Crime Bureau, Delhi give some indication of the incidence of juvenile crimes in India. Up to 1987, every year about 50 thousand crimes were committed by the juveniles under the Indian Penal Code (IPC) and about 85 thousand under the local and special laws (LSL). Crime cases attributed to juveniles naturally have been reduced now. This is why juvenile delinquency in and after 1988 (after the enactment of Juvenile Justice Act, 1986) compared to 1987 and earlier years has decreased both under IPC and LSL. At present 14,500 juveniles are apprehended (about 8,500 or 59% under the IPC and about 6,000 or 41% under the LSL) in a year for different crimes. The percentage of juvenile crime to total cognizable crime in India in 2002 was about 0.5 per cent (in 1988 it was 1.7%). Before 1988, this percentage (of juvenile delinquency to total cognizable crime) was about 4.

The incidence of juvenile crime varies widely in different states. Four states—Maharashtra (22.9%), Madhya Pradesh (23.7%), Bihar (10.6%) and Gujarat (11.9%)—account for 69.1 per cent of the total juvenile crimes under the IPC in the entire country. For crimes under LSL, two states—Tamil Nadu (59.1%) and Maharashtra (10.2%) account for 69.3 per cent of the total offences.

Out of the 17,203 juveniles apprehended and sent to the courts in 1988 for delinquencies under the IPC and LSL, 22.9 per cent were sent to their homes after advice and motivation, 19.7 per cent were released on probation, 5.5 per cent were sent to special homes, 7 per cent were fined and 6.5 per cent were acquitted. About 38.4 per cent cases remained pending (crime in India, 2003). The data presented in Table 15.1 retrieved from *National Crime Research Bureau in 2004.*

Table 15.1 : Incidence of juvenile delinquency in different states of India including union territories

Sl. No.	*States/U.T.*	*Incidence under IPC*	*Incidence under special and local laws*	*Total incidence*	*State-wise percentage*
1	Andhra Pradesh	590	66	656	4.52
2	Arunachal Pradesh	42	1	43	0.30
3	Assam	182	7	189	1.31
4	Bihar	382	85	467	3.23
5	Goa	21	0	21	0.15
6	Gujarat	1075	638	1713	11.84
7	Haryana	300	45	345	2.39
8	Himachal Pradesh	47	2	49	0.34
9	Jammu & Kashmir	0	0	0	0.00
10	Karnataka	286	27	313	2.17
11	Kerala	51	1	52	0.36
12	Madhya Pradesh	2380	267	2647	18.31
13	Maharashtra	1848	274	2122	14.69
14	Manipur	0	0	0	0.00
15	Meghalaya	15	0	15	0.10
16	Mizoram	11	36	47	0.33
17	Nagaland	0	0	0	0.00
18	Orissa	195	1	196	1.36
19	Punjab	20	2	22	0.15
20	Rajasthan	674	36	710	4.91
21	Sikkim	6	0	6	0.04
22	Tamil Nadu	403	4051	4418	30.55
23	Tripura	17	0	17	0.12
24	Uttar Pradesh	14	16	30	0.21
25	West Bengal	15	0	15	0.10
26	Andaman & Nicobar Islands	3	0	3	0.02
27	Chandigarh	16	3	19	0.13
28	Dadra & Nagar Haveli	0	0	0	0.00
29	Daman & Diu	0	0	0	0.00
30	Delhi	288	11	299	2.07
31	Lakshadweep	1	0	1	0.01
32	Pondicherry	6	0	6	0.14

Table 15.1 reflects the state-wise distribution of juvenile delinquents under IPC and under special and local laws. It may be mentioned that the newer states like Uttranchal, Chhattisgarh and Jharkhand were not included because of non-availability of data. Table 15.2 shows mild downward trend in the delinquency rate.

Table 15.2 : Trends of juvenile delinquency in the future

Sl.No.	*Year*	*Actual Incidence*	*Incidence Projected*
1	1995	9766	9673
2	1996	10024	9430
3	1997	7909	9187
4	1998	9352	8944
5	1999	8888	8702
6	2000	8765	8459
7	2001	9634	8216
8	2002	10340	7973
9	2003	7645	7731
10	2004	8765	7488
11	2005	9875	7425
12	2006	4567	7002
13	2007	5643	6759
14	2008	6754	6517
15	2009	7894	6274
16	2010	10456	6031
17	2011	8765	5788

Table 15.3 reflects that how juvenile delinquents are treated by the existing legal systems. It has been observed that majority of them, i.e. 18045 delinquents are sent to courts after being arrested followed by 5272 are released on probation (care of parents). Apart from above systems there are juveniles who are released on probation (care of Fit), sent to special home, charged fine, acquitted/other disposals and pending disposal.

Table 15.3 : Juvenile disposed by different systems

Sl.No.	*Disposal options*	*Number*
1	Arrested and sent to courts	18045
2	Sent homes after advice/admonition	1656
3	Released on Probation (care of parents)	5272
4	Released on Probation (care of Fit)	768
5	Sent to special home	1166
6	Fine	820
7	Acquitted/other disposals	3258
8	Pending disposal	5105

An attempt has been made here to have zone-wise distribution of incidence of juvenile crimes in India after subscribing to secondary data analysis. This data will provide us more comprehensive magnitude of the problem.

Zone-A (High delinquency prone area)

State	*Incidence*
Tamil Nadu	4418
Madhya Pradesh	2647
Maharashtra	2122
Gujarat	1713

This zone comprises of States/UTs, which have high delinquency rates. The following 12.5 per cent of the total States in India cover 75 per cent of the incidence of juvenile delinquency in the whole of India.

Zone-B (Medium or moderate delinquency prone area)

State	*Incidence*
Rajasthan	710
Andhra Pradesh	656
Bihar	467
Haryana	345
Karnataka	313
Delhi	299
Orissa	196
Assam	189
Kerala	52

Zone B comprises of States/UTs, which are medium delinquency prone. The following 28.125 per cent of the States cover 23 per cent of the incidence of juvenile delinquency in the whole of India. Remaining 59.375 per cent of the States cover 2 per cent of the incidence.

Zone-C (Low delinquency prone area)

State	*Incidence*
Himachal Pradesh	49
Mizoram	47
Arunachal Pradesh	43
Uttar Pradesh	30
Punjab	22
Goa	21
Chandigarh	19
Tripura	17
Meghalaya	15
West Bengal	15
Sikkim	6
Pondicherry	6
Andaman & Nicobar Islands	3
Lakshadweep	1
Jammu & Kashmir	0
Manipur	0
Nagaland	0
Dadra & Nagar Haveli	0
Daman & Diu	0

Table 15.4 : Number of Homes in the Country, 2006

Observation Homes	280
Juvenile Homes	251
Special Homes	36
After-care Organizations	46
Total	613

Juvenile Justice Act

The whole juvenile justice system in India is governed by JJA. It is an Act for the care, protection, treatment, development and rehabilitation of neglected juveniles and for the adjudication of certain matters relating to, and disposition of, delinquent juveniles. The main objectives of the Act are :

1. To lay down a uniform legal framework for juvenile justice in the country so as to ensure that no child under any circumstances is lodged in jail or police lock-up. This is being ensured by establishing Juvenile Justice Boards and Juvenile Courts.
2. To provide a special approach towards the prevention and treatment of juvenile delinquency keeping in view the developmental needs of the child found in any situation of social maladjustment.
3. To establish norms and standards for the administration of juvenile justice in terms of investigation and prosecution, adjustment and disposition, and care, treatment and rehabilitation.
4. To constitute special offences in relation to juveniles and provide for punishment.
5. To develop appropriate linkages and coordination between the formal system of juvenile justice and voluntary agencies engaged in the welfare of neglected children.
6. To spell out the machinery and infrastructure required for the care, protection, treatment, development and rehabilitation of various categories of children coming within the purview of the juvenile justice system.
7. To bring the operation of the juvenile justice system in the country in conformation with the United Nations Standard Minimum Rules for administration of juvenile justice.

The Act propounds a concept of juvenile justice within the overall framework of social justice as enshrined in the Constitution of India. It symbolizes response to the changing socio-cultural and economic conditions that affect juveniles in terms of an equal sharing of opportunities for their growth and fulfilment. Besides a thorough restructuring of juvenile correctional system, the Act contemplates a vigorous use of the inherent potentials of the community for dealing within the mainstream of social life. The new approach undoubtedly places an onerous responsibility on the state to mobilize all resources of the family, the community and social organizations in tackling the problem of juvenile social maladjustment in its full range.

Thrust areas of the JJA

1. The definition of "neglected juvenile" has been construed more precisely so as to ensure only those juveniles who are to be abused, exploited and inducted into criminojenic life and are in need of legal support to be weaned away from such situations are processed through the law. At the same time, legal protection has been extended to all juveniles being abused or exploited for immoral or illegal purposes or unconscionable gain.
2. The procedures of handling neglected or delinquent juvenile at various stages—apprehension, processing and placement—have been rationalized from the view of the protection of human rights as are not inconsistent with the requirements of the law. A neglected child may be brought before the competent authority not only by a police officer but also by any other person or organization authorized for the purpose. This provision should enable social worker and voluntary organizations to increasingly assume the responsibility of the referral of neglected juveniles to appropriate care.
3. The Act provides for a differential approach in the processing of neglected juveniles *vis-à-vis* the delinquent. While neglected children produce before the Juvenile Welfare Board, the delinquents are to be dealt with by the Juvenile Court. The Juvenile Welfare Board and the Juvenile Court have been empowered for the transferability of cases brought before them on the basis of the necessary screening.
4. Observation Homes are contemplated for the temporary reception during the pendency of an

enquiry when their placement with parents, guardians or places of safety has not been feasible.

5. The Act lays down a wide range of dispositional alternatives open to the competent authority, with preference to family/community-based placement. The neglected juvenile will be sent to a Juvenile Home only if his care with a parent, guardian or fit institution is not found conducive. For juvenile delinquents also, institutional care will be resorted to as the last measure, only if his restoration to parent, release on advice/admonition, placement on probation, care under fit person/institution or discharge on fine is not considered appropriate for a normal growth and development of the juvenile.
6. For delinquent and neglected juveniles, Special Homes are required to be set up or voluntary institution certified as such. Special Homes have to offer suitable facilities for accommodation, maintenance, education, vocational training and rehabilitation as well as for development of their character and ability and reformative training, so as to ensure an all-round growth and development of their individual responsibility.
7. The Act contains a comprehensive provision regarding the establishment or recognition of aftercare organizations for taking care of juveniles discharged from Juvenile or Special Homes and for the purpose of enabling them to lead an honest, industrious and useful life. Specific rules are to be formulated for the relevant scheme as also for the nature and standards of organizations. The mandate calls for a systematic approach towards bridging the gap between the institutional treatment and the process of reassimilation into the society.
8. Consequent upon the enactment of the Narcotic Drugs and Psychotropic Substances Act, 1985 providing *inter alia* for the establishment and notification of treatment centres for drug addicts, a provision has been made for the transfer of juveniles addicted to drugs to such

treatment centres, as in the case of juveniles of unsound mind and those suffering from leprosy.

9. A new provision has been incorporated for the creation of a fund to be exclusively utilized for the welfare and rehabilitation of juveniles dealt with under this Act. Such fund may be raised from voluntary donations, contributions or subscriptions made by individuals or organizations. This surely opens up a definite avenue of generating public support and participation in building up an effective system of juvenile justice.
10. The Act requires the State Government to constitute advisory boards to advice on matters relating to the establishment and maintenance of homes, mobilization of resources, provision of facilities for education, training and rehabilitation of neglected and delinquent juveniles and coordination among various officials and non-official agencies concerned.

The Juvenile Justice (Care and Protection of Children) Act, 2000—Some Reflections

- The first uniform law on juvenile justice (Juvenile Justice Act, 1986) did not result in any dramatic improvement in the treatment of juveniles.
- The law continued to provoke a lot of concern, in human rights circles, pertaining particularly to the way juveniles were treated in detention centers designated as special homes and juvenile homes.
- The Government of India ratified the convention of the rights of the child in the year 1992 and amended various legislations to recognize children's right adopted in the convention.
- Juvenile Justice (Care and Protection) Act, 2000 is one of the Acts that was amended after this ratification.

What is special in this Act?

- It gave a new dimension to the juvenile justice system of the country.

- Focus has also been given on voice of children towards identification and solution of their own problems.
- It also encourages children in need of care and protection to produce themselves before the juvenile committee in case of violation of their basic rights.
- The Act provides more significance on treatment, care, protection and developmental needs of children by adopting a child friendly approach in the adjudication and disposition of the matters in the best interest of the children.
- The Act redefined children as an individual below the age of 18 years.
- The Act has also categorized children as—(a) children in need of care and protection, and (b) children in conflict with law.

The Juvenile Justice (Care and Protection of Children) Amendment Bill, 2005

- The Juvenile Justice (Care and Protection of Children) Amendment Bill, 2005 was introduced in Lok Sabha on August 29, 2005 to amend the Juvenile Justice (Care and Protection of Children) Act, 2000 (Principal Act). The Standing Committee on Social Justice and Empowerment submitted its report on December 12, 2005.
- The Bill seeks to modify the Principal Act in order to offer a wider scope of rehabilitation for the child through not only institutional but also non-institutional approach. Therefore, the words 'through various institutions established under the enactment' have been removed from the Preamble of the Principal Act.
- The Bill clarifies that the Act would be applicable for all cases involving detention or criminal prosecution of juveniles under any other law.
- The Bill adds a provision stating that a juvenile can be confined in a special home for a maximum period of three years or until he ceases to be a juvenile.

- The Bill prohibits any newspaper, magazine or visual media from publishing the name, address and other particulars of a juvenile in conflict with the law as well as a child in need of care and protection.
- The Bill excludes any police officer from the inquiry process. Child Welfare Committee would conduct an inquiry in the prescribed manner. If the child does not have family or any support system he can remain in a children's home till he is rehabilitated or attains the age of 18 years.
- There is a provision to allow a fit insutitution to take charge of a juvenile in conflict with the law as an additional alternative to detention in an observation home. A fit institution is defined as a governmental, registered non-governmental or a voluntary organization, which is prepared to own responsibility of a child and is authorized by an authority.
- The Bill lays down a minimum time period of twenty-four hours within which a juvenile should be produced before the Juvenile Justice Board. The 24 hours excludes the time necessary for the journey from the place where the juvenile was caught. The same provision applies in case of a child to be produced before the Child Welfare Committee.
- Along with single parent and parents with biological children, the Bill seeks to extend the scope of adoption to childless parents. However, it restricts to children of Indian citizen only.
- The Bill amends the definition of "juvenile in conflict with law" to make it more explicit that the relevant date for a person to be considered a juvenile would be the date on which the alleged offence was committed. According to the Bill, the person should not have completed 18 years to be considered as a juvenile. The Bill also lays down the procedure to be followed in case a person claims to be a juvenile in a court.
- The phrase "local authority" has been removed from the Bill. The authority to discharge or transfer a child rests solely with State Government.

The implementation of juvenile justice

It is evident that juvenile justice system has been designed to respond to the developmental needs of juveniles and youthful offenders. The Act evokes a response and calls for undertaking several corrective actions. It poses a challenge for the country and provides an opportunity to fulfil constitutional obligations towards all such children, who on account of their own doings or of others, wittingly or unwittingly, come into conflict with law. However, commenting on the constraints of the juvenile justice system, it has been observed that:

(i) Juvenile institutions are not always manned and administered by qualified and trained staff. The general morale of the institutional staff is often very low.

(ii) The shortage of juvenile courts, the multiplicity of their functions, the heavy workload of police and judiciary and the lack of necessary infrastructure for the care, treatment and rehabilitation of various categories of children dealt with through the formal system continue to be the main impediments in the development of a progressive system of juvenile justice administration.

(iii) In many places, juvenile courts are still presided over by ordinary magistrates without proper regard to the specific needs of the juvenile justice system. The quality of pre-sentence investigation and supervision placed in foster care, sponsorship or on probation leaves much to be desired.

(iv) Apart from the problems of proper coordination among various agencies concerned with juvenile justice, a variety of inter-system conflicts mar the quality of services as envisaged in the law. The police, in most of the cases, inherit an image, which hardly fits with the modern concept of juvenile justice. Only a few States have been able to organize special police units to appropriately deal with the wide range of problems pertaining to juvenile deviance. In the general police structure, the maintenance of law and order, investigation and prosecution of crime and preservation of juvenile delinquency and crimes often generates contradictory trends.

(v) While the juvenile laws provide for legal defence of the juvenile involved in crime, even at the expense of the State, if he or she cannot afford it, in actual practice, it is often left to the commitment, capacity and competence of the presiding officer of the juvenile court to protect both the law and the juvenile.

(vi) Among the various components of the juvenile justice system, the development of correctional system personnel seems to have received the low priority in most of the developing countries. As a result, the juvenile justice system tends to function in isolation from other vital sectors of social development, to the detriment of both the juvenile involved and the society at large.

(vii) It has to be realized that the formal juvenile justice system, however, thoughtfully conceived and carefully designed cannot be expected to take over the responsibility of correcting observations of the wider socio-economic system as a re-associated with juvenile social maladjustment when the former is the product of the later.

(viii) Despite assumptions that the juvenile justice system, in the sense of social justice, may reach all children in need of care, protection and rehabilitation, in actual practice it cannot go beyond the categories of the children recognized as offenders or endangered to be so because of its inherent limitations.

Promising commitments in the new millennium

Juvenile justice system in the next century has already been a topic for discussion in our country. So let's have a glimpse as on some of the future directions of better functioning of the juvenile justice system in India in the concluding part of this article. The term 'Juvenile' as currently used in JJA should be substituted by the word 'Child'. The usage of the word 'Juvenile' instead of 'Child' gives a negative picture about a young person, more so, when it is continuously being used with the term 'delinquency'. There is a need to have a holistic law relating to juvenile justice as a large number of laws such as family law, labour law, property law, environment law, constitutional law, have specified special provisions conferring rights and entitlements for children which need to be converged under one umbrella as this would facilitate a comprehensive treatment to the juvenile justice system and other survival, development and participation rights of children.

It is thought that as an alternative to the Juvenile Court System, Family Court System could be evolved wherein the Judges assume the parental role of not only serving the best interests of the child but also that of the state.

More importance is to be given to the overall role of probation in the juvenile justice system. It is because probation plays a pivotal role in the treatment and rehabilitation of children.

More consolidated participation of local community and non-governmental organizations are required in realizing human rights in general and children's rights in particular.

Administration of juvenile justice system through a decentralized mechanism that reaches the rural population throughout the country would serve as an important via media specially where the formal system is remote and access limited. This would also entail community involvement.

It was felt that there would be an immediate need to professionalize the manpower responsible for the implementation of JJS in the country in conformity with new trends in the field, which among other things emphasise requirement in their own right but could also perform their roles and responsibilities in a scientific manner.

There is a need to prioritize and strengthen non-institutional methods such as adoption, foster care and sponsorship through legal procedures so that placing a victim of abuse in an institution is not perceived as the only goal of protection.

Parents and families must be encouraged to shoulder the responsibility of child care and development with a sense of commitment and the State acting as 'parents patriae' should intervene to protect the child if the family fails to fulfil its responsibilities towards the child.

Besides awareness of the general public, the law maker, decision maker and the implementing authority would have to be thoroughly grounded in the basic essentials required for an effective implementation of the Act. The dilemma between social welfare and social control approach would have to be done away with by reconciling the efforts with the preventive strategies to be strengthened at the community level.

The system has to be used sensitively, selectively and with proper care and caution. It cannot be used as a dumping ground for all problem cases. It will have to re-examine its policies, especially those that relate to institutional commitment of children in adverse social and economic circumstances. It will have to further appreciate the need to diversify and change alternatives to closed correctional facilities. This would require the development of a wide variety of divergent programme to keep as many juveniles as possible from entering the JJS. Institutional commitment may be deemed necessary only:

(a) where the child is mentally defective.
(b) a badly spoiled child whose history of misconduct is so serious or persistent as to indicate the necessity of providing him with specialized and intensive institutional treatment.
(c) a child who has failed under prior treatment of other sorts.

With functionally inadequate building, limited budget, untrained staff and absence of adequate public scrutiny, most of the correctional institutions have gradually deteriorated without any public notice or concern. Inadequate appropriation and lack of viable framework for reforming the inmates and other constraints under which these institutions are administered combine to reduce them to a status of little better than a prison for juniors. The need, therefore, is to improvise the quality of commitment consistent with their given ends and objects. It necessarily calls for adequate funding, proper staffing, and functionally adequate building and scientifically conceived and operated treatment and rehabilitation programme.

The JJS has largely been a non-priority area having a step-child status in the scheme of criminal justice. The paramount need, therefore, is to create an organizational set up wherein juvenile and adult correction programme be administered within a single agency, so as to make it responsible for the administration of all correctional programme under a unified set up. Such a step would also help in cadre building, unified recruitment rules, adequate promotional avenues and planned in-service and refresher training.

The bureaucratic inertia characteristics of an obsolescent of correctional management has to yield place to a scientific managerial culture that may introduce into correctional administration the principle of 'management by objectives'. The whole system of traditional mechanisms in juvenile justice has to be abandoned in favour of progressive programme changes that promise better results.

Another area which needs urgent attention is the fact that the present statistics pertaining to the number of inmates in the institutions under the JJA point out that more than 80 per cent of them fall under the category of neglected juveniles. By putting them in institutions which are custodial in nature, they are being thwarted of their normal growth. It is in this regard that non-institutional services have to be strengthened.

The following intervention strategy also needs to be adopted as felt by our policy-makers:

1. provide family surrogates to nurture children when no functional family unit is available.
2. strengthen the ability of the family to fulfil its primary obligations to instill social values in younger generation.
3. support-*cum*-social institutions (i.e. the school, religious institutions and community organizations) in their role of developing capable, mature and responsible youth.

4. intervene immediately and effectively when delinquent behaviour occurs in order to successfully prevent delinquent offenders from becoming chronic offenders.
5. identify and control the small group of serious, violent and chronic juvenile offenders who have committed felony offences or who have failed to respond to intervention and community based treatment and rehabilitation services.

Role of social worker

As per Section 5(3) of the JJA, every Juvenile Court is to be assisted by a panel of two honorary Social Workers possessing such qualifications as may be prescribed. In practice, the role of the panel of Social Workers in the present scheme of the Act is very limited and may overlap or replace the work of a Probation Officer. The Social Workers may be asked to assist the Juvenile Court in fact-finding as well as decision-making, especially when the report of the Probation Officer is not forthcoming. In view of the purpose for which panel of social workers is appointed under the JJA, it is desirable that the Juvenile Court should give serious consideration to the advice of the panel; if the advice is unacceptable, the reasons for that ought to be recorded.

Conclusion

In conclusion, it is reiterated that the juvenile justice system reaffirms its positive faith in the fundamental human rights and in the dignity and warmth of the individual. It recognizes that children by reasons of their physical and mental immaturity need special safeguards and care, including appropriate legal protection. It lays considerable stress on the society to provide facilities to the juveniles who are in need of the care and protection of the welfare services. The State owes a different duty to children than to adults. What is critical in this regard is not the 'guilt' or innocence of the juvenile, but the considerations as to who is, how he has become, what he is, and what could best be done in his interest. In the implementation level, it would require a thorough restructuring and revamping of the existing set up to make it viable and sensitive to the needs of the children in especially different circumstances.

SUGGESTED READINGS

1. Awasthe, S.K., (2005); The Juvenile Justice Act, 1986 with important judgments; *Law and Vision*, Allahabad, pp. 29-48.
2. Antony, M.J., (1999); *Landmark Judgment on Children's Rights;* Indian Social Institute, New Delhi.
3. Bakshi, P.M., (2003); *The Constitution of India;* Universal Book Traders, New Delhi.
4. *Crime in India*, (2003); National Crime Records, New Delhi.
5. Diwan, Paras and Peeyushi Diwan, (2000); *Human Rights and the Law;* Deep and Deep Publication, New Delhi.
6. Goonesekere, Savitri, (1999); *Children, Law, and Justice—A South Asian Perspective;* Sage Publication, New Delhi.
7. Kumare, Ved, (1993); *Treaties on the Juvenile Justice Act 1986;* The Indian Law Institute, New Delhi.
8. Mitra, N.L., (2005); *Juvenile Delinquency and Indian Justice System,* New Delhi, Deep and Deep Publication.
9. Nagpaul, Hans, (1996); *Social Work in Urban India*, Rawat Publication, Jaipur.
10. Rosenheim, K. Margaret, (2001); "Organization and Process of Juvenile Justice", in Samford Kadish (ed.), *Encyclopaedia of Criminal Justice;* Vol. 8, New York; The Free Press.
11. Srivastava, S.P. (1989); *Juvenile Justice in India—Policy, Programmes and Perspective;* Ajanta Publication, New Delhi, pp. 234-238.

16

Current Trends in Child Labour
A Study of *Beedi* Industry in Bharatpur-II Block, Murshidabad District of West Bengal

Introduction

My name is today. All of you believe and proclaim that we, the children, are the future of our society. But I work day and night just to survive. My childhood is maimed. I am living an un-seasonal adulthood. I see some children of my age at play, at school, in mother's lap and in father's arms. I wish I should have had all. My dreams are unfulfilled. Resentments are bottled up and I cannot find an outlet to express them. My green childhood is cruelly replaced with the responsibility of supporting my very poor family. If you look into my eyes, you cannot expect to see hope, innocence or trust. All these signs of childhood are replaced by betrayal, hunger and fear. My country, India, has earned the dubious distinction of having the highest number of child labourers like me. You can find me in every nook and corner of our country.

The term child labour, has been defined differently by different organizations, agencies and countries and many a time the terms **"child labour"** and **"child work"** have been used interchangeably. This has often led to a lot of confusion and a failure to focus and mobilize significant attention on the real priorities within the field. Child labour, distinguished from child work, is that which "impairs the health and development of children". Francis Blanchard, the former Director General of the International Labour Organization (ILO), has defined child labour as that which includes "children prematurely leading adult lives, working long hours for low wages under conditions damaging to their health and to their physical and mental development, sometimes separated from their families, frequently deprived of meaningful education and training opportunities that could open up for them a better future." According to the Encyclopaedia of Social Science: "when the business of wage earning or of participation in itself or family support conflicts directly or indirectly with the business of growth and education, the result is child labour".

Child labour is increasingly becoming an important issue of concern for the world community, with over 250 million children working around the world. India is one of the world's leading countries in terms of employing children with an estimated number between 60 and 115 million children working. Most of these children work in the agricultural sector, leaving about 15 per cent of these children in the service and small-scale industries. It is not a significant form of organization of production in India, though the absolute numbers of child labourers are quite large. Child labour in India is largely engaged in subsistence activities in family based production units, which are often linked to the market and exchange mechanisms through the transfers of commodities and also labour power.

Children those are working in *beedi* rolling industries consist of roasting, sorting, grading and packaging the *beedi*. According to government estimate (2004), *beedi* rolling employs nearly 4.45 million people, of whom 65 per cent are women and 15 per cent to 25 per cent are children. Women often face discrimination and are paid less than men. Children are even worst off with no wage structure and usually get paid the least. It has also been estimated by the Government of India that there are 43,99,644 *beedi* rolling workers out of which only 35,85,018 are having 'Identity Card'.

India, the largest democracy in the world has mammoth child labour population in the age group between 6-14 years. Majority of them are girls. In the recent Supreme Court Judgment on abolishing child labour it is observed that none of the official estimation includes child labour in the unorganized sector, and therefore, are obviously gross underestimates. Estimates from various non-governmental sources as to the actual number of working children range from 44 million to 100 million.

Child labour is the result of multiple factors. These children come from the most economically and socially disadvantaged sections of the society. Poverty is cited as the main reason for child labour. However, these children earn too little to contribute substantially to their family income and in the face of inexplicable exploitation.

National Policy on Child Labour

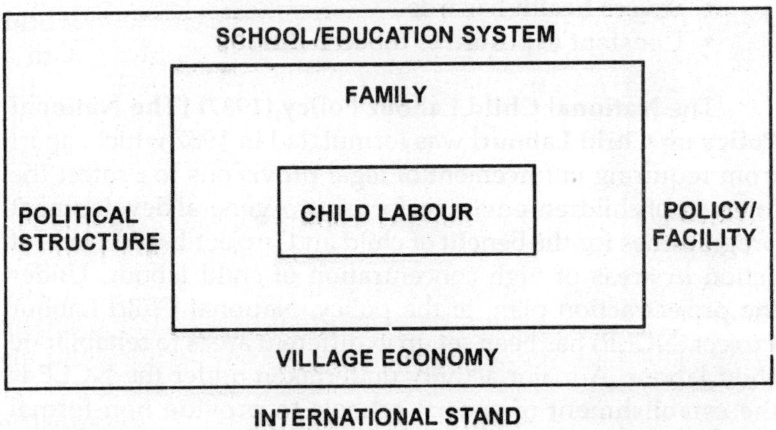

Paradoxically, government interventions have worsened in West Bengal in regard to *beedi* rollers. After the promulgation of the Beedi and Cigar Act, 1960, factory-based *beedi* rollers (all men) were thrown out of the factories, and the work shifted to home-based among children and women. The Minimum Wages Act is not strictly followed. Owing to the significant rise in cost of *tendu* leaves (required for *beedi* rolling) after the nationalization of their collection in West Bengal, improving the returns to the *tendu* pickers, the *beedi* industrialists managed the increased costs by slashing the wages of the child *beedi* rollers.

Beedi workers of forty years ago said that their livelihood had been adequate, whereas the *beedi* rollers of today have precarious livelihood. Major problems faced by the *beedi* rollers are:

- Perpetual poverty
- Very low wages
- No wage bargaining system
- No access to entitlements
- No benefits and gratuity
- Delayed payments
- Illiteracy
- Hidden child labour
- Severe health hazards
- Constant exposure to tobacco dust

The **National Child Labour Policy (1987) [The National Policy on Child Labour]** was formulated in 1987 which, apart from requiring enforcement of legal provisions to protect the interests of children, envisage, focusing of general development programmes for the benefit of child and project-based plans of action in areas of high concentration of child labour. Under the project action plan, of the policy, National Child Labour Project (NCLP) has been set up in different areas to rehabilitate child labour. A major activity undertaken under the NCLP is the establishment of special schools to provide non-formal education, vocational training, supplementary nutrition etc. to children withdrawn from employment emphasizes the role of education and its core rehabilitation programmes through joint venture of GOs and NGOs, but actually its implications has very mere existence.

By ratifying the ILO Convention No.182, governments would be pressured to put an end to all forms of illegal child labour through enforcement and monitoring of child labour laws. The goal of the ILO is for all member countries to adopt and ratify this new convention, and work on ways to help ensure its effectiveness. The government should work with non-governmental organizations and other non-profits in leading information campaigns that will educate society as a whole. Ratifying the convention is just the first step. Governments must agree to strict enforcement and prosecution of offenders. Civil society should also play a major role in helping alleviate the problem by actively helping with the monitoring process and informing the general public about the statistics, realities, and current situations regarding child labour. Although India is one of the leading countries in terms of having a problem with child labour, the country has not yet ratified this important convention that would help eliminate the child labour. Prior to Convention 182, **The Minimum Age Convention 138 (C138), 1973** which enforced ratifying countries to eliminate child work by raising the working age 'to a level consistent with the fullest physical and mental development of young persons'. This age was dictated as the age did students reach 15 or the age after completing the country's mandatory educational requirements. As of till to date, India has also not yet ratified this convention.

Objectives

- To unveil the social and economic realities that forces the children to start *beedi* rolling at an early age.
- To highlight the living and working conditions of *beedi* workers in general and child workers in particular.
- To understand the current trends in child labour in *beedi* industry and to find a proper explanation as to why child labour in *beedi* industry is growing, while it is showing a clear-cut decline at national level as a general trend.
- To enumerate GO-NGO collaboration towards protection of rights and rehabilitation programmes for the *beedi* rolling child labour.

Methodology and research settings

Research design

In this study, exploratory research design was followed because the main purpose of such design was to formulate a problem for more precise investigation or to develop some working strategies from an operational point of view. The major emphasis was to explore ideas and insights. The research design was therefore flexible enough to provide opportunity for considering different aspects of the child labour problem under study.

Universe

Several studies have shown that Murshidabad district is one of the largest *beedi* manufacturing districts in the country. It has also been an established fact that Muslim population dominates Murshidabad and majority of them are surviving on the *beedi* industry. Bharatpur-II block was selected purposively because it was in the close vicinity of other two districts such as Burdwan and Birbhum, which are also having a huge number of *beedi* manufacturing units. This particular block among all the blocks in the district has been designated as the highest employment of child worker working in *beedi* industry. The study was conducted in ten villages within the geographical area of the said block.

A glimpse of the Bharatpur Block (2001 Census)

This Block is under Kandi Subdivision of the Murshidabad District. There are fifty-two villages under the jurisdiction of the block. The study was mostly concentrated on the villages under the Talibpur Gram Panchayat of the Block. The villages, which were taken as operational zone on the basis of the assumption, that, the severity of the problem in these villages were much in abundance.

Area (Sq.km)	*No.of households*	*Population (total)*	*Population (male)*	*Population (female)*
158.50	29492	150133	76713	73420

Population Density: 947-persons/sq. km
Average size of Household: 5.09 persons/household
Sex ratio: 957 female per 1000 male

SC Population	*Male*	*Female*	*ST Population*	*Male*	*Female*
27580	14158	13422	155	84	71

Population (0-6 years):	17.12% of total population (51.45% male and 48.55% female)
Literate Population:	45.31% of total population (57.70% male and 42.30% female)
Illiterate Population:	54.68% of total population (45.50% male and 54.50% female)

Main Worker (total)	*Male*	*Female*	*Cultivator (total)*	*Male*	*Female*
42624	37189	5435	9012	8757	255

Total Worker:	33.15% of total population (81.37% male and 18.63% female)
Main Worker:	85.61% of the total workers (87.25% male and 12.75% female)
Cultivator:	12.07% of total workers (97.17% male and 2.83% female)
Agricultural Labourer:	26.60% of total workers (98.52% male and 1.48% female)
Household Industry Worker:	5.19% of total workers (55.74% male and 44.26% female)
Other Worker:	15.66% of total population (89.34% male and 10.66% female)
Marginal Worker:	12.58% of total population (64,87% male and 35.13% female)
Cottage Industry Worker:	19.77% of total population (13,62% male and 86.38% female)
Non-Worker:	90.83% of total population (36.07% male and 63.93% female)

Apart from the above statistical data; the educational infrastructure, health and drinking water facilities, electric supply and road communication in the block were very poor as we observed and came to know from the villagers after having informal conversation.

Some of the current trends of child labour in the district are:

- The *beedi* rolling child labourers live under the most difficult condition. They work, on an average, 12 hours a day, and contribute significantly to India's GNP.

- But in return they receive:
  - An average salary of Rs. 15 per day.
  - Emotional and physical abuse.
  - Incalculable damages to their health before they are 14 years old.
  - Limited access to the basic rights—education, food, water and shelter.
  - Complete loss of their invaluable childhood.
  - An entire lifetime of frail health and penury.
  - An underpaid or unemployed status as adults.

Sampling method and size

Purposive sampling is a non-random sampling method in which the sample is arbitrarily selected because characteristics, which they possess, are deemed important for the research. This method ensures that those individuals will be included in the sample that is relevant to the research design. This particular sampling method was also used for this study. The collection of sample was done after obtaining secondary level information regarding the existence of *beedi* rolling child labour in the selected villages. The respondents were selected after accumulating necessary information about them from block office, panchayat office and Census of India. The *beedi* rolling child workers were selected purposively and interviewed according to their availability at their houses or workplace. The respondents decided the time and venue for face-to-face interview.

Two types of respondents' views were included in the study—(a) the *beedi* rolling children, the reference group for the study; (b) the stakeholders (local school teachers, panchayat functionaries, government administrators and police personnel) whose opinion were deemed to be very crucial for the study. Four hundred and twenty child workers were selected from ten villages using proportional allocation method considering the number of households in the study villages. Fifteen stakeholders were also taken into consideration from different sections along with twenty respondents were also selected for detailed case study for in-depth analysis of the problem.

Tools of data collection

Semi-structured interview schedule both open-ended and close ended was designed for the collection of data. Close-ended questions were kept for convenience of coding and easy understanding for the respondents to answers. Open-ended questions were mainly for profound realization, root cause of the problems and its counter domain to resolve the issue. Inferences were drawn from the subjective as well as objective facts and figures on the basis of frequency distribution with the help of statistical interpretation.

Pilot study

The research team did an assessment of the situational background of the operational area from every possible and relevant dimension before carrying out the final task. This pilot study, undoubtedly, helped the research team to a large extent to adopt necessary modifications in the interview schedule as well as plan of action.

Fieldwork

Fieldwork was done in two phases. The first phase was devoted for pilot study stretching into two months to understand the real life situation in the operational area. The final fieldwork was carried out for almost six months. The whole fieldwork process was periodically monitored.

Data processing and analysis

After collection of data, it was coded on the code sheet and transferred into the codebook developed for this study. Data was processed with the help of computer using SPSS software package. Various tabular and graphical representations were used for meaningful interpretations of the facts and figures. Both univariate and bivariate tables as well as graphs, wherever required, were taken its way for some of the comparative analysis.

Limitations of the study

The study was conducted in a particular block of a vast district. *Beedi* rolling child workers in other blocks of the district were not covered due to time constraints and paucity of funds. So the situation of child workers in other blocks was not known. The stakeholders were also not found to be very serious and genuine in their responses. They were deemed to suppress many facts and not interested to disclose before the research team. In majority of the cases the respondents were not allowed to give interview in absence of either their parents or relatives. With these few obstacles, the research team made all efforts to bring out the best results from the study.

Major findings and conclusion

Table 16.1 ascertains that the majority of the *beedi* rolling children worker belongs to the age group of above 12 to 15 (36.67%) years followed by 25.71% who belong to the age group of above 9 to 12 years. The other striking feature, which is emerging out from the table, is that out of total samples of 420 *beedi* rolling workers of which 346 (82.38%) are girls.

Table 16.1 : Gender and age of the respondents

Age	*Gender*		*Total*	*Percentage*
	Male	*Female*		
Below 6 years	3	9	12	2.86
6 years-9 years	15	52	67	15.95
Above 9 years-12 years	20	88	108	25.71
Above 12 years-15 years	14	140	154	36.67
Above 15 years	22	57	79	18.81
Total	74	346	420	100
Percentage	17.62	82.38	100	

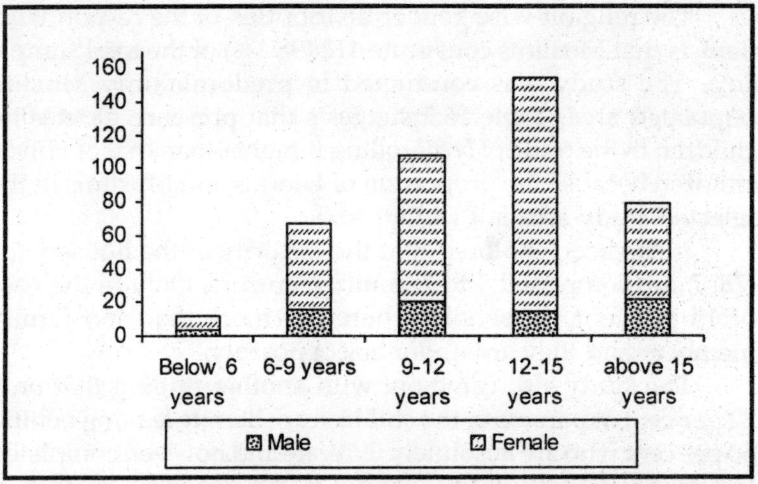

Fig. 16.1 : Gender and age of the respondents

Table 16.2 : Gender and religion of the respondents

Gender	*Religion*		*Total*	*Percentage*
	Hindu	*Muslim*		
Male	2	72	74	17.62
Female	6	340	346	82.38
Total	8	412	420	100
Percentage	1.90	98.10	100	

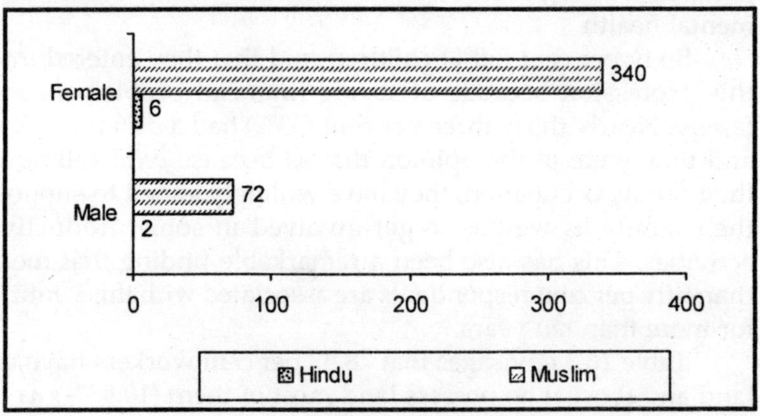

Fig. 16.2 : Gender and Religion of the Respondents

The religion-wise gender distribution of the respondents depicts that Muslims constitute 412 (98.1%) of the total sample size. The study was conducted in predominantly Muslim populated area. Table 16.2 suggests that presence of Muslim children in the trade of *beedi* rolling is higher than that of Hindu children because the proportion of Hindus and Muslims in the selected study area is 1 : 4 (approx).

It has been explored that the majority of the households (78%) are comprised 4 to 7 family members. Only in the case of 13 per cent households there are more than ten family members and they are under abject poverty.

The study also came out with another finding that only 22 per cent of parents of the children are literate leaving behind 60 per cent who are absolutely illiterate and not even completed the primary level of education. On the contrary, in case of children—58 per cent were found to be dropped out from the school before completing their primary education. Only 40 per cent of the children just completed primary education and 2 per cent continued their education after eighth standard.

Majority of the respondents (88%) were in the opinion of absence of bonded labour in their community in contrast to 10 per cent respondents who replied positively stating that hidden and unreported bonded labour prevails. It was also known that 92 per cent respondents rated *beedi*-making profession as high risk oriented both in terms of physical and mental health.

Sixty per cent (60%) children said that they entered into this profession because of severe financial problem in the family. Nearly thirty three per cent (33%) had a different view and they were in the opinion that as because *beedi* rolling is their family occupation, they have willingly joined to support their family as well as to get involved in some productive activities. This has also been a remarkable finding that more than fifty per cent respondents are associated with this venture for more than ten years.

Table 16.3 envisages that 78.57 per cent workers have no land and those who possess land most of them (10.48%) have within 1 bigha of land. Table 16.4 clearly speaks of that mostly the fathers of the children are engaged in the same *beedi* rolling profession. This is also to note that bread earners of the family are also involved in agriculture, small business, construction work as well as daily labour for profitable trade with a paltry amount. If we see from another perspective, it is evident that 59.05 per cent children are above poverty line in contrary to 38.33 per cent who belong to below poverty line. Only very small percentage (2.62%) belong to affluent families.

Table 16.3 : Distribution of agricultural land owned according to family size

Agricultural land	*Family size*				*Total*	*Percent-age*
	1-3 Persons	*4-7 Persons*	*8-10 Persons*	*10 and above*		
Landless	23	262	39	6	330	78.57
1 Bigha	4	36	4	0	44	10.48
1-2 Bighas	0	16	3	1	20	4.76
2-3 Bighas	0	4	2	0	6	1.43
Above 3 Bighas	2	10	5	3	20	4.76
Total	29	328	53	10	420	100
Percentage	6.90	78.10	12.62	2.38	100	

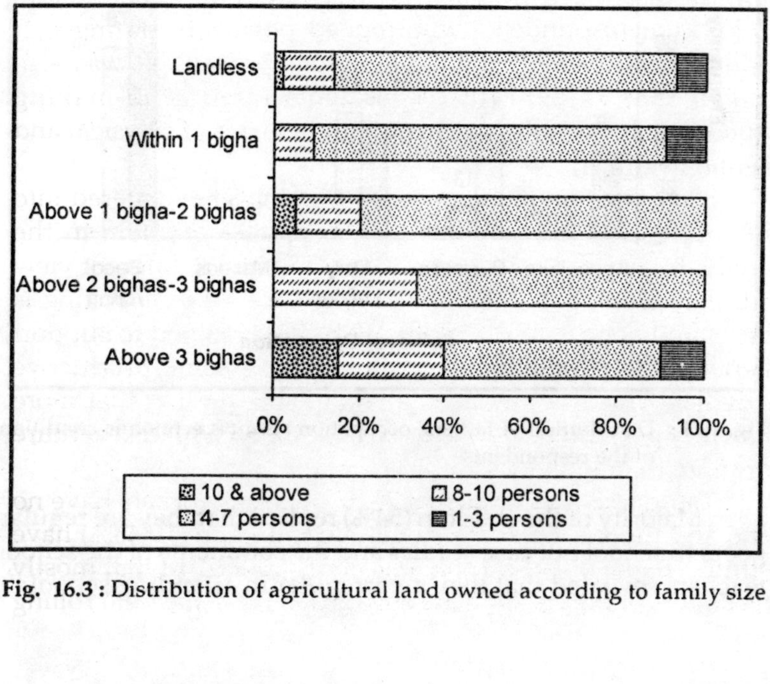

Fig. 16.3 : Distribution of agricultural land owned according to family size

Table 16.4 : Distribution of fathers' occupation *vis-à-vis* economic condition of the respondents

Fathers' occupation	Socio-economic condition			Total	Percent-age
	Above poverty line	Below poverty line	Affluent		
Agriculture	36	17	3	56	13.33
Business	42	13	4	59	14.05
Daily labour	46	51	0	97	23.10
Masons	1	2	0	3	0.71
Beedi rolling	123	78	4	205	48.81
Total	248	161	11	420	100
Percentage	59.05	38.33	2.62	100	

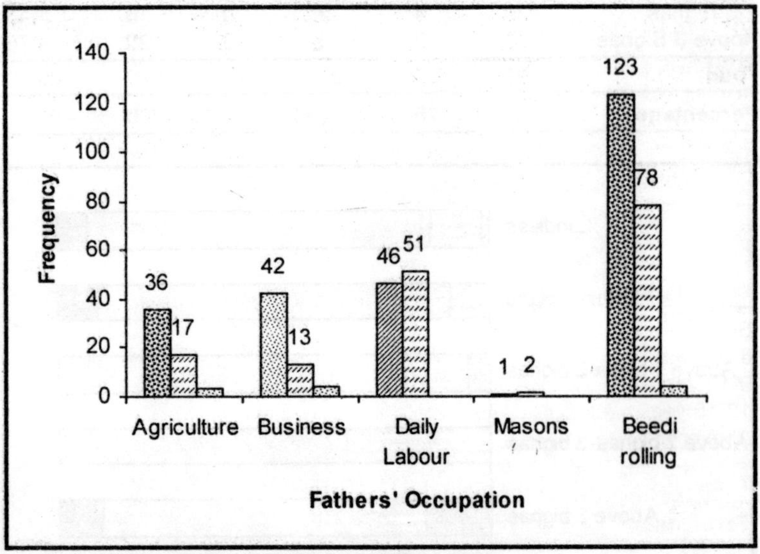

Fig. 16.4 : Distribution of fathers' occupation *vis-à-vis* economic condition of the respondents

Majority of the children (54%) replied that they are regular goers to school but case studies and the comments of the school teachers revealed that they are irregular in attending school. It has also been explored that a high percentage (45%) children have stopped going to school either because of the inability of the parents to afford education or because of family work pressure.

Every child worker at their tender age is suffering from both physical and mental health hazards. Physical problems include shoulder and neck pain, pain in the spinal chord due to prolonged working hours in sitting head-down position while rolling *beedis*. Respiratory problem, eye infection due to tobacco dust is also very common among them. In terms of mental health problems; they are always under constant stress and strain, frustration and which all lead to the development of bad habit of smoking. They have no time or resources to deal with such occupational hazards. If the situation aggravates, they resort to quack doctors or at the most they visit primary health centres for the treatment. Every child said that they don't have any leisure time for recreation or other social interactions.

Table 16.5 : Age of the respondents and monthly income

Age	*Monthly income*			*Total*	*Percentage*
	< Rs. 200 line	*Rs.200-500*	*Rs. 500-1000*		
Below 6 years	9	2	2	13	3.10
6-9 years	48	18	1	67	15.95
9-12 years	49	53	5	107	25.48
12-15 years	42	87	25	154	36.67
Above 15 years	7	52	20	79	18.81
Total	155	212	53	420	100
Percentage	36.90	50.48	12.62	100	

Table 16.5 clearly shows that the majority of the children (50.48%) earn between Rs. 200-500 and a very few percentage (12.62%) earn between Rs. 500 to Rs. 1000. It also reflects that forty-nine children in the age group between 9-12 years earn less than Rs. 200 per month. On the other hand children in the age group of 12-15 years of which 87 and 25 children earn between Rs. 200 to 500 and Rs. 500 to 1000 respectively. The

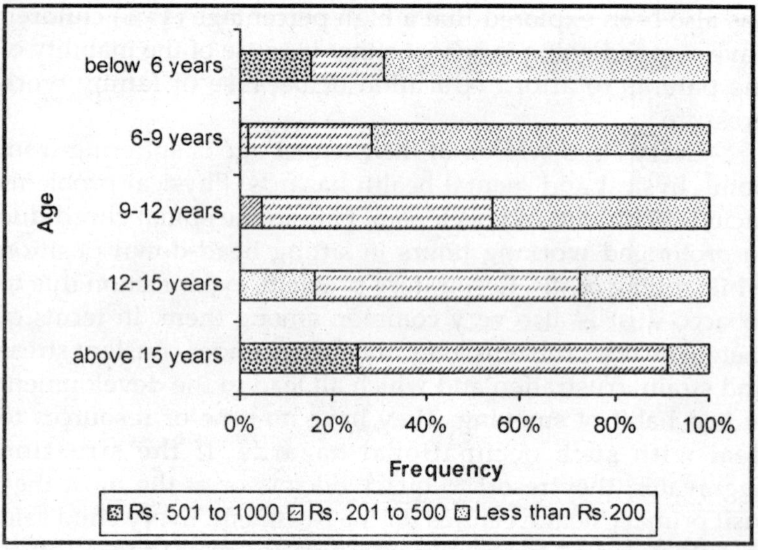

Fig. 16.5 : Age of the respondents and monthly income

income is very poor in comparison to the hours of work, which is depicted in Table 16.6.

Table 16.6 : Monthly income and daily working hours of the children

Monthly income	*Daily working hours*					*Total*	*Percent-age*
	Up to 4 hours	*4-6 hours*	*6-8 hours*	*8-10 hours*	*Above 10 hours*		
Less than Rs. 200	57	73	17	7	1	155	36.90
Rs. 200-500	12	110	75	8	7	212	50.48
Rs. 500-1000	5	7	24	13	4	53	12.62
Total	74	190	116	28	12	420	100
Percentage	17.62	45.24	27.62	6.67	2.86	100	

Table 16.6 envisages that 45.24 per cent children work above 4 to 6 hours daily and the next higher percentage (27.62%) work above 6 to 8 hours daily. There are children who

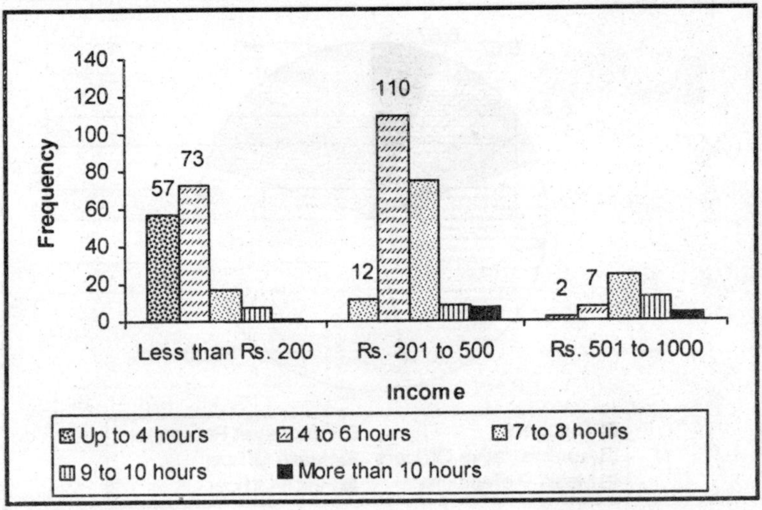

Fig. 16.6 : Monthly income and daily working hours of the children

work more than 8 hours, which is against the international labour rule. It is also seen that 57 per cent children work up to 4 hours in a day and in exchange they earn less than Rs. 400 per month. The highest percentage (50.48%) of the children earn between Rs. 200 to 500. On the contrary, only a small percentage (12.62%) earns Rs. 500 to 1000 per month.

Stakeholders' views were also given much emphasis for the study as mentioned in the methodology section. Two important findings will be discussed here. Table 16.7 shows the different types and numbers of stakeholders whose opinions were taken into consideration.

Table 16.7 : Distribution of the types of stakeholders

Stakeholders	*Frequency*	*Percentage*
Teachers	3	20.00
Panchayat Personnel	5	33.33
Administrative officers	4	26.67
Health officers	1	6.67
Medical professionals	1	6.67
Police personnel	1	6.67
Total	15	100

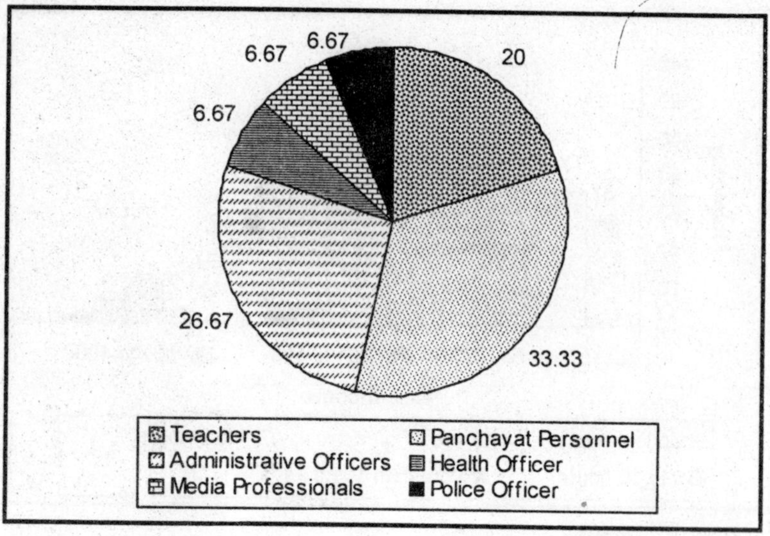

Fig. 16.7 : Distribution of the types of stakeholders

Table 16.8 ascertains that 26.19 per cent stakeholders perceived that working long hours for low wages and physical and mental hazards involved in the profession faced by the children are the worst part of the child *beedi* rolling workers. Children leading adult lives at premature age and deprived of education, childhood and vocational training are also noticeable opinion of the stakeholders about the issue.

Table 16.8 : Perception of stakeholders about the condition of child labour

Perception on child labour	*Frequency*	*Percentage*
Children leading adult lives at tender age	6	14.29
Working long hours for low wages	11	26.19
Working condition is damaging their physical and mental development	11	26.19
Frequently deprived of education and vocational training	6	14.29
Involvement in the profession due to direct or indirect family conflict	1	2.38
Work within or outside the family	4	9.52
Minimum time for leisure	3	7.14
Total	42	100

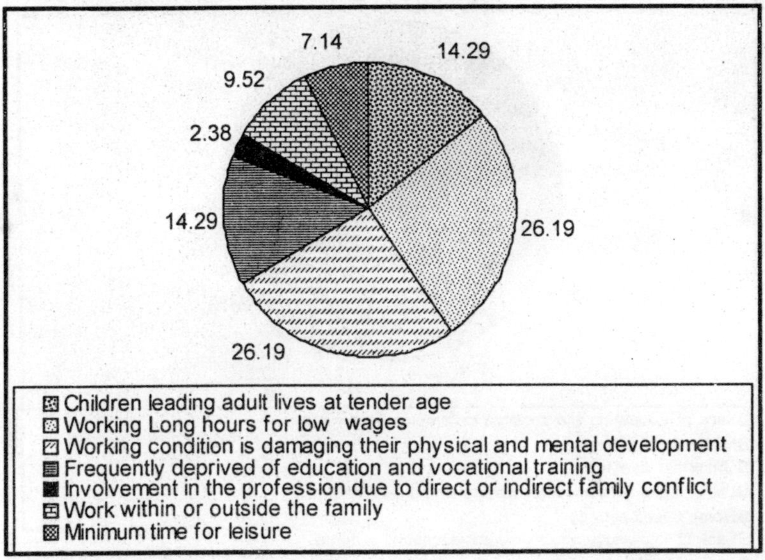

Fig. 16.8 : Perception of stakeholders about the condition of child labour

Table 16.9 : Causes of becoming child labour as the stakeholders perceived

Causes of child labour	*Frequency*	*Percentage*
Lack of education and socialization	14	22.58
High rate of poverty	15	24.19
Uncertain disasters	5	8.06
Lack of alternative income	13	20.97
Home based activity	9	14.52
Lack of family planning	4	6.45
Lack of knowledge about government policies and programmes on socio-economic scheme	2	3.23
Total	62	100

The stakeholders (24.19%) opined that high rate of poverty is the principal cause of child labour as shown in Table 16.9. 22.58 per cent and 20.97 per cent stakeholders are of the opinion that lack of education and alternative income generation respectively leads to child labour. So, mainly what is extracted from the table that socio-economic condition is solely responsible for these children to be crept into this profession.

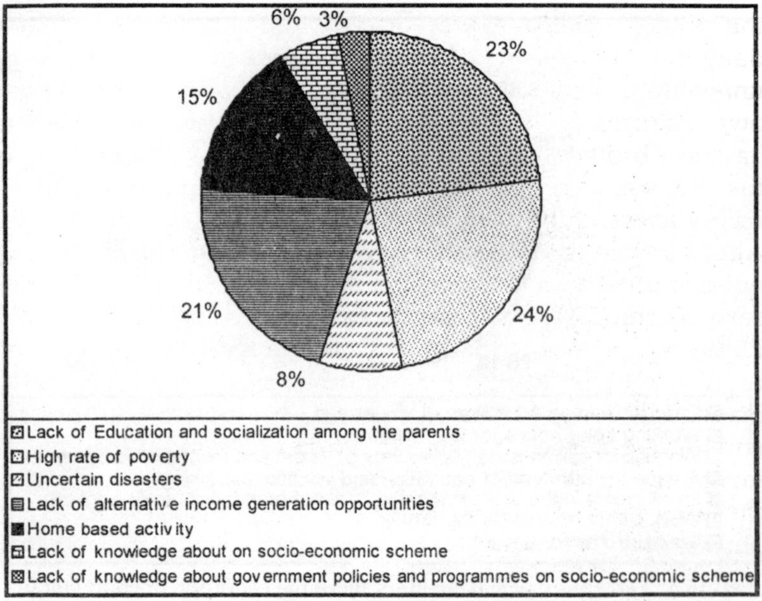

Fig. 16.9 : Causes of becoming child labour as the stakeholders perceived

To wrap up the discussion it is to be noted that none of the households is having latrine, pure and safe drinking water or healthy and hygienic living condition. Children are not at all aware of the ill-effects and future implications of *beedi* rolling activities as well as existing child labour prohibition legislations. No initiative has been taken so far by the government or NGOs to improve their condition and make them free from these evils of life.

Case Study

"I want to play with my friends..."

Akurma Khatun (F) is the eldest daughter and the only earning member of the family. Though she is twelve years old, she has to shoulder the responsibility of maintaining her family of five members. Her father is chronically ill-patient and almost bed-ridden and cannot move and work. Mother is equally not in good health condition and often falls ill. With great difficulties, the mother manages to work in *beedi* rolling to supplement her daughter's income. They live in a small mud hut in a very unhealthy environment and having no agricultural land of their own. Akurma is illiterate and does not go to school and she is having a brother and sister of very tender age. *Beedi* rolling is the only source of income for the family. The family is leading a very stressful life with no time to spend for other activities. Akurma spends most of her time and effort to roll maximum number of *beedis* to earn much in a day. She has to work from early morning to late in the evening even when she is terribly ill. If she does not work she will loose the earning of the day. In return she gets scanty amount, which is absolutely inadequate for their sustenance. She has no time to interact with her peer. She often gets frustrated with her life and feels mental fatigued. If proper care is not taken at this stage it can cause a persistent mental problem. She has also started facing physical problems because of long hours of work as back and neck pain, eye problem and respiratory problem. She has no option left in her life except to continue the *beedi* rolling for the survival of her family with meagre amount in exchange of her assiduous labour. She is an exploited child and has lost all spices of her life.

"I get sick very often... but I still keep working"

Rupchand Sekh (M) is a young boy of six years old. He is associated with *beedi* rolling activities from his childhood to add more income to his family. His family income is very low in comparison to the family size. So to support his parents he joins in the *beedi* rolling whenever he is free. He studies in the first standard in the school. Immediately after coming from school he starts working with his father. As a result he has no time to study, play or do other activities. His both parents are illiterate. They are not so much aware of his education and poor financial condition has forced them to involve Rupchand in this profession at such an early age. His father is a farmer by profession but having no land of his own and works as a labour in others field. Rupchand's mother and elder sister are also associated with *beedi* rolling. He is also physically not strong enough; often suffers from persistent fever, which takes long time to cure. He is also suffering from eye problem having permanent blood clot in his eyes and which restricts his clear vision. However, his poor health condition has never been got proper attention. A family which is struggling hard to ensure their existence by meeting square meal a day is not in a position to go for medical examination for Rupchand. So, in such a tender age and with all adverse socio-economic and health condition he is forced to be with *beedi* rolling activities.

Recommendations

Considering the analysis and the findings of the present study, a multidimensional approach needs to be designed for effective intervention and properly addressing to the problem of *beedi* rolling child labour.

(a) Direct household level intervention

- Bridge course education for potential *beedi* rolling child labour for their re-enrolment to the schools.
- Opportunities for afternoon recreational activities for the children.
- Massive and intensive awareness and sensitization programmes in the communities through posters, meetings, rallies etc.
- Capacity building and advocacy programmes of the school teachers so as to enable them to orient the students in the school and to counteract the problem.
- Vocational training for children for opening up future employment opportunities.
- Motivating the mothers for formation of self-help group and undertake income generation programmes after careful assessment of their resource availability and skill orientation.

(b) Constant review and research

- Conducting Participatory Rural Appraisal (PRA) meetings in the study area including every village.

- Intensive survey of the households of child labours for pinpointing of the variables, which influence the children to be a potential *beedi* rolling worker.
- Information, Education and Communication (IEC) workshop at the community level with the legal instruments.
- Review of existing policies and legislations for necessary modification and amendments.
- Research and collection of facts and figures on the issue of child labour with emphasis on *beedi* rolling occupation at state and national level.

(c) Policy influencing and public advocacy

- State and national level interactions with different major stakeholders and actors.
- Formation of neighbourhood groups against employment of child labour in *beedi* rolling occupation.
- Networking with Community Based Organizations (CBOs), local bodies, judiciaries and law enforcement agencies.
- Networking at the local level with Panchayati Raj Institutions (PRIs), block as well as district level administration.

(d) Curative and rehabilitative approach targeting the households of the* beedi*-rolling children

- Re-enrolment of the dropouts to the schools.
- Preparing parents groups towards formation of co-operatives of *beedi* rolling workers.
- Greater stress should be given on increasing the children's access to good quality relevant education.
- Mobilizing the employers for introduction of social security measures including provident fund account.
- Motivating and mobilizing the agents/brokers and employers for payment of proper and minimum wages to the parents.
- Efforts to be taken to ensure participation of children and their families in the implementation, monitoring and evaluation phase.

(e) *Preventive and promotional approach comprising of alternative income generation avenues for the parents*

- Changes in policies and practices affecting children and young people.
- Changes in equity and non-discrimination of children and young people.
- Changes in children and young people's participation and active citizenship.
- Changes in civil society and communities' capacity to support children's rights.
- Mobilizing credit institutions for financial support to the head of the households after assessment of the availability of resources and skill orientation.
- Development of constant joint monitoring mechanism, comprising government agencies, PRI representatives and community leaders for follow-up of the process.

SUGGESTED READINGS

1. Khatu, K.K. (2005); *Working Children in India;* Rawat Publications, New Delhi.
2. Bardhan, Pranab, "Social Justice in Global Economy"; *Economic and Political Weekly*; Vol.XXXVI. Nos. 5 and 6, February. 3-9/10-16, 2001.
3. Saksena, Anu (2003); *Human Rights and Child Labour in Indian Industries,* Shipra Publications, New Delhi.
4. Bhandari, J. "Child Labour: the challenges ahead", *Yojana*; Vol. 44, No. 9, September 2001.
5. Bhatt, K.N. "Eliminating child labour through primary education: Indian scenario"; *Mainstream,* Vol. XXXVIII, No. 49, November 25, 2006; p. 27.
6. Satyarthi, Kailash; "Child rights' protection: the triangular paradigm". *The Hindu,* January 6, 2005, p. 15.
7. Jha, Dhirendra K. (1997); "A catastrophe in slow motion". *The Pioneer,* March 7, p. 9.
8. Burra, Neera (2001); *Born to work: Child Labour in India,* Oxford University Press, New Delhi.
9. Gupta, Shriniwas (2003); "Child Labour and Law: An Overview"; *Social Defence,* Vol. 50, No. 145, July, pp. 18-29.
10. *The Times of India,* (1999), 'Child Beaten to Death', 15 July.
11. *The Statesman New Service,* 1 December, 1996, p. 3.
12. *The Statesman,* 8 July, 1997, p. 6.
13. *The Times of India,* 22 December 1996, p. 18.

PART D

AGEING

17

Problems of Elderly Abuse
Some Reflections and Implications for Social Work Practice

Introduction

Every person—every man, woman, and child—deserves to be treated with respect and with caring. Every person—no matter how young or how old—deserves to be safe from harm by those who live with them, care for them, or come in day-to-day contact with them. Older people today are more visible, more active, and more independent than ever before. They are living longer and in better health. But as the population of older people grows everywhere, so does the hidden problem of elder abuse, exploitation, and neglect.

Most elder abuse and neglect takes place at home. The great majority of older people live on their own or with their spouses, children, siblings, or other relatives—not in institutional settings. When elder abuse happens, family, other household members, and paid caregivers usually are the abusers. Although there are extreme cases of elder abuse, often the abuse is subtle, and the distinction between normal interpersonal stress and abuse is not always easy to discern.

There is no single pattern of elder abuse. Sometimes, the abuse is a continuation of long-standing patterns of physical or emotional abuse within the family. Perhaps, more commonly, the abuse is related to changes in living situations and relationships brought about by the older person's growing frailty and dependence on others for companionship and for meeting basic needs.

It is not just infirm or mentally impaired elderly people who are vulnerable to abuse. Elders who are ill, frail, disabled, mentally impaired, or depressed are at greater risk of abuse, but even those who do not have these obvious risk factors can find themselves in abusive situations and relationships.

Elder abuse, like other forms of violence, is never an acceptable response to any problem or situation, however stressful. Effective interventions can prevent or stop elder abuse. By increasing awareness among physicians, mental health professionals, social workers, home health care workers, and others who provide services to the elderly and family members, patterns of abuse or neglect can be broken, and both the abused person and the abuser can receive needed help.

Definitional paradigm

Elderly abuse covers any behaviour or pattern of behaviour by a person or persons, which results in harm to an elder person. Definitional categories are often diverse, including combinations of physical abuse, psychological abuse, medical abuse, economic abuse, violation of rights, sexual abuse, and neglect and self-neglect. Elder abuse is part of the intra-familial violence and society as a whole is reluctant to acknowledge and accept this as a problem. The factors that make family life intimate may also make it prone to conflict and if the conflict is not resolved by negotiation and compromise then it may lead to violence.

Thus, in view of the problems faced by the elderly in the changing family context, the elder abuse and neglect becomes a topic of significant interest and focus for researchers, social workers and policy-makers.

Scenario of elderly population

Our world is growing old. Worldwide there are 600 million people aged 60, which is expected to reach 2 billion by 2050. In India also the life expectancy has increased from 40 years in 1951 to 64 years today. Thus, there are 77 million older persons today, which is expected to touch a figure of 177 million in another 25 years. It is important to recognize that about 80 per cent of the elderly population in India lives in the rural areas and 30 per cent of the elderly are below the poverty line. 40 and 200 out of 1000 elderly are experiencing physical violence and verbal abuse respectively (*Newsletter,* 2003). The population of 80 years (age) and above constitute 11 per cent of the elderly population. This is also to note that there are 2,00,000 centenarians in India alone. It is also to be mentioned that 60 (+) population is projected to shoot up to 100 million, which is likely to double in the next 17 years (198 million).

The number of elderly people worldwide will reach 1000 million. Europe would continue to be "oldest" region in the world with 25 per cent representation of world elderly. Three quarters of all deaths in developing countries could be ageing related. Out of 10 countries with largest population 60 (+) will be from the Asian continent—China (230 million), India (142 million), Indonesia (29 million) and Pakistan (18 million).

Theoretical underpinnings

Some of the theoretical explanations regarding elder abuse can be categorized as follows (Desai and Raju, 2000):

1. Social isolation

When elderly are isolated from the society or the social network is such that which is not permitting the elder people to come into the mainstream of the society. As a result they feel lonely and cannot interact with the larger segments of the society. This cloistered life pattern lead to increase their risk of being abused. Many research studies in this area are found to be in support of this theory (Phillips, 1993; Pillemer, 1985).

2. Stress

A stress perspective on elder abuse, on the other hand, emphasizes the interplay between intra-individual and social structural variables such as caregiver stress resulting from work or unemployment, life crises, economic conditions and so on. When an elderly parent lives in a family and if all the members except children go out for work for the entire day which may arise conflict, stress, misunderstanding, lack of discipline, disruption in communication; culminate in elderly abuse (Desai and Raju, 2000).

3. *Intra-individual dynamics*

According to this explanation, the abusers sometimes possess a few personality traits, habits or some pathological characteristics, which make them abusive. This has been reiterated from time to time (Pillemer and Suitor, 1990). Of course, this explanation is subject to criticism (Gelles and Pedrick-Cornell, 1990).

4. *Dependence because of impairments*

Elderly people with severe physical or mental impairments tend to become more dependent as well as more vulnerable to be abused (Block and Sinnott, 1979). The basic reasons behind it that care-givers who are responsible to take care of these types of elderly people undergo tremendous physical and mental pressure which make them impatient, a sense of irritation develops and which all get manifested in a form of abuse and neglect.

5. *Negative attitudes towards elderly*

Another explanation may be that peoples' prevailing negative stereotype attitudes towards the elderly and their roles in society. The conventional way of looking at the older people as somebody who is unproductive and useless human being and burden on the society. These negative attitudes tend to dehumanize old people and make it easier for an abuser to victimize them without feeling remorse (Giordano and Giordano, 1984).

6. Cycle of abuse or inter-generational transmission of violence

Abuse breeds abuse. It means that some point of time abuse is cyclical in nature. If a child gets abuse at his or her early age by the parents that sometimes manifests in a form of abuse by the children towards the parents. So child abuse leads to elder abuse (McCuan, 1980). People learn to be violent when they grow up in violent homes.

Types of abuse

The proportion of ageing and security are on the decline. Instead of treating the elderly people as valuable resources they are treated as a burden. The present generation has developed a feeling that the older people are rendered unproductive during their entire post-retirement period, which can be considered long, covering about one-third to one-fourth of a person's entire life span.

There is no uniformity regarding 'what constitutes abuse'. Many researchers refer to all kinds of problems elder people face are to be considered as abuse including lack of proper housing, misuse of money or property of the elderly, forcing the elderly to leave their own houses, or creating situations that the elder persons are forced to go and take refuge in an old age home. Under given situation the author would like to classify the types of abuse as follows:

- *Physical abuse*—Using physical forces that result in physical pain or injury:
  - Refusal to go to same emergency department for repeated injuries.
  - Repeated unexplained injuries.
  - Dismissive attitude or statements about injuries.
  - Rope marks or welts on the wrists and/or ankles.
  - Bruises or grip marks around the arms or neck.
  - Repeated time lags between the time of any "injury or fall" and medical treatment.
  - Inconsistent explanations of the injuries.

- *Emotional/Psychological abuse*—Verbal assaults, humiliation, threats, harassment, intimidation or abusive behaviour:
  - Evasiveness.
  - Lack of interest in social contacts.
  - Uncommunicative and unresponsive.
  - Unreasonably fearful or suspicious.
  - Chronic physical or psychiatric health problems.
  - Depression, hopelessness, helplessness, thoughts of suicide.
  - Hypervigilance.
  - Trembling, clinging, cowering, lack of eye contact.

- *Neglect*—Failure to make provisions for personal care (food, shelter, medical care, social contact), or forceful confinement or restraint of the older adult (either intentionally or unintentionally):
  - Sunken eyes or loss of weight.
  - Extreme thirst.
  - Bed sores.
  - Signs of malnourishment.
  - Chronic health problems both physical and/or psychiatric.
  - Overmedication or oversedation.
  - Caregivers exhibit high levels of indifference or anger towards the older adult.
  - Elder is not given the opportunity to speak without the caregiver being present.

- *Material/Financial abuse*—The misuse or withholding of an adult's resources by another adult:
  - Signature on checks don't match elder's signature.
  - Life circumstances don't match with the size of the estate.
  - Large withdrawals from bank accounts, switching accounts, unusual ATM activity.
  - Recent acquaintances, housekeeper, caregiver, etc. make promises of lifelong care in exchange for

deeding all property and/or assigning all assets over to the acquaintance, caregiver, etc.

- The caregiver only expresses concern regarding the financial status of the older person and does not ask questions or express concern regarding the physical and/or mental health status of the elderly.
- Documents are being drawn up for the elder to sign but the elder cannot explain or understand the purpose of the papers.
- The elder's living situation is not commensurate with the size of the elder's estate (e.g. lack of new clothing or amenities, unpaid bills).

• ***Sexual abuse***—Non-consensual contact with an older person:

- Bruised breasts.
- Torn or bloody underwear.
- Unexplained vaginal or anal bleeding
- Veneral diseases or vaginal infections.

• ***Violation of basic rights***—This is also an important area of elder abuse and which needs lot of attention:

- Caregiver withholds or reads the elder's mail.
- Caregivers have removed all doors from the older adult's rooms.
- Caregiver intentionally obstructs the older person's religious observances (e.g. dietary restrictions, holiday participation, visits by ministers, priest etc.).
- As violation of basic rights is often concomitant with psychological abuse the indicators of basic rights violations are similar indicators as those for psychological abuse.

Possible causes of elderly abuse

Elder abuse is an extremely complex problem. Below is simply a listing of some of the possible contributory factors related to elder abuse. It is important also to remember that these factors usually do not operate in isolation but rather interact in unique ways depending on the victim and perpetrator's situation.

Caring for a non-well older adult suffering from a mental or physical impairment is highly stressful. Individuals who do not have the requisite skills, information, resources etc. and who are otherwise ill-prepared for the caregiving role may experience extreme stress and frustration. This may lead to elder abuse and/or neglect.

It has been argued that as an older adult's dependency increases so does the resentment and stress of the caregiver. Studies have found that individuals in poor health are more likely to be abused than individuals who are in relatively good health. In addition, caregivers who are dependent on the elder financially is also more likely to perpetrate abuse.

External stress such as financial problems, job stress, and additional family stressors have been hypothesized to also increase the risk for abuse. Abuse, whether spousal abuse, child abuse, or elder abuse occurs most often in families characterized by social isolation. Of course, this may be both an indicator of potential abuse as well as potential contributing cause of abuse.

Individuals who are abused as children are hypothesized to become part of a cycle of violence. Violence is learned as a form of acceptable behaviour in childhood as a response to conflict, anger, or tension. Thus, when these feelings arise during caregiving, the caregiver is at risk for becoming a perpetrator of elder abuse or neglect. If the older person receiving the care previously abused their child, that child now in the role of caregiver simply is returning the abuse they suffered.

Some caregivers may be at risk for abusing elders as a function of their own difficulties. For example, a caregiver who suffers from such problems as alcoholism, drug addiction, and/or an emotional disorder (e.g. a personality disorder) is more likely to become an abuser than an individual who do not suffer from such problems.

What has been emerging out from the above discussion, the author would like to summarize for its convenience as follows:

Family situations

- Marital stress between an older couple,
- Social isolation,
- Family stress,
- Financial burden,
- Discord in the family, and
- Women's violence in the family.

Caregiver issues

- Personal problems of the caregivers,
- Stress of the caregivers,
- Caregiver's own self-image,
- Emotional and psychological problems of the caregivers,
- If caregiver is responsible for an older person who is physically and mentally unfit, and
- Dependency is a contributing factor in elder abuse. When caregiver is dependent financially on an impaired older person, there may be financial exploitation or abuse.

Cultural issues

- Certain societal attitudes,
- Lack of respect for the elderly,
- Religious or ethical systems sometimes allow for mistreatment of elderly, and
- The ideas that what happens at home in 'private' can be a major factor in keeping an older person locked in an abusive situation.

Implications for social work practice and preventive measures

Current trends in ageing suggest that 21st century social work advocates should be prepared to work with healthier and more socially skilled elders as well as with a sizeable proportion of old who are incapacitated, frail, and poor. Social scientists (Hooyman and Kiyak, 1993; Raffoul and McNeece, 2000) project that changes in medicine and medical technology, marital status and family structure, work and leisure, and government intervention, will ensure that elders of the 21st century are older and healthier. They will also be active participants in ensuring a high quality of life for themselves and for others. As society shifts away from its youth orientation, we will view elders as both consumers and resources. Their power base will increase as they move into positions of control and become an integral part of daily social system activities.

Social workers in India need to develop the skills of working with elderly. A range of supportive services and financing streams are involved in managing elderly care. It is recommended that at the level of community, the planning of long-term care must focus on four themes (Beland and Arweiler, 1996): (1) Developing priorities to reflect values, (2) Setting-up human services organizations governed by a set of rules and procedures, (3) Choosing objectives to which participants and organizations are committed, and (4) Mobilizing the various resources.

Awareness, Education and *Advocacy* are having lot of implications for social work practice. Creating awareness about the elder abuse is the first step in formulating response to the abuse of older persons. Sensitizing media about such heinous task and to propagate properly against elder abuse and its consequences is a very important aspect. Educational programmes to enable participants in the assessment and detection of abuse and neglect for effective intervention needs to target lawyers, politicians, law enforcement officers, social workers, and other professionals. WHO has developed awareness materials to assist them with screening tools to identify abusive and potentially abusive situations, protocols for referral and intervention, and training resources kits for service providers.

In terms of preventive measures as well as role of social workers for elderly abuse; the issue can be perceived from different angles. An attempt has been made to reckon those in a synoptical manner as follows:

Towards prevention for the individual

- Maintain social contacts; increase network of friends.
- To encourage participation in social and community activities.
- Ask friends to visit at home.
- To review will periodically.
- Don't leave your home unattended.
- Don't sign a document unless someone you trust has reviewed it.
- Arrange to have your social security check or pension deposited directly into your bank account.
- Get legal advices concerning arrangements you can make not for future disability (e.g. power of attorney).
- Volunteer.
- Develop a buddy system with a friend outside the home.
- Keep in touch with old friends and neighbours even if you move.

Towards prevention for families

- Maintain close ties with ageing relatives and friends.
- Find sources of help and use them.
- Explore alternative sources of care.
- Don't hamper the older person's independence or intrude unnecessarily upon his/her privacy.
- Don't ignore your limitations and overextend yourself.
- Don't expect family problems to disappear once the elder moves into home.
- Examine closely your family's ability to provide long-term, in-home care.
- Don't offer personal home care unless you thoroughly understand the demands and can meet the responsibility and costs involved.
- Anticipate potential incapacitation and make plans based on discussion of the elder's wishes.

Towards prevention for communities

- Develop a new ways to provide direct assistance to care giving families.
- Ask other community groups to become more involved in ageing service programmes.
- Encourage both public and private employers to help caregiving families.
- Publicize available support services and professionals available to caregivers.
- Give public agency employees basic training in responses and case management.
- Provide training for community "gatekeepers" and service providers.
- Recognize that many forms of abuse or mistreatment are crimes.

In addition the following suggestions can also be well thought of by the social workers to prevent elderly abuse:

- Awareness and facilitation of positive and productive ageing.
- Coalition building.
- Alcohol and substance abuse treatment programmes available to all in need of such services.
- Adequate caregiver training and services.
- Mental health and family counselling services available to all in need of such services.
- Adequate and available financial management and planning services.
- Violence-reduction, conflict resolution, and meditation programmes and services available to all in need of such services/programmes.
- Assertive training, promotion of elder rights and self-advocacy training for all elder adults.
- Public awareness and professional training in relation to elder abuse and other adult issues.
- Sufficient income, health care, and social services for all older adults.

SUGGESTED READINGS

1. Beland, F. and Arweiler, D. (1996); "A frame of reference for elaborating policies of long-term care: a conceptual model"; Canadian *Journal of Aging*. 15 (4): 532-648.
2. Raffoul, P., and McNeece, C. (2000); *Future issues for social work practice*; Boston: Allyn and Bacon.
3. Hooyman, N., and Kiyak, H. (1993); *Social gerontology: A multidisciplinary perspective*; Boston: Allyn and Bacon.
4. Desai, M., and Raju, S. (2000); *Gerentological Social Work in India—Issues and Perspectives*; B.R. Publishing Corporation, Delhi.
5. Rathbone-McCuan, E. (1980); "Elderly Victims of Family Violence and Neglect"; *Social Casework*, 61, 296-304.
6. Pillemer, K. and Suitor. (1990); "Personnel to Serve the Aging in the Field of Social Work: Implications for Educating Professionals"; *Social Work*, 35 (5), 412-415.
7. Gelles, R. and Pedrick-Cornell, C. (1990); *Intimate Violence in Families*, (2nd Ed.), New Delhi: Sage.
8. Giordano, N., and Giordano: (1984); "Elder abuse—A Review of the Literature"; *Social Work*, 29 (3), 232-236.
9. Block, E. and Sinnott, J. (1979); *The Battered Elders Syndrome*, College Park, MD: Center on Ageing, Unpublished manuscript.
10. Phillips, I. (1993) "The Dangers of Dependency: New Findings on Domestic Violence Against the Elderly": *Social Problems*, 33, 146-158.
11. Pillermer, K., (1985); Prevention of Elder abuse. In R. Ammerman and M. Herser (Eds.) *Treatment of Family Violence*, (406-422), New York: John Wiley.
12. The National Elder Abuse Incidence Study. (1988); U.S. Department of Health and Human Services, Administration on Aging.
13. *Newsletter;* National Institute of Social Defence: Vol. 4, No. 12; December 2003.
14. *Newsletter;* National Institute of Social Defence: Vol. 4, No. 4; April 2003.

18

Combating the Problem of Ageing with Dignity

Introduction

Ageing is now recognized as a major global—social, economic and humanitarian—issue. If we go in a somewhat chronological manner with regard to the development of various initiatives taken by the United Nations and its agencies it would become apparent that though UN declaration of the year 1999 as International Year of Older Persons has once again stirred the conscience of the world to the problems of ageing and the aged but several major initiatives had already been taken during the last fifty years.

It was way back in 1948 that the question of ageing was first taken up by the United Nations at the initiative of Argentina, which proposed a ***Draft Declaration on Old Age Rights***. The question was taken up again and placed on the agenda of the General Assembly at the initiative of Malta in 1969. But it was only in 1972 that the Economic and Social Council of the United Nations deliberated at length for the first time on the issues of ageing and the aged. However, it was only after a gap of ten years that the first World Assembly on Ageing could be held in Vienna in 1982 wherein the UN member-states formulated and adopted the ***International Plan of Action on Ageing,*** which was later on endorsed by the UN General Assembly in the same year. Again, almost a decade later, the UN adopted the ***Principles for Older Persons*** in 1991. The eighteen Principles were grouped into five clusters, namely

independence, participation, care, self-fulfilment, and **dignity** and are best summed up in the logo : ***To add life to the years that have been added to life.***

In 1990, the UN General Assembly designated October 1 as the **International Day of Older Persons** for celebrating and acknowledging the contribution of older people to society. The Conceptual Framework for **IYOP (International Year of Older Persons),** which is based on the International Plan of Action on Ageing (1982) and the Principles for Older Persons (1991), was formulated and submitted by the Secretary General to the 50th sessions of the General Assembly in 1995. The 1997 Operational Framework also assisted in setting the scene for the **International Year of Older Persons, 1999.** The overall theme for IYOP was " ***Towards a Society for All Ages".*** India has followed by nominating the Year 2000 as the National Year of Older Persons.

This makes us reflect back into what is old age. The Oxford Dictionary defines old age as the later part of normal life. There are main two approaches to the identification and definition of old age—**Biological** and **Chronological.** Biologically, normal ageing is characterized by progressive and irreversible changes in both structure and function with time. In modern society, we use chronological age, i.e. the length of time (usually counted in years) that a person has lived, as a social indicator.

Current status of the elderly

We have started living in the Age of ageing but it is only the dawn of that age. From 12 million in 1901, we rose to be 20 million in 1951 and there are now nearly 77 million older persons in India today (Desai and Raju, 2000). About 11 per cent of elderly are above 80 years. By 2025 (United Nations Projections, 1998) we would have 25 per cent who would be above 80 years.

At a moderate estimate, there are likely to be 177 million older people in India by 2025 (United Nations Projections, 1998). This in itself is no cause for alarm. However, the country is totally unprepared to handle the human problems associated with such a situation. There is no comprehensive national policy for elderly care. Old age pensions are meager and not all elderly are eligible for it. The National Sample Survey Organization's data shows that 4.5 per cent of elderly males and 6.7 per cent of elderly females in India were physically immobile (NSS, 1991). Nearly 45 per cent of rural and 44.8 per cent urban elderly suffer from seven major chronic diseases. A recent study of urban and rural elderly in Bangalore found 60 per cent of the older people to be suffering from long term illnesses. More than a fourth (28.2%) of women aged over 60 years needed help in managing activities of daily living. Many rural women who require care complained that they did not get such help. And to add to that, if a woman is widow, which is the case with 55 per cent of elderly women today, the world may not be a pleasant place to live (*Employment News* 12-18 August, 2000). More than half (50% to 55%) of the rural elderly have problems in seeing and walking, two things that are essential to keep the elderly active and independent (Prakash, 1997).

About 90 per cent of older persons today are from the unorganized sector that just means that at the age of 60, they have no regular source of income, no provident fund or gratuity; no medical insurance or any social security after formally or informally retiring from active earning

Ageing has important implications, both at the macro and micro levels. While at the micro level, it affects individuals and their families; at the macro level it affects the entire nation. With about 33 per cent of the elderly living just below the poverty line and another 33 per cent just above it, but belonging to lower income group, the financial situation of about 66 per cent of the older persons today is fragile. This relates to serious livelihood insecurities caused by factors including growing incidence of prolonged old age ailments, disabilities, dysfunctions, lack of opportunities in gainful activities and no or little familial support.

Changing status of elderly in the context of globalization

Globalization means accentuated change. If ageing makes adjustment to change difficult then we would expect globalization of change to increase life stress across all groups and income levels of the elderly though naturally there would be individual and group related variations.

The elderly in every country tend to be looked upon as among the relatively weaker segments of the population. Our fears for the elderly in India as for other weaker sections are born out of this scenario of developments in the world economy. The fears may not be entirely misplaced but they would need greater understanding and definition if they are to serve as a basis for preventive or corrective action.

Here again it would be important to consider which aspects of social and cultural change are likely to affect the elderly and in what manner. It may also be that not all of the ideas communicated through improved communication may help the elderly to utilize their extended spans or to add creativity to their lives.

Family plays a major role in looking after the elderly. Family is viewed as one of the most unique entities; it holds together dynamic relationships of members of different ages and generations. The concept of respecting the elders was ingrained in children during their younger years of upbringing. With the shift of household platform from extended families to nuclear families because of industrialization and modernization, there is an increased demand on family resources, making it necessary for individual family member to have more than one job. This reduces the time family members spend together. With the migration of working members in search of employment, the older persons are left behind-alone. This means that they have to look after themselves. So, the welfare of older persons is gradually shifting from family to community and government.

Problems and needs of the elderly

The problems of elderly can be categorized in India such as—(i) Health, (ii) Financial, (iii) Status and his emotional ties with the family members, and (iv) Housing. All these problems are interrelated. One affects the other in a cyclical nature. Health problems over a period of time generally have some bearing on the financial and socio-psychological problems as well. For instance, if an elderly person has been suffering for a long time, it not only entails a drain of financial resources but also affects social relationship with the members of the family who have to look after the ailing aged for a long time.

Further, ailing aged is likely to become more irritating and depressed further strain and mental agony to others as well, in the family. Similarly, a financially dependent elder particularly in lower middle class or poor families, usually suffers from malnutrition and continued malnutrition may result in ill-health and even chronic diseases. Socio-psychological suffering occurs in the elderly as well as in other members of the family both in case of continued sickness and where family income is inadequate to provide for the day-to-day needs of the dependent elderly parents.

A glimpse of programmes and policies for elder care

The well-being of the older persons has been mandated in the Constitution of India. Article 41 of the Directive Principles of the State Policy states that the State shall protect the well-being of senior citizens. Apart from this, Hindu Adoption and Maintenance Act, 1956 provides a legal safeguard to the elderly from their financially independent sons/daughters, who are required to provide a maintenance allowance. However, the priority for the welfare of the aged has not been seen much at government level in the Ministry of Social Justice and Empowerment, previously known as Ministry of Welfare.

The Government announced the **National Policy on Older Persons** in January 1999. The policy provides a broad framework for intersectoral collaboration and cooperation both within the government as well as between governmental and non-governmental agencies. The policy has identified a number of areas for intervention i.e. financial security, health care and nutrition, shelter, education, research, welfare, protection of life and property of media.

National Council for Older Persons (NCOP) was constituted in May 1999 to operationalize the National Policy.

There are 39 members in the Council from all-over the country, which includes a 7 members working group. The **NCOP** receives suggestions, complaints and grievances from individual older persons.

The Ministry has also commissioned "AADHAR", as a secretariat for the NCOP. This is being coordinated by Agewell Foundation. AADHAR is an initiative in the direction of empowering the elderly population of India to find satisfactory solutions to the problems as per their felt needs through co-ordination of voluntary efforts and administrative initiatives.

In June 2000, an Action Plan to implement the National Policy on Older Persons was released by the Ministry of Social Justice and Empowerment. As a result of growing concern for old age social and income security due to change in demographic, social and traditional structure, Ministry of Social Justice and Empowerment commissioned the National Project titled **OASIS (Old Age Social and Income Security).** The project was mandated to make concrete recommendations for actions that the Government can take today, so that every young worker can build up enough saving during his/her working life, which serve as a shield against poverty in their old age and reduce the burden on the State (Subha, *Employment News*, 12-18 August, 2000).

Some of the responsibilities extended to the elderly by the State are the following :

1. Income-tax rebate for senior citizens are provided under section **88B, 80D** and **80DDB.** Section 80DDB pertains to deduction in medical treatment of certain specific diseases.
2. **Annapurna** is distribution of free foodgrains up to 10 kg per month to those older who are destitute.
3. Different states also give **Old Age Pensions** to those who do not receive it through the Central Government. The amount varies from Rs. 60 in Bihar to Rs. 300 in Rajasthan.
4. Among the most important privileges and benefits given to the older citizens is the **National Old Age**

Pension Scheme. This is given to destitutes, i.e. those who do not have a regular source of income. The amount is a meagre Rs. 75.

5. Life Insurance Corporation of India is also extending services to the citizens through saving schemes such as :

(a) **Medical Insurance Scheme** known as **Medical Facility** is available within the age range of 50 to 75 years. This provides for reimbursement of medical expenses incurred by an individual towards hospitalization/domiciliary hospitalization for any illness, injury or disease contracted or sustained during the period of insurance.

It has been reported from various sources (not based on any particular source) of geriatric science from time to time that the common physical disorder the elderly population face quite often. A glimpse of it has been tabled below with existential percentage.

Percentage of elderly reporting various ailments

Ailment	*Reported percentage*
Visual impairment	88.0
Locomotive disorder, Joints, muscles	40.0
Neurological complaints	18.7
Cardiovascular disease	17.4
Respiratory disorder	16.1
Skin Conditions	13.3
Gastro intestinal/abdominal disorders	9.0
Psychiatric problem	8.5
Hearing loss	8.2
Genitourinary disorder	3.5

(b) **Jan Arogya** is primarily meant for a larger segment of population who cannot afford the high cost of medical treatment.

(c) **Jeevan Akshay** is a lifelong **Pension Plan** and lump sum death benefit as also survival benefit at the end of 7 years.

(d) **Jeevan Dhara** which is a pension plan for the individual who are self-employed—artists, cine-artists, technicians, businessmen and professionals—as these individuals cannot have **'Pension'** benefits after they cease to earn.

(e) One needs to make financial provisions to care for both the risk dying clearly as well as the risk of living too long. Statistics prove that with increased longevity, a man's retired life today is nearly half of his active life. LIC's pension plan, **Jeevan Suraksha** helps to ensure a pleasant and self-reliant life, even after retirement.

(f) **Senior Citizens Unit Plan** is a scheme under which one has to make one time investment depending on one's own age and one has the benefit of medical treatment for self and spouse at any of the selected hospitals on completion of 58 years of age.

6. Concession are available for travel with the railways who grant 30 per cent concession to all senior citizens (i.e. 65 years) in all cases. Indian Airlines grants 50% discount on normal adult fare on all domestic travels to those who have attained 65 years of age.

7. The Maintenance and Welfare of Parents and Senior Citizen Act, 2007 has brought an end of tyranny, abuse and exploitation of their helplessness by their sons and daughters. Not only that the Act has pronouncedly made an attempt in the direction that grandsons and granddaughters have equal role to play, i.e. they are legally responsible to take care of their grandparents. It has empowered the parents to appeal against any injustice caused to them in the tribunal set up in every sub-division and the sub-divisional officer is the head of the tribunal. If the verdict is not accepted by them,

the neglected parents can approach to appellate authority for fair decision. District Magistrate himself/ herself is the appellate authority. Every district must have 100 bed old age home with all opportunities for healthy living. The point to note that rigorous punishment have been prescribed in the Act for children in violation of carrying out their responsibility. towards older parents. No stay order is accepted from any court during the process of litigation.

Neglect of older persons is more often a part of a broader context of poverty, structural inequalities and other human rights violations. A lack of resources and the absence of societal mechanisms to respond to violence against older persons obviously results in low detection of cases of mistreatment.

Intervening into social, economic and political conditions that provide fertile ground for disrespect of elders along with creating enabling structure to empower older persons to prevent their plight can lead to improvement in the quality of life of older persons. With this view in mind there have been a number of initiatives taken in this respect to formulate a world response to the problems of elderly.

Recognizing the need to develop a global strategy for the prevention of old age related problems the World Health Organization (WHO) has set up the International Network for the Prevention of Elder Abuse (INPEA) in partnership with Help Age International and other academic institutions. As an initial step WHO set up a study in eight countries: Argentina, Austria, Brazil, Canada, India, Kenya, Lebanon and Sweden.

The WHO study has come out with some recommendations which can be summarized as follows:

1. Develop a screening and assessment tool for use in primary health care settings.
2. Develop an education package on elder abuse for primary health care professionals.
3. Develop and disseminate a research methodology 'kit' to study the problems of elderly.

4. Develop a minimum Data Set concerning violence and older people. Ensure dissemination of the research findings through scientific journals.
5. Develop a global inventory of good practices.

Implications for social workers

Social work practice with elderly is a field of practice called gerontological social work. Here, we would like to see how the social work intervention could be effective in dealing with the problems of elderly.

Assessment of the problem

1. **Type and extent of disability** (physical, cognitive, psychological, or combination of different types of problems).
2. **Type of support** (practical, monetary, emotional support, help with activities of daily living).
3. **Quantity of care** (occasional, or on daily basis, or around the clock care).

Resources needed

1. **Economic resources** (pension, monthly allowances, property).
2. **Availability of cares** (spouse or children).
3. **Cognitive capacity** (absence of dementia or deterioration).
4. **Physical** (absence of disabling disorders and capacity for mobility)
5. **Psychological** (life satisfaction, morale and absence of depression).

Planning for care

1. **Possibility** of providing care at home.
2. **Exploring** carers and potential carers.

3. **Assess** the need for institutionalized care.
4. **Tailor made *versus* standardized services** (Elders are a heterogeneous lot and their needs and resources vary. Of course, there are common human needs of the elderly, yet marked individual variations are also observed. So services provided have to be individualized, depending upon one's own needs and environmental configuration and need not to be uniform for everyone).

Apart from the above there are some more *key concerns for social workers* in terms of dealing with elderly in geriatric setting are the following :

1. Social work clinics and psycho-social and informational preparedness are essential. Social work healing is possible in social work clinical settings.
2. Counselling and social work treatment are very important in balancing of the environment.
3. Integration of social work and journalism strategies in technology transfer and technology utilization are essential in the care of the aged (Sivakumar, D., 2001)).
4. Finding out synoptic, intermediate, and ultimate causes of illness and immediate, intermediate and ultimate treatment models based on living and working conditions.
5. Promotion of health and welfare, literacy campaigns for the enhanced social functioning of the elderly.
6. Collaboration, coordination and linkage with other professions like nutrition, psychology, psychiatric, nursing, pharmacology and community participation are essential.
7. Policy analysis and cooperation with public and civil administration for the care of the aged and for the full development of their personality.
8. Fighting social maladies like superstitions, human and substance abuse, cheating, crime, delinquency and

squalor and preventing of social deviance, information deficiencies, suicides, conflicts, violence etc.

Promising future recommendations for better elderly care

1. Strengthening of family betterment committees.
2. Geriatric experts may be made available at all levels of service.
3. The NGOs and para-professionals may have to be increasingly involved in health efforts of older persons.
4. Journalists and the mass media should cover care programmes of the older persons in its totality.
5. Workshops, seminars and conferences on the care of the aged may be organized frequently at various levels (village, district, state and national) as a multi-disciplinary and multi-professional programme.
6. Psycho-social and economic betterment and empowerment of women and families are essential to cater to the care of the older persons.
7. Physical beautification, environmental sanitation, personal hygiene, horticulture therapy, music therapy and occupational therapy have to be promoted and strengthened.
8. Daycare centres should be scientifically run and professionally equipped.
9. Both State Government and Central Government should come out with different policies and social security measures.
10. Professional and scientific social work intervention has to be promoted in the prevention, treatment and rehabilitation of physical, mental and social ill-health.

SUGGESTED READINGS

1. Desai, Murli and Raju Siva: (2000); *Gerontological social work in India*, B.R. Publishing Corporation, New Delhi.
2. Prakash, I.J. (1997); *Functional competence and well-being of elderly—Indian Data*. Report submitted to Help Age India, New Delhi.

3. Soneja, Shubha, (2000); "Caring for Senior Citizens", *Employment News*, 12-18, August.
4. Modi, Iswar, (2001); *Ageing and Human Development*, Rawat Publications.
5. Morgan Leslie and Kunkel Suzanne: (2001); *Ageing;* The Pine Forge Press.
6. Sivakumar, D. (2001), *Role of People's Participation in Empowering Families for the Care of the Elderly*, International Congress on Ageing, Centre for Gerontological Studies, Thiruvananthapuram.
7. Brinks, S. (1997); The Greying of our communities worldwide; *Ageing International*, 23 (3 and 4), 13-31.

19

Encountering the Problems of Older Workers in Industries

Significance for Social Workers

Society continues to expect and often requires the majority of people older than 65 to retire. Historically, human considerations were claimed to be the main reason. Because much of the labour in the early and middle stages of the industrial revolution consisted of heavy, physical effort over a long work-day and work-week, relief through retirement became a desirable goal.

The age-old tradition of determining retirement from work (employment) by age irrespective of the productivity of the individual worker (in spite of age) has not changed. The industrial revolution caused a dramatic change in occupational pattern in the society. Much of the population could be no longer inheriting occupations like their parents had because occupations had changed drastically. Industrial society required workers to be highly mobile and not bound to any locale or set of traditions. Industrializations represented a multifaceted attack on tradition, an attack symbolized by the word *'change'* and *'movement'* (Wilensky and Lebeaux, 1965). The attitudes resulting from these changes created an environment in which older people found it difficult to keep up with the changing time and requirements. In this context four general areas are examined:

- definition of older workers,
- demographic trends,

- problems of the aged—general as well as occupational, and
- the role of social workers in dealing with such problems.

Older Workers: Definition

It is always better to have a working definition of the group under consideration but the term *'older worker'* tends to be an elusive query.

Labelling oneself as old often seems to be dependent on the perception of the worker concerned (Drury, 2007). At the age of 35 a female worker may consider herself as old while a male worker may look at 40 as the threshold of the old age (Reark, 2005). Perception apart, definition of older worker also gets complicated by the nature of occupation in which they are engaged, for example, a worker might be occupationally old at 30 in a heavy industry in comparison to 60 plus in a pharmaceutical concern.

Sterns (2005) suggests five general approaches to the definition of the older worker starting with:

- standard chronological approach, which he points out, starts at age 40,
- according to functional age, that is, a performance based definition,
- psychological age covering social perceptions and attitudes of society towards older workers,
- organizational age, which he looks at the workers time on the job and the technology used to indicate current or absolute skills, and
- finally a life-span approach which acknowledges historical influences and individual differences in aging.

Standard chronological approach is still the dominant determinant of labelling a person as old or young. Even in the industrial sector as mentioned already this approach influences the policy decision. However, the nature of job, especially the skills that are required to perform a job, also influences in categorizing the workers as old or young in the present-day context. It is not only how the employers determine but also how the workers perceive themselves irrespective of the skills required to perform the job, chronological age as the dominant factor. In the context of the modern technological revolution, skills as well as retention of skills are no doubt important factor. In this essay, the chronological approach as well as the functional age based on performance would address the issues confronting the older workers.

Demographic trends

The impact of aging on contemporary society is occurring at such a rapid pace that even gerontologists are surprised, and available data require continuous updating. Only in 1975, 20 million people in the world (10 per cent of the population) were older than 65. Demographers warned at that time that planners should prepare for large increase in the number of older people and predicted that by the year 2010 there would be as many as 28.8 million older people. This segment of the population is increasing so rapidly that even the specialists have been caught off guard.

To add with, the two important trends in the global scenario are that the younger worker group (15 to 24) is decreasing while older workers (45 to 54) are the fastest growing group and this will continue in the second decade of the next century (McCormick, 1996). The rise in the percentage of older people has occurred principally because of improved health care and advances in medical technology help more people live longer. At the same time, lower birth rate has resulted in a smaller percentage of younger people in the world.

To illustrate, during 1981-1991 population in India increased by 24.75 per cent and that of the aged by 31.60 per cent. It has been projected during 1981-2001; population of the aged has increased by 38.02 per cent (Table 19.1).

Table 19.1 : Decadal percentage increase of general population and that of the aged (60 years and above)

Decade	*Increase in general population*	*Increase in 60+ population*
1951-1961	21.51	22.40
1961-1971	24.86	32.32
1971-1981	24.75	31.60
1981-1991	18.89	38.02
1991-2001	20.67	37.89

At present in India the percentage of older male workforce is 77.74 and for the female it is 48.39.

Problems of the aged

It would be truism to state that the aged have a set of problems which are somewhat unique to them. The problems of aged could be viewed from two perspectives—**general** and **occupational.** With advanced age they experience psychomotor difficulties and disabilities of vision and hearing; develop orthopaedic and cardiac ailments, diabetes and respiratory complications. Many aged also suffer from a variety of mental symptoms and diseases. Anxiety states, hypochondriasis, depression and melancholia are ailments common among the aged.

Social problems faced by the aged are by no means small. The aged find it difficult to adjust them with changing social values, institutions and environment itself. Often the phenomenon of the **'generation gap'** may render them irrelevant.

In terms of occupational problems it may be stated that age usually brings in work curtailed participation in productive and economically gainful work. With this, the phenomenal changes in the world of work by rapid industrialization and globalization of world economy bring a lot of occupational problems for older people. Deregulation of financial markets and protected industries, in an effort to be internationally competitive in this new environment, has brought critical changes in:

- the structure of industry,
- the composition of workforce,
- change in the nature and organization of work, and
- technological innovation.

How each of these is affecting older workers and how to get re-adjusted with them in industrial scenario will be highlighted now.

Implications for social workers

The notion of functional age has received a great deal of attention in industrial gerontology by the prolific work of Ross McFarland (1973). Subsequently Florence Safford (1999), John McCormick (1996) and others who also have done extensive work in this area and shown the economics of aging in industry can be reduced to the consideration of work, retirement, income and other related issues.

Adherence to several social work values is essential for effective work with older workers. Respect for the worth and dignity of every older employee must be assured. A non-judgmental attitude further protects them from being stigmatized. The social work value of democratic principles protects the employee's rights and assists the managements in formulating policies for the benefit of the older people. Insistence on preserving client confidentiality instils confidence among employees to seek services from the social workers.

Emphasizing on functional aging and applying the above social work values and ethics, social workers can very well make an attempt to deal with various types of common problems as discussed below often encountered by the older workers in industries.

The problem of work and employment of older workers has led to certain solutions, including redesigning the job (the tasks as well as the technology and technological aids that suit the incumbent) and in the development of special training principles and technique for helping older workers adapt to changing technology and/or to new occupations. An effort can be undertaken by the social workers in this regard to explore how all these can be mobilized for the benefit of the older workers.

To add with this, older workers are frequently absent from training programme and often simple problems like inconvenient location, time and many others are the reasons. It so happens that on many occasions older workers do not see the need for such programmes. The reluctance may be due to an insecurity and lack of confidence to attend training programmes for reasons associated with anxiety about their own aging and learning abilities or fear of rapid technological change and its effects on their job. Educational programmes about normal *versus* pathological aging can be useful here and, age or gender specific programmes as well as partner sessions are conducive to sharing normative experience. A systematic data collection is also necessary as the needs of older workers can also appraise management of the feasibility of flexible work options for this group.

In recent years job re-design has become a more frequent subject for research experimentation because of such workplace problems as absenteeism, turnover, morale and quality of output along with productivity (Davis and Taylor, 2003; Stephen Griew, 1964; Barkin, 2007) has shown the importance of this approach to work environment improvements as applied to problems of ageing. Retraining has also been proposed as one approach in any multiprolonged set of solution to problems of older workers.

Counselling is another function that could be effectively used by the social workers who become knowledgeable in industrial gerontology. Counselling may relate to emotional problems, employment related health problems or numerous other problems of the older workers.

Stress management and time management are two vital concerns for older workers. Social workers can play a pivotal role in this regard. Very common stressors include anxieties about their own aging, fear of rapid technological change and its effects on their work, worry about inflation and its potential effects on their impending retirement, concern about the well-being of their grown-up children, and responsibility for dependent elderly parents and even grandparents can be addressed effectively in stress management programme. Timely work completion, prioritization of work, daily routine is a few areas which could be dealt with effectively by the time management programme.

In any industry there are a wide range of services available but many of the workers are not knowledgeable about the array of services or the eligibility requirements. At this juncture social workers can function as brokers to link the elderly with available services. It is worth mentioning here that outreach is another way of intervention for dealing with the older workers problems. This includes identifying and offering services to those aged workers who need financial assistance, better housing, recreational and leisure-time service, transportation, companionship, consumer protection services, sex-education and many others.

For some older workers, continuing work is either not possible or desirable. Thus, programme such as job banks for the retired could be an unique programme to be tried out by the industrial social workers. This venture is to encompass life beyond paid work through volunteering whereby the older workers can make a quantifiable economic contribution.

Questions relating to retirement—who retires, when and why—are not as simple as they seem. Among the important factors to consider are mandatory as well as voluntary retirement provisions, social security and other pension system, the state of the economy, personal health and motivation and cultural level values. Anyone person's decision on whether or not to retire may be affected by any or all of these considerations. So, some amount of counselling, consultancy services, need-based support programme could be very good idea to be conceived by the social workers in these situation.

The part of a stress-management programme addressing retirement should explore the emotional impact of the transition from the known, familiar world of work to the unfamiliar work of retirees, with its lack of structure, undefined roles and uncertain economics. For those whose central life interest was work, retirement may be an ego-alien experience. So, pre-retirement counselling is essential where social workers have much role to play.

Conclusion

There is a socio-economic need for older workers to help them at their workplace as well as in the family to help them continue their productive contributions to society. Research indicates that older workers who are in good health could benefit from a prolonged work experience, which may positively affect their mental health, life satisfaction and marital satisfaction. Some companies in western countries have initiated innovative older worker programmes such as ***Early Retirement Income Security (ERIS), Elder Care Programme (ECP), Senior Community Service Employment (SCSE)*** that seem to benefit both older workers and employers. Initiative could be taken in this regard and the programmes might be implemented in Indian industries.

The social work profession can have an important role in raising awareness of the issues and initiating changes. Social work intervention can make a difference for the older workers by working with individuals, groups and work organizations to change attitude, initiate policies and programmes, and open up new horizons for older workers and work organizations.

SUGGESTED READINGS

1. Barkin, Soloman (2007); "Retraining and Job Redesign: Positive Approach to the Continued Employment of Older Persons", In H.L. Sheppared (ed.), *Industrial Gerontology*, Schenkman, Cambridge.
2. Davis, Lowis and Taylor, James (eds.) (2003); *Job Design*; Middlesex, Penguin Books, England.

3. Drury, D. (2007); *Age Discrimination against Older Workers in the European Community*: Russel Sage Foundation, New York.
4. Griew, Stephen (1964); *Job Redesign: The Application of Biographical Data on Aging to the Design of Equipment and the Organization of Work;* Organization for Economic Co-operation and Development, Paris.
5. McCormick, J. (1996); "Older Workers: Roles for Occupational Social Work", *Australian Social Work;* March; Vol. 49, No.1.
6. McFarland, Ross, A. (1973); "The need for functional age measurements in industrial gerontology"; *Journal of Industrial Gerontology,* Fall.
7. Reark, Research (2005); "Attitude of People Aged 55-64 to Employment, Unemployment and Early Retirement". *Monograph,* Sydney, NSW.
8. Safford, Florence (1999); "Value of Gerontology for Occupational Social Work"; *Social Work;* January-February; Vol. 33, No. 1.
9. Sterns, H. (2005); "The Impact of Technological Change on Employment—Prospects of Older Persons", In Habib, J. and Jusberg, C., *Rethinking Worklife Options for Older People;* International Federation on Ageing, Washington, DC.
10. Wilensky, H.L. and Lebeaux, C.N. (1965); Industrial Society and Social Welfare; Russel Sage Foundation, New York.

PART E

GENERAL ISSUES

20

Alcoholism and Social Work Intervention

A Perspective in the 21st Century

The problem of alcoholism, until a few decades ago, was considered a moral problem and a sign of social irresponsibility. After the introduction of the prohibition policy in some states of India, it was viewed as an illegal act. Now, it is considered as a complicated, chronic and immensely costly disease than a type of a deviant behaviour. The victim needs not the punitive treatment but treatment by specialists—psychiatrists, doctors and specially social workers who will help him in his personality reconstruction.

What is Alcoholism?

The literature provides a multitude of definitions of alcoholism. Recently, however, alcoholism has been seen as a disease. Authorities contend that alcoholism is both a physical and psychological use of the substance over a prolonged period of time (Lester, 1997, Hafen and Brog, 1998).

Although no formal or universal definition of alcoholism has been accepted, most experts agree that alcoholism is "a disease—a disabling condition, progressive in nature and manifested as a syndrome with interrelated biological, emotional, social, spiritual, and behavioural aspects" (Hafen and Brog, 1998). Broadly speaking, alcoholism has been characterized by four factors (Ahuja, 1998):

- excessive intake of alcoholic beverages,
- individual's increasing worry over his drinking,
- loss of the drinker's control over this drinking, and
- the disturbance in functioning in his social world.

The disease of alcoholism is characterized by stages. A three-stage definition of alcoholism is normally used. Common names for the three stages of alcoholism are:

1. prealcoholic,
2. promodal, and
3. crucial or chronic alcoholic.

Each stage has identifiable traits, and transition from one stage to the next have also been identified (Chlms, 1983). Classifying alcoholism as a disease was something dramatic. As a result of the disease concept of alcoholism, alcoholics are now viewed as patients, or suffering victims of the disease. Furthermore, alcoholics are currently viewed as sick people who have not chosen to be sick. It is assumed that it is unpleasant to be an alcoholic, and that treatment should be provided to these individuals to help them restore their health. The use of the disease model of alcoholism has lessened the stigma attached to being an alcoholic, and has paved the way for the development and implementation of medical and psychological approaches to treatment (Kinney and Leaton, 1993).

Problems and causes of alcoholism

In interpreting the causes of alcoholism, the important thing to bear in mind is that, of those who use alcohol, about 90 per cent do not become alcoholics. The key to alcoholism is in the motive for repeating the drinking. Therefore, explaining alcoholism only in terms of factors like personality structure will be inadequate. One psychological view is that practically all alcoholics show the mark of deprivation of emotional needs during childhood. Clinebell (1956) reports four main types of parental attitudes which happen to be associated with alcoholism in adulthood and all of which tend to produce trauma and emotional deprivation in the child:

(a) authoritarianism,
(b) over rejection,
(c) moralism, and
(d) success worship.

That these factors are the key ones in the formation of an insecure personality resulting in falling prey to alcohol is indicated by the fact that psychological studies of alcoholics repeatedly mention the following personality traits (Clinebell, 1956):

1. a high level of anxiety in interpersonal relationships,
2. emotional immaturity,
3. low frustration tolerance,
4. low self-esteem,
5. feelings of isolation and guilt, and
6. ambivalence towards authority.

These psychological traits are not the result of alcoholism but are the causes of alcoholism. The main sociological causes of alcoholism are:

(a) environmental pressures,
(b) peer-pressures, and
(c) a dominant sub-culture.

A question is raised whether pressure can be located in the culture itself both to cause and to control alcoholism. It is said that same culture are better able to develop effective control over the individual than others. A research in the United States shows that there are very few teetotallers among the *Jews* (13%) compared to *Catholics* (21%) and *Protestants* (41%). In France, Germany, and the United States, the use of wine has been very common. It is only recently that alcoholism has become a major crisis in the life of the people of these countries. Once people start using alcohol because of the cultural sanctions, they use it frequently, especially in situations of insecurity and anxiety.

The problems of alcoholism, in terms of personal misery, family budget, family discord, loss of wages, failure of health, accidents and cost in damage claims, cost of hospital treatment, cost in custodial treatment in jail, monetary damage in courts, and inducement to crime are almost disastrous. Social deviance and social problems emerge from the use and abuse of alcohol.

Another problem of alcoholism is that it has increased illicit bootlegging. Since independence, hundreds of tragedies have taken place throughout the country in which many people have died on consuming liquor produced illicitly. This phenomena is still on at an alarming rate.

Magnitude of the problem

In India, about 15 to 20 per cent of the people take alcohol. According to a study made by the "All India Institute of Medical Sciences", Delhi, where it has been recorded that, over the past 20 years, the number of drinkers in our country has increased from one in 300 to one in 20. However, alcoholics comprise 5 per cent while the occasional drinkers account for 95 per cent (*The Hindustan Times,* June 5, 2005).

In India, the intake of ***Indian Made Foreign Liquor (IMFL)*** is growing at the rate of 15 per cent per annum, according to industry sources. It has also been found that about 65 per cent of the Indian liquor market is controlled by whisky (*The Hindustan Times,* July 14, 2000). The production and sale of liquor at present in the whole country has increased almost 20 times. The revenue from liquor is Rs. 50 crore at the time of independence and now it has gone up to Rs. 12,000 crore in a year.

In India, Kerala today stands first in the per capita consumption of liquor (9.3 litres), followed by Punjab (7.9 litres) against the national average of 5.7 litres (*Frontline,* April 3, 2005). Similarly, Kerala Government's revenue from liquor (i.e. excess revenue) has continuously increased from 1960-61 to

1997-98 and it is from Rs. 2.62 crore to Rs. 10.02 crore. The excise revenue comes mainly from the auctioning of liquor shops, licence fee for bars and distilleries, tax on trees in the toddy sector, sales tax, and excise duty on country liquor.

If we compare the alcohol users above twenty years of age (that is adult) in different countries, the highest number are found in France (62,000 per one lakh population), followed by the U.S.A. (4,760 per lakh); Sweden (2,280 per lakh); Switzerland (2,605 per lakh); Denmark (2,260 per lakh); Norway (2,250 per lakh); Canada (2,140 per lakh); Australia (1,640 per lakh); England (1,530 per lakh) and Italy (1,100 per lakh).

The cause of increase in the drinking population in the young age groups were stated as: the disappearance of the stigma associated with drinking, the emergence of a new group of social drinkers including women and girls, and government's tourism-oriented policy of starting beer parlours in many of the states. A study of 284 under trials (Ahuja, 1998) in one sub-jail (Thiravananthapuram) showed that 57 per cent were under the influence of alcohol at the time of committing the crime, including hooliganism, rape and murder. The menacing effect of alcoholism also gets manifested in the form of family and marital problem, health and financial problem.

In the background of a huge multifacets problems of alcoholism in different dimensions we can have a very close look on general treatment measures before embarking upon the implications for social workers—should be the call of this millennium.

Treatment of alcoholics

Alcoholism is more treatable than drug addiction. There have been many successful treatment programmes such as psychotherapy, environment therapy, behaviour therapy, medical therapy which could be used for different types of drinkers. In psychotherapy, resocialization is reinforced through counselling and through group therapy. In environment therapy; the drinker is made to change the environment where his behaviour may be easily controlled. In behaviour therapy, his fears and inhibitions are removed to enable him to develop self-confidence and self-reliance. Detoxification in hospital using tranquilizers, high potency vitamin, fluid electrolyte and oral pills ('Antabuse-Tetra Ethylthiv Ramdisul Fide) (Walsh and Furfey, 2006) come under the medical therapy.

Involving an alcoholic's family in his treatment and rehabilitation enhances the chances of success by 75 to 80 per cent. The family members do not preach, nor do they blame or condemn the alcoholic. They minimize his problems, offer him sincere and unselfish help and guidance, and never abandon him. So, role of family in dealing with the problem of alcoholism undoubtedly bears paramount importance.

Another most effective social therapy which uses group interaction is *Alcoholic Anonymous* (*AA*). It is an organization, a group of people, fellowships of men and women, who share their experience, strength and hope with each other that they may solve their common problem and help others recover from alcoholism.

Implications for social workers

Social work education provides the social worker with a broad range of knowledge, values, and skills relating to alcoholism. Adherence to several social work values is essential for effective work with alcoholics. Respect for the worth and dignity of every individual ensures that the individual with a drinking habit is not seen as a bad person. A non-judgmental attitude further protects the individual from being stigmatized. The social work value of democratic principles protects the individual's rights. Preserving confidentiality is a prime duty for social workers.

Social workers also possess many other skills which make them unique and ideal professionals for work with alcoholics. When working with alcoholics, social workers make use of his/her skills in the areas of alcohol and substance abuse counselling, marriage and family counselling, general-emotional counselling, assisting with legal problems, and based on interviewing and counselling techniques (Dickman, Emener, and Hutchisum, 2005). Social workers also help in establishing on-site self help group such as *Alcoholic Anonymous* (AA).

Social workers also use his/her skills to make changes as both the micro and macro levels. Social worker effect changes in individuals, families and group at micro level. Ecological perspective or environmental factors contributing to one's problem of alcoholism needs to be dealt at macro level.

The social work curriculum provides the knowledge required to recognize that the problem of alcoholism is not necessarily limited either to the individual or the environment, but needs to be seen at both of these levels. The individual is not totally blamed for his/her alcoholism, for the social worker is able to recognize that frequently the environmental influence also contribute to the alcoholism as we. The current social work curriculum provides social workers with valuable knowledge concerning human behaviour in the context of a person's social environment; knowledge about the disease of alcoholism is increasingly included in the social work curriculum.

Social workers should administer clinical skills to assess a broad range of problems, the ability to do motivational counselling and to identify appropriate treatment resources, and expertise in dealing with issues relating to problem of alcoholism.

Social worker with sound knowledge of human behaviour, of different intervention modalities and social policy and with social research skills has the competence to deliver the needed services to the alcoholics. The ecological perspective of social work provides a holistic base for intervention at the individual level.

It is incumbent on human service agencies to offer basic education and training to their staff. Social workers, being part and parcel of human service organizations have instrumental role to play in this regard. Social workers, through organizing short-term, in-service training can impart training to staff of the organization to be adequately trained in identifying, controlling and treating alcoholics and their families. The major objectives of any in-service training programme should evolve around the areas of attitudinal change, basic information about alcohol and alcoholism, and skills particular to working with alcoholics.

Social workers can impart knowledge as well as develop themselves more productively in organizing and strengthening *AA or AI Anop Group,* in-service staff seminars where issues like defining alcoholism as a disease, symptom of alcoholics when they are intoxicated, rudiments of etiology of the problem, data on prevalence and incidence, pharmacology, treatment techniques processes and modalities are discussed.

Although most social workers have the skills necessary to work with alcoholics, there are a series of skills relating to confrontation that should be introduced. The successful treatment of alcoholism often requires confrontation to break down the strong denial and alibi system that operates in the disease. On the other hand, it is unfortunate that many social workers have not incorporated this strategy into their treatment repertoire and thus became overwhelmed with the protracted and convoluted series of excuses, denials and confabulations that alcoholic weave (James Royee, 2008).

There should always be a written policy as necessary component for all the human service agencies. This would give directions to the staff and social workers in regard to how to go about with alcoholics. Through role playing and skill exercise social workers can learn these confrontational skills and incorporate into clinical practice.

The problem of alcoholism is as much a social and community problem as it is an individual illness. By coordinating the various caregivers, providers, and gate-keepers within a community, an agency as well as social workers can assure both continuity of care and network of concern that can address the community problem of alcoholism (Googins, 1984).

Future promises to combat alcoholism

- More treatment centres should be developed as alternatives to hospital treatment. Each centre should have about 10-12 residents. Here not only counselling takes place in a supportive environment but residents are made to follow certain anti-drinking rules too. ***Alcoholic Anonymous (AA) group*** also must be strengthened.

- Voluntary organizations should undertake educational and information programmes to alert the alcoholics to the dangers of excessive drinking. Social workers help drinkers in coping with life and changing the social values and attitudes about drinking.
- After independence, some states took up the programme of prohibition earnestly and some half-heartedly. In Andhra Pradesh anti-arrack agitation which was started in one district (Nellore) in 1992 gradually spread to other districts and ultimately snowballed into a major prohibition movement. In Tamil Nadu, arrack was banned in 1994. In Haryana, the widespread movement for prohibition organized by Arya Samaj was supported by political parties. In Karnataka, anti-liquor movement was also started. Gujarat has been a dry state since 1938. Except some scattered efforts, neither the central nor state government is taking any serious venture in this regard and that due to mainly political influences, and revenue earned. So the above two areas should be given serious threat and put lot of endeavour to fight against the problem.

Our governments are fail to realize the revenue earned from the sale of liquor is far less than the expenditure increased on the social consequences of alcoholism. According to a couple of studies in the United States and other countries it was worked out that if the revenue earned is one dollar; the expenditure on its consequences is 35 dollars (*The Hindustan Times*, April 10, 2004). In India, even if the expenditure on the consequences is not 3.5 times, it may be about twice of what the state gets as revenue. Obviously, scrapping prohibition can be called 'penny-wise, pound-foolish' policy. What is suggested is that politicians should come out from their vicious thread of narrow political interest and join hands together on a common objective to make the country free from such a devastating consequence of alcoholism.

- Women activists, women's organizations and even ordinary housewives in rural as well as urban areas have already been struggling hard over the past several years to convince men against liquor consumption and force governments to introduce prohibition. They should demand that they will vote only for parties committed to prohibition in their poll manifestos.
- There should be total ban on any type of advertisement shown on TV in regard to different kinds of liquor which directly stimulate people to go for it.
- As it has been suggested by the doctors as well as in the world of medical science research that a limited amount of alcohol is good for heart and overall health. But, ultimately it turns out to be very dismal. People get encouraged by the words of doctor and start consuming alcohol everyday. Then it becomes a habit and the amount keeps on increasing. At the end, the person becomes alcoholic and instead of having good health, the person starts having numerous physical problems and life is in danger. So, this kind of attitude needs to be changed.
- Student community, teachers, writers could be the very powerful soldiers in this battle. They should think and act together for the benefit of the entire nation.

Unlike many other social problems, the solutions of the problem of alcoholism are not difficult or expensive. They involve promoting attitudinal change; demythologizing the mystique of alcoholism treatment replacing an over-reliance on specialized alcoholism agencies with a community network of providers, caregivers and gate-keepers; and in-service training. None of these measures require radical individual or structural change, what is required are professional commitment and a willingness to examine and change attitudes that deny the problem of alcoholism while allowing alcoholics and their families to suffer the ravages of the disease. Social workers represent the largest proportion of the professional working in special hospitals and clinics for alcoholism treatment and in general mental health facilities. This, in itself, offers an opportunity for the social workers to have a significant impact on one of the nation's largest social problems through concerted efforts.

SUGGESTED READINGS

1. Ahuja, Ram (1998); *Social Problems in India;* Rawat Publications, New Delhi.
2. Clinebell, Howard, J. (1956); *Understanding and Counselling the Alcoholics,* Abingdon Press, New York.
3. Dickman, F.J.; Emener, W.G.; and Hutchison, W.S. (2005); *Counselling the Troubled Person in Industry;* Springfield, IL: Charles, C. Thomas Publisher, New York.
4. *Frontline,* April 3, 2005
5. Googins Bradley (1984); "Avoidance of the Alcoholic Client", *Social Work;* March-April.
6. Hafen, B. and Brog, M. (1998); *Alcohol.* St. Paul, MN: West Publishing; UK.
7. Lester, L. (1997); "The Special Needs of the Female Alcoholic"; *Social Case Work,* 63, pp. 456-461.
8. Chlms, D.L. (1983); *The Disease Concept of Alcoholism",* Belle Ville, IL: Gary Whiteaker Company.
9. Royee, James (2008); *Alcohol Problems and Alcoholism: A Comprehensive Survey*: New York, Free Press.
10. Walsh, Maty E. and Furfey, Paul, H. (2006); *Social Problems and Social Actions,* Prentice Hall Inc. Englewood Cliffs. N.J.
11. *The Hindustan Times,* June 5, 2005.
12. *The Hindustan Times,* July 14, 2000.
13. *The Hindustan Times,* April 10, 2004.
14. Kinney and K. Leaton (1993); "Alcoholism and drug abuse in the workplace", *Social Work,* Vol. 10; No. 5.

21

Strategies for Encountering the Menace of Absenteeism

Over the past decade, human service programmes created specifically for the complex of work, workers and workplace have been embraced by the private and public sector organizations and trade unions. These programmes are not in themselves unique, nor do they address recently identified problems. Alcoholism, drug abuse, absenteeism, indebtedness and emotional disturbance are aspects of the human conditions that have held the attention of the medical profession and policy-makers for some time. What is unique is the setting in which these issues are now addressed. Historically, production goals of the corporation and the human and social needs of employees have existed in uneasy tension. Work concerns and personal concerns were assumed to be separate spheres, apparently (according to conventional wisdom) distinct. Consequently, the introduction of various human service programmes and the proliferation of social workers within the occupational setting mark a new development for social work profession to deal with plenty of personal problems. Absenteeism which is growing rapidly both in developed and developing societies pose a challenge to professional social work.

Hence the focus of this chapter is to present the role of professional social workers in encountering the problem on industrial absenteeism. In this context four areas are examined—(a) what is professional social work? (b) a general description and the magnitude of the problem; (c) impact of absenteeism on industry; and (d) the role of professional social work in dealing with absenteeism in industry.

What is professional social work?

The growth of professional social work in the past several years has been dramatic. Less than 100 practitioners could be identified to participate in the 1978 conference on 'Social Work Practice in Labour and Industrial Settings' jointly sponsored by the Columbia University and Hunter School of Social Work. The situation has changed a great deal. The changing needs and realities of the workplace have opened a new frontier for the social work profession and created opportunities, inspiring new and creative forms of practice.

Googins and Godfrey (1985) very beautifully defined professional social work as "the field of practice in which social workers attend to the human and social needs of employees in the work milieu by designing and executing healthier individuals and environments." The very essence of professional social work is that "troubled employees should be treated rather than relied" (Trice and Sonnerstuhl, 1987).

Professional social work offers practitioners the opportunity to rationalize and humanize contemporary society by increasing responsiveness of organizations to equality, opportunity and respect for their employees. Professional social work require collective action for job-related service which will improve and humanize not only the quality of work life but also the relationship between the management and trade unions.

Magnitude of the problem

Absenteeism is the failure of workers to appear on the job when they are scheduled to work. A worker is to be considered as 'scheduled to work' when the employer has work available for him and the worker is aware of it. The Labour Bureau views absenteeism as the extent of total time lost due to human factors as a percentage of total time schedule to work. The Labour

Bureau does not regard spells of absence from work due to authorized vacation and privilege leave, strikes, lock-out and lay-off, and *ex post facto* regularized period of overstay following authorized leave, as falling within the scope of the term 'scheduled to work'. Absenteeism depends on multifarious factors which could be categorized as ***extrinsic*** and ***intrinsic.***

Extrinsic factors

Factors extrinsic of work situation include background orientation of the workers—their culture, festivals, way of life, rate of literacy, aspiration of life, personal problems such as health, family burden, earning capacity, indebtedness, living conditions, sickness and emotional maladjustment which forces workers to remain away from work.

Intrinsic factors

Factors intrinsic of the work include the working conditions, plant administration, job satisfaction and lack of recognition. Appreciation for efficiency and expertise, if denied to worker, would cause frustration which in turn leads to absenteeism. The supervisors being close to workers have much influence on workers' satisfaction which inversely related to absenteeism. If the supervisor is inadequately trained or unsuited for his job, poor morale and absenteeism are likely to result. The extent of the problem, i.e. the statistical evidence of the rate of absenteeism in Indian industries finds its variation from one industry to another depending upon innumerable factors among which the following are worth mentioning:

- type of industry (steel, textile, engineering, mining, plantation, food processing, printing etc.).
- seasonal variation.
- monthly variation.
- regional differences.
- small-scale or large-scale.

- Prevalence of anyone or a combination of more than one extrinsic or intrinsic factors and its sub-factors.
- Engagement in other occupations.

Rate of absenteeism

The existing studies and reports show that in almost all the cases the average rate of absenteeism in textile industry is the highest (35%) in comparing to all other types of industries. The Bombay Cotton Mills are more prone to absenteeism than the cotton mills in other states. The rate of difference is almost five per cent (5%).

The most important cause of absenteeism in almost all types of industries is social and religious functions which amounts to be 12 per cent of total absenteeism. The rate of absenteeism increases generally in the month of June, July, August, September and November.

Next to the cotton mills, the steel industry is also facing the problem of absenteeism to a great extent. It can be discernible from the Table 21.1. Lastly the current trend of the problem of absenteeism in a few major industries is given in Table 21.2.

Adequate data does not exist on the rate of absenteeism in each and every industry in India. Nor the comparative analysis is available. The readers should not get biased only by observing the magnitude of the problem on the basis of data presented in the above tables.

Table 21.1 : Percentage of absenteeism in cotton mill and steel industry

Year	*Absent in Steel Industry*	*Absent in Cotton Mills*
2000-2001	16.4	18.2
2001-2002	13.4	25.4
2002-2003	15.3	18.3
2003-2004	15.4	19.2
2004-2005	14.6	20.3
2005-2006	16.4	18.5
2006-2007	16.8	18.8

Source: *Indian Labour Journal*; March 2007.

Table 21.2 : Problem of absenteeism in major industries

Year	Month	Cotton Mills				Engi-neering	Gold mining	Plan-tation
		Mum-bai	Sola-pur	Ahme-dabad	Karna-taka			
1	2	3	4	5	6	7	8	9
2006	January	16.0	23.9	13.9	20.2	13.5	13.9	21.1
	February	18.2	34.4	14.8	-	15.1	—	—
	March	18.2	—	13.0	25.1	13.6	13.9	18.7
	April	20.6	25.0	13.1	—	16.3	—	—
	May	30.1	40.3	14.1	—	23.3	12.3	31.0
	June	28.3	41.1	13.6	—	30.8	12.8	26.0
	July	19.8	—	12.0	—	12.9	-	18.9
	August	16.7	37.7	12.1	—	15.0	56.6	18.7
	September	19.7	37.6	12.2	11.0	13.0	17.4	19.6
	October	18.9	32.0	12.4	20.5	20.0	9.2	20.3
	November	19.2	35.3	12.6	30.0	15.9	12.5	18.9
	December	17.8	41.9	12.8	—	15.7	—	—

Source: *Indian Labour Journal*; March 2007.

Impact of absenteeism on industry

Absenteeism is one of the economic evils of industrialization. One social scientist was in the opinion that for an industry, strikes and lockouts is a case of heart disease and absenteeism a cancer. Absenteeism adversely affects not only the worker but also the industry, its production and growth and ultimately the economy of the nation.

Absenteeism is a malady which disrupts work schedule, imposes burden on co-workers and the supervisory staff, causes unnecessary overtime and thereby results in overall increase in the labour cost. It also reduces efficiency and moral of the workers. It hinders proper planning of production, productivity, profit and investment. It is a major obstacle for industrial growth and development.

Effects of absenteeism on various factors

On workers

- Income loss
- Efficiency loss
- Loss of morale
- Labour turnover and resultant work allotment

On employers

- Additional burden on reserves (workers are needed to be deployed which in turn increases financial burden)
- Payment of overtime resulting into increase in the cost of production
- Employment of unskilled workers due to the absence of regular skilled workers which affect the quality and quantity of the production

On production and productivity

- Production loss
- Low productivity
- Loss of credit and goodwill of the industry
- Problem of standing in market competition
- Reduction in growth rate

On consumers

- Price hike
- Non-availability of consumer goods
- Low quality and less durability of the products

On national economy

- Non-fulfilment of targeted production
- Rise in the market price
- Decrease in export

- Difficulty to compete in the international market
- Affects the overall growth of industrialization

The effects on various factors of production clearly show that the problem of absenteeism cannot be dealt with in isolation because the impact of absenteeism as mentioned has a chain reaction. Therefore to counter the problem, holistic approach needs to be adopted. As such the conventional ways of dealing with the various problems of the workers by labour welfare/personnel officer in almost all the industries may get different dimension by the application of emerging concept of professional social work.

Importance of professional social work

The social workers could come out as effective persons to deal with this problem in a constructive manner. They would provide the knowledge required to recognize the problem of absenteeism in a broader perspective. They would see the individuals in their totality. They would examine the work environment which contributes to the absenteeism and would influence the human behaviour in the context of the social environment of the workers including the work place.

Adherence to several social work values is essential for effective work with the absentees. Respect for the worth and dignity of every individual ensures that the employee with a problem of absenteeism is not seen as a bad person. A non-judgmental attitude as one of the principles of social case work is very effective in dealing with such problem. The social work value of democratic principles protects the workers' rights and assists the management in formulating policies which are not punitive and repressive. Insistence on preserving client confidentiality among employees to seek services from the professional social workers.

Problem solving mechanism

While working with the absentees as well as the other troubled workers, the professional social worker can make the best use of the 'problem solving mechanism' or 'problem solution cycle' which seems to be very effective.

The solution cycle begins with awareness as shown in the figure below that there is a problem. Once awareness exists, it begins to seek information which will help problem definition. The next stages are analysis and diagnosis, which means identifying the key aspects and establishing the causes. Analysis breaks down the problem into its component parts, and the diagnosis means seeing the relationship between them. An understanding of the causes will provide an indication of the range of solutions, and give a reasoned basis for decision and action, which ultimately can have the effect of changing the situation in a positive way.

Problem solution cycle

SITUATION : B

7. EFFECT
↑
6. ACTION
↑
5. DETECTION
↑
4. DIAGNOSIS
↑
3. ANALYSIS
↑
2. DEFINITION
↑
1. AWARENESS

SITUATION : A

Social workers possess many skills such as motivational, family counselling, identifying appropriate treatment resources, delivering the needed services, different interventional modalities, social research which make them unique professionals to deal with the problem of absenteeism.

Social workers use their skills to make changes at both the micro and macro levels by effecting changes in individuals, their family, groups and sub-groups while formulating and implementing industrial programmes and policies.

To conclude every establishment should treat rather than terminate the services of absentee employees. Consequently, industries should begin to employ persons trained in dealing with problem workers. Social workers with their professional training and education, coupled with their commitment to professional values and ethics are ideally suited to combat absenteeism in industry.

SUGGESTED READINGS

1. Googins, Godfrey (1985); "Avoidance of the Alcoholic Client"; *Social Work*; March-April.
2. Kershner, A.M. (2006); *A report on job analysis*. Washington DC Office of Naval Research.
3. Lawler, E.E. (2006); *Pay and organizational effectiveness: A psychological view*, New York: McGraw-Hill.
4. Morsh, J.E. (2005); "Job analysis in the United States Air France"; *Personnel Psychology*, 37, 7-17.
5. Trice and Sonnerstuhl (1987); *Handbook of Industrial and Organizational Psychology*; Chicago: Rand McNally.

22

Conflict Management
A Holistic Perspective

The term human relations in its broadest sense cover all types of interactions among people—their conflicts, cooperative efforts, and group relationships. It is the study of why our beliefs, attitudes, and behaviours sometimes cause interpersonal conflicts in our personal lives and in work-related situations. Human relations emphasize the analysis of human behaviour, prevention of strategies, and resolution of behavioural problems.

Conflict management in human relations refers primarily to conflict within an organization, although it can also mean disputes among organizations or between an organization and the public (as is also people's striving for their own preferred outcome, which if attained, prevent others from achieving their preferred outcome, resulting in hostility and a breakdown in human relations). It is true that whenever people work together, some conflict is inevitable. But disputes, personal clashes and disagreements left unresolved can hurt an organization's operations and reduce its effectiveness as a provider of goods or services. Conflict tends to obstruct cooperative action, create suspicion and distrust and decrease productivity.

Conflict management also refers to the long-term management of intractable conflicts. It is the label for the variety of ways by which people handle grievances—standing up for what they consider to be right and against what they consider to be wrong. Those ways include such diverse phenomena as gossip, ridicule, lynching, terrorism, warfare, feuding, genocide, law, mediation, and avoidance. Which forms of conflict management will be used in any given situation can be somewhat predicted and explained by the social structure—or social geometry—of the case.

Conflict management is often considered to be distinct from *conflict resolution*. In order for actual conflict to occur, there should be an expression of exclusive patterns, and tell why the conflict was expressed the way it was. Conflict is not just about simple inaptness, but is often connected to a previous issue. The latter refers to resolving the dispute to the approval of one or both parties, whereas the former concerns an ongoing process that may never have a resolution. Neither is it considered the same as conflict transformation, which seeks to reframe the positions of the conflict parties.

However, conflict should not be regarded as a solely negative experience. In fact, some amount of creative thinking and true innovation are the core of the conflict. The heart of effective management lies not in trying to eliminate conflict, an impossible task, but in turning the energy released by conflict to constructive ends. Creatively managed, conflict can shake people out of their mental ruts and give them new frameworks, new assumptions and new points of view.

Types of conflict

The author has experienced that there are generally four types of conflicts observed in almost all organizations irrespective of the type and nature of the organizations. **Interpersonal conflicts** are serious problems to many people because they deeply affect a person's emotions. There is a need to protect one's self-image and self-concepts which are threatened, serious upset occurs and relationship deteriorates. Sometimes, the temperaments of two persons are incompatible and their personalities clash. This type of conflict arise from a variety of sources such as:

- Miscommunication
- Differences in perception

- Personality clashes
- Threats to status
- Organizational changes
- Different sets of values

Every group comes into at least one potential conflict with every other group with which it interacts. This is called **intergroup conflict**. There are four factors which contribute to group conflict such as interdependence, differences in goals and perceptions and increased demand for specialist. Conflict can also be categorized as **functional conflict** and **dysfunctional conflict**. A functional conflict is a confrontation between groups that enhances and benefits the organization's performance. A dysfunctional conflict is any confrontation of interaction between groups that harms the organization or hinders the achievement of organizational goals.

Consequences of conflict

It has both *advantages* and *disadvantages.* One of the benefits produced by conflict is that people are stimulated to search for improved approaches that lead to better results. It energizes them to be more creative and to experiment once hidden problems are brought to the surface, where they may be confronted and solved. And once the conflict is resolved, the individuals may be more committed to the outcome through their involvement in solving it.

There are also possible disadvantages, especially if the conflict lasts a long period of time or becomes too intense. At the interpersonal level, cooperation and teamwork may deteriorate. Distrust may grow among people who need to co-ordinate their efforts. For individuals, some may feel defeated, while the self-image of others will decline. Periodically, the motivation level of some employees will be reduced. It is important, then for managers to be aware of the potential for interpersonal and intergroup conflicts, to anticipate their likely outcomes, and to use appropriate conflict resolution strategies.

Conflict resolution is a range of processes aimed at alleviating or eliminating sources of conflict. The term 'conflict resolution' is sometimes used interchangeably with the term dispute resolution or alternative dispute resolution. Processes of conflict resolution generally include negotiation, mediation and diplomacy. The processes of arbitration, litigation, and formal complaint processes such as ombudsman processes, are usually described with the term dispute resolution, although some refer to them as 'conflict resolution'. Processes of mediation and arbitration are often referred to as alternative dispute resolution.

There are many tools available to persons in conflict. A way would be not to fight over it, no violence, only talking out the problem. How and when they are used depends on several factors (such as the specific issues at stake in the conflict and the cultural context of the disputants). The list of tools available to practitioners include negotiation, mediation, community building, advocacy, diplomacy, activism, non-violence, critical pedagogy, prayer and counselling. In real world conflict situations, which range in scale from kindergarten bullying to genocide, practitioners will creatively combine several of these approaches as needed. Additionally, practitioners will often specialize in a particular scale (e.g. interpersonal, community or international), or a particular variety of conflict (such as environmental, religious or organizational), and repertoires of tools they find most useful.

Conflict resolution as both a professional practice and academic field is highly sensitive to culture. In Western cultural contexts, such as the Canada and the United States, successful conflict resolution usually involves fostering communication among disputants, problem-solving, and drafting agreements that meet their underlying needs. In these situations, conflict resolves often talk about finding the *win-win* solution, or mutually satisfying scenario, for everyone involved. In many non-Western cultural contexts, such as Afghanistan, Vietnam and China, it is also important to find *'win-win'* solutions; however, getting there can be very different. In these contexts, direct communication between disputants that explicitly addresses the issues at stake in the conflict can be perceived as very rude, making the conflict worse and delaying resolution. Rather, it can make sense to involve religious, tribal or community leaders, communicate difficult truths indirectly through a third party, and make suggestions through stories. Intercultural conflicts are often the most difficult to resolve because the expectations of the disputants can be very different, and there is much occasion for misunderstanding. A firm position in diplomacy must be maintained.

When personal conflict leads to frustration and loss of efficiency, *counselling* may prove to be a helpful antidote. Although few organizations can afford the luxury of having professional counsellors on the staff, given some training, managers may be able to perform this function. Non-directive counselling, or "listening with understanding", is little more than being a good listener—something every manager should be.

Sometimes, the simple process of being able to vent one's feelings—that is, to express them to a concerned and understanding listener, is enough to relieve frustration and make it possible for the frustrated individual to advance to a problem-solving frame of mind, better able to cope with a personal difficulty that is affecting his work adversely. The non-directive approach is one effective way for managers to deal with frustrated subordinates and co-workers.

There are other more direct and more diagnostic ways that might be used in appropriate circumstances. The great strength of the non-directive approach (non-directive counselling is based on the client-centred therapy of Carl Rogers), however, lies in its simplicity, its effectiveness, and the fact that it deliberately avoids the manager-counsellor's diagnosing and interpreting emotional problems, which would call for special psychological training. No one has ever been harmed by being listened to sympathetically and understandingly. On the contrary, this approach has helped many people to cope with problems that were interfering with their effectiveness on the job.

Prospective strategies for intervention

There are a few basic assumptions which must be kept in mind before we embark upon in the conflict resolution process.

1. Every individual is unique.
2. Certain amount of confidentiality must be maintained.
3. Non-judgmental attitude is always accepted.
4. Differences of opinion are healthy and beneficial.
5. An attitude of patience must be maintained.
6. Every individual has the in-born potentiality to resolve the conflict.
7. It is to be understood that either party could compete with the other but because a mutually acceptable outcome is so important; each side should choose to cooperate.
8. Anger and conflict, as common responses that create the opportunity to share opinions and get things done, are to be accepted.
9. All participants in the conflict resolution process are entitled to their opinions. Each person's opinion must be respected regardless of his or her level of experience, personality, communication style, or position in the organization.
10. There is a win-win solution to the problem and the positive results from the solution must be focused on.

Based on the above assumptions the following diagram represents the direction one can take in resolving conflict. The following steps could be adopted for conflict resolution mechanism.

(i) The saying 'a problem well defined is a problem half solved' is not far from the truth. Everyone involved needs to focus on the real cause of the problem. At this stage, it is helpful to have everyone write a one or two sentence definition of the problem, when everyone is allowed to define the problem; the real cause of the conflict will often surface.

(ii) Once the problem is defined the next step is to gather the facts and opinions needed to understand the situation. Collection of all the facts may be impossible in a particular case; but as long as the major points and opinions are identified, the process can keep moving.

SITUATION : A

↓

Define the problem

↓ (i)

Collect facts and opinions

↓ (ii)

Consider all solutions proposed

↓ (iii)

Define the expected results

↓ (iv)

Select the solutions

↓ (v)

Implement the solutions

↓ (vi)

SITUATION : B

(iii) When the problem has been defined and the facts surrounding it has been brought out, the group should brainstorm solutions. It is important to remember that the group is not looking for one final solution but for creative ideas about solving the problem. No one should be allowed to evaluate, judge, or rule out any proposed solution, no matter how unorthodox or improbable it may seem.

(iv) Obviously, not all solutions to a problem are feasible or desirable. So, poor solutions are to be eliminated and the most appropriate ones settle on.

(v) Which solutions will give the desired results? In light of the goals the group has set, one or perhaps two or three of the solutions will stand out as the most appropriate. The group can then systematically select the best solutions to achieve the desired goals.

(vi) Establish timetables for implementing the solutions and provide some way to evaluate the results. On a regular basis, make a point to discuss with others how things are going. Even the best solutions can fail unless all involved make the attempt to follow them through. When the conflict is to be resolved any of the four inevitable outcomes will occur. The following diagram illustrates the different outcomes :

Win	Win-Lose 3	Win-Win 4
Individual Outcomes	1	2
Lose	Lose-Lose	Lose-Win

Other person's outcome

The first situation is termed **'Lose-Lose'**. In which a conflict deteriorates to the point that both parties are worse off than they were before. The second quadrant is **'Lose-Win'** a situation in which one person (**individual A**) is defeated. While the other one (B) is victorious. In quadrant three (**Win-Lose**) the situation is reversed with **individual B** losing to individual A. The fourth outcome is **'Win-Win'** in which both persons perceive that they are in a better position than they were before when the conflict begins. This is the ideal outcome to try to achieve.

When we talk about conflict resolution in the light of human relations the concept of occupational social work could be very effective in this regard. Occupational social work offers practitioners the opportunity to rationalize and humanize industrial organizations by increasing responsiveness or provide equality, opportunity, and give respect to their employees. Occupational social work also will require collective action for job related services that will improve and humanize the quality of work life by establishing cooperative relationships with management and trade unions.

Conclusion

The healthy emotion of anger is at the root of many conflicts. Even though anger can be expressed in non-productive ways, one can choose to turn one's own anger into energy that helps find solutions to problems in ways that benefit everyone.

Conflict between people can arise over breakdowns in communicating, value clashes, and personality conflict. Organizations may create conflicts through their work policies and practices and adversarial management. There are several approaches for dealing with conflicts, which may be grouped into three basic strategies, **win-lose, lose-lose** and **win-win. Win-win** strategy not only can resolve a conflict but can also preserve good human relations.

Regardless of the strategy implemented the level of assertiveness and desire for cooperation are key factors towards effectively resolving conflicts with others. When people can not solve their conflicts in an informal manner, many organizations create solutions through a conflict resolution process. The process is dependent on win-win attitudes, a strong, sensitive leader, and a clear outline of the steps that need to be taken in order to resolve the conflict.

SUGGESTED READINGS

1. Augsburger, D. (1992). *Conflict mediation across cultures*. Louisville, Kentucky: Westminster/John Knox Press.
2. Bannon, I. and Paul Collier (Eds.). (2003). *Natural resources and violent conflict: Options and actions.* Washington, DC: The World Bank.
3. Ury, F. and Rodger Fisher. (1981). *Getting to yes: Negotiating agreement without giving in*. New York, NY: Penguin Group.
4. Wilmot, W. and Jouyce Hocker. (2007). *Interpersonal conflict*. New York, NY: McGraw-Hill Companies.
5. de Waal, Frans B.M. and Angeline van Roosmalen. (1979); "Reconciliation and consolation among chimpanzees". *Behavioural Ecology and Sociobiology* 5: 55-66.
6. de Waal, Frans B.M. (1989); "Peacemaking Among Primates". *Harvard University Press*, Cambridge, MA.
7. Judge, Peter G. and Frans B. M. de Waal. (1993); "Conflict avoidance among rhesus monkeys: coping with short-term crowding". *Animal Behaviour* 46: 221-232.
8. Veenema, Hans *et al.* (1994); "Methodological improvements for the study of reconciliation". *Behavioural Processes* 31:29-38.
9. de Waal, Frans B.M. and Filippo Aureli. (1996); "Consolation, reconciliation, and a possible cognitive difference between

macaques and chimpanzees". *Reaching into thought: The minds of the great apes* (Eds. Anne E. Russon, Kim A. Bard, Sue Taylor Parker), Cambridge University Press, New York, NY: 80-110.

10. Aureli, Filippo. (1997); "Post-conflict anxiety in non-human primates: the mediating role of emotion in conflict resolution". *Aggressive Behaviour* 23: 315-328.
11. Castles, Duncan L. and Andrew Whiten. (1998); "Post-conflict behaviour of wild olive baboons: Reconciliation, redirection, and consolation". *Ethology*: 104: 126-147.
12. Aureli, Filippo and Frans B. M. de Waal, eds. (2000). *Natural Conflict Resolution*. University of California Press, Berkeley, CA.
13. de Waal, Frans B.M. (2000). "Primates—A natural heritage of conflict resolution". *Science* 289: 586-590.
14. Silk, Joan B. (2002). "The form and function of reconciliation in primates". *Annual Review of Anthropology* 31: 21-44.
15. Weaver, Ann and Frans B.M. de Waal. (2003). "The mother-offspring relationship as a template in social development: reconciliation in captive brown capuchins (Cebus apella)". *Journal of Comparative Psychology* 117: 101-110.
16. Palagi, Elisabetta *et al.* (2004). "Reconciliation and consolation in captive bonobos (Pan paniscus)". *American Journal of Primatology* 62: 15-30.
17. Palagi, Elisabetta *et al.* (2005). "Aggression and reconciliation in two captive groups of Lemur catta". *International Journal of Primatology* 26: 279-294.
18. Lorenzen, Michael. (2006). "Conflict Resolution and Academic Library Instruction". *LOEX Quarterly* 33, no. ½, 6-9, 11.
19. Winslade, John and Monk, Gerald. (2000). *Narrative Mediation: A New Approach to Conflict Resolution*, Jossey-Bass Publishers, San Francisco.
20. Bar-Siman-Tov, Yaacov (Ed.) (2004). *From Conflict Resolution to Reconciliation*, Oxford University Press.

23

Faculty Development Strategies for Social Work Teachers

Challenging Priority before the Profession

There are about 110 schools of social work offering degree courses both at the Baccalaureate and Master level in different parts of India. Among them some of the schools of social work are also offering Master of Philosophy (M.Phil) and Doctoral Programme (Ph.D.). These schools employ approximately 800 teachers, who strive to integrate teaching, research and extension education. To perform multifarious roles, such as curriculum designers, course developers, field-work instructors, researchers; extension educators and administrators, more efficiently and effectively, these teachers have to develop newer professional and personal competencies and skills in several areas like educational technology; human relations, research, management etc. No system of education or research in any university or academic institution can rise above the level of the teachers. However sound the curriculum including the fieldwork, the integral part of social work education and research ultimately depends on the competence and confidence of the teachers. Currently, the quantitative dimension of teachers probably claims priority over the qualitative dimension. The quantitative expansion cannot go on forever. It has necessarily to be commensurate with qualitative improvement of the teachers (Gupta, 2006).

Need for faculty development

Today's students virtually become tomorrow's teachers in the schools of social work. All good researchers or persons having excellent academic qualifications may not necessarily be good teachers. A teacher with adequate qualifications and a research bent of mind may be proficient in the knowledge of the subject matter but this is only a part of teaching. The rest he/she has to acquire through concerted efforts. As change agents, the teachers can bring about quantum changes in the students, provided they possess the required competence and, more importantly, they feel like doing so. The performance of students mainly depends on what the teachers do. If the teachers can be trained to do better, then the achievement of students is bound to rise (Tandon, 2004).

Our educational panorama in social work is marked by rapid changes in the society. Different new individual and social problems are emerging due to dynamic pattern of the society, changing government policies and programmes, and due to revolution in educational technology and innovations. Evaluation of suitable strategies to improve the teaching effectiveness in social work profession is mainly based on the principles of educational technology and keeping the teachers abreast of the changes taking place in the professional field in terms of rendering services to the clientele. Recent developments in educational technology like the use of programmed instruction, simulation, computer application etc. have been shown to enhance the teaching-learning process. Experiential learning, interdisciplinary team teaching, etc. demand a new instructional technology. The impact of recent advancements in the areas of social services on the social work teaching and learning process as well on the research effectiveness cannot be ignored. The social work teachers are often criticized for their excessive dependence on more routine methods, and for their lack of emphasis on and awareness of other emerging and more effective methods of teaching and research. They have to pay greater attention to rapid adoption and dynamic change, rather than to pattern maintenance. The endeavour, should, therefore, be to provide them with the best possible opportunities for personal and professional development to prepare them better to meet the emerging needs.

As the quality of social work education and research in the country can be no better than the quality of teachers in the schools of social work, every possible effort should be made to improve the quality of teachers, through appropriately designed faculty development programmes. Such an effective programme makes the teachers aware of their strengths and weaknesses, and may provide them with enough opportunities to develop their competence to overcome their deficiencies. Although faculty development has a direct bearing on the quality of social work education and research in the country, it has so far received very little attention. It is time for schools of social work to pay greater attention to this vital activity in the face of rapid developments taking place all-rounds.

Principles of faculty development

Faculty development is mainly concerned with the means by which the teachers acquire new knowledge and develop those skills, whose application will improve the efficiency and effectiveness of whatever functions they perform. It aims at improving the competence and confidence of the teachers in performing their duties. It is a deliberate and continuous process that involves the identification of anticipated needs of the individual teachers for furthering their job satisfaction and career prospects, and the timely provision of the required opportunities.

Functions of faculty development

1. It helps the teachers to acquire and maintain appropriate expertise to meet current as well as projected needs that their job demands.
2. It ensures that each faculty becomes competent in his/her field of specialization.

3. It enables the faculty to broaden and update their knowledge, and to advance their personal and professional achievements.
4. It encourages in the teachers, a positive response to various changes that are occurring within and outside their institution.
5. It enables the teachers to achieve personal satisfaction in their work by making full use of their capabilities throughout career.
6. It encourages the teachers to contribute to the maintenance of academic culture and professionalism.
7. It equips the teachers with necessary skills to meet the emerging needs in the areas of educational technology and research.
8. Above all, it helps to maintain the commitment and vitality of teachers in achieving the goals of their institutions.

Policy issues

To develop sound faculty development programmes for the social work teachers, the schools of social work will have to pay adequate attention to the following policy issues.

Professional training

As newer developments are taking place at a faster rate, adequate provisions should be made for professional training of social work teachers, both short-term and long-term, in critical areas so that they are well prepared to utilize the opportunities whenever they come. A list of organizations, where the needed specialized training is available, has to be maintained. Every academic institution is caught in between the increasing number of teachers to be trained on the one hand, and rising expectations.

Foundation training

Each school of social work should explore possibility of introducing a foundation course for the beginners, who take teaching assignment after their post-graduation (UNESCO 1990a; UNESCO 1990b; Gupta, 2006). Such a course should focus on:

- Theoretical aspects at the general level as a basis for higher social work education.
- Guidance for practical aspects like preparing lesson plans, developing the courses, designing the materials and defining the student teacher activities.
- Guidance for fieldwork practice, supervision, research methodology and other related areas.
- The pedagogical aspects including the latest and more effective technique of teaching like individual learning, interdisciplinary team teaching, programmed instruction, computer aided instruction; and
- Educational technology cells to be created in each of the schools of social work which can be entrusted with this responsibility.

Seminars, Symposia, Workshops and Summer Institutes

For the qualitative improvement of in-service teachers, they should be encouraged to attend seminars, symposia, and workshops etc. that are organized nationally or internationally by local as well as outside institutions. Every teacher has to be encouraged to participate in these programmes as and when one feels the requirement. This will enable them to foster interaction and cross-fertilization of ideas among the teachers from different schools of social work.

Refresher course

It has been made mandatory by U.G.C. (University Grants Commission) that a Lecturer is required to attend two refresher courses to be promoted to the post of Senior-Lecturer (exemption of one refresher course for those lecturers who are having Ph.D. degree—before the implementation of 6th Pay Commission). A Senior Lecturer needs to attend two refresher courses to be promoted to Reader. But Reader onwards a teacher does not require any refresher course for the next promotion. So, sometimes attending refresher course has become credential for promotion and higher scale for pay but not for attaining knowledge. It is, therefore, necessary to have a standing policy that every teacher, irrespective of designation has to attend refresher course on every three years in his/her service career.

It has also been observed that a very few schools of social work, namely Jamia Millia, Tata Institute of Social Sciences and Visva-Bharati, Santiniketan are entrusted to organize refresher course. It should be made mandatory by U.G.C. that every school of social work should periodically conduct refresher course. This would enable each school to develop its man-power potentially in organizing a programme, sharpen the skills and responsibilities of each faculty member and, above all, exchange of ideas among the schools of social work.

Study leave

Depending on the situation, each school has to work out suitable mechanism to provide study leave so that quality upgradation of teachers is possible. While awarding such leave, the university has to pay due attention to the nature of the programme for which the teacher proposes to attend; the capacity of the teachers to make effective use of the opportunity that the programme will provide; and the needs of the school. The teachers should be encouraged to undertake their higher studies by availing study leave in institutions other than the one in which they are working.

Self-development

It is possible to provide personal help to teachers for self-development through evaluation and feedback. In this teaching improvement programme, the teachers can be helped by the colleagues in the identification and improvement of their instructional strengths and weaknesses through the collection and analysis of data from a variety of sources like student questionnaire, classroom feedback etc.

Apprenticeship

Since the freshers need more reassurance and guidance, they have to be made to work with experienced teachers for at least two years in the beginning of their career. The schools of social work have to encourage teacher apprenticeship wherein the more experienced senior teachers, through teaching and research experience and monitoring, assist the new and young teachers to improve their job effectiveness.

Sabbatical leave

This leave is with full salary and is counted as a period of their service. Here, the teachers get freedom from routine duties and are able to undertake special studies at some other institutions of their choice. The experiences thus gained will promote their professional competence. The teachers of each school of social work should be encouraged to avail this leave after completing ten years of service, both within and outside the country, up to a maximum of one year at a time.

Inter-visitation

This involves the exchange of visits of teachers between and among the schools of social work. The teachers could be encouraged to visit other schools of social work for a particular period of the time to work on a specific problem and interact with the teachers there. Training takes place through exchange of ideas, knowledge and experience.

Apart from these prime areas for faculty development programme, some more areas could be explored by all the schools of social work for the effective implementation of faculty development programmes. The process of acquiring new knowledge and developing special skills in a continuous one; it should never be considered as a one-time activity. Periodic orientation of teachers is of vital importance in enabling them to keep abreast of the latest development in their area of specialization (Main, 2008). So goal oriented programmes have to be planned systematically on a scientific basis for better results.

It may be worth considering the idea of setting up ***'Human Resource Development Cells'*** in each school of social work according to its capacity which can be entrusted with the responsibility to design, implement, co-ordinate and monitor various faculty development programmes.

In the present competitive situation, 'publish or perish' is the slogan often heard in the academic world (Gupta, 2006). Policy-makers and administrators do not appear to be bothered so much about teaching effectiveness as with publishing research results. In case of career advancement, including, merit promotion, publication score is much above the teaching effectiveness. Obviously, the teachers tend to give secondary importance to teaching. The schools of social work must look into this matter and treat the teaching and publications equally.

It would be worthwhile to consider the possibility of developing a system wherein the teachers who have participated in various training programmes, conferences and meetings could be asked to organize seminars for the benefit of other teachers in the schools of social work. Such seminars have to be organized within a given time frame, say fifteen days from the date of return. Suitable norms have to be worked out by each school of social work. Implementation of various faculty development programmes is a costly exercise that involves teachers; time and cost. It becomes, therefore, necessary to evolve suitable follow-up action plans to closely monitor and assess the impact of various programmes on the performance of teachers. They should be provided with necessary facilities and encouragement to introduce what they learnt from the progamme (Gupta, 2006). This experience will also help the schools of social work to design more meaningful programmes in future.

Teachers have to be honoured for their outstanding accomplishments in teaching. Suitable reward system for imaginative and creative instruction by the teachers has to be worked out by the schools of social work. This can avoid teaching getting ***'routinised'***. Best teacher awards may be instituted by the schools of social work to motivate the teachers.

Conclusion

Unless the policy-makers of the schools of social work develop understanding and appreciation for the usefulness of faculty development efforts in improving the professional competence of the teachers, nothing useful will emerge from such efforts. They have to be more optimistic and provide all facilities and encouragement necessary for meaningful implementation of various faculty improvement programmes.

Finally, any type of faculty development effort will become effective only when the policy-makers become sensitive to the usefulness of various faculty development strategies. It is usually the teachers' awareness and readiness that make faculty development a success or a failure. Teacher's commitment together with adequate support system and conducive policies will ensure the effectiveness of faculty development strategies.

SUGGESTED READINGS

1. Ahmad Shakeel (2001); *Human Resource Development in Universities;* A.P.H. Publishing Corporation, New Delhi.
2. Ary, P.P. and Tandon, B. B. (2004); *Human Resource Development;* Deep and Deep Publications, New Delhi.
3. Gupta, A.K. (2006); *Teachers' Education: Current and Prospects;* Sterling Publishers Pvt. Ltd., New Delhi.
4. Gupta, D.K. (2006); *Glimpses of Agricultural Education;* Northern Book Centre, New Delhi.
5. Harding, A.G. and Kanewsouthi, S. (1981); *Professional development in higher education—state of the art and the artists,* Educational Development Series, Bradford, London.
6. Main, A. (2008); *Education Staff Development,* Croom Helm, London.
7. Raman, K.V. and Balaguru, T. (2007); "National Agricultural Research System in India"; *Journal of Indian School of Political Economy,* 2 (3), 464-474.
8. UNESCO (1990); *Innovations and initiatives in teacher education in Asia and the Pacific Region,* Volumes I and II, Overview, UNESCO Regional Office, Bangkok, Thailand.

24

Developing Employee Assistance Programme in Industry

Challenging Priority in the 21st Century

Work is a powerful force in the lives of human beings and their strongest ties to reality. It is work that meets the basic needs of economic survival as well as other human needs such as satisfaction, social status, and emotional security. Where we live, how we live, and who we see socially are to a great extent dominated by the work we do (Jerome, 2004). The work performance of the individuals is greatly influenced by their feelings about work, their supervisors and other such details. These feelings become an important part of behaviour and performance at work. It was also realized that a contended individual would perform better results, than a production oriented supervisors (Skidmore, 1974). This was the very essence of human relation movement as well as the basic philosophy of the Employee Assistance Programme (EAPs).

What is EAP?

Traditionally, even at present, employers feel that employee problems should be dealt with privately, at a distance. Employees for their part, feel that their employers are disinterested in personal concerns and difficulties. To bridge the gap and to change these kinds of attitudes and perception, employee assistance programmes (EAPs) are designed to deal with employee problems that may affect workplace performance. The major impact has been to change the views of the workplace from that of a producer of problems to a source of help. So, EAPs are programmes to assist employees (and sometimes their families) with personal problems that interfere with employment. EAPs are a professional assessment and referral and/or short-term counselling service offered to employees with mental health and or problems related to substance addiction that may be affecting their work. They also include managerial-supervising consultation and employee education. Employees may either be self-referred to the company's EAP or are referred by employers or their respective supervisors.

EAPs help the employee who are affected by substance abuse, mental health problems, or other emotional issues either their own or those of loved ones. They are shown how to cope with the anxiety, fear, and other emotions that emerge in response to these problems. EAP staff can work as team members with the personnel and medical staff of the organization, and they can also provide support services to unions for members who are dealing with personal problems (Masi, 2008).

A company's EAP can serve as a valuable resource in developing employee policies, and it can help allay employee anxieties and fears as the company develops its philosophy and policy surrounding new issues. As society evolves, the workplace must be flexible and open in its commitment to help its employees. On the other hand as society becomes more complex, the workplace must be prepared to offer employees assistance in coping with such issues as drugs, AIDS, sexual harassment and prejudice, EAP personnel are in a unique position to offer this kind of support, since they should be trained in mental health counselling, social work, policy implementation, and education. EAPs can also help companies to interpret and implement labour as well as social security legislations for the benefit of the employees.

Recent estimates reveal that there are at present approximately 15,000 EAPs in American work organizations as compared to 5,000 in 1981 (Masi, 1999). In addition, a couple of other studies have also been carried out in Western countries especially in the U.S.A. which shows how effective the EAPs are.

General Motors of the U.S.A. and *Goldsmith Company of U.K.* after implementing EAP programmes have been able to reduce absenteeism by 70 per cent and 55 per cent respectively. Apart from that, the rate of alcoholism has fallen from 56 per cent and 49 per cent respectively in General Motors and Goldsmith Company. Marked improvements has also been noticed in other areas such as reduction in mental health problems and on-the-job accidents and increase in job performance, team spirit, loyalty to the organization and public image (L. Stern, 2007).

EAP—Conceptual framework

- EAPs are based on the premise that work is very important to people (it is ego reinforcing), the work itself is not the cause of the employee's problem; consequently, the workplace can be a means to get people help (Stern, 2007).
- Information about the employee's job performance is extremely important—diagnosis and treatment. It can be used to measure and track whether treatment is successful.
- Workplace peers and union stewards are very important; however, they too can deny the problem and enable the employees to continue the behaviour. Teaching them to confront and consequently breaking the denial barrier is an important element.
- EAPs concentrate on personnel issues and job performances.
- Job leverage is the key ingredient. The counsellors must be able to use this with the supervisors.
- Cost-effectiveness is an important consideration and must be addressed with staff of the management.
- The EAP practitioner's knowledge about addiction is paramount. Every EAP should be staffed by clinically licensed professionals from the mental health field who

are familiar with addiction and can help EAP practitioners in their intervention in dealing with addicts. The mental health professionals can also provide help to EAP personnel in dealing with emotional and psychiatric problems of the employees.

- The supervisors play a key role in getting help for the employees. Often, however, the supervisor denies the problem and even enables the troubled employee to continue the problem behaviour. The supervisor is critical in the confrontational process with the troubled employee. Therefore, education is necessary to eliminate the supervisor's tendency to enable the employees by denying the problem (Masi, 2008 and S. Friedland, 2008).
- EAPs should be the part of the organizational structure of management and unions should be an important participant in the development and smooth running of EAPs.

Extended areas of EAP intervention

The changes that are occurring in the world of business and on the industrial scenario are projected to continue at a more rapid pace into the 21st century. These can pose problems of great magnitude and concern to the EAP model. Certain policy measures and legislations have been introduced/amended including the deregulation of financial markets, technological innovation, the open market policy, exit policy and amendments to the ***Monopolistic Restrictive Trade Practice Act (MRTP)***. These are bound to have critical changes in global and internal competitions that will affect the structure of the industry; unionization, feminization and composition of work-force, erosion of social security benefits and ecologically sustainable jobs (increasing technology and socially useful work).

The above-mentioned changes in the work place are bound to aggravate or to some extent, create a set of new issues and problems affecting the employees and their families. The problems of drug abuse, occupational stress and emotional illness, pre and (golden handshake policy) post-retirement issues, termination and relocation of work place, career advancement, financial and legal counselling, and care of the elderly and other family related problems are the manifestations of such changes. With these changes in the industrial scenario, the roles of EAP personnel need to change and extend from that of the earlier objectives of treating only alcoholic employees to those with diverse affairs.

EAPs can be divided into "**Internal**" and "**External**" programmes (Lawrence, 2003). *Internal EAPs* could be staffed by individuals who are regular employees of the company. Internal programmes can have the advantage of greater integration into the workings of the company, leading to more effective organizational development and outreach. *External EAPs* could be provided by outside agencies or on a contractual basis. Many countries in the Western world have already started this practice. In India they could be started for those companies which are not in a position to manage the welfare of employees with their existing resources.

Beth Lewis (2005) has explained the importance of EAPs from another dimension, namely a two-tier pattern of EAPs. EAPs will become more common generally, but vary enormously in their role and function depending on the employment context.

Basic EAP services will be broadly available in a variety of jobs. They will be intended to meet the needs of the employer in addressing personnel issues arising from the personal problems of the employees. Basic programmes will include diagnostic/referral services and short-term treatment. Plant closings and mass lay-offs could be the important target of basic EAPs to see the devastating effects on workers, their families and the community and to deal with these issues. Unemployment caused by plant closings and mass permanent lay-offs is an important area we often come across in the present world of business and industry owing to massive *globalization process and technological innovation*. Economic insecurity and deprivation following job loss tends to result in a decline in physical and mental health. Symptomatology such as depression, anxiety, alcoholism, hypertension, gout, and ulcers have been observed for the displaced workers and their spouses (Joyce, O. Beckett, 1999). Family and social problems such as withdrawal, child and spouse abuse, and divorce have been found as well; the larger the plant closing period, the more severe the problem. At the other extreme, **deluxe EAPs** will provide comprehensive programmes to employees in better-paying jobs, primarily full-time employees of medium and large firms.

Another enormous task the EAP personnel can meet is the stress and strain faced by employees of almost all the industrial organizations and of the computer revolution (Craig Brod, 2008), which has been causing mental and physical health problems of the employees. This problem has been termed as technostress (Brod, 2008). A research study conducted by the Administrative Management Society Foundation in the U.S.A. (Reece, 1998) showed that the key role could be performed by EAP personnel to reduce technostress-cyberphobia (excessive fear of new computer technology) and cyberphrenia (addiction to new computer technology to the extent that it totally dominates one's life) and the result was quite encouraging (no statistical data available).

At this juncture it would be worthwhile to distinguish between the role of the personnel department and EAP personnel which would justify the importance of EAPs in the 21st century. The role of the personnel department starts from **Management Functions** which include (Flippo, 1984):

- planning,
- organizing,
- directing, and
- controlling.

On the other hand **Operative Functions** include:

- procurement,
- development,

- compensation, and
- integration.

Through all these performing roles the personnel department perceives an employee only as an individual of an industry with little or no human touch. On the other hand, the EAP personnel consider an employee not only as an individual of the industry but also as a product of a larger society. The personnel department is more concerned about an employee while he/she is on the job, i.e. during working hours but the basic focus of the EAPs is also to see what is happening to an employee when he/she is out of the industry. Lastly, the EAP personnel are better equipped with the concept of counselling, mental health and other aspects of human relations to deal with personal as well as the job related problems more effectively and humanly which the people from the personnel department are not able to.

Essential ingredients of EAPs

The success of an EAP must depend on the following ***ingredients.*** These elements are all equally important and are not listed in the order of priority:

1. Historically, unions have been concerned that employee counselling programmes might be a management method for circumventing collective bargaining. Companies can gain union support by including them in programme planning.
2. Supervisors, especially if they make referrals to the assistance progamme, must be properly trained. They should understand the programme policies, procedures, and services and be clear about their role in relation to the plan. It is important that the supervisor is trained to view the referral as a service that helps rather than embarrasses or humiliates the employee. Supervisory training is equally necessary to make the EAP servi(e available to the concerned employees.

3. If the EAP is to be effective, employees must be informed of its availability and services. Memos, posters, and programmes including slide shows or films could be used to inform employees about the existence of the EAP. They are usually more effective and well received if they are presented at the proper time, namely during the lunch hour or the coffee break. These should be offered regularly. Plans that encourage family members' participation should be carried out regularly and such information should be sent to the employee's home.

   In addition, the EAP should provide separate educational sessions and material on different issues as updated from time to time. Employee education programmes could use written materials, short talks, workshops, or films and should be well fitted in which the other methods of communication and information dissemination.
4. Most employees will not participate in the programme unless they feel assured that their case remains confidential. Therefore, secure records and training for professional and support staff are essential. Everyone including secretaries, interns, and volunteers must understand the importance of confidentiality. Files should be locked, access should be limited and monitored, and identifying information kept to a minimum.
5. An EAP located within the organization should be under the auspices of the company's human resource or personnel department. It should be situated in such a way that it is accessible to employees who are in need of EAP services. EAP location should be inconspicuous enough to help confidentiality. It should be well furnished and situated in pleasant surroundings to demonstrate the commitment of the EAP. If the EAP is located offside, there should be an office on the premise where supervisor and clients can meet with the EAP personnel if and when necessary.

6. The written policy statement of the company should clearly define the purpose of the programme, organizational and legal mandates, employee eligibility, the roles and responsibility of various personnel in the organization and procedures. This statement should have the formal support of unions.
7. The basic services an EAP can provide are information, assessment and referral, and/or short-term counselling. It is important for the counsellor not only to listen to the employee but also to evaluate the nature and seriousness of the employee's problems before the employee is assisted and a focus for help defined.
8. The staff should be required to have at least two years experience working with alcoholism, other addictions, human resource development, labour welfare, and community development. The staff should be qualified with adequate work experience in the recognized mental health professions, psychology, social work, psychiatry and should have the appropriate credentials. In addition, these professionals should demonstrate the ability and flexibility to work with managers, supervisors, employees and unions.
9. One of the EAP's responsibilities is to evaluate the community resources for appropriate employee referrals and to keep the list up-to-date. For example, in the case of an employee with AIDS, support groups for the employee and family are required.
10. EAP personnel must pay attention to the needs and problems of women, the physically, mentally and socially handicapped people, old and minority people in order to deal with group-specific issues such as sexual harassment, family violence, role conflict and work related problems.

Programme evaluation

All EAPs should be evaluated to justify their existence and demonstrate their effectiveness. An evaluation allows the company to assess the extent to which its objectives are being met and to find ways to improve the effectiveness. In addition, an evaluation can help ensure that the company EAP is legally protected. It is better to have a third party evaluator, an individual or corporation without connection to the company to make an adequate and unbiased evaluation. EAP evaluation could be of two types—**(a) process evaluation; and (b) an outcome evaluation.**

Process evaluation should encompass the review and analysis of monthly statistics, including the number of cases, categories of diagnosis, and supervisory referrals. The purpose of this evaluation component is to ensure that the EAP reaches the appropriate number of employees, including those with different types of addiction: that the client population reflects the workforce composition in relation to age, sex, race, job level, and so on; and there is a baseline data in job performance for comparing performance after going to the EAP. An outcome evaluation is both ***quantitative*** and ***qualitative.*** The quantitative evaluation determines whether the EAP is cost effective. Areas are to be evaluated may include:

(a) Absenteeism,
(b) Advanced leave,
(c) Leave without pay,
(d) Industrial accidents,
(e) Health Insurance claims (if any),
(f) Sick leave,
(g) Workers' Compensation claims, and
(h) Performance appraisal records.

EAPs can be evaluated qualitatively through a peer panel approach conducted by recognized experts in the fields of psychiatry, psychology and social work who can provide a professional, comprehensive, and constructive review of individual case records. This panel should review a number of randomly selected EAP records and provide a written and oral report to management.

Conclusion

It is needless to say that production and profit are the prime objective of any industrial organization. Employees are the key elements for the success of an organization. So employees must be properly taken care of in every respect as if they can perform best on the job and lead to the success of the organization. In this context, the employee assistance programmes have immense importance in industry and especially in the light of the changing complexities of the industrial scenario.

SUGGESTED READINGS

1. Brod, Craig (2008); *Effective Human Relation in Organization;* Houghton, Mifflin Company, Boston.
2. Bryant, M. (1990); "Ways to Make EAPs More Cost Effective", *Business and Health,* September.
3. Berry, C. (1990); *Good Health for Employees and Reduced Health Care Costs for Industry* (Washington, DC); Health Insurance Institute, pp. 28-29.
4. Beckell, Joyce, O. (1999); "Plant Closings: How Older Workers are Affected", *Annals of the American Academy of Political and Social Sciences,* September.
5. Duda, M. (1990); "Banking on EAPs Brings Companies Big Dividends", *Safety and Health.*
6. Flippo, B. Edwin (1984); *Personnel Management;* McGraw-Hill Book Company, New York.
7. Gaylord, Maxine (1979); "Relocation and the Corporate Family: Unexplored Issues", *Social Work,* Vol. 24, No. 3, May, pp. 186-191.
8. Lawson, Billie (1987); "Work-related Post Traumatic Stress Reactions: The Hidden Dimensions"; *Health and Social Work,* Vol. 12 (4), pp. 250-258.
9. Levis Beth (2005); "Social Work in the 21st Century" in Michael Reish and Eileen Gambrill (eds.); *Social Work in the 21st Century;* Pine Forge Press, California.
10. McCormack, John (1998); "Older Workers: Roles for Occupational Social Work", *Australian Social Work,* Vol. 49, No. 3, March.
11. Masi, Dale (1999); "Evaluation of Occupational Alcoholism and Drug Abuse Programmes". Paper presented at 36th International Congress on Alcohol and Drug Dependence; Glasgow, Scotland, Published by International Council on Alcohol and Addiction (ICAA).

12. Masi, Dale and Friedland, S. (2008); "EAP Actions and Options", *Personnel Journal*, June.
13. Ozawa, Martha (1980); "Development of Social Services in Industry—Why and How"? *Social Work*, Vol. 25, No. 6, November, pp. 464-470.
14. Reece, L. Barry (1998); *Personnel/Human Resource Management*, Houghton Mifflin Company, Boston.
15. Rosow, Jerome (2004); *The Worker and the Job;* Englewood Cliffs, New Jersey, Prentice Hall.
16. Rosenthal, Neal (1995); "The Nature of Occupational Employment Growth—1983-92"; *Monthly Labour Review*, June, pp. 45-54.
17. Root, S. Lawrence (2003); "Social Work and the Workplace" in Michael and Eileen Gambrill (eds.); *Social Work in the 21st Century;* Pine Forge Press, California.
18. Stern, L. (2007); "Why EAPs are Worth the Investment"; *Business and Health*, May.
19. Skidmore, R. (1974); "Social Work Practice in Industry; *Social Work*, Vol. 14, No. 4, pp. 28-29.

25

Status of Implementation of National Rural Employment Guarantee Act (NREGA) from Community Perspective

A Situational Analysis Study with Special Reference to Birbhum District of West Bengal

Introduction

Birbhum District is one of the mono-cropped agricultural districts of West Bengal where employment opportunities have got paucities due to various economic imbalances which gradually is engulfing a colonial section of our society. This has left the rural people in a precarious condition. Especially it has insurmountable impact on the marginal farmers and landless labourers. They are unable to fulfil their basic livelihood needs which has forced them to migrate to the nearest cities or even to other parts of the country in search of their living for their families. In veritable sense this incessant migration exposes them in perfidious situation and in turn ultimately endangers their lives and are denied of their basic democratic and fundamental rights.

The idea of an Employment Guarantee Act is not new, but a series of unlikely events has captured it from obscurity to the top of the political agenda. Indeed, the first pledge of the Common Minimum Programme which read: "The UPA Government will immediately enact a National Employment Guarantee Act. This would provide a legal guarantee for at least 100 days of employment to begin with on asset creating public works programme every year at minimum wages for at least one able-bodied person in every rural, urban poor and lower middle-class household." The need for an Act has been questioned. Why is it not enough to initiate massive employment schemes? The main answer is that an Act places an enforceable obligation on the State, and gives bargaining power to the labourers. By contrast, a scheme leaves labourers at the mercy of government officials. There is another major difference between a scheme and an Act. Schemes come and go but laws are made durable.

In the light of the above, the **NREGA** has been seen as an attempt to address and provide some employment avenues to the poor people and specially the landless and marginal farmers in the district. It is expected that this state operated scheme which is meant for the economic upliftment of rural people would help in raising their families above the poverty line, and also bring them out from the vicious circle of abject poverty.

The Act will be applicable to areas notified by the Central Government and cover the whole of the country within five years. The scheme will be implemented as a centrally sponsored scheme on a cost-sharing basis between the centre and the states. The Centre-State ratio in sharing the costs for providing wage employment is 90 : 10. In a nutshell, under this scheme any adult who is willing to do unskilled manual work at the minimum wage is entitled to be employed in public works within 15 days of tendering application. If the employment is not provided within 15 days, the applicant is entitled to an unemployment allowance. At least one-forth of the minimum wages for the first 30 days and at least one-half of the minimum wage thereafter will be given to the employed person (male or female). In the eligibility criteria, anyone above the age of 18 years and resides in rural areas, 100 days employment will be granted per household per year. The work site will fall within 5 k.m. from the applicant's residence and if work is provided beyond 5 k.m. a travel allowance should be paid by the concerned authorities. The minimum wage entitled under this Act is Rs. 68 per day. The wage is to be paid on a weekly basis or in any case not later than a fortnight. The mandatory work site facilities which are to be provided are safe drinking water, shade, medical aid and crèche if more than five children below the age of 6 year are having by the employed female person.

There would be no gender discrimination under any circumstances and especially in terms of wages—equal wage for both the gender. At least 33 per cent of labourers should be women in the allocation of employment as a mark of priority for women. The works which are to be performed under the scheme are related to water conservation, watershed management, drought and flood proofing, social forestry, land development, rural connectivity and wasteland development. NREGA is an attempt by the Central Government in invigorating grassroots democracy and bringing about good governance.

Driving force behind the emergence of the Act

The Employment Guarantee Act is a step towards the right to work, as an aspect of the fundamental right to live with dignity. The 'right to life' is a fundamental right of all citizens of the country; which is incorporated under **Article 21** of the **Constitution of India**. Right to life includes the right to live with human dignity: it will include all the aspects, which would make life meaningful, complete and living.

On the other hand, the right to work falls under Directive Principle of the Constitution. This Act elucidates **Article 39A** of the Constitution of India which directs the state that its responsibility towards the citizens—both man and woman—should be treated without any gender discrimination and have the right to adequate means of livelihood. In the furtherance of this context **Article 41**, states that the State shall make effective provision for securing the right to work.

Poverty reduction strategies along with sustainable, durable assets creation in rural areas

Taking into account India's contemporary degrading socio-economic condition, the **NREGA** is a sincere attempt of the Union Government to eradicate those problems. It came into account mainly to explore the socio-economic conditions in relations to poverty and hunger and understand the coping mechanism of the rural poor.

For the overall development of any region a sustainable development strategy is to be adopted. The NREGA gives stress on durable creation in rural areas for sustainable development and reduction of poverty. A list of eight categories of works that are supposed to be the focus of the scheme are water conservation and water harvesting, drought proofing (including afforestation), irrigation canals including micro and macro irrigation works, provisions of irrigation facility to land owned by households belonging to the Scheduled Caste and Scheduled Tribes, beneficiaries of land reforms or beneficiaries of Indira Awas Yojana, renovation of traditional water bodies including desalting of tanks, land development, flood control and protection including drainage in waterlogged areas, rural connectivity to provide all weather access.

Autopsy of the above-mentioned programme shows that these are the creation of durable assets in rural areas and employment generation among rural people. All the schemes are interrelated among each other and all are significantly meant for durable assets creation and eradication of poverty.

The relation between durable assets creation and sustainable development can be presented through a chart. There is an interlinking between durable assets creation and reduction of poverty. (Diagram 25.1)

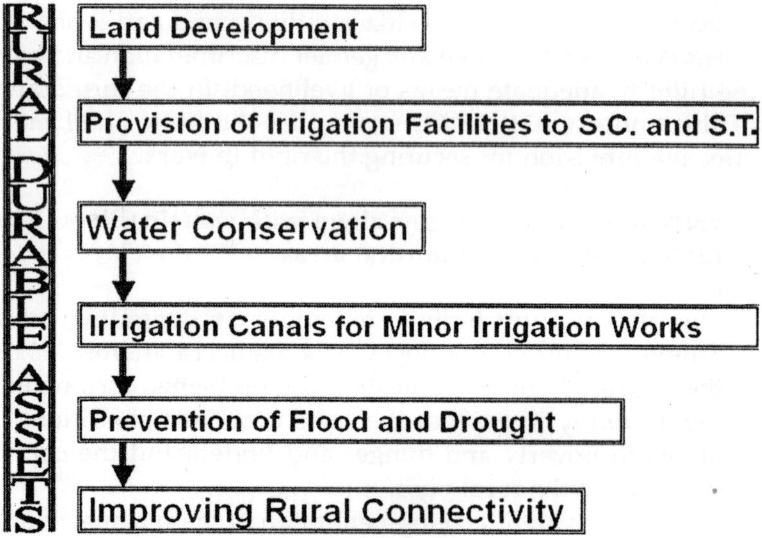

Diagram 25.1

Land should be developed in rural areas and to be provided to poor rural people for irrigation. To make the land suitable for cultivation, water conservation is to be done and to support irrigation more canals are to be built. To prevent the irrigated land from natural disaster like food and drought, suitable steps are to be taken. For the overall development of any place, the improvement of rural connectivity, i.e. good roads are to be constructed.

On further analyzing this chart it can be found that the landless farmers are provided with land suitable for irrigation. If land is made suitable for agriculture, the production of food grains rises and through the better connectivity, there is easy access to the local market, making it easy for marketing. On a critical examination of this scheme, it reflects that in the whole process a huge number of labourers are deployed and which in turn generates a considerable amount of employment. This will facilitate this working people to interact more with external world and can have access to handful of information.

In relation to the above views the NREGA emerged as a **'People's Act'** from various dimensions because it has been developed for upgrading livelihood condition among the rural households, whereas it intends to ensure the fundamental right of the working people, i.e. sustainability with dignity and it also empowers the rural people to play an active role in creation of durable livelihood assets by their democratic functioning.

Basic arguments/assumptions whether this Act is able to reduce poverty and enhance sustainable development for the rural poor

This particular scheme has been rolling on since 2006. And now, the government and panchayat bodies are at loggerheads over the *'success'* of the Act. While government claims that NREGA has achieved a success rate of over 90 per cent, panchayats are not ready to accept that. According to them, it is only a clinical assessment which means an estimate derived by studying physical statistics only and not the utter reality. The reality gives a completely different scenario. Even the fundamental principles of the Act have not been implemented homogeneously in the state of West Bengal.

Launched on February 2, 2006 across 200 poorest districts spreading over 27 states, the Act guarantees 100 days of unskilled manual work in a year to one adult member of every rural household. The Act aims at eradication of extreme poverty and making villages self-sustaining through productive asset creation. Under the Act creation of productive assets like water tanks and soil conservation works get preference. This is to regenerate the village's natural resources, which in turn result in sustainable livelihood for residents. The Act puts the Panchayati Raj Institutions (PRIs) at the helms of the affairs starting from identifying the eligible household to planning the works to be undertaken.

The Union Rural Development Ministry had allocated Rs. 11,300 crore for the year 2006-07. The Central Government had already released Rs. 4401.57 crore to States during the last six months. The Ministry of Rural Development spent Rs. 2367.56 crore on the NREGA during 2005-06. Madhya Pradesh and Rajasthan, according to Ministry of Rural Development officials, are the only two States to ask for the second instalment of the funds pointing out slow pace of implementation. Uttar Pradesh, Bihar, Jharkhand, Assam and West Bengal which constitute 41 per cent of total districts implementing NREGA, have been able to spend hardly 15 per cent of the initial instalments allotted.

On August 25, 2007, the Union Rural Development Minister, Sri Raghuvans Prasad Singh added close to 10 lakh more jobs to the NREGA, when he informed the Lok Sabha that more than 83.05 lakh rural households have been provided with employment under the Act up to August 22. He informed that 2,54,73,820 job cards had been issued. Out of these 89,43,703 demanded employment. It reflects that 92.85 per cent success in terms of job provided *vis-à-vis* job demanded.

The Union Ministry of Rural Development (MoRD) had another slightly vague assessment of NREGA which clearly and erroneously (in terms of data) differs from the statistics issued by MoRD itself. "Almost 100 lakh people have been employed so far. People are gradually learning about the benefits of the Act and the results are encouraging", said Renuka Vishwanathan, the then Secretary to MoRD. She refused to comment on the 90 per cent success rate claimed by the ministers slamming it as 'baseless and not coming from any official document'.

Diagram 25.2 : Emerging trends

- NREGA is in implementation in 200 districts.
- Inordinate delay in distributing job cards.
- 41 per cent districts have been able to spend 15 per cent fund allocated to them.
- Many States are yet to come out with mandatory guidelines on the Act.
- State governments are diluting powers of Panchyats under the Act.
- Water conservation consists of 54 per cent of total works undertaken.
- Overall expenditure on NREGA is around 31 per cent.
- Panchyats and all other nodal authorities are without staff and thus unable to handle the workload.

Diagram 25.3 : Status of NREGA

No. of rural households (in the 27 states implementing the NREGA)	5,75,41,426
Applications	3,33,87,046
Job cards	2,42,30,592
Employment demanded	95,58,234
Employment provided	88,24,994
Fund released till now for 2007-08 in Rs. Lakhs	1,35,798.611
Fund released till now for 2008-09 in Rs. Lakhs	4,38,642.065

Source: As of August 21, 2009 (Ministry of Rural Development).

Diagram 25.4 : Performance standards of 13 States

States	*Implementation in percentage*
Assam	18
Bihar	12.79
Gujarat	26
Haryana	26
Himachal Pradesh	12
Jharkhand	22
Karnataka	23
Mizoram	7
Nagaland	21
Tamil Nadu	5
Uttaranchal	13
Uttar Pradesh	18
West Bengal	14

Source: As of August 21, 2009 (Ministry of Rural Development).

Justification of the study in relation to livelihood and food rights and need of the hour

- The NREGA is a special effort in Birbhum District to assess the needs and expectations of rural people in terms of their participation in Gram Sabha, involvement in democratic planning, implementation and evaluation and monitoring process (social audit). It is also significant to assess the roles and functional responsibilities of different institutions (GP, Block, Districts) in relation to empowering rural households by providing 100 days of job security for their livelihood and food security.

- The proposed situational analysis study was conducted in Birbhum District as one of the NREGA districts; where out of 19 Community Development Blocks; 10 Blocks were selected as the study area. The research team conducted the extensive survey for acquiring various information relevant for the study by using various tools such as Structured Interview Schedule, Focus Group Discussion, Participatory Rural Appraisal and Case Studies.
- NREGA does not focus on the benefit of the deprived people, rather on the political members because of the subvert practices of the elected members and their political polarization.
- Distribution of work is highly gender based as observed. There is lack of information among the people specially the women who are not aware of the reservation policy and other benefits meant for them under the NREGA scheme and other policy measures by the government.
- The most astonishing event is that the job cards are always with the political leaders or panchyat personnel. It is never with the authenticated jobholder. It is because of extreme politicization, political manipulation and other unaccepted social practices.
- Most of the villagers are not aware of their basic livelihood rights that are provided to them. They are illiterate, backward and primitive in every regards of life.

The shortcomings of the NREGA need to be addressed

A. For the civil society, NREGA's implementation is marred by crucial faults. The assessment study indicates that Panchayati Raj Institutions (PRIs), the nodal bodies under the Act, have not yet been empowered in operationalizing the Act. If we have a couple of specific glimpses of the assessment, it is observed that political intervention at local level is taking a toll on the authority of PRIs. Besides, the objectives of creating productive assets under the Act are not being adhered to, thus limiting its impact on local development.

B. The Act has made it mandatory for all states to formulate state-specific rural employment guarantee (REG) schemes and operational guidelines within six months of its implementation conforming to the *Schedule 1* of the NREGA. Also under the Act, all states are supposed to have the nodal advisory body called State Employment Gurantee Council (SEGC).But unfortunately this has not been in operation in Birbhum as well as some other districts.

C. According to the Act, panchayats should implement at least 50 per cent of total works. Assessment shows that steps have not been taken in this regard. The guidelines prescribed in the Act clearly state that an *employment guarantee assistant* for each village panchayat must be recruited for the implementation of the scheme. But this has not been done in most of the states. As a result, panchayats have not completed selection and registration of employment seekers, thus leaving behind a large gap between registrations and providing jobs.

D. The NREGA has guidelines on preferred works to be taken up. Out of the nine types of works prescribed by the NREGA, the number seven deals with water conservation and management. The research team observed that this important sphere of development is eventually very much unattended for a plethora of reasons. The states are free to evolve their own specific preferred work within the broad guidelines. This is to make sure that the local development needs are to be reflected in the scheme. If not, but a futile attempt has been made in this regard which never be amount to the instrument of success.

NREGA: Some hidden facts

It guarantees 100 days of employment in a financial year to every rural household whose adult members are willing to do unskilled manual work. As mentioned earlier that the NREGA is an important step towards realization of the right to work and right to life. It is expected to enhance people's livelihood security on a sustained basis, by developing economic and social infrastructure in rural areas. One of the most distinguishing features of the NREGA is its approach towards empowering citizens to play an active role in the implementation of employment gurantee schemes through gram sansads, social audit, participatory planning and other activities.

Is NREGA a service delivery agency?

If the recommendations of the second Administrative Reforms Commission (ARC) are implemented where ARC has suggested that all service delivery schemes like rural health mission, universalization of education and rural water and sanitation schemes should be converged into NREGA. The Commission argues that only 100 days of employment guarantee may not ensure livelihood security and it should be supplemented by making the scope of the Act widespread. The impact of the NREGA will be fully realized if all other service delivery mechanisms meet the expectations of the people. ARC has also recommended that all funds available with Panchayats be brought under the NREGA management for creating durable assets. The other suggestion is that earthwork component could be executed under the NREGA and the rest of the development works be taken up under regular departmental schemes. The earthwork components of assets creation under Bharat Nirman can also be converged with the NREGA.

West Bengal seeks change in NREGA preferred works

The West Bengal government has asked the Union Government to allow (*NREGA has a list of permissible works*) other works to be undertaken under the NREGA. The argument put across by the Ministry of Panchayat and Rural Development; Government of West Bengal that it is extremely difficult for the State to provide jobs in accordance with the *National Rural Employment Gurantee Act, 2005* because of the factors—lean season, flood, drought, other natural calamities and agricultural issues etc. The permissible work list has already been mentioned earlier. It will be better if alternative categories of work could be included in the scheme. If work is not allotted to the applicants, the State will have to pay an unemployment allowance. The Government of West Bengal has shown hesitation in giving cash unemployment allowances. Instead it has requested to give food grain.

Definition of a household

It has been pointed out that the operational guidelines of the NREGA detail a household as a nuclear family comprising mother, father and their children. In addition, a household refers to a single-member family. Despite this explanation, there is still a lot of confusion about the definition of this critical term. For instance, in many villages of the district show that gram panchayats treat joint family as one household, thus issuing them a single job card. Our country has historically followed the system of joint families; such practices have both advantages and disadvantages.

Denial of registration

Registration was denied to single-woman-headed households and physically challenged individuals. Discrimination based on caste has also been noted in some villages.

Distribution of job cards

According to data provided on the NREGA website (www.nrega.nic.in), maintained by the Ministry of Rural Development, Government of India the percentage of job cards issued to registered households varies across the district and state.

Delay in distribution of job cards

Though job cards have been prepared but those have not reached to the people in due course of time, thereby restricting their right to work. The probable cause for this is that panchayat worker who are responsible in distribution are not seriously taking note of it and lack of efficient manpower in the panchayat office and block office as well.

Non-issuance of receipts

Another common problem noted in the villages was the absence of a system to issue receipts to applicants. This could be because of lack of awareness on the part of the panchayat worker and the villagers. Receipts, however, are very important as a proof of work demanded.

Shortage of staff and delay in appointments

When the Act was launched, it was not accompanied by the appointment of additional staff for its implementation. This had resulted in the existing staff being burdened with additional responsibility. At the panchayat level, the specific guidelines were given and it was mentioned that the appointment of 'rozgar sevak', was mandatory for smooth running of the project. Disappointingly it has not been done. The lack of manpower is having a negative impact on the workings of the NREGA. Such additional appointments are a rare opportunity to provide employment to the youth in the villages and should not be allowed to be squandered due to administrative hurdles.

Presence of contractors

Like in many other rural development programmes, contractors are increasingly becoming a threat to the NREGA. Though this may not be very much apparent on the surface, but private contractors are slowly finding their way into the system. The Act clearly states (Schedule-1; Section-1) that no contractor is permitted in the implementation of the project or should not be associated in any capacity with the whole range of NREGA activities.

Non-availability of Muster Rolls at the Worksite

It is rare indeed to find that officials at worksites are maintaining muster rolls/attendance sheets. Rough notebooks and diaries are being used to mark attendance and make wage payments.

Absence of worksite facilities

The NREGA provides for facilities for safe drinking water, shade for children, periods of rest and a first-aid box at the worksite (Section-27, Schedule-II). But it has been observed that small children remain unattended and there is no place for them to stay except under the tree even in the scorching heat. As a result women are hesitant to bring their children to worksites while coming for work. The situation, sometimes forces the women group to abstain from work even though they loose job and wage as well. The Commissioners of the Supreme Court (in the case of PUCL *vs.* UOL and others in 2006) advised the state that if need arises, temporary shelters must be built for those working as NREGA labour. The NREGA emphasizes on the general need to uphold the 'right to food', which follows from the fundamental 'right to life' enshrined in Article 21 of the Constitution of India. But a lot has to be done to ensure these facilities. The notable absence of worksite facilities is a problem that cuts across the districts.

Delay in wage payments

Delay in wage payment has always been a matter of concern in the NREGA. Wage payments are delayed for weeks, sometimes months. The time lag varies from Block to Block. For instance, in Nanoor Block, a month long delay was noted. In some areas like Sainthia Block the delay was for a period of 15 to 30 days to more than a month.

Less payment than the minimum wage

In many villages, workers do not get minimum wages. For instance, in Jubutia village of Nanoor Block, the paid wage is as low as Rs. 30 to Rs. 40 per day. Whereas the minimum wage is as prescribed Rs. 68 per day. Women are paid even less—about Rs. 30 per day.

Under the NREGA scheme, the workers are supposed to dig a pit of pre-specified size (for example, 100 cubic feet in the case of soft soil) in order to earn the minimum wage. In practice, the system raises several problems. To start with, it typically takes more than a day for an average labour to complete the specified task, making it hard to earn the statutory minimum wage. This is a violation of the Act which states that the 'schedule of rates' should be such that a lobour working for seven hours normally earn the minimum wage (Schedule-1; Section-8).

Social Audit and Muster Roll

From the discussions with the rural people during FGD session, it was explored that the people's participation in Gram Sansad level meeting was very meagre; most remarkably the members of Gram Sansad were not interested to promote decentralized planning process for assessing the need of durable assets in the rural areas and the villagers don't have any democratic right to give decision in this context. It was also reported by the research team that a considerable number of rural people were getting only 15 days of work in Kusumjatra village at

Diagram 25.5 : Progress of NREGA in West Bengal

State	Districts	Rural households	Applications	Job cards	Employment demanded	Employment provided	No. of works	Funds released (Crore)	Expenditure
West Bengal	10	7374151	4181330	2728773	1551613	1343414	7908	18358.84	5692.91

Progress of NREGA in West Bengal (District-wise)

S. No.	District	No. of Rural Households (2001 census)	Estimated Rural BPL Families	Applications registered	Job cards issued: Number	Job cards issued: % to Rural Households	Job cards issued: % to Application registration	Demand for Employment: Household	Demand for Employment: % of Households Job-cards issued	Demand for Employment: Individual	Demand for Employment: No. of Person per households	Employment provided: Household	Employment provided: % of Households to Employment Demanded	Employment provided: Individuals	Employment provided: No. of Persons per households
1	Jalpaiguri	560931	178657	496989	472231	84.19	95.02	180252	38.17	201995	1	154331	85.62	180183	1
2	West North Dinajpur	411735	131138	418298	412165	100.10	98.53	292164	70.89	465754	2	278385	95.28	403913	1
3	South Dinajpur	279682	89079	219372	212172	75.86	96.72	86782	40.90	100954	1	86005	99.10	100402	1
4	Malda	582117	185404	448939	257657	44.26	57.39	66779	25.92	92642	1	40628	60.84	73706	2
5	Murshidabad	1000713	318727	833429	680873	68.04	81.70	163847	24.06		0	90099	54.99		0
6	24 South Parganas	1068976	346839	567602	409912	37.64	72.22	40349	9.84	100871	2	40349	100.00	100871	2
7	West Midnapur	1632430	519929	610603	542182	33.21	88.79	91646	16.90	187342	2	87946	95.96	207997	2
8	Bankura	559295	178135	395131	356064	63.66	90.11	185156	52.00	660100	4	182377	98.50	649021	4
9	Purulia	403601	128547	365560	261051	64.68	71.41	49687	19.03	174357	4	50346	101.33	199200	4
10	Birhbhum	545000	173583	527063	512163	93.97	97.17	341374	66.65	415683	1	341374	100.00	419272	1
	Total	7064480	2250037	4882986	4116470	58.27	94.30	1498036	36.39	2399698	2	1351840	90.24	2334565	2

Ahmedpur Gram Panchayat. On the other hand local political leaders irrespective of the party they belong to illegally used to grab the job cards in their hands which they were not supposed to enjoy and handed over to their party supporters for some vested interest.

It was also observed that there were ample misuse occurred in maintenance of muster rolls by the panchayat authorities. For instance, in most of the cases muster rolls were filled-up by the panchyat nominated local political leaders and sometimes they used to show 3 to 6 people more in the muster rolls on a particular workday. Similarly, one single job cardholder earned Rs. 68 in two days, but actually the person supposed to receive Rs. 136 in two days. Rupees sixty-eight has been provisioned as the minimum wage rate in West Bengal per labour/per day as per the PWD unskilled labour wage guideline.

The most frightening instances have been reported that the rural people do not have the right even to see the muster rolls or ask about their minimum wages to the Panchayat nominated workers. The research team has also come to know that the beneficiaries do not even get the scope to practice social audit in spite of implementation of unplanned activities without common people's concern and decision. As a whole two important ingredients of NREGA, i.e. transparent maintenance of muster rolls and democratic practice of social audit are completely denied in the rural areas, which further rise question on the accountability of the Panchyat and Block authorities to ensure NREGA and REGS as a sustainable livelihood security programme for poverty alleviation.

While it has been highlighted some of the problems in the implementation of NREGA, it is important to note that the Act is still in its infancy. It takes years to put in place. The tools and instruments are needed to actualize the right to employment through a scheme; even in the best of the circumstances will be great promise before the government.

The NREGA addresses itself chiefly to working people and their fundamental right to live with dignity. The success of NREGA, however, will depend on people's realization of the Act as a right. Effective level of awareness and sustained public pressure are crucial to ensure that the problem of implementation is properly addressed and the objectives met.

Study Design

The mandate enshrined in the National Employment Guarantee Act (NREGA) is a **'People's Act'** from various dimensions because it has been developed for strengthening better livelihood condition among the rural households, as it intends to ensure the fundamental rights of the working people for sustainable life with dignity, and it also empowers the rural people to play an active role in creation of durable livelihood assets by their democratic functioning. Intitially 200 districts have been covered in different states of the country. Birbhum is one of the Districts of West Bengal has been considered for implementation of the said Act.

In assumption of high range of rural households in Birbhum District, the District still lacks adequate information in relation to their direct involvement for better access and economic benefit from the scheme. Therefore, the information status and accessibility of the provisions of the scheme among the common people are very poor. This insufficient information has really made the implementation of the scheme in static state and not in a position to improvise.

So, a special effort has been made to assess the needs and expectations of rural people from REGS in context of their participation in Gram Sansad, involvement in democratic planning, implementation, evaluation and monitoring process (social audit). It has also assessed the different institutional (**Gram Panchayat, Block and District**) roles and functional responsibilities in relation to empower rural households by providing 100 days of unskilled work for their livelihood security.

This situational analysis study was conducted in 2009 in Nineteen (19) **Community Development Blocks** and **Panchayat Samities** along with 167 Gram Panchayats. Out of 19 CD Blocks as mentioned above; 10 Blocks were much familiar with the research team prior to the study because of the earlier work experience as collaborating research unit. One GP from each selected Block, i.e. 10 GPs were in the list. The next step was adopted, that is, one village from 10 GPs and subsequently 40 households were selected by the purposive random sampling method. This amounts to 400 rural households who were the primary stakeholders for the study. The purposive sampling method was adopted for the convenience to cover maximum number of GPs in Birbhum District within a short span of time and also to cover a reasonable number of GPs and villages for getting perceptions of rural households on implementation on NREGA in their locality. Primary stakeholders of the study were selected in accordance with the following criteria(s):

(a) households are interested to do unskilled work;
(b) households still do not have access for registration number/job cards;
(c) households are having no assets;
(d) households are selected with equal gender priority;
(e) households are selected according to the priority of Scheduled Caste, Scheduled Tribe and Other Backward Classes; and
(f) households are selected with their migratory nature.

To have a better insight of the study the secondary stakeholders comprising BDO and other concern authorities directly responsible for implementing the scheme were taken into consideration for discussion.

Primary data were collected through **Structured Interview Schedule** along with **Participatory Rural Appraisal (PRA)** and **Focus Group Discussion (FGD)** sessions. Three thematic case studies were prepared by the team. PRA and FGD were exercised primarily to assess the situation and expectations of the rural people towards the new scheme. The study was completed within six months (January-June 2009).

At the beginning the team paid visit to the selected villages, GPs and Block officials for rapport establishment and collection of secondary data on current status of NREGA in the respective areas. In the next phase, the team collected primary data from the selected villages as much as possible to keep it authentic and the final stage was the preparation of writing report on the basis of collected data. The collected data was processed through using **SPSS software** for cross-tabulation on selected variables between two family categories, i.e. **APL (Above Poverty Line)** and **BPL (Below Poverty Line)**. Both the family categories have been equally prioritized for the study because of the following reasons:

- to differentiate these family categories in accordance with availing more facilities and preference from NREGA in terms of job card, registration, types of job, wages etc.;
- it has tried to explore that whether BPL people have got the equal opportunity of empowerment in terms of participation, decision making and livelihood security through NREGA in comparison to APL;
- it has also made an attempt to see whether BPL people especially SC and ST have faced any problem of political suppression or discrimination in comparison to APL category.

On the basis of the available quantitative and qualitative data as well as collected reviews and critiques from websites, journal articles and other source of written documents, the research team had made an outstanding effort to prepare the report. As an example how participatory rural appraisal method along with **Social Mapping** and **Venn Diagram** right through the data collection phase in every village were used by the research team have been shown in Diagram 25.7.

Major findings and analysis

The research team, after meticulously assessing and investigating the exact reality of the operational status of NREGA, came to their findings and critical appraisal. The attempt has been made here to highlight only the striking features of the assessment which are enough to internalize for the readers what is going on about NREGA.

Diagram 25.7 : Details of participatory rural appraisal exercise in the study area

Village	:	Kendula	Gram Panchayat	:	Hetampur	Block	:	Dubrajpur

Participatory Livelihood Assessment Through Preference Ranking

Rank Indicators		(A) Safe Drinking water	(B) Irrigation	(C) Rural Roads	(D) PDS	(E) Employment	(F) Watershed	(G) Social Forestry	(H) Rural Drainage	(I) Active GS/GP	(J) Disaster Mitigation	(K) Agricultural Land	Score	
Safe Drinking water	(A)	×	B	C	A	E	A	A	H	A	J	K	08	
Irrigation	(B)	B	×	B	B	B	F	B	B	B	B	B	[illegible]	1st Preference
Rural Roads	(C)	C	B	×	C	E	F	C	C	C	C	C	12	4th Preference
PDS	(D)	A	B	D	×	E	F	D	H	D	J	D	05	
Employment	(E)	E	B	E	E	×	E	E	E	E	J	E	16	2nd Preference
Watershed	(F)	A	F	F	F	E	×	F	F	F	F	F	15	3rd Preference
Social Forestry	(G)	A	B	G	D	E	F	×	H	I	J	K	01	
Rural Drainage	(H)	H	B	C	H	E	H	H	×	H	H	K	12	4th Preference
Active GS/GP	(I)	A	B	C	I	E	F	I	H	×	I	I	06	
Disaster Mitigation	(J)	J	B	C	J	J	F	J	H	J	×	J	10	
Agricultural Land	(K)	K	B	C	K	E	F	K	H	I	K	×	07	

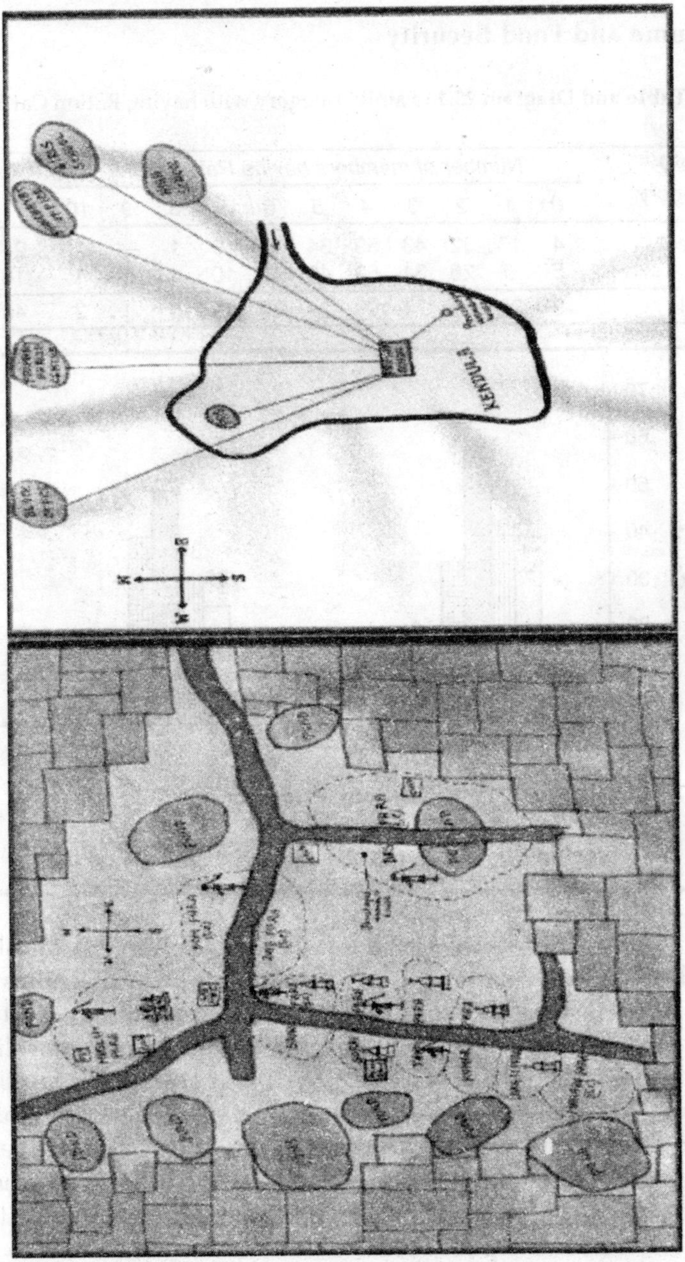

Diagram 25.8 : Social Map and Venn Diagram

Income and Food Security

Table and Diagram 25.1 : Family category with having Ration Card

Family category	*Number of members having Ration Card*											*Total*
	0	*1*	*2*	*3*	*4*	*5*	*6*	*7*	*8*	*9*	*10*	
BPL	4	13	32	43	59	34	17	9	1	—	1	213
APL	5	7	25	31	50	40	13	10	4	1	1	187
Total	9	20	57	74	109	74	30	19	5	1	2	400

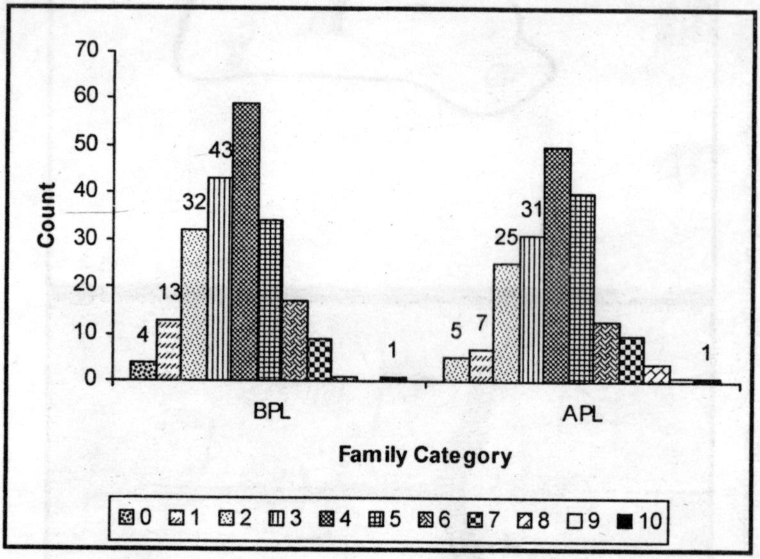

Table 25.1 indicates that out of 400 families, 391 families are having ration card and only meagre number of families do not possess it. This table further calibrates that the Public Distribution System (PDS) is availed by most of the families. Two hundred and thirteen BPL (213) and (187) APL families are in the possession of ration cards. It clearly reflects that there is no such biasness in distribution of ration cards to APL and BPL category people. As opined by the ration card holders there are huge gaps in demand and supply of essential commodities under PDS for the poor rural households.

Table and Diagram 25.2 : Family category and average family income

Family category	*Average family income (in Rs.)*				*Total*
	500-1000	*1001-2000*	*2001-3000*	*3001-4000*	
BPL	151	59	1	2	213
APL	103	77	6	1	187
Total	254	136	7	3	400

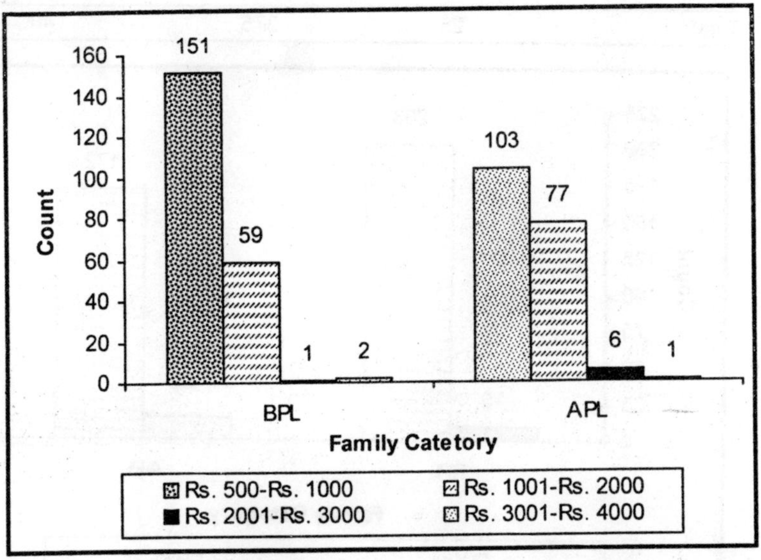

Table 25.2 indicates that out of 400 families, 254 and only 3 families lie between the income range of (Rs. 500-1000) and (Rs. 3001-4000) respectively. If we take a close look at the table and diagram, it is clearly evident that 151 and 103 families fall under BPL and APL category respectively. These 103 families should have access to ration cards.

This states that there is embezzlement in the distribution of BPL cards by the concern authorities. Whereas on the other hand, out of 3 families falling under the higher income group, 2 families are from BPL category and 1 from APL. This projects that political biasness persists among the panchayat and local leaders in terms of distribution of BPL cards. Nepotism and biasness do play a great role in the whole process.

Table and Diagram 25.3 : Family category with different sources of income in a year

Family category	*Earning from different income in a year*		*Total*
	Yes	*No*	
BPL	10	203	213
APL	15	172	187
Total	25	375	400

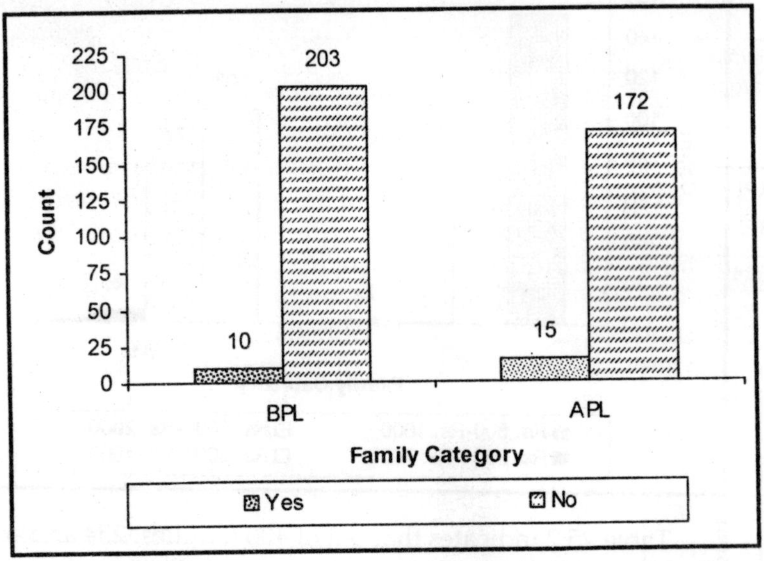

Out of 400 families (Table 25.3) only 25 families stated that they have the alternative income sources. It can be further stated that if REGS is implemented properly, it can provide a stable source of income to the needy families and raise the per capita income. This will also create durable assets in the villages and provide sustainable income to the rural households in future.

From the Table 25.4 it can be seen that out of 400 families, majority of them, i.e. 166 are engaged in other activities (working at construction sites, local shops, household servants etc.) One important finding is that 62 families starve and 43 families migrate temporarily in search of better livelihood. A reasonable number, i.e. 129 families continue their living with the money they save during their tenure of work. Due to improper and directionless implementation of the scheme it is unable to emancipate rural people from the clutches of poverty. On the other hand, migration often leads to various social imbalances like child labour, increasing rate of illiteracy, health problems, bearing communicable diseases etc.

Table and Diagram 25.4 : Family category and coping mechanism at the time of inadequate income

Family category	*Coping mechanism at the time of inadequate income*				
	Often starve	*Migrants temporarily*	*Saving money during the season*	*Others*	*Total*
APL	35	31	48	99	213
BPL	27	12	81	67	187
Total	62	43	129	166	400

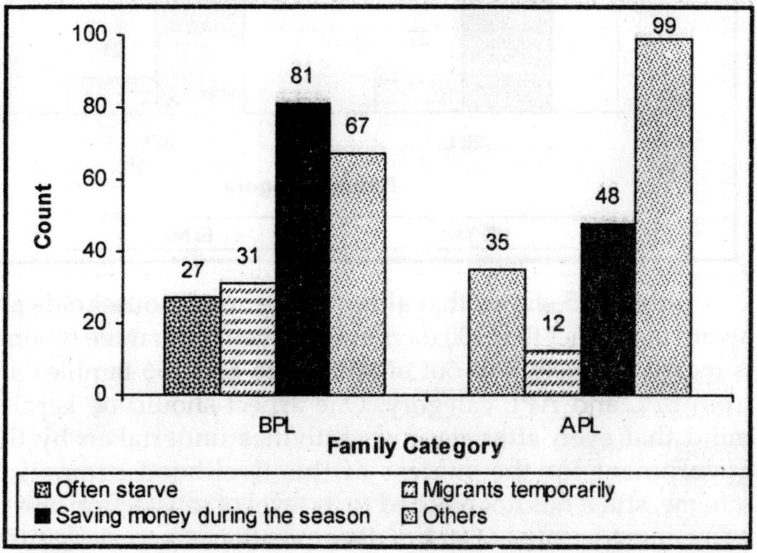

People's Awareness about 'NREGA'

Table and Diagram 25.5 : Type of family and level of awareness about 'NREGA'

Family category	*Level of awareness*		*Total*
	Yes	*No*	
BPL	186	27	213
APL	166	21	187
Total	352	48	400

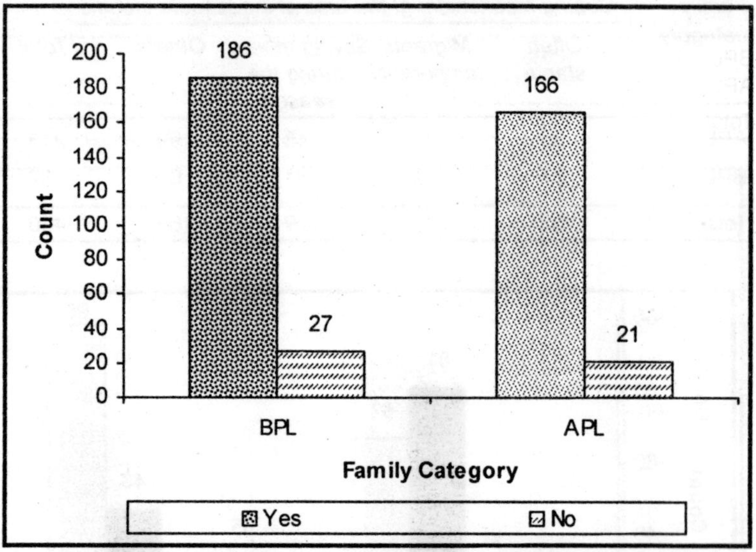

Table 25.5 shows that almost 88 per cent households are aware of the fact that 100 days employment guarantee scheme is meant for them and out of which 186 and 166 families are from BPL and APL category. One aspect should be kept in mind that even after rigorous activities undertaken by the government for the success of this livelihood promotion scheme, still it has not reached to its level of satisfaction due to tremendous amount of lack of dissemination of knowledge and remarkable gaps of communication. People are not clear about the types of work they are supposed to do, what is the

minimum rate of wage for each labour, length of working hours in a day etc. are some of the issues which are to be considered as stumbling block and all these need to be cleared out if the 'NREGA' is to be successful. Panchayat authorities should also be sincere and take much more initiative to make it a fruitful venture.

Table and Diagram 25.6 : Family category and source of information on 'NREGA'

Family category	*Source of information about 'NREGA'*			*Total*
	BDO office	*Panchayat*	*Local political leaders*	
BPL	10	121	82	213
APL	8	123	56	187
Total	18	244	138	400

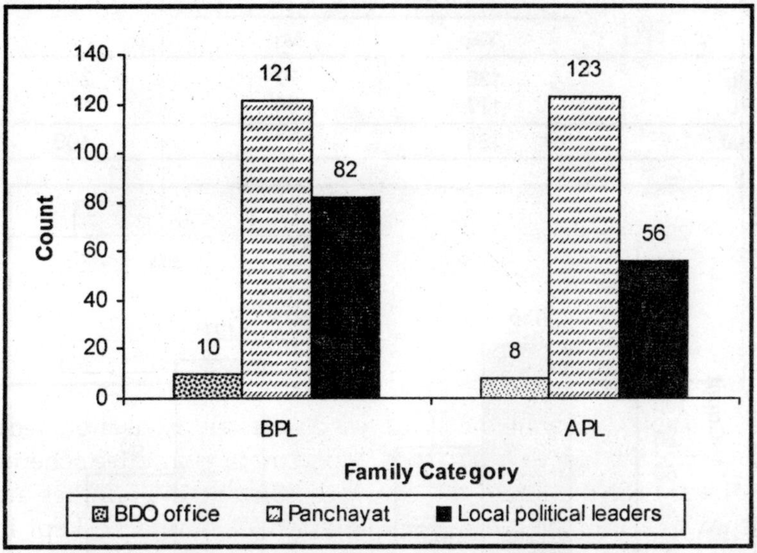

Table 25.6 offers us multidimensional view regarding the sources of information about NREGA. Out of four hundred respondents almost half of them, i.e. 244 came to know about NREGA from panchayat and out of which 121 are from BPL

category and the rest from APL. Insufficiency of BDO office in disseminating information about NREGA is highly demoralizing because it was reported that only 18 families were assisted by BDO office in this regard. On the other hand, 138 families received information from local political leaders and it shows their immense involvement in the government scheme and implementation as well. But the point to be remembered that none of the concern official as reported by the research team is well informed to share all information regarding NREGA with community people.

Registration and Job Cards

Table and Diagram 25.7 : Family category and application for job cards

Family category	*Application for job cards under Gram Panchayat office*		*Total*
	Yes	*No*	
BPL	136	77	213
APL	127	60	187
Total	263	137	400

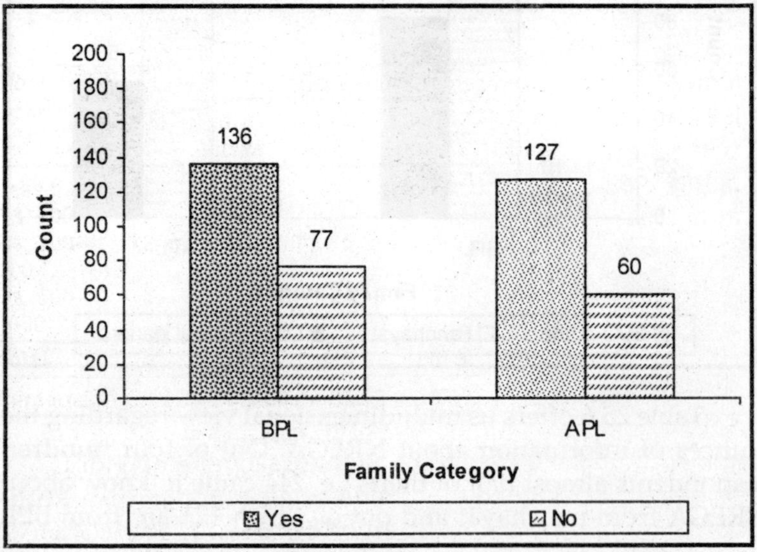

Table 25.7 indicates that out of 400 households, 263 had registered themselves for job cards in the Gram Panchayat office including both BPL and APL category. On the other hand, a reasonable number of respondents were still not being registered for the cards. So, all the community households are not aware of the scheme, provisions and the process.

Another important finding by the research team was that 78.75 per cent households still have no idea about getting employment within fifteen days from the date of submission of application. This reflects that there is a colossal failure of the Gram Panchayat in providing adequate information about the provisions under NREGA. According to the data provided by the Ministry of Rural Development, the Panchayats who are the nodal authorities of implementing the scheme are without staff and thus unable to handle the workload. Many states are yet to come out with mandatory guidelines to work on the Act. In general, perception of the primary reference group of NREGA shows us their opinion against the Panchayat system and lack of awareness among the Panchayat members who are the key stakeholders in implementation of the scheme.

Table 25.8 tells us that 254 families are having job cards. Out of which 130 and 124 families are from BPL and APL category respectively. The number of households not having job cards are 146. A large number of households are still unable to access job cards in spite of having registration. But the fact is to unearth in the context of how many of them are provided with job even after registration. There lies the actual challenges before the Gram Panchayats and concern authorities in proper allocation of job to all the rural populace if the 100 days employment guarantee scheme is to be achieved. According to the statistics (rough estimation) provided by the Ministry of Rural Development that 2,42,30,592 job cards were issued in India and the employment provided to 88,24,994. Job distribution system is not in tune with the scheme as it is expected. In this regard, on autopsying the fact it is revealed that most of the families are not aware of the five years validity of the cards because in time of distribution, no communication was made by the Panchayat office in this regard.

Table and Diagram 25.8 : Family category and having job cards

Family category	*Family having job cards*		*Total*
	Yes	*No*	
BPL	130	83	213
APL	124	63	187
Total	254	146	400

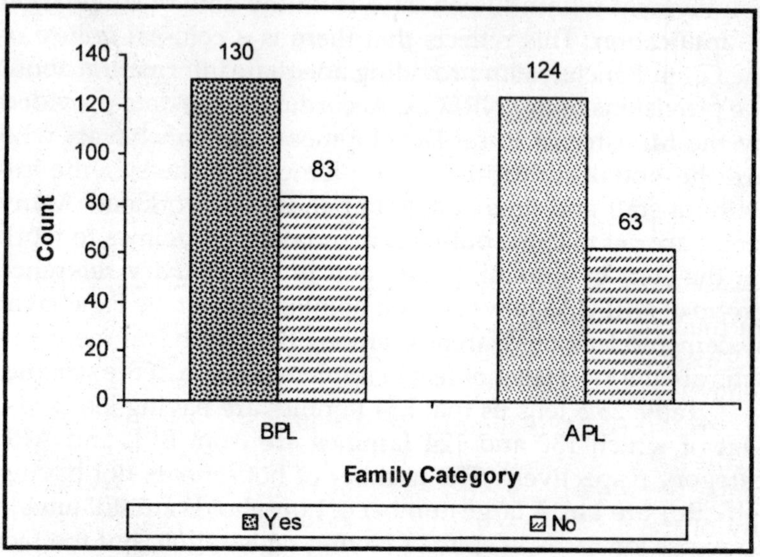

Availability of Work and Minimum Daily Wages

Table and Diagram 25.9 : Distribution of jobs in the locality

Family category	*Receive jobs in the locality*		*Total*
	Yes	*No*	
BPL	101	112	213
APL	106	81	187
Total	207	193	400

Table 25.9 indicates that out of 400 households, 207 (51.75%) were very happy to get job in the vicinity of their residence. On the other hand, 48.25 per cent got it quite far

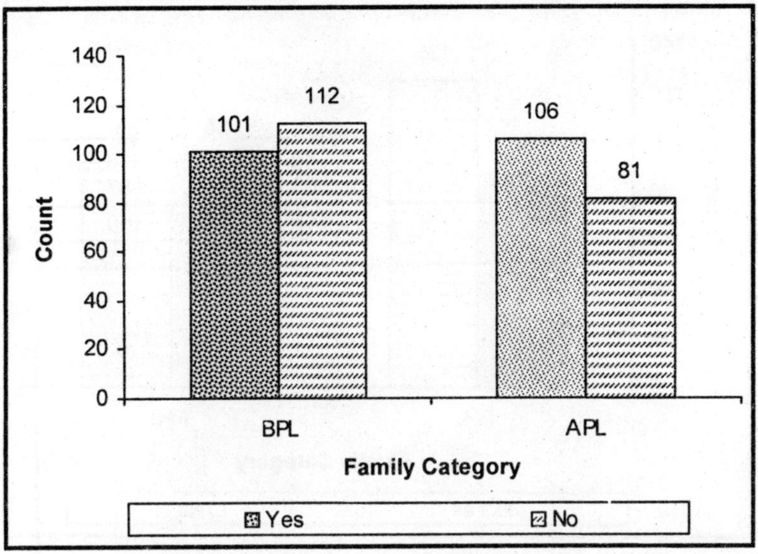

from their place of residence, which, of course is against the law. This is very much frightening because the mandate of the scheme that all community people should be provided job at the nearest possible to their residence. But what is coming out from the data that due to inactive participation and inadequate planning of the Panchayat members and the concern authorities many of the people get the job at the farthest corner of the community which amount to be a great problem in their day-to-day communication.

Table and Diagram 25.10 : Awareness among the households about the daily wages

Family category	*Level of awareness about daily wages*		*Total*
	Yes	*No*	
BPL	88	125	213
APL	95	92	187
Total	183	217	400

Table 25.10 enlightens the skeleton of the level of awareness among the rural populace. The figures indicated by the table show that out of 400 households, 217 i.e.

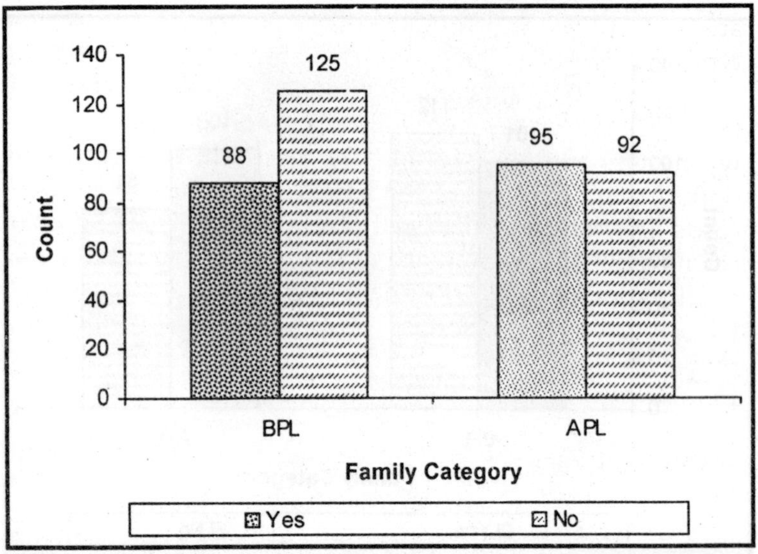

54.25 per cent of the people do not know even what is the rate of minimum wage under NREGA. Only 45.75 per cent are aware of the rate of minimum daily wage. So, it is discernible that Gram Panchayats are unable to make the people aware and understand of their rights. There is ample political influence and massive corrupt practices of the political leaders which dismantle the whole scheme in terms of its fruitful implementation.

It was also reported that 80 per cent (out of total surveyed households) rural households do not complain to any authorities if daily minimum wages are not paid to them. Only 20 per cent do complain about this unhealthy practice. Out of 400 households, 286 (71.5%) responded that they prefer to complain against the daily wage to any local influential person of the ruling party. On the other hand, only 19.5 per cent and 9 per cent go to Panchayat and BDO office respectively to lodge complaints against their wage dispute. The rural people who are the main reference group still prefer to liaison with implementing agencies by the help of influential political leaders. These leaders enjoy the power game and present before them as father figure to help them restore their voice for livelihood rights. It was also told that these political leaders are the deciding factor in fixation of daily wage rate as well as type of work to be done and working hours for the rural people.

During the study four important constraints were noted—(a) panchayat and block authorities do not encourage rural women to get registered and avail daily employment opportunity; (b) most of the households who are having job cards are not assured to get job on a daily basis because of strong political interference as mentioned repeatedly earlier in allocation of the work and manpower; (c) as a consequence, if a person works on Monday, he/she would get further chance on Friday or even after; (d) most of the households do not get more than 15 days employment.

Livelihood Security through Rural Employment Guarantee Scheme (REGS)

Table and Diagram 25.11 : Awareness among the people about the types of work are to be performed

Family category	*Awareness of type of work to be performed*		*Total*
	Yes	*No*	
BPL	68	145	213
APL	98	89	187
Total	166	234	400

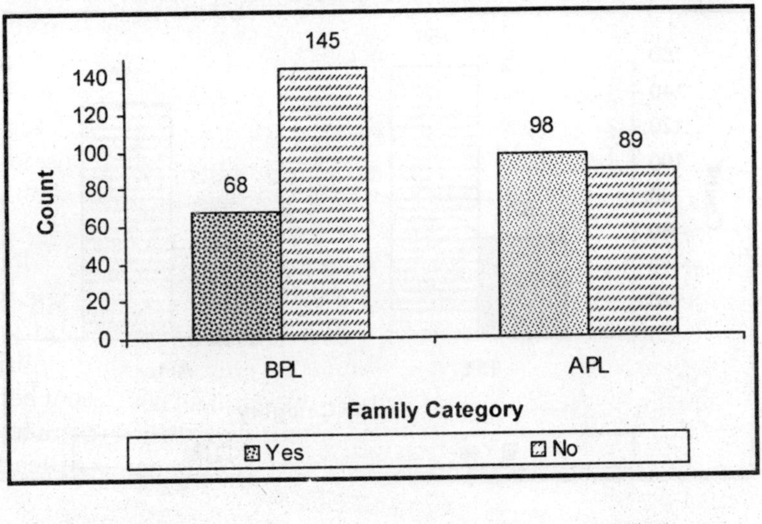

It can be seen from the Table 25.11 that out of the total 400 households, 234, i.e. 58.5 per cent have no such information in relation to the types of work under NREGA. Only 41.5 per cent have inadequate information. As per the mandatory provision of the Act, rural durable asset creation work i.e. minor irrigation, rural road preparation, social forestry, etc. have been suggested for sustainable income generation for the rural poor in future course of time. Most of the Gram Panchayats, Gram Sansads have been formed but remain inactive. Consequently, there is no practice of need based participatory planning, resource identification or preparatory strategy formulation for rural asset building. The primary gap in this process is inadequate information to the rural people and even Gram Panchayat members. In spite of having Right to Information Act, 2005, the Government authorities have still not developed any strategies for information dissemination to the primary reference group of NREGA.

Table and Diagram 25.12 : Perception of the people towards REGS

Family category	*Perception of the people towards REGS*		*Total*
	Yes	*No*	
BPL	57	156	213
APL	52	135	187
Total	109	291	400

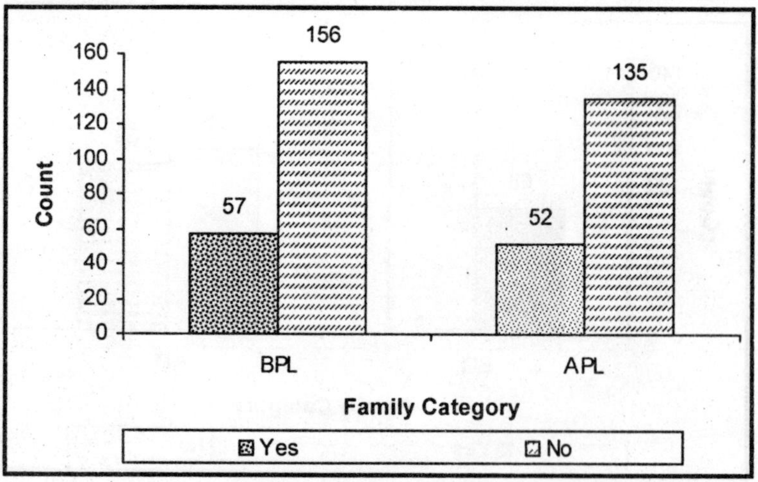

On gleaning the facts from the Table 25.12 it is found that 72.75 per cent households are in the opinion that NREGA is unable to increase household income and create sustainable, durable assets in their vicinity. A small section of them i.e., 27.25 per cent holds some positive views on the same, even they are still getting only 15 days of work out of 100 mandatory days. As mentioned earlier that REGS has been introduced as one of the important livelihood support programme for poverty reduction and establishing food rights. But in reality several constraints and impediments are making its ways full of tentacles to see the hope of success. "**NREGA is unable to increase the income level of the rural poor and create sustainable, durable assets in the rural areas**" because of a couple of reasons which were mentioned earlier.

Gender, Equality and Equity

Table and Diagram 25.13 : Gender discrimination in providing job cards

Family category	*Gender discrimination in providing job cards*		*Total*
	Yes	*No*	
BPL	120	93	213
APL	106	81	187
Total	226	174	400

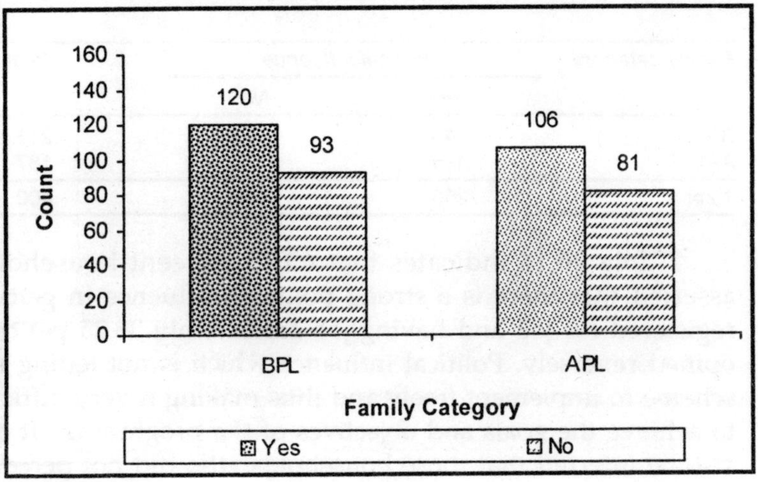

Table 25.13 reflects that 56.5 per cent households have asserted that there is a strong gender disparity on providing job cards to the rural women. Only 43.5 per cent opined positively and stated that there no disparity has been observed by them. Women and physically challenged are the two sections having been prioritized in the access of equal employment opportunities and equitable wage benefit. But in practice the scenario is different, for example in a work place the work sharing ratio is 20 men : 3 women. This is not only because of political intervention but also our traditional paradigm of men control over women.

It was found that 94 per cent households were not aware of the issue that 33 per cent reservation for the rural women in employment avenue and on the contrary only 6 per cent have heard about it very vaguely. The Government and Panchayat are the two main implementing agencies of NREGA, where they have joint responsibility to enforce the provision of 33 per cent reservation for the women in the said act in the light of socio-economic empowerment of the rural women. But, in practice this provision has not been taken seriously at all.

Political Influence in REGS

Table and Diagram 25.14 : Political influence in registration and card distribution process

Family category	*Political influence*		*Total*
	Yes	*No*	
BPL	140	73	213
APL	115	72	187
Total	255	145	400

Table 25.14 indicates that 63.75 per cent households asserted that there is a strong political influence in getting registered for job and having job cards. Only 36.25 per cent opined reversely. Political influence which is not letting the scheme to implement freely and thus making it very difficult to achieve the goals and objectives of the programme. It can also be inferred that those households who did not perceive

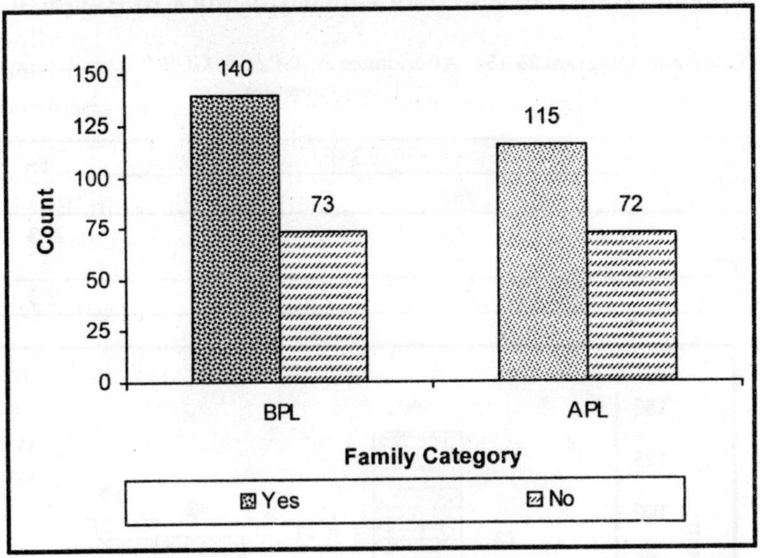

any political influence have a nexus with the Panchayat members and in the process it is creating an ominous sign of darkness and not allowing the all-round development of the villages. The implementing agencies have not been seen very apt in properly regulating the scheme and making all the provisions under the scheme in operation. Rather their approach is more poll-oriented and as a result they deprived people or for whom the scheme is meant for are completely ignored.

Out of the total households, 79.25 per cent have still no space to express their views on better implementation of NREGA or any other grievances against the scheme. This is to a great extent amounts to be the violation of Article 19 of the Constitution of India, i.e. "*Right to Expression*". Those people who have close proximity with the Panchayat members and local political leaders do get the opportunity to express their views and they comprise 20.75 per cent only. If this unhealthy trend of political suppression continues for a longer period of time the rural people will find it difficult to emancipate themselves from the abject poverty and hunger.

Role of Gram Sansad/Gram Panchayat/Block in REGS

Table and Diagram 25.15 : Attendance in GP/GS/GUS (Gram Unnayan Samiti) level meeting

Family category	*Attendance in GP/GS/GUS level meeting*		*Total*
	Yes	*No*	
BPL	73	140	213
APL	89	98	187
Total	162	238	400

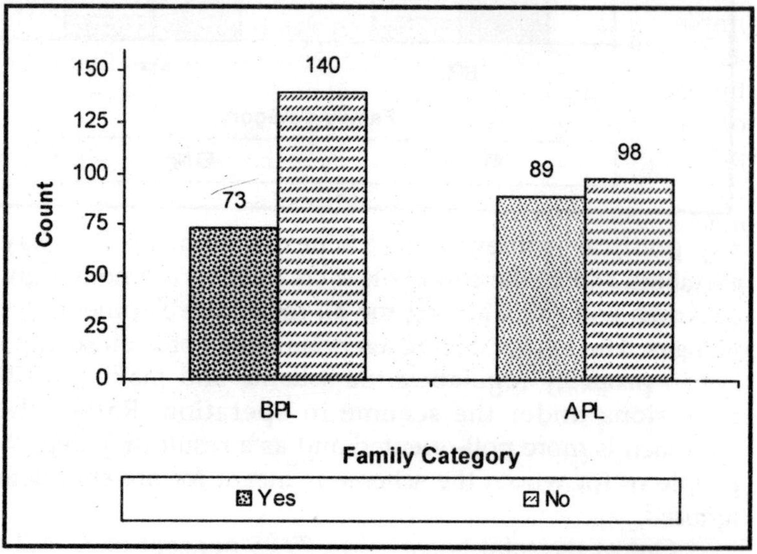

Table 25.15 depicts that 238, i.e. 59.5 per cent households have not received any space/scope to attend any sort of GP/GS/Block meeting on NREGA. Only 40.5 per cent enjoyed the opportunity to attend such meeting. In relation to the above features, the ineffectiveness and lack of initiative of the implementing agencies have been reported—(a) the significant tool of the success of NREGA, i.e. people's participation is not encouraged; (b) the number of meetings between the community people and concern officials are very few in rotation which in turn make the people disinterested about the scheme; and (c) those people who all participate in the

meeting are unable to express their views because of political pressure and apprehension of denouncement by the party members.

Another important aspect is that 90.75 per cent households perceived that the key stakeholders of REGS were unable to formulate plan, strategies and not even create sustainable job opportunities for them. Only 9.25 per cent were very satisfied by the way scheme was going on and they felt they were benefited.

There is no paucity of fund in each block of the district, but it lacks in work culture and positive interest of the implementing agencies to restore the livelihood rights as well as food security measures. Another reason is that inadequate human resources for enactment of the Act and implementation of the scheme. It is further revealed that the scheme/ programme is still not able to present as pro-poor credential in the area of participatory planning and implementing mechanism.

Reflections

- The Act and Scheme have been introduced without disseminating information to the stakeholders and proper orientation to the implementers who are supposed to be the two most important groups of players in the whole process.
- Serious disparities have been observed in payment of minimum daily wages and management of manpower and muster rolls.
- In spite of having adequate fund for each block, most of the job cardholders are enjoying 15 days of work out of eight months as stipulated in the scheme. This means the Act is unable to create guaranteed employment for the rural people.
- Local political leaders are the main constraints in democratic decentralization of NREGA and REGS (Rural Employment Guarantee Scheme) in the light of rural development.

- Most of the Gram Sansads are still inactive or not serious in promoting employment generation through identification of need based rural assets, participatory planning and social audit due to their lack of orientation, poor level of awareness and inefficient manpower.
- Gram Panchayats are unable to maintain records properly as well as help the rural people in time due to shortage of professional staff. Lack of coordination between Gram Panchayat and Gram Sansad has also been observed.
- Several misconceptions (discussed in the analysis part) have been reported in terms of minimum wages, type of works to be performed, working hour, 33 per cent reservation for women, and job card distribution among the BPL cardholders (average household income Rs. 500 to Rs.1000).
- Participation of rural youth is also very discouraging.

Thematic Case Studies

CASE STUDY-1

Block and Gram Panchayat Interface

The reason for significant drawback of crippled and unsuccessful NREGA to address the livelihood needs of the people is because of static work culture and stagnant interest of the Block officials and Gram Panchyats for the public good. The interaction with GP members revealed that they are still in dark in terms of pros and cons of the scheme. So, the question is that if the concern authorities are not clear about the scheme how it is expected that people who are illiterate and neo-literate even the literate can access the benefits of the Act.

As it is known that works under NREGA are to be provided on the basis of people's demand with a specific goal of creating durable assets in their village from where they would be benefited in future. But practically, the Gram Sansad who is behind the bar is found to be very weekly constituted and unable to function democratically as it is expected, due to political interference of the local leaders and which further make the common people voiceless, demandless and lastly loosing all hopes of life.

There is no dearth of funds. Ample funds have been allocated by the Distrct Programme Coordinator for each block but in spite of that a reasonable number of people are not having job cards and getting not more than 15 days of work. This is a very dismal scenario as the research team found and the most crucial reason they had pointed out that the implementing stakeholders are absolutely incapacited for whatsoever reasons.

Sl. No.	*Name of the Block*	*Fund allotted (Rs. in lakhs)*
1.	Suri-I	50
2.	Suri-II	80
3.	Sainthla	60
4.	Md. Bazar	50
5.	Rajnagar	60
6.	Dubrajpur	150
7.	Khoyrasole	80
8.	Illambazar	100
9.	Bolpur-Sriniketan	200
10.	Nanoor	80
11.	Labpur	60
12.	Mayureswar-I	60
13.	Mayureswar-II	60
14.	Rampurhat-I	50
15.	Rampurhat-II	50
16.	Nalhati-I	90
17.	Nalhati-II	50
18.	Murarai-I	80
19.	Murarai-II	40
	Total	1450

[Fund allotted for each Block by the order of District Magistrate/Programme Coordinator as on 19.9.2009]

CASE STUDY-2

Gender Disparity in the Light of 33 per cent Reservation for Women

Gender disparity is a common social issue but the magnitude of the problem costs a lot in the society. Though, it was realized that the discrepancy between a man and a woman in terms of their status in the society would be reduced after the implementation of NREGA; but the scenario remains same. This is needless to say that the status of women has definitely been ameliorated irrespective of NREGA venture after the introduction of the concept of SHG or Mahila Mandals.

During the tenure of the study, some rural women reported that whenever they have asked for work, it was never been encouraged and they were told by the local leaders/ political leaders/panchayat personnel about the paucity of work. Some women, who worked under REGS for some time, informed us that they face problem while working as they have to take their children along with them. There were no facilities of crèche for their children and they were also differentiated by wages for similar type of work with men. It was also the attitude which prevails that men are better worker than women. This age long attitude needs to be changed and then only women will be more praiseworthy and the success of NREGA will be built on.

CASE STUDY-3

People's Movement for Livelihood Security

Poverty and hunger due to unemployment and food insecurity are the interrelated factors still exist in different villages. Generally hunger caused deaths remain hidden and have never been publicized before the media. In view of that, NREGA was introduced with some commitment to address the livelihood and food security issues of the marginal section of the rural society. Nevertheless, this section of people still live in vulnerable condition because they have no assured and regular jobs, low level of income and purchasing power to fulfil their basic livelihood needs.

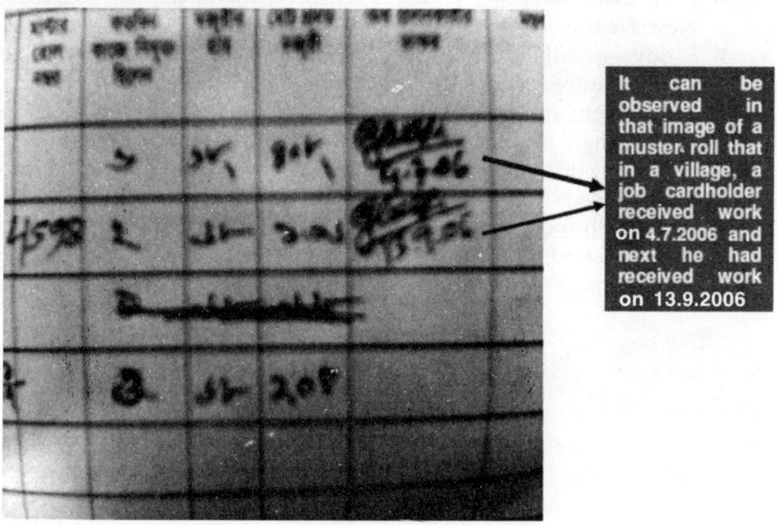

The consequence is generation of dissatisfaction arousing in the minds of the common people regarding various animosities of the officials which led to an ugly predicament in some of the villages. Villagers of Hetampur GP under Dubrajpur Block led a mass movement in their GP office to express grievances against unequal and irregular payment of daily wages and unavailability of work on regular basis.

The villagers of Kusumjatra under Sainthia Block organized a rally in district headquarter to place their demands to the District Magistrate/District Programme Coordinator of Birbhum and complained about the unequal payment of wages and discrimination against women in providing job to them. They also placed a deputation to the District Authority on various subvert practices of the local implementing authorities.

SUGGESTED READINGS

1. Bhagyalakshmi, J. (2005); "Towards Equality at Work", *Kurukshetra*, Vol. 23; No. 3, May.
2. Dreza, Jean. (2005); "Employment Guarantee Act", *Kurukshetra*, Vol. 23; No. 3, May.
3. ISST (Institute of Social Studies Trust), *Newsletter* (April-June, 2008); New Delhi.
4. E-pov—*Monthly Newsletter on Environment and Poverty* (November, 2008); Centre for Science and Environment, New Delhi.
5. www.nrega.nic.in for collection of updated data on NREGA in West Bengal and Birbhum District.
6. www.birbhum.nic.in for collection of information in relation to block-wise NREGA budgetary allocation.
7. www.rightfoodindia.org for collection of reviews and information on REGS and NREGA as well as Right to Food.

26

Integration of Urban Informal Sector in the Public Policy Process

A Case Study of Urban Street Vendors in the Birbhum District of West Bengal

Introduction

The informal sector is known by many different names according to different contexts and points of view. It is referred to as the informal economy, unregulated economy, unorganized sector, or unobserved employment, to cite but a few of its titles, this sector typically refers to both economic units and workers involved in a variety of commercial activities and occupations that operate beyond the realm of formal employment (Williams and Windebank, 2005).

In most countries, both developing and developed ones, activities in the informal sector were not included in national employment statistics (Suharto, 2002). In an attempt to bring this sector to national attention as well as to reduce the concern over high unemployment, the inclusion of the sector in national figures has now become a common feature in many developing and developed nations alike (Portes, Castells and Benton, 2003). However, their activities, which are mostly unregistered and unrecorded in national income accounts, are still the main determinant in referring to the sector as informal. The main reason is that the activities are almost always outside the scope of state regulation and protection. Even if their activities are registered, the informal sector does not follow any labour protection, job security and other protective measures of the workplace (World Bank, 1998; UNDP, 2000).

In the urban context, the informal sector refers to small enterprise operators selling food and goods or offering services and thereby involving the cash economy and market transactions. This so called "**urban informal sector**" is more diverse than the rural one and includes a vast and heterogeneous variety of economic activities through which most urban families earn their livelihood. The main forms are retail trade, small-scale manufacturing, construction, transportation, services and domestic work operating either as home-based or public-based activities. Activities of the informal sector in the public arena of cities are particularly apparent in street-based trading which is known as street vendors. Although these street enterprises are mostly hidden from the state for tax, they are involved in very visible structures and often subject to certain limited administrative processes such as simple registration or daily collection fees.

Putting the distinction of street traders under the umbrella concept of urban informal sector, this study had gone through with some ingredients as street traders compared to the other urban informal activities. These ingredients are:

- They operate in public premise which are not intended for business purposes such as the simple roadside, pavement and other connected to street premises (e.g. public market, square green areas).
- They trade a variety of items categorized as food, goods or services for economic benefits involving market transactions.
- They do not pay tax but pay daily fees to the city authorities mainly for sanitary and security purposes.
- They involve family members in their businesses in both ownership and management systems.
- Their enterprises are small and mostly self-driven or sometimes employing (if so required) less than five workers including unpaid family members or apprentices.

- Their employment is not protected by any sort of employment benefit either from government (e.g. social services, social security measures or anything of those kinds) or labour union (e.g. insurance, fixed and standardized salaries or any other).
- Their establishments are characterized by inadequate infrastructure, no technological intervention; and limited economic and human capital.
- They are unlicensed but never be considered as criminal by law or the regulation of the city administration.
- They often form linkages with rest of the economic sections especially backward linkages with the modern formal sector (e.g. many commodities they sell which are industrially manufactured items).

Despite the fact that the informal sector provides a livelihood for huge numbers in the national labour force, this sector continues to have low productivity, poor working conditions, low income and few opportunities for advancement. Although some of the more structured groups of the informal sector such as street traders tend to have an entrepreneurial character and sometimes high income, it is still widely recognized that the informal sector is vulnerable with little capital, limited markets, inadequate economic returns and low levels of living standards.

With reference to street enterprise, the issue of the informal sector is particularly related to its business operation. As it was mentioned earlier that street traders operate their business in the areas that can be classified as public spaces and are originally not intended for trading purposes. As most street trading occupies busy streets, sidewalks or other public spaces, it is often considered illegal. This vagabond and homeless status makes these traders victims of harassment and threats from police and other government authorities. In Bolpur town of Birbhum district, for example, the municipality continues to perform cleaning operations in the five busiest areas. It is believed that these areas should be free from the 'nuisance' of street traders especially during even days.

It is a common belief among the majority of the people that street vendors as faceless individuals, strangers in the city selling small items, at times carried on head, in baskets or small carts. They could be squatters in the marketplace or in residential areas or may be mobile in search of customers. The areas where the vendors operate could be affluent, middle-class or lower-middle class colonies or slums. Most of the slum dwellers, in fact, depend on them for their day-to-day provisions.

Looking at the Indian economy at all levels, particularly the household economy of the middle and lower class, a major part of our commerce in terms of day-to-day trade is accounted for by vendors. Yet, neither they are taken serious notice nor their roles are being recognized as such that they are most useful and dynamic agents of the economy. They are recognized only when people need them for their immediate concern. In professional perception, that is in the interaction of the vendors with policemen, at most times they come across as transgressing the limits of law.

The authorities themselves are caught within conflicting interests depending on their perception and respective role assignment. Of course, sometimes, their perception is also guided by the political master and their ideological framework. The perpetual conflicts between the police and municipal authorities are often aggravated in the context of restoration of rights of vendors when municipal and land owning authorities grant them some kind of licence or permission to operate in public places; and the police, on the other hand, feel duty-bound to clear the obstructions being caused by the vendors on footpaths, streets and public land. This is a major dilemma frequently faced by the vendors.

In the prevailing situation, certain questions confront everyone concerned. Is it proper for the vendors to squat on the roads and places meant for vehicular traffic or for pedestrians to walk? Should they make use of the given limited spaces, which are meant for other uses? Is it appropriate for the traffic and the policemen to be indifferent and let the vendors to continue with their business? Is it appropriate for the municipal and the land owning authorities to issue licences thereby creating conditions wherein obstructions attain a legal sanction? On the other hand, in given human considerations, is it appropriate for the authorities to thoughtlessly remove the vendors for whom these public places and streets happen to be a lifeline? Perhaps these questions are always remain unanswered.

Since municipal bodies and land owning department are the designated agencies to permit through licence or otherwise, vendors to operate in public places; one must see into certain important aspects which are often being overlooked and discussed below:

1. It is not that such people are being granted permission only for the reason that it is their fundamental right to carry on their trade unhindered, with reasonable restrictions, at any place during a given time. It is more because there are certain political leaders and pressure groups behind their continued existence. So, sometimes it becomes a political game for different political parties to attract these hapless vendors to cast vote for their respective political parties. These all are invisible allurement for street vendors. Such pressures often compel local bodies to make some kind of arrangement even though law enforcement agencies like police or those concerned with providing civic amenities dishonour the vendors' right from the point of view of legal security.
2. The municipal authorities often grant licence and collect fee from the vendors to conduct business on the roads, in the market place or even for setting up markets on weekly off days in certain specified places or localities.
3. Vendors are often permitted to carry on with their trade at specified places on account of a 'stay order' from the court.

The perception of the court may be based on humanitarian or other considerations but they are often at cross-purpose with the perceptions of the local/municipal authorities and the police. In any case, perceptions of police are usually at variance with those of the municipal authorities or the court. However, when it comes to jeopardizing wrongly or rightly the interests of the vendors, municipal authorities and police have to work in tandem.

The police are expected to act in accordance with their legal and official commitments to keep the roads, streets and public places free from obstruction and encroachment. **Section 283** of the **Indian Penal Code** applies nationally, permits action against vendors and such others who cause impediments in the free flow of traffic or obstruction to movement on footpaths. Identical laws exist in other metropolitan cities where the vendors and the police confront each other as adversaries.

In contrast to the legal obligations of the police, the basic interest of vendors is survival, since their life and business depends on access to the streets and footpaths from where alone they can operate and earn the livelihood. It appears almost impossible to come to any concrete conclusion to resolve such a massive problem of vendors and allied dimensions of the issue. The law enforcement agency is not expected to be humane all the time going beyond the stipulation of the laws. And so, at certain point of time, they have to adhere to very drastic steps which go against the vendors and deadly affect their existence as a human being.

Whatever the legal status of vendors, the municipal corporation and police authorities, particularly in crowded metropolises and bigger cities, are under constant pressure to act. It also sounds to be impractical that for every small issue and conflict pertaining to vendors would be brought back to court and wait for the court order to resolve the problem. So, there has to be a consensus on a legally acceptable solution to both safeguarding the business interests of the vendors and create conditions under which they are not constantly hounded and subjected to undignified treatment by the authorities and common people. Obviously, at the same time, the city profile or the public convenience on the streets, footpaths and spaces of common use cannot be completely sacrificed.

Indeed, it is possible to find spaces not far from the busy roads and footpaths wherein vendors could squat in order to carry on with their business, while at the same time keeping in mind the administrative paradigm of all authorities. Such adjustments could be made by permitting free use of the marketplace for the vendors on the weekly off days. In fact, on account of their lower prices, a large number of people would prefer to shop on such days. However, this move would in all likelihood meet with the disapproval of local shopkeepers, since they stand to loose potential customers.

In almost all the situations, the interaction between the traffic policemen, municipal officials with the vendors on the streets are hostile. The clash between the traffic police and vendors is inevitable since most of them, albeit due to necessity, cause destruction. Nevertheless, some kind of common strategy needs to be believed since no authority, police or municipal, can operate without public support. Since vendors constitute a significant presence and are an active segment of society they have to be brought in as partners in governance. The conduct of the police *vis-à-vis* vendors is most uncharitable since they perceive them as strangers or suspects. Needless to add that a compassionate or humane approach is missing in the realm of legal obligations. But then, the police are often blamed, even perceived as the so-called *'hafta'* collection agency. While a ding-dong battle goes on, possibly, a number of unscrupulous and corrupt policemen on the streets do not miss out the opportunity to earn some money in dishonest manner. Some time before, a committee was constituted as recommended by the State Government to look into the functioning of such agencies and studying the problem. It was also realized by the committee to identify the police personnel who are involved in such matter. Unfortunately nothing concrete came out of it.

As long as there is a gap exists between the law and reality, such problems cannot be counteracted. Laws sce vendors only as 'public nuisance'. The human and socio-economic aspects pertaining to their livelihood and the top of that the restoration of human rights has never been appreciated. Within the given legal situation there is a little scope for improving understanding as there exists a major hiatus between expectations and reality. Even experiments and policies to accommodate and rehabilitate the vendors by the government authorities may prove to be futile unless the perception and attitude of the government personnel and general public change towards the vendors and respect them as human being.

Behind police, ill-treatment and exploitation by gangsters and anti-social elements towards the vendors are also a matter of serious consideration. Under the crime prevention programmes, *Crime Control Bureau* always takes into account that strangers are always suspicious, i.e. individuals without a definite identity or fixed abode or occupation are seen as suspicious. The mobile vendors invariably and the squatting vendors in a majority of cases, neither have proper identification nor regular permission to trade, duly verified by the authorities. The organizations espousing the interest of the vendors have demanded that identity cards need to be issued to them by the police department or municipal authorities so that they may move around in an area or remain at a fixed place and continue the business.

Yet another phenomena has also been observed that it is not only the police but the different residential areas/ association/complex do not permit vendors to come in on the plea of security. Sometimes, it is painful to see the inhuman behaviour of the security of various housing complex with the vendors. A police officer with over two and a half decade of service was in opinion that he never came across many vendors committed serious crimes. It was basically our perception and anticipation without much rational input. But, decidedly, there is a need to give them some kind of identification for their self-protection and to keep themselves away from any sort of torture. Hopefully, the verification will be proved worthwhile to the police personnel, municipal authorities and vendors.

Understanding the ground reality as it prevails today a common platform and strategic planning are essential to combat with such problems; of course, keeping in mind the different perception of the vendors, police and municipal authorities towards each other and among themselves as well, their legal and professional obligations and last but not the least the human and socio-economic considerations. There is a definite need to identify each and every vendor, whatever their mode of operation in the metropolitan cities and to give them some kind of identity through verification.

Similarly, when left unguided or at large in search of a livelihood, pursuing their survival interests, the vendors are likely to operate in a manner which may create conflict with the interest of the authorities. The authorities should find alternative places for them or spaces in the vicinity of their business areas or provide them some kind of opportunity where they operate without obstructing traffic or inconvenience cause to the public. The problem of street vendors is definitely one, which cries for solution for the reason that it involves human beings and their basic rights. Althogh the problem appears mind-boggling and intractable, it is not beyond limited and temporary solutions at least in parts of the city.

This research-for-policy project aimed to provide information on social and economic factors underlying street vending activities as a basis upon which to generate policy issues and options in the urban development planning. As such, the study had focused on ***five areas*** of inquiry:

- Socio-economic characteristics of street traders;
- Reasons to participate in street vending;
- Preferences of their business site;
- Policy-maker's perception on the operation of street enterprises; and
- Existing policy measures and legislations relating to the operation of street enterprises.

Under this conceptual clarity of the ingredients of the street vendors, these were the ***objectives*** of the study:

1. To identify major socio-economic and administrative variables related to operation of street vending and environmental conditions of the enterprise including business profile, social and economic determinants of street vending activities and factors influencing the selection of worksites of the street traders.

2. To examine and review the policy-making process within urban development planning highlighting existing policy development measures and legislations related to the operation of street enterprises, such as approaches of the measures, problems and implementation patterns, stakeholders (advocates, opponents, decision-makers) involved, and participation and communication procedures in policy-making.
3. To identify and discuss scope of research in solving policy issues within the context of urban development planning in Birbhum district.
4. To increase the awareness and involvement of different stakeholders so as to enhance the efficient process of public policy making.
5. To outline and propose open and integrated policy measures and interventions to public policy administrators concerning the operation of street enterprises within the adequate framework of urban built environment.

Methodology

Research Design

In this study, exploratory research design has been followed because the main purpose of such design was to formulate a problem for more precise investigation or to develop some working strategies from an operational point of view. The major emphasis was to explore ideas and insights. This research design is therefore flexible enough to provide opportunity for considering different aspects of the problems of street vendors under study.

Universe of Research

The study was conducted in the district of Birbhum, West Bengal during 2007-08. A glimpse of Birbhum district is given below. Its area [1,757 sq mile (4,550 sq km)] comprises two distinct regions. To the west lies an undulating, generally barren upland, part of the eastern fringe of the Chota Nagpur Plateau, rising to 3,000 ft (900 m); to the east is a densely populated, alluvial plain of the Gangetic Delta. The Ajay, Mor, Mayurakshi, Bakreswar, and Dwarka are the principal rivers. A project on the Mayurakshi provides irrigation for about 600,000 ac (240,000 ha) and 2,000 kW of electric power. Rice, legumes, wheat, corn (maize), and mangoes are the chief crops in the east; coal, china clay, and iron-ore deposits are found in the west. The district's principal industries include cotton and silk weaving, rice and oilseed milling, and metal ware and pottery manufacture. Suri is the district headquarters.

This district is not so agriculturally developed because majority of the agricultural land is mono-cropping due to unavailability of irrigation water in *rabi* and summer seasons. Due to soil pattern and natural land slope and so employment opportunities for the majority of rural population in other than rainy season are very little. Generally, this particular district was selected because of the familiarity of the research team, high accessibility before the respondents and complete understanding of the intricate fabrication of the district and its subdivisions in terms of all the components required for the study.

The district of Birbhum is administratively divided into three Subdivisions, viz. Bolpur, Suri and Rampurhat. Among these three subdivisions, Bolpur has the prime importance in terms of circulation of economy, strong market based business transactions, population variation and its close proximity with other two prosperous neighbouring districts, i.e. Burdwan and Murshidabad. Suri is ranked second because it is the district headquarter and it has got easy accessibility with the neighbouring state Jharkhand. Rampurhat subdivision is third down the line in terms of its priority before the population, market economy and geographical location.

In particular, it could be ascertained that both Bolpur and Suri subdivisional towns were selected for the present study for the following reasons:

- availability of large number of street vendors,
- availability of vendors in wide variety in terms of type of vending, and
- availability of street vendors in different age groups.

Few important statistics of Birbhum district and its sub-divisional towns are given below:

Important Statistics of Birbhum District

1. Area and Population

Area	square km	4,545.00
Forest	square km	158.22
Population	'000	2,555.66
Male	'000	1,313.29
Female	'000	1,242.38
Urban	'000	229.56
Rural	'000	2,326.10
Population growth (p.a.)	%	2.01
Population density	Persons/sq.km	562.30
Relative Index of Development		68
Urbanization	%	8.98

2. Literacy and Workers Statistics

Literacy	%	48.56
Male	%	59.26
Female	%	37.17
Workers as % of total population	%	33.15
Workers as % of main workers		
Agriculture and allied activities	%	73.28
Mining and Quarrying	%	0.95
Mfg. (Non-household) industries	%	4.60
Household industries	%	3.60
Construction	%	0.96
Services	%	16.61
Major Rivers	Ajoy, Kopai, Mayurakshi, Bakreswar	
Forest area as % of reporting area	%	3.50
Gross irrigated area as % of gross cropped area	%	54.20
Fertilizer consumption per ha.	kg	127
Per capita food grain production	kg	306

3. Infrastructure

Road Length per 100 sq. km	km	47.74
Railway route length per 100 sq.km	km	4.80
Post offices per 100,000 persons	No.	17.65
Telegraph offices per 100,000 persons	No.	3.60
Bank branches per 100,000 persons	No.	6.77
Per capita Bank deposits	Rupees	910
Per capita Bank credit	Rupees	401
Per capita Bank credit to SSIs	Rupees	40
Per capita Bank credit to industries	Rupees	72

4. Major Crops

Crop	*Quantity (tonnes)*	*Value as % of district total*
Rice	729,773	77.75
Potatoes	193,850	8.30
Rapeseed	35,923	7.60
Wheat	46,786	3.38
Sugarcane	80,613	0.84
Gram	4,170	0.70
Sesame	1,889	0.46

5. Minerals

Mineral	*Quantity in tonnes*	*Value in Rs. Millions*
Coal	243,000	60.50
Kaolin	108,377	15.48
Fireclay	35,465	1.68

Source: As specified Data in No. 1, 2, 3, 4 and 5 are sourced from Birbhum District Website as www.birbhum.nic.in

A. Area (in sq.km) and Total Population

Subdivision	*Area (Sq.km)*	*No. of Households*	*Population (Total)*	*Population (Male)*	*Population (Female)*
Bolpur	10.73	14008	65693	33337	32356
Suri	8.98	12816	61806	31801	30005
Rampurhat	3.95	10542	50613	26110	24503
Total	**23.66**	**37366**	**178112**	**91248**	**86864**

Average Size of Household: 4.76 persons/household
Sex Ratio: 952 female per 1000 male

B. Population of 0-6 Years Children and SC Population:

Subdivision	*Population (0-6 Years) (Total)*	*Population (0-6 Years) (Male)*	*Population (0-6 Years) (Female)*	*SC Population (Total)*	*SC Population (Male)*	*SC Population (Female)*
Bolpur	6958	3547	3411	14994	7510	7484
Suri	6735	3460	3275	12255	6245	6010
Rampurhat	5839	3023	2816	13126	6647	6479
Total	19532	10030	9502	40375	20402	19973

C. ST Population and Literate Population

Subdivision	*ST Population (Total)*	*ST Population (Male)*	*STPopulation (Female)*	*Literate Population (Total)*	*Literate Population (Male)*	*Literate Population (Female)*
Bolpur	1037	514	523	47059	25903	21156
Suri	884	458	426	45142	24829	20313
Rampurhat	991	494	497	36406	20340	16066
Total	**2912**	**1466**	**1446**	**128607**	**71072**	**57535**

D. Illiterate Population and Total Workers

Subdivision	*Illiterate Population (Total)*	*Illiterate Population (Male)*	*Illiterate Population (Female)*	*Total Workers*	*Total Workers (Male)*	*Total Workers (Female)*
Bolpur	18634	7434	11200	22206	17770	4436
Suri	16664	6972	9692	19999	16336	3663
Rampurhat	14207	5770	8437	15112	12985	2127
Total	**49505**	**20176**	**29329**	**57317**	**47091**	**10226**

E. Main Workers and Cultivators

Subdivision	*Main Workers (Total)*	*Main Workers (Male)*	*Main Workers (Female)*	*Cultivators (Total)*	*Cultivators (Male)*	*Cultivators (Female)*
Bolpur	20112	16624	3488	116	98	18
Suri	18564	15558	3006	125	120	5
Rampurhat	13945	12238	1707	138	129	9
Total	**52621**	**44420**	**8201**	**379**	**347**	**32**

F. Agricultural Labour and Worker in Household Industry

Subdivision	*Agri-cultural Labour (Total)*	*Agri-cultural Labour (Male)*	*Agri-cultural Labour (Female)*	*Worker (House-hold Industry)*	*Worker (House-hold Industry) (Male)*	*Worker (House-hold Industry) (Female)*
Bolpur	191	162	29	556	323	233
Suri	94	81	13	296	147	149
Rampurhat	464	349	115	258	195	63
Total	**749**	**592**	**157**	**1110**	**665**	**445**

G. Other Workers and Marginal Workers

Subdivision	*Other Workers (Total)*	*Other Workers (Male)*	*Other Workers (Female)*	*Marginal Workers (Total)*	*Marginal Workers (Male)*	*Marginal Workers (Female)*
Bolpur	19249	16041	3208	2094	1146	948
Suri	18049	15210	2839	1435	778	657
Rampurhat	13085	11565	1520	1167	747	420
Total	**50383**	**42816**	**7567**	**4696**	**2671**	**2025**

H. Marginal Cultivators and Marginal Agricultural Labourers

Subdivision	*Marginal Culti-vators (Total)*	*Marginal Culti-vators (Male)*	*Marginal Culti-vators (Female)*	*Marginal Agril. Lab-ourers (Total)*	*Marginal Agril. Lab-ourers (Male)*	*Marginal Agril. Lab-ourers (Female)*
Bolpur	22	18	4	68	42	26
Suri	25	6	19	126	48	78
Rampurhat	15	13	2	68	39	29
Total	**62**	**37**	**25**	**262**	**129**	**133**

I. Marginal Household Industry Workers and Marginal Other Workers

Subdivision	*Marginal House-hold Industry Workers (Total)*	*Marginal House-hold Industry Workers (Male)*	*Marginal House-hold Industry Workers (Female)*	*Marginal Other Workers (Total)*	*Marginal Other Workers (Male)*	*Marginal Other Workers (Female)*
Bolpur	353	48	305	1651	1038	613
Suri	201	20	181	1083	704	379
Rampurhat	81	32	49	1003	663	340
Total	**635**	**100**	**535**	**3737**	**2405**	**1332**

Maps of West Bengal and Birbhum

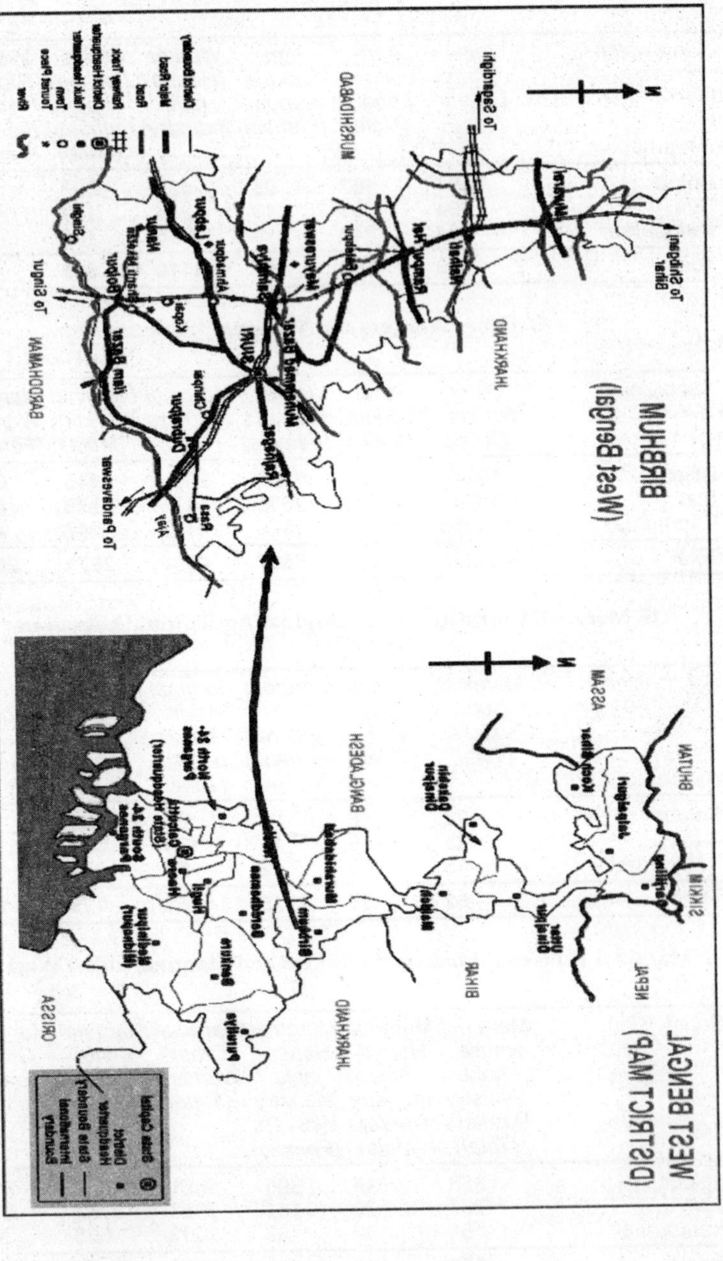

J. Non-Workers

Subdivision	*Non-Workers (Total)*	*Non-Workers (Male)*	*Non-Workers (Female)*
Bolpur	43487	15567	27920
Suri	41807	15465	26342
Rampurhat	35501	13125	22376
Total	**120795**	**44157**	**76638**

Source: As specified Data in No. A, B, C, D, E, F, G, H, I and J are sourced from District Statistical Handbook 2007 of Birbhum under Bureau of Applied Economics and Statistics, Government of West Bengal.

Selection of Samples and Sampling Method

Stratified random sampling is a sampling technique where the target population is first divided into a number of homogenous strata. A simple random sampling of appropriate size is drawn from each stratum in order to make the whole sample. This method ensures that the sample is a representative of the population, when the population consists of units of heterogeneous characters.

This method of stratified sample has been adopted to select the final sample in Bolpur and Suri subdivisional towns. Stratification has been done on the basis of type of vending. Sample from each stratum has been according to proportional allocation rule and without replacement method. Let N_h be the number of street vendors under h^{th} vending type in the population, then the number of vendors drawn from the stratum n_h follows the rule,

$$n_h = \left[\frac{n}{N}\right] N_h$$

Where,
n = Total sample size,
N = Total population size.

The identification of the street vendors to form a sampling frame has been done after obtaining primary level information regarding existence of street vendors in the study area. All the wards under both the municipality area were included for the study. The respondents have been selected after obtaining relevant information about them from municipality, market regulatory committee, businessmen, peer groups, ward counsellors and common people.

Sample Size

Initially six hundred (300 from each subdivisional towns) street vendors were identified from Bolpur and Suri subdivisional towns covering all the wards and as many as category of vendors possible to get a good representation in the final sample. Two hundred (100 from each town) street vendors were then selected from two towns using stratified random sampling technique (without replacement). Special care was taken to include all major types of vending in the sample.

Methods of Data Collection

After completion of the pilot study, the actual work was done after minimum of modification in the schedule. Relevant reviews of literature were carried out in order to develop questions on socio-economic conditions of the respondents. Questions on the status of the respondents as street vendors were given utmost priority. A **structured interview schedule** was developed and administered according to the objectives of the study. The method of focus group discussion was also used for facilitating the response received in an informal setting. The variables selected for the statistical tests were also been selected after careful examination. Simple interview method was also adopted to collect some important data. Data were presented through tables (univariate, bivariate as needed) and statistical tests for interpretations of data and facts.

Data processing and analysis

As mentioned earlier that data were collected through interview schedule and coded on the code sheet. Later on, it was transferred to the codebook developed for the study. Data were processed with the help of **SPSS software**. Statistical tests were done (**SPSS and MINITAB software**) to establish the relationship among the variables.

Interpretation of key words

1. Urban Informal Sector

In the urban context, the informal sector refers to small enterprise operators selling food and goods or offering services and thereby involving the cash economy and market transactions which is more diverse than the rural one and includes a vast and heterogeneous variety of economic activities through which most urban families earn their livelihood.

2. Public Policy

There are directives laid down by the Government for governance of the issues related to public interest. In the context of this study, public policy refers to the policy framework for maintenance, control and operation of the vendors in the urban areas. Here, urban area refers to the places where governance and development planning are done by Municipality or Corporation.

3. Urban Street Vendors

Street vendors have been defined as 'an individual who offers goods and services to be sold to the public in the urban area without having any permanent structure or fixed place for vending activity'.

Variables and their Measurement

Some interdependent variables were identified in relation to street vending in Birbhum district. These variables have the significance in order to explore the problems the street vendors are encountering in urban areas. Each dependent and independent variable has been closely associated with the street vending activities along with addressing different constraints as the street vendors faced in their daily life. For the measurement of dependence and influence between these dependent and independent variables on street vending; two statistical methods were used—**cross-tabulation (frequency distribution) and chi-square test** for having proper quantitative and qualitative justification of the problems of the street vendors in urban informal sector. Of course, cent-per-cent accurate statistical inferences were not possible to draw because of plenty of uncontrollable phenomenon where the research team was helpless. These dependent and independent variables were:

I. Age and types of vending activities

II. Gender and types of vending activities

III. Religion and types of goods sold

IV. Gender and types of goods sold

V. Family type and habit of working in association

VI. Gender and habit of working in association

VII. Caste and type of goods sold

VIII. Educational status and location of preference for street vendors

IX. Reasons for selecting vending sites and distance of home from vending area

X. Nature of work done in past and reasons for street vending

XI. Amount of daily selling and working hours

XII. Monthly income from street vending

XIII. Income allocation for family expenses

XIV. Received threatening during street vending

XV. Other occupation, if any, apart from street vending

XVI. Vending and formal tax paid

XVII. Vending and informal tax paid

XVIII. Help to improve business condition and their affiliation to union or association.

Statistical Techniques used

(i) Frequency Distribution

(ii) Chi-square test has been used to test the independence of attributes.

Chi-Square is defined by

$$_{W1}X^2 = \sum^{k} \frac{(f_0 - f_e)^2}{f_e} \sim X^2_{(k-1)}$$

Where,

f_o = Observed frequency

f_e = Expected frequency

K = Number of classes

Critical value approach—Reject H_0 at level $\propto = 0.05$ if $x^2_{obs} > x^2_{0.05,\ k-1}$ p-value approach: p-value = p ($x^2 > x^2$ observed)

Reject H_0 if p-value $\leq \alpha$

An attempt has been made to highlight some of the prudent findings of the study in relation to the objectives set

Table 26.1 shows that a considerable number of street vendors (39.5%) in the study area are mobile street vendors and they sell their products by roaming or walking; while a large number of them (60.5%) use cart, bicycle etc. as their vehicle for vending.

The point is also to be noted that majority of the street vendors are found in Suri because it is the district headquarters as well as preferable business location for them. This is also the largest municipality area.

Table 26.1 : Subdivision and categories of mobile street vendors

Subdivision	*Categories of mobiie street vendors*		*Total*	*Percentage*
	Walking Street Vendors	*Street Vendors with Cart, Bicycle, etc.*		
Bolpur	38	62	100	50
Suri	41	59	100	50
Total	79	121	200	100
Percentage	**39.5**	**60.5**	**100**	

Table 26.2 : Age and type of vending activities

Age	*Types of vending activities*		*Total*	*Percentage*
	Mobile	*An Enterprise or Workshop*		
17 to 23 years	8	8	16	8
24 to 30 years	14	47	61	30.5
31 to 37 years	19	55	74	37
Above 37 years	7	42	49	24.5
Total	48	152	200	100
Percentage	**24**	**76**	**100**	

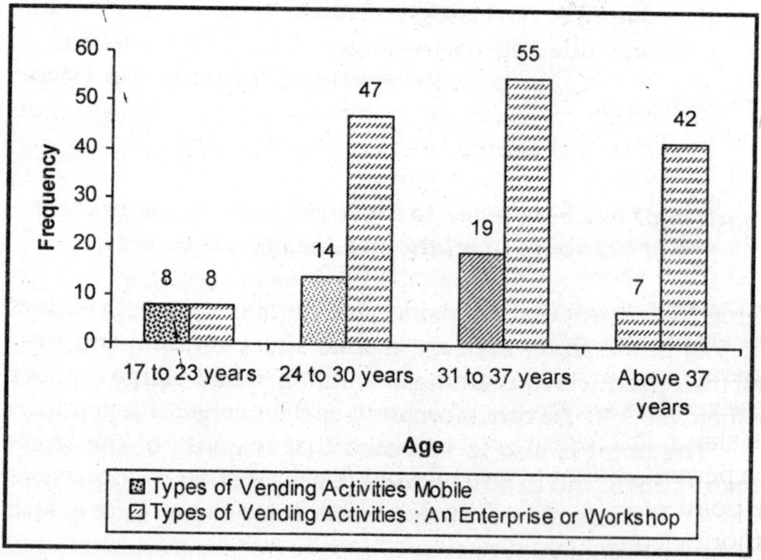

Table 26.2 depicts that most of the street vendors belong to the age group (24-37 yrs), which amounts to (67.5%). There are also considerable number of street vendors who are more than 37 years old. So, a very clear trend is observed that people do not enter into the vending profession at a very young age as it is found in other unorganized sectors. It is probably because most of the street vendors operate their vending activities as an enterprise (76%) and (24%) are mobile and unorganized.

To test whether age and vending type are independent

Age	*Types of Vending Activities*	
	Mobile	*An Enterprise or Workshop*
Up to 30 yrs.	22	55
Above 30 yrs.	26	97

Chi-Square Results

$$\chi^2_{(observed)} = 1.434$$
$$\text{p-Value} = 0.0231$$

Chi-square test rejects the null hypothesis at level $\propto = .05\%$ but fails to reject null hypothesis at level $\propto = .01\%$. So age and vending type are dependent at 5 per cent level but at 1 per cent level they are not dependent.

It is evident that a considerable number of vendors of 24 to 37 years of age group are preferred to operate their business activities through enterprise or workshop because of sustainable income in a safe place. The above age group is most vulnerable due to unemployment or lack of alternatives to generate employment for livelihood security. Consequently, these vendors are preferred to encroach a small space in market, bus stand and railway station to start their vending activities on a permanent basis. This encroachment is purely illegal from the point of view of legal framework. Sometimes, municipal authorities destroy the illegal encroachment for expansion of roads and therefore, those vendors are shifted as mobile street vendors.

Table 26.3 : Gender and types of vending activities

Gender	*Types of Vending Activities*		*Percentage*
	Mobile	*An Enterprise or Workshop*	
Male	24.18%	75.82%	91
Female	22.22%	77.78%	9
Percentage	24	76	

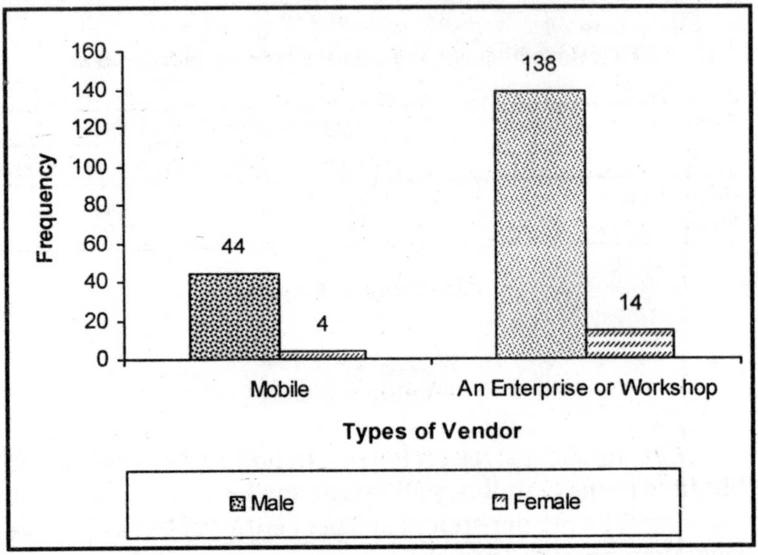

Table 26.3 reflects that this sector is mainly male dominated and only 9 per cent of them are females. Out of them, 22.22 per cent operate their business as mobile vendors because mobile vending is a gruelling task for them. Majority of them (77.78%) prefer to run their business as enterprise or workshop. It is also worth mentioning here that men earn more than women because of two reasons—(1) most of the females have less capital to invest; and (2) they cannot spend much time in vending due to family responsibility. Women vendors are often harassed or molested by their counterpart and no action is generally taken by the local authority against this issue.

Table 26.4 : Religion and types of goods sold

Religion	*Types of Goods Sold*					*Percentage*
	Vege- tables	*Snacks and Tea*	*Daily Household Goods*	*Food*	*Others*	
Hindu	6.37%	14.01%	7.01%	28.03%	44.59%	78.5
Muslim	4.65%	9.30%	0.00%	18.60%	67.44%	21.5
Percentage	**6**	**13**	**5.5**	**26**	**49.5**	

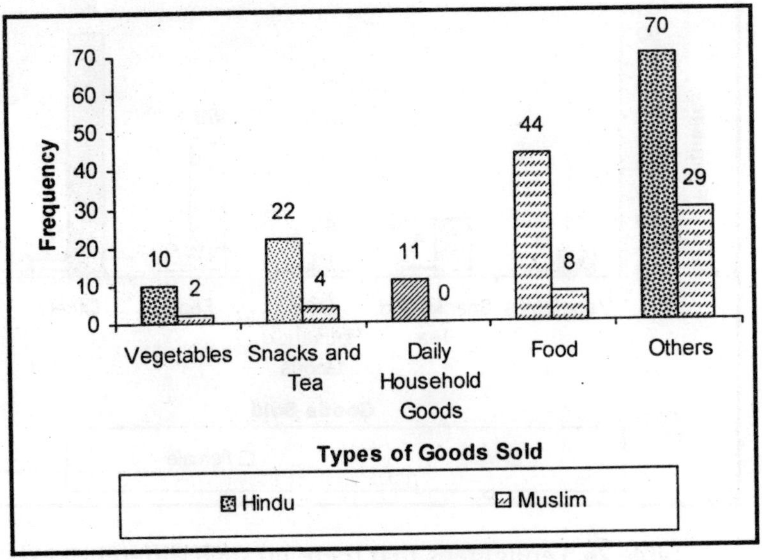

Table 26.4 depicts that among the street vendors 78.5 per cent are Hindu in comparison to Muslim (21.5%). Majority of the street vendors (75.5%) sell foods and other items and only 13 per cent sell snacks and tea. In the sample it was not found that any Muslim selling daily household goods. Hindu street vendors are more preferred than Muslims due to cultural and age long traditional beliefs and practices.

Table 26.5 : Gender and types of goods sold

Gender	*Types of Goods Sold*					*Percentage*
	Vege-tables	*Snacks and Tea*	*Daily Household Goods*	*Food*	*Others*	
Male	5.49%	12.09%	4.40%	27.47%	50.55%	91
Female	11.11%	22.22%	16.67%	11.11%	38.89%	9
Percentage	**6**	**13**	**5.5**	**26**	**49.5**	

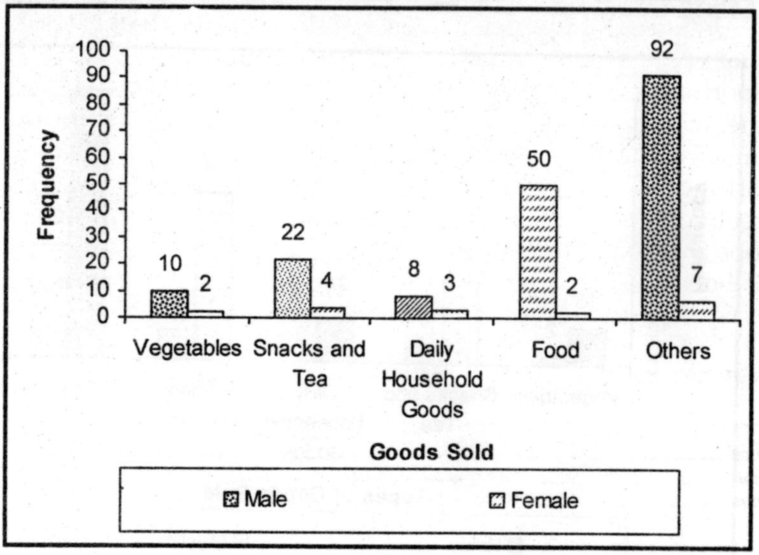

Table 26.5 enlightens that there no such difference exists in type of goods sold in relation to gender of the street vendors as it is found in the study though representation of women in the profession is very less.

Table for Chi-Square Test

Gender	*Types of Goods Sold*		
	Daily Household Goods	*Food*	*Others*
Male	18	72	92
Female	5	6	7

To test the null hypothesis regarding gender of the street vendors and the types of goods sold are independent

Chi-Square Results:

$$\chi^2_{(observed)} = 5.170$$
$$\text{p-Value} = 0.075$$

Chi-square test fails to reject the null hypothesis both at level $\propto$ = .05 and .01. So gender and types of goods sold are not at all dependent on each other both at 5 per cent and 1 per cent level of significance.

In street vending activities, gender priorities are almost equal whereas men and women street vendors access similar opportunities to sell their goods in the market. At the same time women street vendors are most accepted in daily household goods selling in comparison to food related workshop or enterprise. Though in the present market, male street vendors are in majority and women have very limited scope and space in all types of vending activities. Therefore, it has been tried to analyze weather the women street vendors are equally recognized and enjoy considerable status as men.

Table 26.6 : Educational status and location preference for street vending

Educational Status	*Location Preference for Street Vending*									*Total*	*Percentage*
	Enterprise	*Shop or Workshop Building*	*Sites Or Road Works*	*Fixed Market*	*Mobile Market*	*Home with Specific Outfits*	*Street*	*Mobile*	*Others*		
Illiterate	0	6	0	2	1	0	1	7	0	17	8.5
Literate	0	14	0	4	0	0	5	10	0	33	16.5
Primary	2	43	2	5	2	0	6	6	0	66	33
Up to Class-VIII	2	35	0	4	1	0	6	8	1	57	28.5
Secondary	0	7	0	2	0	0	2	0	0	11	5.5
H. Secondary	2	5	0	0	0	1	0	1	0	9	4.5
Graduate	2	5	0	0	0	0	0	0	0	7	3.5
Total	8	115	2	17	4	1	20	32	1	200	100
Percentage	4	57.5	1	8.5	2	0.5	10	16	0.5	100	

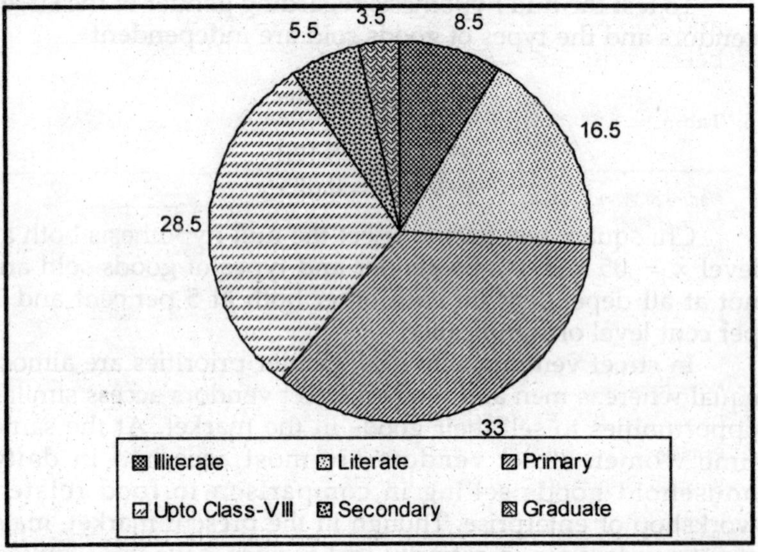

Table 26.6 suggests that majority of the street vendors 57.5 per cent prefer to run their business as enterprise or workshop irrespective of their educational status and 16 per cent of them also like mobile street vending for earning. But mobile street vending is mostly preferred by relatively less educated street vendors. During the study it was found that the vendors who have relatively high educational level tend to concentrate on one fixed business. But in case of the vendors, who have low level of literacy, may have to depend upon more than one business. Therefore, they prefer mobile vending.

Table 26.7 reflects the fact that among the street vendors, 36.5 per cent had no work experience before joining the profession; 23.5 per cent were engaged in farming and as daily labourers and 22 per cent were engaged in other profession. Most interestingly 9 per cent of the street vendors worked before as industrial worker and they joined in this profession due to closure of factory. So, almost all the street vendors had no prior experiences in street vending before joining this profession. These street vendors opined that they joined in this profession because, it is difficult to get a job in a formal sector (20%), easy to enter in the street enterprises (24.5%). Sixteen per cent (16%) of the respondents did not have required skills and knowledge prior to entering into the profession as it has been envisaged from the table.

Table 26.7 : Nature of work done in the past and reasons for street vending

Nature of Work Done in Past Status	*Reasons for Street Vending*								*Total*	*Percentage*
	Difficult to get a job in a formal sector	*Easy to enter in the street enterprises*	*Easy to operate street enterprises*	*Job suited to my knowledge and skills*	*Following Predecessors*	*Job interesting to me*	*Job provides adequate income*	*Job provides high social status*		
No work done	3	23	10	18	16	0	3	0	73	36.5
Daily labour	3	6	9	1	2	0	1	0	22	11
Farming	10	4	8	2	0	0	1	0	25	12.5
Small business	8	3	2	2	1	0	0	1	17	8.5
Industrial Worker	3	3	6	2	1	2	1	0	18	9
Others	13	10	6	7	4	2	3	0	45	22.5
Total	40	49	41	32	24	4	9	1	200	100
Percentage	20	24.5	20.5	16	12	2	4.5	0.5	100	

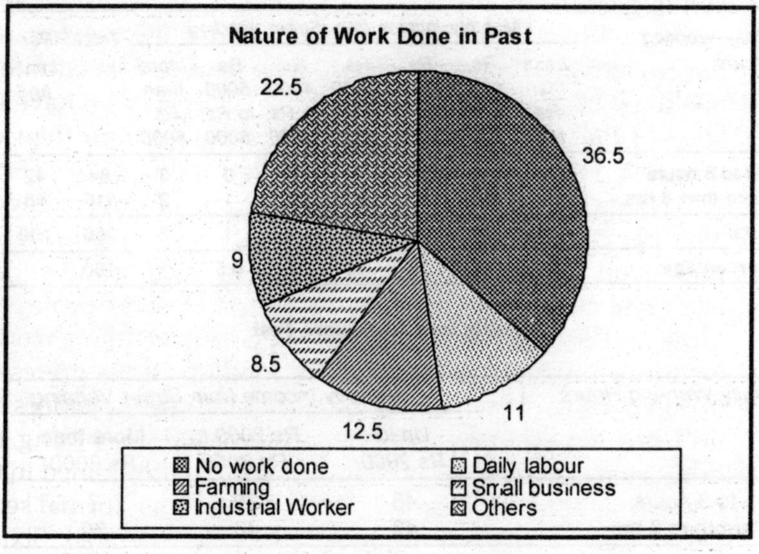

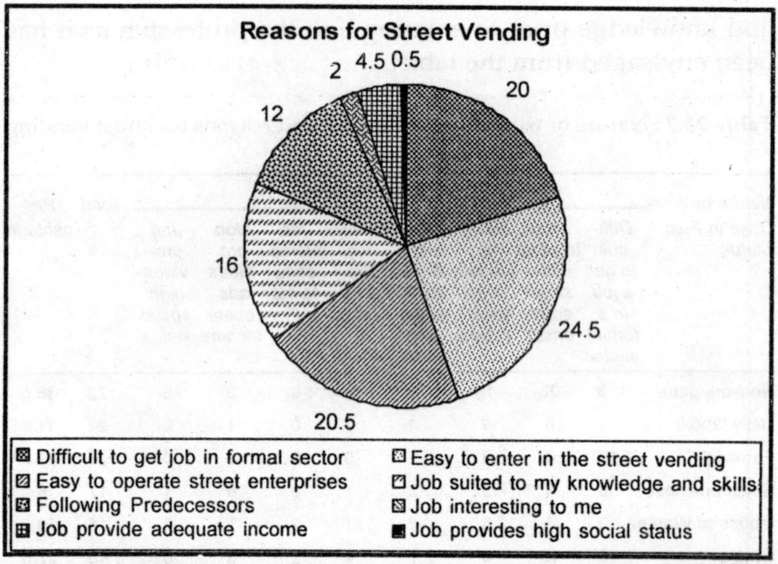

From Table 26.8 we see whether the working hours and monthly income from street vending are closely related.

Table 26.8 : Daily working hours and monthly income from street vending

Daily Working Hours	*Monthly Income from Street Vending*							*Total*	*Per-cent-age*
	Less than Rs. 1000	*Rs. 1000 to Rs. 2000*	*Rs. 2000 to Rs. 3000*	*Rs. 3000 to Rs. 4000*	*Rs. 4000 to Rs. 5000*	*Rs. 5000 to Rs. 6000*	*More than Rs. 6000*		
Up to 8 hours	8	40	29	7	0	0	0	84	42
More than 8 hrs.	3	40	43	23	4	1	2	116	58
Total	11	80	72	30	4	1	2	200	100
Percentage	5.5	40	36	15	2	0.5	1	100	

Table for Chi-Square Test

Daily Working Hours	*Monthly Income from Street Vending*		
	Up to Rs.2000	*Rs.2000 to Rs.3000*	More than Rs.3000
Up to 8 hours	48	29	7
More than 8 hrs.	43	43	30

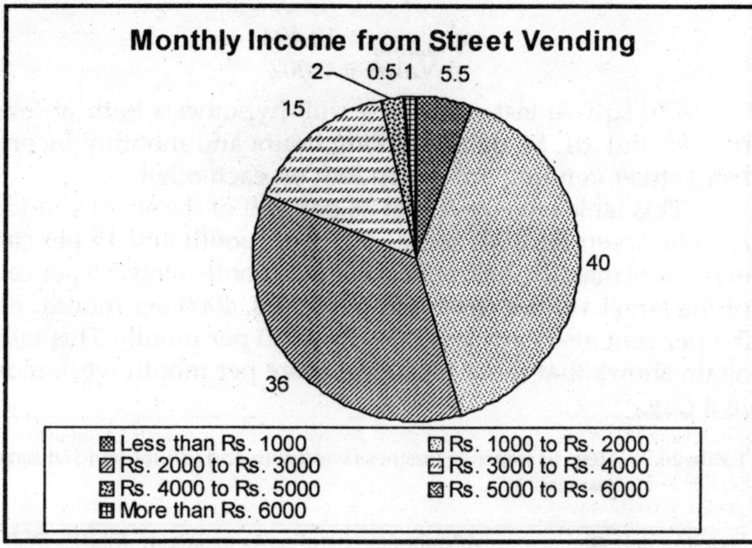

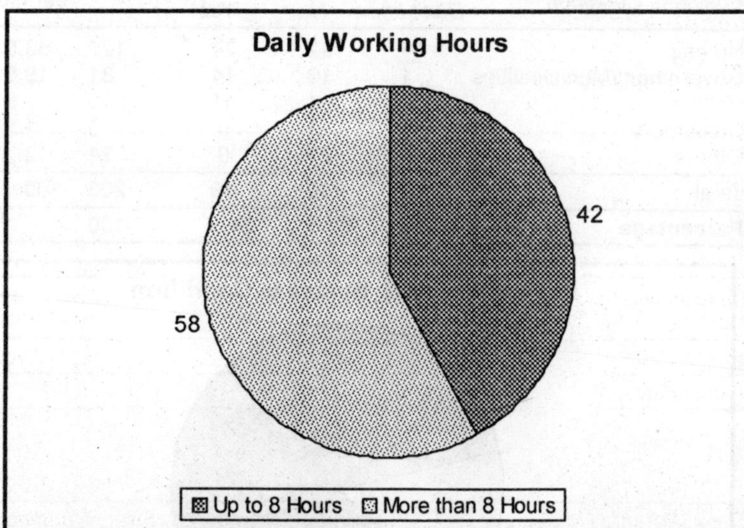

To test whether the working hours and monthly income from street vending are independent or not.

Chi-Square Results

$$\chi^2_{(observed)} = 12.494$$
$$\text{p-Value} = 0.002$$

Chi-square test rejects the null hypothesis both at level $\alpha = .05$ and .01. So daily working hours and monthly income from street vending are dependent on each other.

This table envisages that 76 per cent of the street vendors earn between Rs. 1000 to Rs. 3000 per month and 15 per cent earn more than Rs. 3000 to Rs. 4000 per month. Only 3.5 per cent of the street vendors earn more than Rs. 4000 per month. But 5.5 per cent also earn less than Rs. 1000 per month. This table again shows that those who earn more per month work more in a day.

Table 26.9 : Help to improve business condition and affiliation to union or association

Help to Improve Business Condition	*Affiliated to Union or Association*			*Total*	*Percentage*
	Don't know	*No*	*Yes*		
No help	11	92	24	127	63.5
Government/Municipalities	1	16	14	31	15.5
Unions	0	4	11	15	7.5
Customers	0	3	0	3	1.5
Others	0	24	0	24	12
Total	12	139	49	200	100
Percentage	6	69.5	24.5	100	

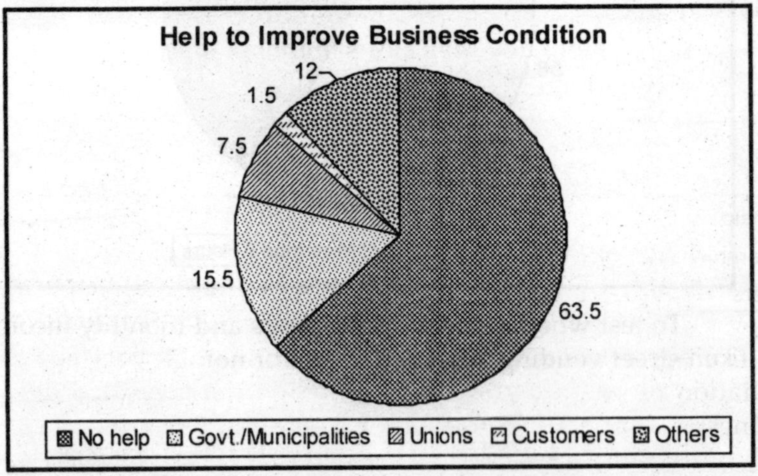

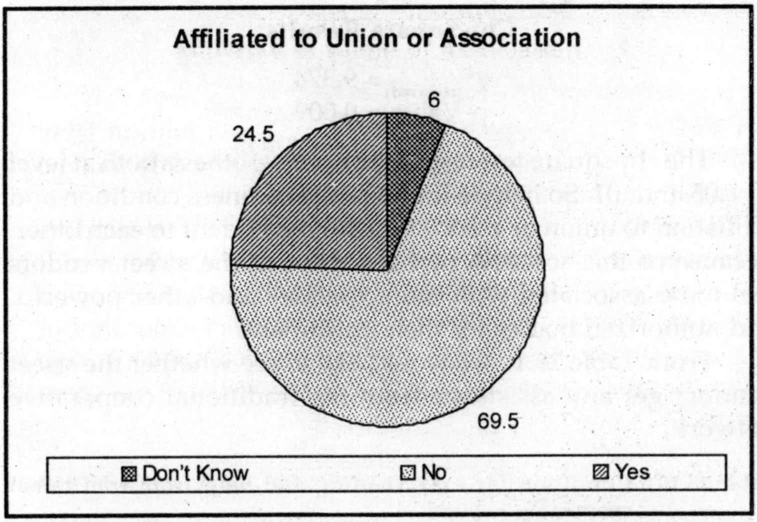

Table 26.9 suggests that 69.5 per cent street vendors are not affiliated to any union or association and only 24.5 per cent are affiliated. This table also ascertains that 63.5 per cent street vendors do not get any kind of help to improve their business condition and only 15.5 per cent get help from Government or Municipalities. Even those who are affiliated to some union or association, majority of them do not get any help. So it clearly indicates that the lack of proper awareness prevails among the vendors about the importance of affiliation to any authorized body.

Table for Chi-Square Test

Help to Improve Business Condition	*Affiliated to Union or Association*	
	No	*Yes*
No help	103	24
Government/Municipalities	17	14
Others	31	11

To see whether there is any relationship between affiliation to union bodies and improving the condition of business.

Chi-Square Results

$$\chi^2_{(observed)} = 9.374$$
$$\text{p-Value} = 0.009$$

The chi-square test rejects the null hypothesis both at level ∝ = .05 and .01. So help to improve the business condition and affiliation to union or association are dependent to each other. Because of this scenario perhaps most of the street vendors feel to be associated with municipalities and other powerful and authorized bodies for their upliftment.

From Table 26.10 we would like to see whether the street vendors get any assistance from the traditional cooperative network.

Table 26.10: Condition for easy vending and help from traditional cooperative network

Condition for Easy Vending	*Help from Traditional Cooperative Networks*		*Total*	*Percentage*
	No	*Yes*		
Completely free to set up	24	123	147	73.5
Received help from other people	13	40	53	26.5
Total	37	163	200	100
Percentage	18.5	81.5	100	

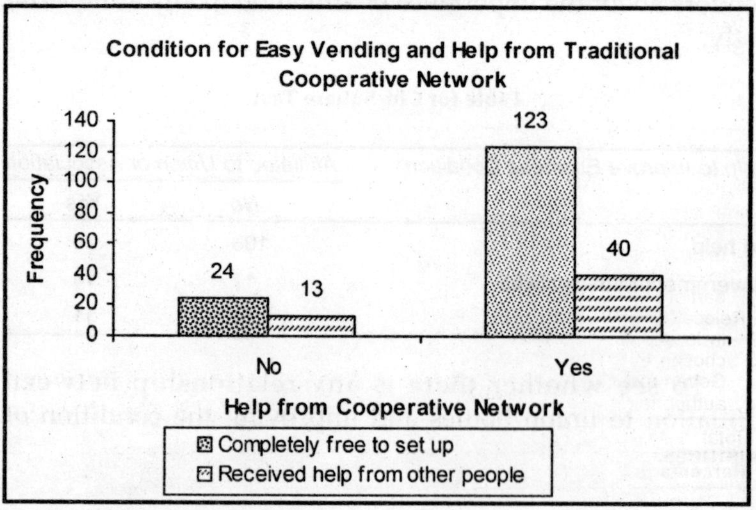

Table 26.10 reflects that 81.5 per cent street vendors receive help from traditional cooperative network for their business. Those who want to be completely free to run their business, majority of them receive help from the traditional cooperative networks as it is found in the study.

We want to test whether condition for easy vending and help from traditional cooperative networks are independent or not.

Chi-Square Results

$$\chi^2_{(observed)} = 1.738$$

$$\text{p-Value} = 0.187$$

Chi-square test fails to reject null hypothesis both at level $\alpha = .05$ and .01. So condition for easy vending and help from traditional cooperative networks are not dependent to each other. So from this data it can be observed that vendors are much aware of the traditional cooperative network. It has also been found that there is a close relationship between the condition of vending and help from traditional cooperative network. It is clear that the more the financial assistance from the traditional cooperative network, the more the opportunity of easy vending.

Table 26.11 : Option for choosing vending sites and formal tax paid

Option for Choosing Vending Sites	*Formal Tax Paid*						*Total*	*Percentage*
	No Tax Paid	*Service Tax to Electric and Water Dept.*	*Business Space Tax to Municipality*	*Income Tax*	*Sales Tax*	*Others*		
Sell legally from location they desire	50	26	65	2	1	1	145	72.5
Sell legally from some of their locations evacuated earlier	8	1	30	2	0	0	41	20.5
Relocate them in location chosen by Government authorities	5	4	4	1	0	0	14	7
Total	63	31	99	5	1	1	200	100
Percentage	31.5	15.5	49.5	2.5	0.5	0.5	100	

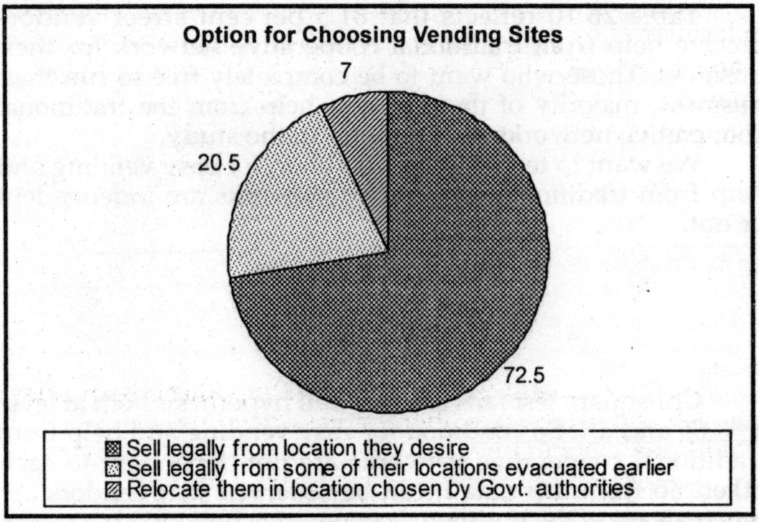

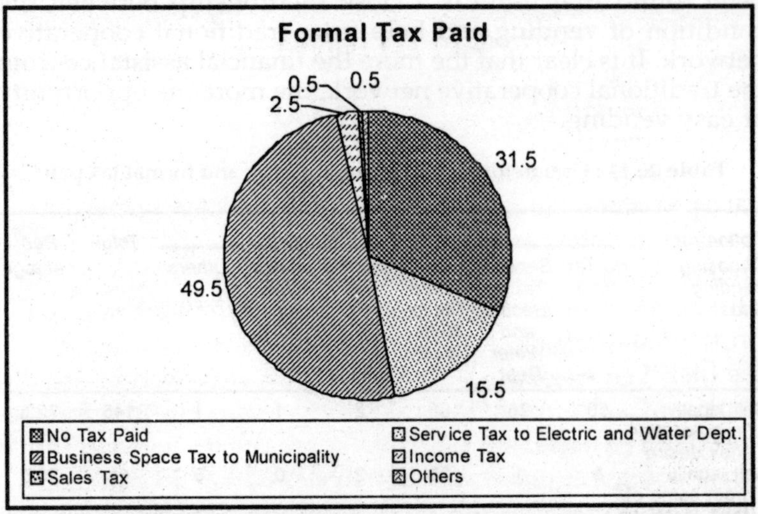

Table 26.11 indicates that 31.5 per cent street vendors do not pay any kind of **formal tax** for their business. Those who pay tax, majority of them (49.5%) pay for their business space tax to the municipalities. Vendors accounting for 15.5 per cent also pay tax to the electricity and water department as service

tax. This table also shows that those who want to sell legally from location they desire, a large number of them also do not pay any kind of tax. Most interestingly those who were evacuated earlier from their vending places, majority of them used to pay tax to the municipality for their business.

Modified Table for Chi-Square Test

Option for Choosing Vending Sites	*Formal Tax Paid*	
	No Tax Paid	*Tax Paid*
Sell legally from location they desire	50	95
Sell legally from some of their locations evacuated earlier	8	33
Relocate them in location chosen by Govt. authorities	5	9

To test whether option for choosing for vending sites and formal tax paid are independent or not.

Chi-Square Results

$$\chi^2_{\text{(observed)}} = 3.444$$

$$\text{p-Value} = 0.179$$

Chi-square test again fails to reject the null hypothesis both at 5 per cent and 1 per cent level of significance. So formal tax paid and options for choosing vending sites are not dependent to each other.

It has been found that none of the vendors have to pay tax on the basis of their income. As majority of the vendors choose their vending sites according to their desire and need not to pay any kind of tax. As most of them are mobile vendors they need not to pay electric and water service tax as well

In this regard, one important aspect is that 55 per cent vendors also do not have to pay any kind of **informal tax,** whereas 34 per cent and 11 per cent of them pay union subscription and other taxes respectively (festival subscription, fees for occupying space of the shop owner, illegal demands of police authorities and anti-social elements from time to time).

From Table 26.12 we see the percentage of street vendors opting for other occupation besides main occupation.

Table 26.12 : Other occupation and monthly income from street vending

Other Occupation Besides Main Occupation	*Monthly Income from Street Vending*							*Total*	*Per-centage*
	Less than Rs. 1000	*Rs. 1000 to Rs. 2000*	*Rs. 2000 to Rs. 3000*	*Rs. 3000 to Rs. 4000*	*Rs. 4000 to Rs. 5000*	*Rs. 5000 to Rs. 6000*	*More than Rs. 6000*		
No	11	64	61	30	3	1	2	172	86
Yes	0	16	11	0	1	0	0	28	14
Total	11	80	72	30	4	1	2	200	100
Percentage	5.5	40	36	15	2	0.5	1	100	

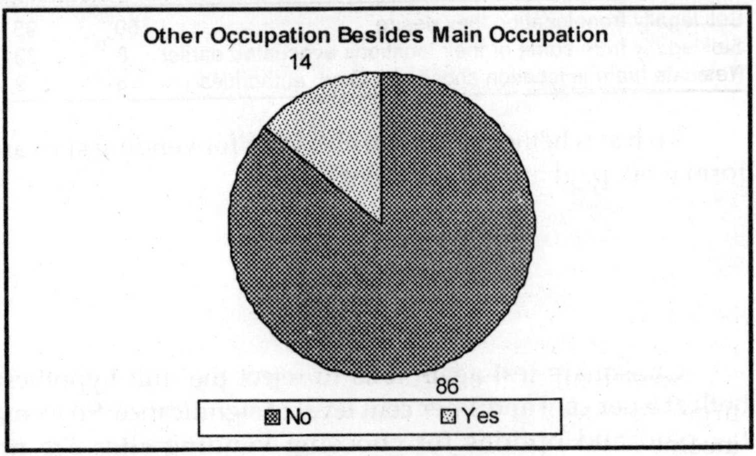

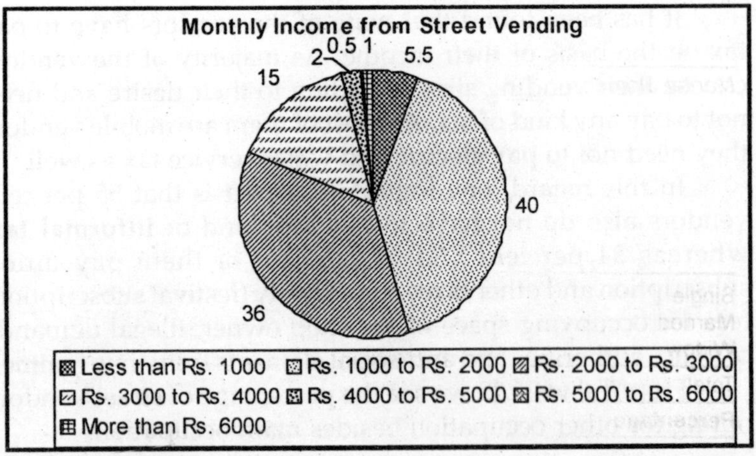

This table ascertains that 86 per cent street vendors do not have other occupation except 14 per cent who all are engaged in some other activities. But most surprisingly, those who earn better in a month have generally no secondary occupation. This is probably they want to concentrate more on their business and their efforts are curved in the single direction, which fetches better earnings.

Modified Table for Chi-Square Test

Other Occupation Besides Main Occupation	*Monthly Income from Street Vending*	
	Up to Rs.2000	*More Than Rs.2000*
No	75	97
Yes	16	12

Chi-Square Results

$$\chi^2_{(observed)} = 1.780$$
$$\text{p-Value} = 0.182$$

Chi-square test above fails to reject the null hypothesis both at level $\propto = .05$ and .01. So other occupations and monthly income from street vending are independent to each other. This happens because the high income groups have neither the urge/necessity to adopt any alternative occupation as the income is adequate enough to maintain their decent living.

Table 26.13 : Marital status and fate of extra income

Marital Status	*Fate of Extra Income*				*Total*	*Per-centage*
	Deposit in Bank/ Post Office	*Purchase More Goods for Ex-panding Business*	*Save in Home for Safety Purpose*	*Others*		
Single	17	2	24	1	44	22
Married	67	5	74	9	155	77.5
Widow	1	0	0	0	1	0.5
Total	85	7	98	10	200	100
Percentage	42.5	3.5	49	5	100	

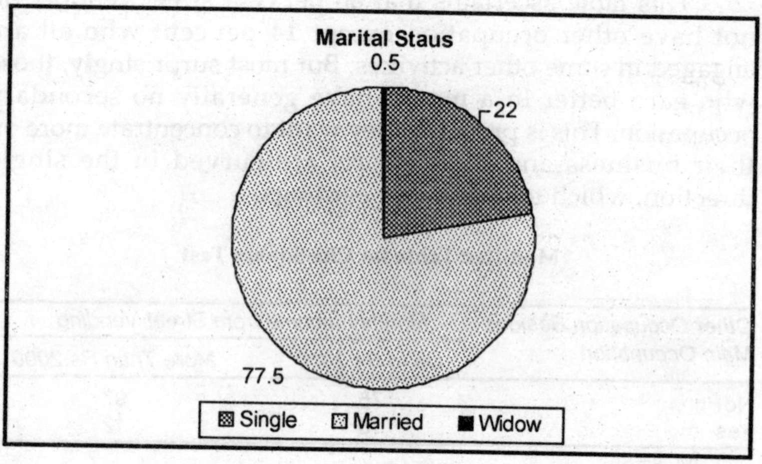

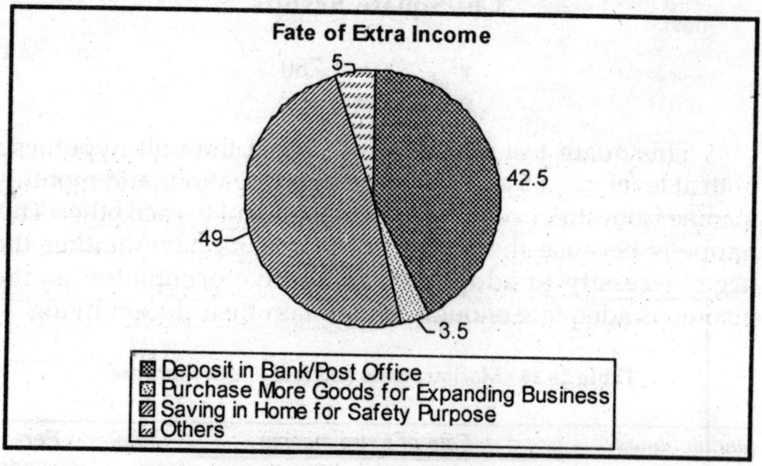

Table 26.13 indicates that 77.5 per cent street vendors are married, and only 22 per cent are single. But hardly any relation between the fate of extra income and marital status of the respondent is found. It clearly indicates from the table that marriage does not create any major impact over the fate of extra income in a sense women would be involved in some productive earning and can supplement to the family income.

Table 26.14 : Activities during financial stress for street vending

Fate of Extra Income	*Activities during Financial Stress Condition for Street Vending*						*Total*	*%*
	No Such Condition	*Borrow from Money Lenders*	*Stop Business and Do Other Work*	*Take Help from Relatives*	*Borrow Money in Mortgage*	*Others*		
Deposit in Bank/Post Office	0	16	4	42	0	23	85	42.5
Purchase more goods for expanding business	0	3	0	4	0		7	3.5
Save in home for safety purpose	0	30	10	42	1	15	98	49
Others	2		3	4		1	10	5
Total	2	49	17	92	1	39	200	100
Percentage	1	24.5	8.5	46	0.5	19.5	100	

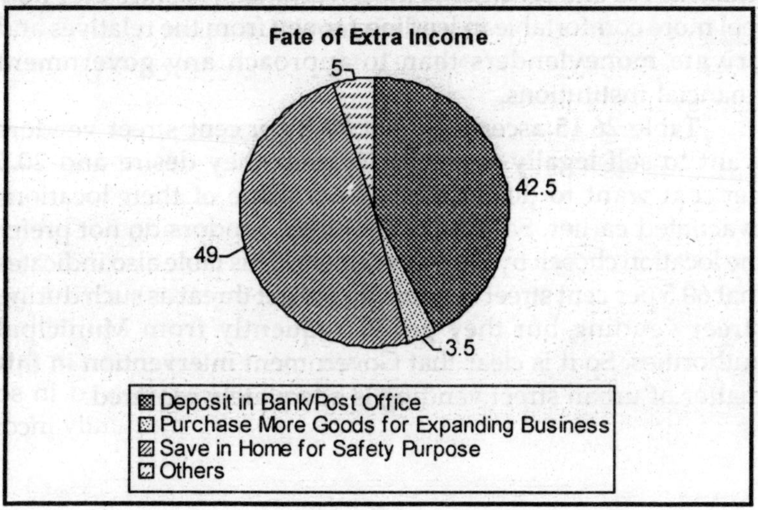

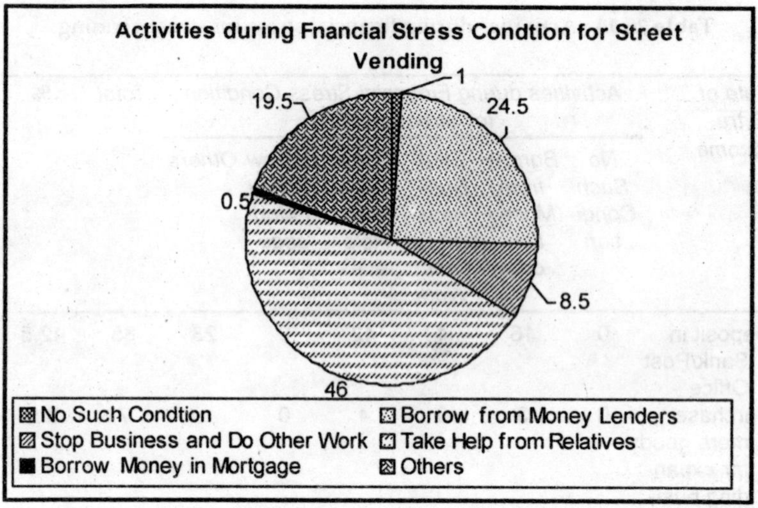

Table 26.14 envisages that 46 per cent street vendors take help from relatives during financial stress and 19.5 per cent manage it differently with lot of difficulties. It is also a matter of fact that a large portion of the street vendors (24.5%) borrow money from private moneylenders. So it clearly states that these street vendors are almost helpless during financial stress. It may happen because they have little awareness of the various financial aid and schemes of the government. Besides they may feel more comfortable in lending money from the relatives and private moneylenders than to approach any government financial institutions.

Table 26.15 ascertains that 72.5 per cent street vendors want to sell legally from the location they desire and 20.5 per cent want to do the same from some of their locations evacuated earlier. So most of the street vendors do not prefer the location chosen by the Government. This table also indicates that 60.5 per cent street vendors do not get threat as such during street vending but they get it frequently from Municipal authorities. So it is clear that Government intervention in this matter of urban street vending is adequately required.

Table 26.15 : Received threatening during business and option for choosing vending sites

Received Threatening during Street Vending	*Option for Choosing Vending Sites*			*Total*	*Percentage*
	Sell Legally from Location They Desire	*Sell Legally from Some of Their Locations Evacuated Earlier*	*Relocate Them in Location Chosen by Government Authorities*		
No Such Threat	101	8	12	121	60.5
Police authorities	5	0	0	5	2.5
Local dadas as Hafta	6	2	0	8	4
Local union members	2	1	0	3	1.5
Municipal authorities	13	25	1	39	19.5
Established shop-keepers	9	4	1	14	7
Others	9	1		10	5
Total	145	41	14	200	100
Percentage	72.5	20.5	7	100	

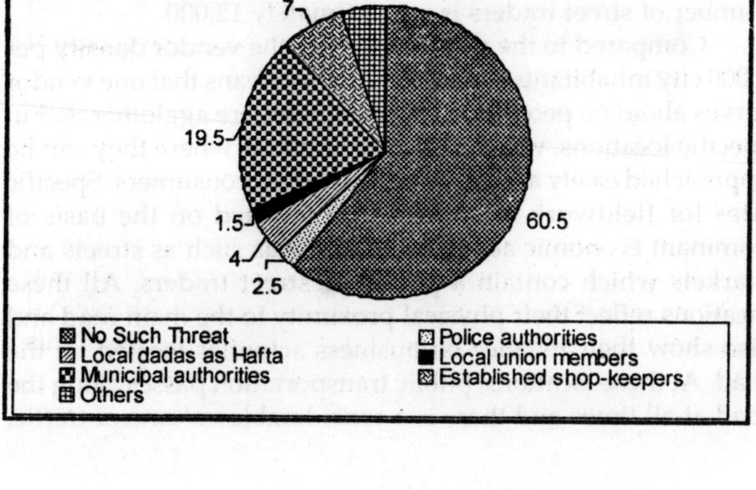

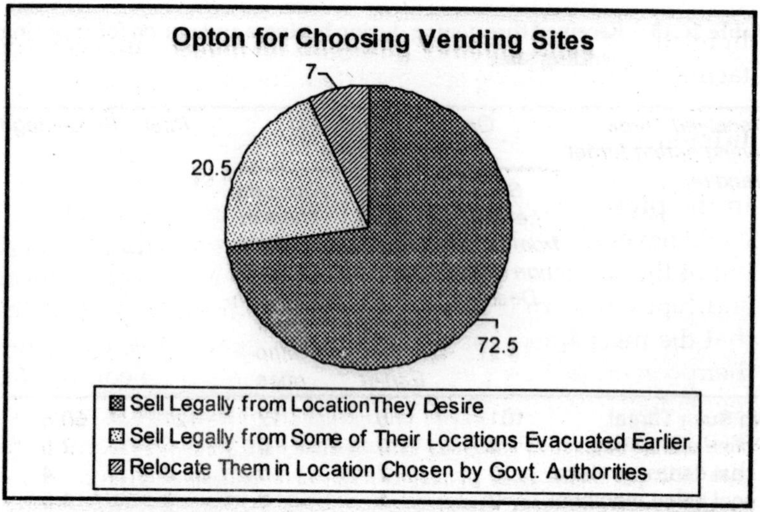

Major Findings and Analysis

It is not possible to determine exact statistics for the urban informal sector in Birbhum district for both Suri and Bolpur subdivisional areas, since recent and extensive survey on this matter are not available. In the case of street enterprises, however, it is possible to figure out their numbers, distribution and some important features. It is a rough estimation that the number of street traders is approximately 12,000.

Compared to the city population, the vendor density per 1,000 city inhabitants is about 15.2. This means that one vendor serves about 66 people. Street enterprises are agglomerated in specific locations, which are close to places where they can be approached easily and favourably by their consumers. Specific sites for fieldwork were therefore selected on the basis of dominant economic activities of the areas such as streets and markets which contain a pocket of street traders. All these locations reflect their physical proximity to the main road and also show their reliance on business activities located on the road. At these locations, public transportation passes along the road at all times and there is a considerable volume of traffic.

In relation to both the central city and the dominant economic facilities, the locations reveal certain marked differences.

Inferences and interventional strategies

In the present scenario, on the basis of research findings, it could never be denied that the urban population do get benefit out of the services rendered by the street vendors of all forms and types and so, it is high time to ponder over and realize that the mechanism for giving them a legal status, extending them certain facilities, specific measures for their control and regulation, equal distribution of resources for self-compliance, recognizing their organization to strengthen and promote for this occupation, their participation in the urban development programmes, rehabilitation avenues for them and mainstreaming their entity and making some arrangement of social security with financial services—must be reviewed with the need of the hour.

The present study has attempted to identify certain dimensions of street vendors where integrated strategy for intervention could be developed. The views of the different stakeholders have been taken into account with high sense of honour and dignity for in-depth understanding of their situation. This study is expected to be good reference in working out future course of action for the development of this disadvantaged population.

Interventional strategies

A. It has been found that the majority of street vendors use bicycle, cart etc. as the conveyance of their vending. But there are many more vendors who have no financial affordability at all to buy any mode of conveyance to sell the goods for their business purpose. Here, government supports in any form, helping hands from banks or some sponsoring agencies come forward to help them out to get any kind of vehicle for their extreme benefit would be a piece of outstanding contribution.

B. As it has been observed that female vendors are hardly encouraged to initiate business of their own. Therefore, this group should have the opportunity to access basic educational facilities, small entrepreneurship training and micro financial support from local banks/ government as well as provision for suitable market place to sell their products.

C. It has been also stated earlier that vendors belong to low income group can hardly spend much of their income in family expenses, as they have to spend money for some other essential purposes. So, in order to give them the opportunity to spend a reasonable amount of their income in family expenses, a small saving and lending scheme could be introduced. This would not only help them to repay debts by easy interest and instalments but also provide a sense of financial security to continue their business without any threats from moneylenders.

D. It has also been pierced through that the steady earning in each week generally increases the monthly income of the street vendors. But, there is a felt necessity of maintaining market price regulated mechanisms of the daily used commodities by the municipal authority to address the issue of consumer friendly market system. It would not only help the consumers in building faith but also enable them to purchase good quality commodities by reasonable price. In other way, this might help the street vendors to maintain steady income and savings as well.

E. It is a proven fact that almost all the vendors belong to low literacy level and tend to opt for multi-occupations as and when required to maintain their livelihood and particularly, so often, when day-to-day vending is affected for whatsoever reason it is. In spite of adherence to multi-occupations they are failing to earn a steady income. Therefore, concern municipal regulated vendor cooperative system could be tailored made to prevent them from such a dismal state of affairs and keep them away from multi-occupations and simply holding vending as their one and single profession to maintain steady life-cycle.

F. It has also been observed that religious disparity and conflict are very much prevalent among the vendors as well as consumers. It needs to be eradicated immediately to bring peace and harmony in the present context of rebellious religious violence across the globe. The fact is that Muslim vendors are not so accepted in Hindu locality because of certain religious bigotry. Therefore, consumer awareness programmes may be launched to address such issues and dispel these static attitudinal and behavioural perceptions.

G. It is also important to see that mostly the street vendors lend money from private moneylenders with an exorbitant rate of interest. In order to protect them from such an exploitative practice a concerted mass awareness programme should be generated by bank, post-office and other government credit institutions. Through these programmes the vendors will be abreast of the benefits of enjoying loan from government enterprises.

H. It is also very clear that the vendors hardly get any assistance for their decent survival from constituted union or government. In this regard, all the unions irrespective of their party affiliation and government must show immense concern for them and try to provide them the means of decent living.

I. It has also been found that this disadvantaged group of people are neither aware of nor they get any guidance about saving money in bank or post-office. Eventually, it is also true that they have very limited scope to save money due to different constraints. So, an initiative could be taken in order to ensure small savings of these vendors in local bank and post-office. The concern banks and post-offices should open a new section for the unorganized sectors to provide them necessary guidance and suggestions and also to inspire them for easy savings with reasonable interest. It has also been realized from the vendor's domain that they need an effective social insurance scheme for future financial security.

J. As female street vendors have less capital to invest in their business, they can be encouraged to form self help groups (SHGs), so that, they can access micro credit facilities to avoid the single investment problem and can invest more capital in order to increase their income on sustainable basis. On the other hand, they have also family obligations and as a result are not in a position to devote much time in vending. This group effort will prove to be highly beneficial for them in terms of equal distribution or family responsibility and productive nurturing of the profession.

K. The crucial issue identified by the research team is the absence of any effective public participation or consultation mechanism in the policy formulation process. Community participation is regarded as key to success for the urban development planning and regularization of public spaces. The formation of forum of urban development stakeholders is needed to increase their participation in the urban development planning. The stakeholders may vary from locations to locations but involvement of street traders associations, academia, mass media, NGOs and other respective local organizations are extremely valuable. The forum can be used as a vehicle for different stakeholders to have access to the policy making process on typical urban development issues in general and on the urban informal sector in particular. While the forum can serve as crucial sources of policy input for local governments, it can act as a public caucus to monitor closely the implementation of new policy regulations.

L. Legislative mechanism is also an important issue which seems to cater in shaping the business environment as well as creating conditions conducive for small-scale and informal business activity in Birbhum district. The special legislation is therefore needed to address adequately and comprehensively the issue of the urban informal sector. There are two existing legislations—(a) **[Section 283 of the IPC**—Danger or obstruction in public way or the line of navigation—whoever, by doing any act or by omitting to take order with any property in his possession or under his charge, causes danger, obstruction or injury to any person in any public way or public line of navigation, shall be punished with fine which may extend to two hundred rupees. The offence punishable under this section is the nuisance of causing obstruction.]; (b) **[Section 34 of the Police Act**—No person shall cause obstruction in any street or public place by—allowing animals or vehicle; leaving any vehicle standing or fastening any cattle in the street or in the public place; using any part of a street or public place as a halting place for vehicles or cattle; leaving any box, bale package or other things whatsoever or upon a street for an unreasonable length of time or contrary to any regulation; by exposing anything for sale or setting out anything for sale in or upon any stall, booth, board, cask and basket or in any other way whatsoever].These two provisions create the contradiction between a legal and illegal vendor. These legislations have no adequate rules to address the issue of street vending comprehensively. They are mainly directed to enforce security and abolition strategy to the urban informal sector without proper considerations of its conditions and contributions. Too narrow emphasis has been given on removal action of street vendors mainly in the name of maintaining social order which result in partial and short-term solution that account to little more than costly and unproductive government distortions. The provisions under the legislations should cover various dimensions ranging from 'stabilizing issue' (e.g. properly formulating permit and licensing procedures, special zoning and time regulation for the urban informal sector operation) to a broader issue of 'supporting' the sector (e.g. provision of suitable workshops sites, adequate and appropriate shelter and infrastructural services and the development of access to appropriate technology and credit schemes).

M. It was remarkably found that all street vendors are not always the poorest of the poor. Economically some are well-off than others. Recognizing such diversity and dynamism of the urban informal sector the need of the hour is to choose the most appropriate intervention planning. Policy should not take a heavy regulatory and 'welfare-based' approach to this sector. Plans to help those amongst the poorest should be differentiated from those amongst the better-off vendors. For example, safety net policies are still vital, particularly to 'surviving' traders living in substandard conditions. However, policies should not be focused only on the provision of social welfare services in a narrow sense. The provision of infrastructural and institutional facilities such as business sites, electricity, licensing and access to appropriate technology and credit at relatively lower cost, are some of the suitable examples for the more 'thriving' micro enterprise needs.

N. Formulation of policies and implementation on street enterprises are the concern of different offices in the district administration with the inherent hierarchical structure and accountability. The number of different bodies involved in this regard makes the intervention strategies burdensome, as they have overlapping jurisdiction and differing priorities as to the resources available. In order to streamline and coordinate the planning and development process as well as to minimize possible conflicts, the policy planning and implementation require a core administrative team that can coordinate a wide range of activities, which cut across traditional government structure.

O. Lastly, it can be mentioned that there are a number of ways in which urban informal workers could be integrated into urban planning. If they pay the costs of registration both transactional and other taxes—urban informal operators would definitely demand for some guarantee that they would receive through the benefits of making their trade as formalized one. These benefits would include:

- the right to work,
- the right to a place from where they would have to work,
- legal rights to property,
- fair prices and wages,
- the right to public services and infrastructure,
- fair and legally enforceable commercial transactions,
- fair and legally enforceable employment relations.

P. The following functional areas or determinants of urban policies are worth mentioning which in turn would help the street vendors for their empowerment:

- regulation of public space,
- framework for legalizing private property,
- provision of infrastructure and services,
- roads, transport and communication,
- marketing and export promotion,
- water, electricity and sanitation,
- regulation of commercial transactions,
- regulation of employment relations.

It is important to remember that the working poor in the urban informal economy need representation in the institutions and processes that determine urban policies and related rules and regulations. Moreover, the urban planners should be quite sensitive, alert and must empathize with the multifarious problems of vendors and put the earnest endeavour to streamline them in the society and give them a prominent status in the world of business and trade and the society at large.

SUGGESTED READINGS

1. Portes, A., Castells, T. and Benton, J. (2003); *Survey Research Methods*, Belmont, California: Wadworth Publishing Company.
2. Suharto, A. (2002); *The Competitive Advantage of Nations*, New York: The Free Press.
3. Thomas, G. (1992); *Economic Reform and Social Sector Development*, Oxford University Press, U.K.
4. UNDP (2000); *Attacking Poverty While Improving the Environment: Towards Win-Win Policy Options*. Poverty and Environment Initiative (Mimeograph).
5. Williams, B. and Windebank, C. (2005); *The Rise and Decline of Nations*, New Haven, Conn: Yale University Press.
6. World Bank (1998); *World Development Report*, New York: Oxford University Press.

27

Best Practices of the Organization towards Building an Enlightened Community through Education

The Experiment of Ramakrishna Mission

With the dawn of independence, India has entered a new phase of social consciousness stimulating voluntary action and a number of organizations have sprung up in the recent past. This is not altogether a new phenomenon of a developing nation. For various reasons these organizations continue to be growing, for the purpose of serving the people in different situations. These organizations have their roots in the philanthropic bodies which are an outcome of innate human goodness for centuries past. Particularly in a country like India, steeped in the tradition of philosophy, of love and humanism, great men build-up great institutions and perpetuated organizations enlisting public cooperation, and also promoting ideas of charity, love and brotherhood. From this philosophy was born the motto of service, around which voluntary organizations have thriven and continue to be thriving even to this day.

Terry Allibund in his book **Catalyst of Development—Voluntary Organizations in India (1983),** reviews briefly India's historical record and its past development successes and failures in the field of PVOs, i.e. what he labels as '**Private Voluntary Organizations**'. According to him, from an historical perspective, India's PVOs have provided a valuable series of unplanned (and largely unanalyzed) socio-economic change experiments. Hatch's work with the YMCA in rural

Kerala, Elmhirst and Tagore's efforts with Bengali Peasants, the early Christian Missionary colonies in the North-West region, Bryane's authoritarian approach to change in Gurgaon District, Gandhiji's programme intended as a model for the rural development of independent India, and Mayer's demonstration of successful social and economic changes at Etawah, are all cases that provide one of the richest sources of insight on appropriate and flexible development methods in India.

During the last decade and a half, there has been a steady spurt in the voluntary organizations and it is rather difficult to arrive at their exact number. However, keeping in view the magnitude of growth of these organizations in recent years, even a conservative rough estimate of the number of voluntary organizations both registered and unregistered in the entire country, may work out to anywhere between 30,000 to 35,000. In other words, the entire structure of voluntary effort depends on the strength and genuineness of these organizations. But, to what extent these organizations have been successful in fulfilling the ideals, the objectives and the aspirations expected of them, is a question.

Brief history of time of voluntary movement in India

Throughout history voluntary organizations have endeavoured towards the cause of the underprivileged section of the society and in the recent years voluntary organizations have been increasingly viewed as an integral part of the process of welfare and development of the country. The terms **Voluntary Action** and **Voluntary Organizations (VOs)** are closely interrelated and are often used interchangeably; in spite of the subtle difference between the two. The former is as old as the history of mankind, referring mainly to informal action undertaken to mitigate the sufferings of the people, whereas the latter, is comparatively a recent and formalized phenomenon.

The history of development of voluntary organizations is linked to the history of voluntary efforts and thereby to the history of **social welfare** and **social reforms** in India. In the process of the evolution of VOs; voluntary efforts, along with the changes in the nature of society, started acquiring formalized structures and methods of functioning, leading to their crystallized manifestation as VOs, and these in recent years have come to be variously classified. Though the last decade has given a broader base to the VOs, but travelling down the memory lane reveals the history of VOs to be an interesting chapter in the field of human development.

Though the conceptual roots of voluntarism can be traced to the functioning of the social institutions in the ancient and medieval periods, we focus our study to the modern period only, i.e. after the 19th century. The history of voluntary movement in India therefore can be classified into five phases for simplicity of our understanding.

Age of Social Reforms (1800-1900)

The initiation of the social reform movements began with the culmination of a process of assimilation of the ideas from Western renaissance, socio-political and socio-religious movements, Western ideas and Christian faith. The establishment of the Church in British India, made legal by the Charter Act of 1913, led to the expansion of missionary work **in a big way especially in the remote and secluded tribal tracts of India.**

Social reform movements gained momentum with the percolation of foreign ideas of **liberty, equality** and **fraternity** which gradually blossomed into the **Indian Renaissance Movement** enriched with the contributions of stalwarts like Raja Rammohun Roy, Ishwar Chandra Vidyasagar, Michael Madhusudan Dutta, Swami Dayanand Saraswati, Annie Besant, Keshab Chandra Sen and others. A number of groups/associations/sabhas emerged during this phase marking the era of change and reform in various aspects of social life specially related to education and women. Some of these are the Bramho Samaj (1828), Royal Asiatic Society (1834), Paramhansa Sabha (1849), Sarvajanik Sabha (1871), Prarthana Sabha (1872), Arya Samaj (1875), Widow Marriage Association

(1850), Arya Mahila Samaj (1868), Ramakrishna Mission (1897), Theosophical Society and Indian National Congress (1885) and Indian Social Conference (1887). One of the most important landmarks at this time was the formulation of the Societies Registration Act, 1860, which is an act for registering literacy, scientific and charitable societies.

A number of periodicals also started reinforcement of reformistic thoughts like the Darpan (1832), Digdarshan (1840), Prabhakar (1841), Dayanodaya (1842), and Tattwabodhini Patrika (1843). The main aim of these organizations etc. and magazines was to bring about social change, spread of education, improving the condition of women, abolition of *'Sati'*, widow remarriage, increasing the age of marriage, improving the condition of lower castes etc.

Socio-Political Awakening (1900-1946)

Voluntary movement gained momentum after the failure of the 'first war of independence'. The British policy of systematic plundering of renewable and non-renewable resources and the creation of a system like developing port cities, establishment of communication, creation of a stratum of middle class for subjugation etc. created a system catering and furthering British Economy, a part and parcel of its expansionist policy. The combined impact of all these led to the *socio-political awakening* and *consolidation* among the *intelligentsia* and this flowed through the *institutional movements*. Ramakrishna Mission (1898), Mumbai Presidency Social Reform Association (1897) were also formed during this period. The outreach of these movements has transcended the linguistic and administrative boundaries of their region. Pure political organizations as well as literary and educational associations started emerging necessitating to the development of an influential vernacular press on one hand and beginning of alternative (nationalist) education on the other. This phase also saw the birth of the working class organizations. The Indian National Congress came up as an official platform for the growing national consciousness in 1885.

The impact of the First and Second World War necessitated the upliftment of the rural poor. Gandhi's involvement into *Champaran Satyagraha* (1917) and later on his famous *Dandi March* (1930) aimed at his goal of *Purna Swaraj* which ultimately started into *a mass movement—a non-violent civil disobedience movement.*

A number of voluntary experiments for upgrading the condition of the poor started during this phase, e.g. Sriniketan, Gurgaon, Martandum, Mumbai, Sevagram etc. Tagore, Brayne, Spenser, Hatch, Quaker Groups belonging to both governmental and non-governmental agencies, came forward on societal change.

The major factor influencing voluntary action has been the successful attempt of channelising the voluntary spirit for political action and mass mobilization for the struggle for independence and new problems resulting from the onslaught of industrialization and consequent urbanization. The partition of Bengal in 1905 acted as a catalyst to the national movement. In the initial phases there was a contradiction between Bal Gangadhar Tilak who stressed on freedom and others like Ranade who emphasized on social reforms. The resolution of this problem occurred with the path showed by Gandhiji who emphasized that *freedom struggle* and work for *rural reconstruction* should go hand in hand to attain Swaraj. Social figures like Gokhale, Gandhi, and Tagore emphasized the rural development and reconstruction. Together with the work of Christian missionaries furthered educational and health facilities. This period also saw the growth of *sectoral organizations* of different ideological shades within the National Movement. All India Youth Congress, Kishan Sabha, the radical group of Chandra Sekhar Azad, i.e. Hindustan Socialist Republic Association. The concept of living allowance of Christian missionaries fostered the idea of meeting the living expenses of the voluntary worker and hence the concept of payment to voluntary workers came into existence.

An analysis of the voluntary experiments during the pre-independence period can be summarized briefly as (a) initiated in remote and interior villages; (b) pioneering and experimental in nature; (c) trying to strike a balance between social and economic development; and (d) focusing on leadership development and peoples participation. In spite of limited success, these models were later adopted by the government of India after 1950.

Post-Independence Era of Nation-Building (1947-1960)

The beginning of the 1950s brought in an era of *nation building* where the voluntary action based nation builders joined together with the government's initiatives. This resulted in extension work in agriculture, health, community development, governmentalization of *khadi* and village industries, establishment of training and higher educational institutes like Tata Institute of Social Sciences (TISS) in Mumbai. During this phase, the Indian Government began to promote and strengthen VOs through its different grants-in-aid programmes and formation of Central Social Welfare Board in the early 1950s. The development of VOs has not been uniform. In terms of number the growth has picked up during the period (1942-1955) due to the motivation provided by Gandhi and Vinoba Bhave. After 1955, the growth slackened due to the introduction of the Community Development Programme in 1952. The developments of VOs have also not been uniform geographically. Places where social reform and political movements were strong saw the development of more organizations involving a large number of voluntary works. On the other hand, places, which were not socially motivated, had an inadequate number of organizations and a smaller number of voluntary workers.

Period of Concerned and Diversified Voluntary Action (1960-1980)

There was a spurt in the growth of the VOs again 1965 onwards, due to deteriorating rural conditions, increasing unemployment; and consequently a growing realization on the part of some people especially youth to resist suppression through organized efforts, impact of Naxalite and JP movements etc. During the late 1960s, the country was caught up in dual crisis of economic stagnation and political instability. It was at this stage that alternative and integrated rural development began to be experimented with. The late 1960s and the 1970s saw a rapid growth and development of servicing and consultancy agencies, funding agencies. Especially international organizations played an important role in the formation of many of these organizations. VOs also realized that the government's chosen 'growth pole' development model ushering a growth through the process of 'trickle down' system did not do well. From the mid-seventies the desire to further strengthen the activities of grassroots organizations through coordination and to form close links with their respective client groups has prompted some of the servicing and consultancy organizations to form coalitions.

The important developments during this phase were the increasing realization that community development through government mechanism and through centralized schemes is not possible. The VOs during this phase also started a critical evaluation of the government policies. During this phase **Foreign Contribution Regulation Act** was passed in 1976 preceded by the **Income Tax Act, 1961** both affecting the voluntary sectors. It was being increasingly realized by many VOs that without peoples' participation in the development process, development was not possible; and therefore, they started mobilizing people; which later on emerged as peoples' movement.

During this phase more focused work with target groups, landless labourers, tribals, small farmers, women, scheduled castes/tribes, *dalits* etc., also became the programme of voluntary work. With the growth in number and scope of voluntary organizations, sectorial specialization in health, agriculture, education, literacy, etc. also gained momentum during this period. This phase saw the emergence of the ideas about conscientization and peoples' participation.

The Genesis of Ram Krishna Mission

The Ram Krishna Mission was initially established in Kolkata on 1st May, 1897 by the indomitable leadership of Swami

Vivekananda, the most passionate disciple of Sri Ramakrishna. On the other hand, the Ram Krishna Math (or Baranagar Math as it was called at that time) was established in September 1886 within two months of the passing away of Sri Ramakrishna. Again the inspiration came from Swamiji. Both had its face based on the divine philosophy of Ramakrishna.

During his visit and series of religious lectures in Western world Swamiji realized the need of an organization and through which the organized service—spiritual, mental and material could be provided to the people. After his return from the West he had made a sojourn to Darjeeling to recuperate his shattered health due to his long stay in Europe.

He took with him Swami Brahmananda and a lay disciple of Sri Ramakrishna, Sri Girish Chandra Ghosh, for consultation on the shape and size of the organization to be formed. After his return from Darjeeling he called a meeting at the house of Balaram Bose, an ardent disciple of Ramakrishna. His proposal was unanimously supported. Consequently, the organization under the appellation of **'Ramakrishna Mission Association'** was inaugurated with both householders and *sannyasins* as its members and office-bearers. The programmes and activities of Ramakrishna Mission are propelled by the monks of the Ramakrishna Order. Let us briefly gloss over the very essence of Sri Ramakrishna's mission of life and his perception towards the world of humanity and attainment of God; on the basis of which Ramakrishna Mission was established.

1. The genesis of the Ramakrishna Mission lies in the spiritual practices, realizations and revelations (*sadhana*) of Sri Ramakrishna and the spiritual traditions of India as revived by him. The following facts in support of this contention may be cited:

   (a) The Trust Deed, the Rules and Regulations, aims and objects of Ramakrishna Mission—as drawn up by Swami Vivekananda—clearly state that the practice and preaching of the ideas and ideals that had been illustrated in the life of Sri Ramakrishna for working out one's own liberation and for the welfare of the world are the sole concern of the Mission.

(b) The Mission was started by Swami Vivekananda for spreading the religious ideal of Sri Ramakrishna by interpreting the scriptures in the light of the great Master's life and realizations and with his idea of service to humanity looking upon human beings as images of God, nay as God himself.

2. Demonstration of truth and God-realization or self-realization was the goals of his life. All activities of life are regulated by moral and spiritual principles. He also believed as well as practiced in serving all beings, looking upon them as God.

3. He found that all ways of *sadhana*, all religions for that matter, are like so many paths leading to the same God, called by different names—God, Brahman, Allah, and so on. According to him 'as many faiths, so many paths', and pleaded with the followers of different religions to love and respect each other as fellow travellers to the same goal.

4. He preached a nice blend of four principal ways of *sadhana*, or four *yogas* for getting the proximity of God—**indiscrimination, divine love or devotion, meditation and unselfish and God-dedicated action.**

5. Unlike the other spiritual organizations of the nineteenth century like the Brahmo Samaj, Arya Samaj, or Prarthana Samaj (each of which represented only one aspect of the Indian spiritual tradition), the Ramakrishna Mission and movement reverberated all the age-old spiritual traditions of India in condensed manner.

6. The role of Sri Ramakrishna in the genesis of the organizational shape of the Mission—his divine revelation—bringing together and training his selected disciples.

7. The young monastics of Mission used to live a life of total austerity, meditation, study and prayer. They used to worship Ramakrishna as his living presence.

8. The tearful prayer of the Holy Mother (Sarada Devi, Ramakrishna's wife) reveals not only her affection and compassion but also her clear vision of what the Ramakrishna order was going to be. She wanted it to be an Order where monks would work for their own spiritual liberation according

to the Master's teachings, and simultaneously cater to the needs of the afflicted and downtrodden people seeking solace.

9. The devotion, sacrifice and contribution of the disciples of Ramakrishna were also an enlightening mark for the growth and prosperity of the Mission.

10. Lastly, Vivekananda's wandering experience gathered from the East and West was the final contributory factor behind the scintillating development of the Mission.

To conclude this aspect of the chapter, the author would like to mention here is that today's R.K. Mission is an outcome of Ramakrishna Movement. According to the literature available in the field of social sciences and especially in sociology the movement must satisfy the following characteristics:

(a) Leadership,
(b) Participation by a large number of people,
(c) Ideology, and
(d) Organization.

All these four characteristics of a movement are present in the Ramakrishna Movement. The Movement is inspired and powered by the Holy Trio—Sri Ramakrishna, Holy Mother and Swami Vivekananda—who also form the common goal and ideal for all the members of the movement.

R. K. Mission as a spiritual organization—its mission and vision

Sometimes, R.K. Mission is mistaken for a social welfare organization. Certainly, it is engaged in different types of social services and social work activities, but basically it is a spiritual organization. Its object is to help people attain self-realization and also to help uplift human beings. The oneness of things is the essence of Vedanta. The world is one, and so also, all humanity is one. God is everywhere and in everything. The work is worship. Whatever the Mission does, does it for God. Mission love and worship the poor as God. The Mission preaches Swamiji's three insights or three-fold vision on the basis of which the Mission attains its goals:

1. The first insight was into the true meaning and purpose of Sri Ramakrishna's life.
2. The second was into the real cause of India's downfall and the means of uplifting her.
3. Swamiji's third vision was about India's spiritual contribution to world culture.

So, spirituality is the main activity of the Mission intermingled with social work activities. Some of the spiritual activities undertaken by the Mission on the basis of three fold vision of Swamiji as mentioned above are briefly discussed below. These also reflect the true vision and mission of the organization.

(a) Spreading a spiritual renaissance

It is the spirituality which is maintaining the integrity and solidarity of Indian culture over last five thousand years. The advent of Ramakrishna and birth of Swamiji has rejuvenated the Indian culture and this has also led to efflorescence in other departments of national life and culture. This phenomenon has been described as **'spiritual renaissance'**.

(b) Maintaining the spiritual vigour of the nation

In order to prevent the degradation of national vigour and culture, the spiritual vigour of the nation has to sharpen not by reading and talking but by the spiritual practices of the monks and lay devotees of Ramakrishna order.

(c) Spiritual guidance and counselling

Ramakrishna has generated a new wave of interest in spiritual life of India. By opening the channels of spiritual power through initiation and by giving guidance and counselling regarding spiritual life, the Mission has been rendering a form of spiritual services which is in no way less important than the various forms of social service rendered by Mission.

(d) Counteracting forces of degradation

According to eminent historians, sociologists from time to time have shown that, when sensuality, indulgence in luxury, consumerism and indolence dominate a society as a result of increase in wealth and power, that civilization undergoes decline. In modern times the situation has become worse because of the dominance of atheism and materialism in the minds of people and the rising tide of immorality, violence, neuroses, drug addiction, etc., in society. By disseminating spiritual knowledge through books and in other forms, the Mission is counteracting forces of degradation.

(e) Unification of Hinduism

Hinduism is a vast and complex socio-religious tradition with many schools of thoughts. It is Ramakrishna's openness of approach; Mission serves as a great unifying force in Hinduism. Mission is the only non-political, purely spiritual organization which represents the whole of Hinduism.

(f) Harmony of religions

Ramakrishna believes in harmony of religions so as Mission too. 'As many faiths, so many paths' is not only propagated by the monks of Ramakrishna order through books, but also put it into practice in their community life by celebrating the birthdays of the founders of different religions, and often conduct interreligious conferences. The devotees come from different communities also.

(g) National integration

'Unity in diversity' is the sole characteristic of Indian culture. Diversity of culture, religion, caste, race and so on are unique. Ramakrishna Mission has its branches all-over India as well as in abroad even in the remotest corner. Monks of different culture come and stay there and in this fashion they bring about social and cultural unity at national level. The Mission is trying to retrieve the national integration without any propaganda but by practice itself.

(h) Rejuvenation of monasticism

The very essence of new monastic life was designed by Ramakrishna and Swamiji retaining the best in the ancient Indian monastic tradition but adapts it to the conditions and needs of present-day society. The new ideal emphasizes inner purity and renunciation and not outer show. It aims at all-round development of personality by the practice of complete austerity.

(i) Building an enlightened community

Swamiji wanted to have community of devotees who are inspired by the ideals of Ramakrishna and have developed the potency to practice it. Swamiji also wished to have a close interaction between the monks and the devotees to discuss various social issues which are pertinent in today's context. These discussions are devoid of prejudices of caste, religion etc. and leading to spiritual development and self-actualization.

Contemporary relevance of Ramakrishna Mission as a voluntary organization

At the start of the new millennium, non-governmental organizations (NGOs), along with others, share a sense of excitement about new possibilities, tempered by widespread anxiety about the future. The excitement stems from the quickly expanding opportunities for civic action that global trends are creating; the anxiety arises from the increasingly critical questions being asked about the role of development NGOs will play in the future.

Confronting globalization begins and ends at the grassroots level, where NGOs are developing strategies to help disadvantaged people address their position in global markets and play a creative role in reshaping economic forces. They are improving the endowments of the people, enabling them to compete more effectively and achieve a basic level of education, voice, and equality of rights. This continues the traditional NGO role of developing skills, confidence, and forms of association and improving access to credit, services, and economic and educational opportunities, but also involves a systematic attempt to link different levels and socio-economic sectors.

So, being a voluntary organization the Mission is making a stupendous progress in its various fields of activities and educational upliftment is worth mentioning. Through the level of education the Mission wants to create a band of men and women who would combine in their lives the spiritual idealism of the East and the material practicality of the West. Mission's aim in starting various educational institutions to teach so-called secular subjects like modern sciences, technology, vocational-oriented sciences, arts, English etc. on the one hand, and the so-called spiritual subjects like the ancient Upanisads, Sanskrit, Vedic literature, etc., on the other, is to create a complete human being, all-round and fully developed in three 'h's—**heart, head** and **hand**. Here is the significance of Ramakrishna Mission which is a faith based organization and ideologically very different from other organizations; as well as an instrument of change in the society which is surrounded by innumerable number of problems vehemently affecting the very structure of Indian society.

Relevance of social work profession as perceived by the Mission

Education like other areas of human life, such as agriculture, the public sector or the economy is being subjected to the forces of change as taking place in our modern society. Traditionally, education was perceived as a social process leading to liberal values and a human concern responding to social needs. Scholasticism was a desirable goal, the context was the human society and learning and knowledge could become an end in itself. These values are replaced by 'instrumental values'—education is to be perceived as an investment where returns become important. Marketable skills, technical knowledge, specialization and a high degree of flexibility become the *sine qua non* of the world of education.

Social work as a tiny component of the educational sector is subject to the same forces. The R.K. Mission has currently opened up a university named "Vivekananda University" which is trying to impart knowledge on various social science subjects as well as marketable and vocational courses which fetch a greater size of employment. Introducing social work courses at master's level with the intention of broadening of social work education as well as enhancing human potentiality required for rendering services to the mankind through innumerable educational inputs is worth mentioning. The whole course curriculum and fieldwork component has been fabricated and designed to the current needs and problems of the society and students are trained on the line by which they can develop required skills and expertise to address all those issues affecting our society as well as emphasize on concerted action for the development of the nation. So this attempt by the Mission to integrate the professional social work in the domain of NGO sector has been a great success and highly applaudable.

Best essence and strategies adopted by Ramakrishna Mission in the field of education

The root cause of misery is ignorance which is called *avidya* in Vedanta philosophy. So, to encounter with misery, one has to destroy and dispel the elements of ignorance. How does ignorance go? It is sheer by acquiring knowledge. Ignorance is identified as darkness and knowledge as light. So the light of knowledge vanishes the darkness of ignorance. To quote Sri Ramakrishna:

> "Those, whose ignorance has been destroyed by the awakening of knowledge, have their knowledge shining as bright as the light of the sun."

So, knowledge is sacred and this should be imparted, amassed and disseminated among the people for their enlightment and to explore the meaning of life and this existing world. R.K. Mission has taken the oath of carrying out the very essence and ethos of Ramakrishna's philosophy of life and education. It is also interesting to see at this juncture a glimpse of Swamiji's idea of education which is very much pertinent when we talk about Mission's contribution to the field of education.

The method and process by which knowledge is traditionally acquired by a disciple from a teacher is called education. Without drawing a line of demarcation between superior and inferior knowledge, Swamiji magnified two types of knowledge—*lower and higher* (*objective and subjective contents*) and he was in favour of synthesis of two which could really bring the totality of education and make the mankind out of danger of ignorance.

All materialistic sciences have *objective reality* which is perceived, seen, and experienced. Spiritual science, called the Science of all sciences in the Upanishads, cultivated in the East, deals with the subjective reality, which is the Perceiver, the Seer, the Experiencer. The objective reality is known as the field of knowledge. The *subjective reality* is considered to be the Knower of this field.

To actualize Swamiji's aim of education, the Mission has taken up multifarious educational strategies for the upliftment of all sections of people which include:

1. *Colleges*: imparting graduate and post-graduate education in science, humanities (including languages), commerce, and vocation-oriented subjects, with facilities for higher research at the doctoral/post-doctoral level.
2. *Schools*: primary, secondary, higher secondary levels which are imparting general education.
3. *Upholding and imparting knowledge of the Sanskrit literature*: As Swamiji visualized "**The conception of Vedanta must come out, must remain not only in the**

forest, not only in the cave, but they must come out to work at the bar and the bench, in the pulpit, and in the cottage of the poor man, with the fishermen that are catching fish, and with the students that are studying. In one word, I want to make them popular. I want to bring out these ideas and let them be the common property of all, of every man in India, whether he knows Sanskrit language or not". It was realized by Swamiji that unless Sanskrit is taught, the spiritual and mythological literature of Indian culture and tradition loose its flavour. So Sanskrit language was an impediment of spreading the ideals of Ramakrishna. The Mission is still trying its best to spread Sanskrit language at every level right from primary and secondary education to graduate and post-graduate level. Yet, it is long way to go. Some work in imparting Sanskrit education is being done in Palai and Kalady, both in Kerala. No better place could be imagined for this work than Kerala, the birth place of the great Shankaracharya.

4. *Vedic schools*: which are imparting Vedic education at the secondary/higher secondary level.
5. *Schools of Languages*: imparting knowledge of language skills in Indian and foreign languages.
6. *Polytechnics*: imparting technical education in various branches of engineering at the diploma level. Librarianship training centre imparting training in librarianship to rural trainees.
7. *Junior technical and industrial schools*: imparting technical and vocational education and training at the secondary/higher secondary level.
8. *Agricultural Schools/Institutes*: imparting education/training in agriculture and horticulture at the diploma level.
9. *Teachers' Training Colleges/Institutes*: imparting teachers' training at the basic/graduate/post-graduate level, with facilities for higher research in education at the doctoral/post-doctoral level.

10. *Students' Homes and Hostels*: attached to residential schools/colleges/institutes run by the Mission as well as by others, attempted to be modelled on the **guru-griha-vasa system**.
11. *Orphanages*: housing destitute children and grown-up students, attempted to be modelled on the **guru-griha-vasa system**.
12. *Computer Training Centres*: imparting computer education and training to school and college students.
13. *Blind Boys' Academy and Centre for Visually Handicapped*: offering general education as well as training in music, agriculture, and several other crafts to the blind and visually handicapped boys.
14. *Rural Development/Social Workers' Training Institutes*: imparting education for rural development work.
15. *Social Welfare and Integrated Rural Development Institutes*: conducting research and evaluation studies, and integrated rural development projects, apart from giving training courses.
16. There are some other short-term training courses (tourism, management courses, advertising, media study, development planning, women's studies, environmental studies, rural management, human rights and human resource management) run by the Mission in tune with the demand of the changing society.

Pedagogical model of R.K. Mission

Rendering services to the people is the main field of activity of the Mission. It is based on the motto "**For one's own liberation, and for the welfare of the world**" and the two cardinal principles of Swamiji as propounded—(1) there is no distinction between the sacred and the secular—all work is sacred; (2) service to man is service to God. The Mission has always been trying to adopt intervention models on the basis of these two principles as envisaged by Swamiji.

Swami Vivekananda worked out a detailed strategy for the educational emancipation of the masses. His principles of action in this respect are based on the following ideas and which are also the very ethos of social work practice:

(a) Each soul being potentially divine, given the opportunity, everybody can manifest himself or herself to a level of excellence.
(b) People should be given help not by way of charity but by way of service to them as embodiment of God.
(c) The best way to help people is to educate them so that they may work out their own salvation.
(d) Education has to be meaningful in the sense that it will enable the people to make use of their resources both human and natural to the fullest extent possible.
(e) For the purpose of educational development an attempt should be made to use both indigenous technology available within the country as well as the best possible science and technology available in the Western world.
(f) No development can be sustained unless a sustainable organization is built to carry on different activities.

Development theology of the Mission is based on research, training, retraining and spiritual orientation and re-orientation of key functionaries, without which field operational programme for educational development can succeed. The Mission is always imbibing this spirit and providing various inputs on human resource development which could be smoothly adopted to the development strategies of the Mission. The Mission caters to the need of the functionaries as well as to the personnel from the state and the country. Despite different curriculum and training, there exists a common bond and relationship facilitating interchangeability of the faculties and the technical know-how among its various institutes. Institutions may adopt different mode of functioning, but all have the common goal of human development in its ultimate form.

The pedagogical methodology was adopted for delivering services on the following basis:

- the student's need for self-expression and their need to communicate their feelings,

- the need to develop a positive self-concept,
- the need for a nourishing atmosphere where the students can relate to the teachers without fear,
- the need to find learning exciting, full of fun and relevant, and
- the need to be treated as a complete human being.

For the trained organizer teachers of the various institutions, orientation classes are held once a month to refresh them with their subjects and techniques of joyful learning including basic knowledge in first aid, health and hygiene, environment awareness. The learners are to sustain the programme with parental intervention; mothers are encouraged to form *Self Help Groups* to augment their income. The innovative part of the curriculum of primary and upper primary classes are complete integration of vocational education courses, enrichment of mental ability and recreational activities. This has resulted in the people adopting a positive approach on their future work life.

To enable the implementers to work out a systematic approach to carry forward the programme in life skill education all the targeted areas are intensively surveyed and need assessment made with the help of community participation at primary, secondary and tertiary level. *Participatory Rural Appraisal* (*PRA*) technique as well as *Venn diagram* is often used for eliciting community participation as an interventional method. Working papers on all the areas surveyed and need assessment made have been prepared and exercises on the modalities to be adopted to implement the programme successfully.

Cultural programme, quiz, drawing and paintings, educational tours, staging of drama, annual sports are organized regularly with students' participation for their overall development. Another regular feature is to award prizes for educational and co-curricular activities to sustain high level of motivation to perform better. *Bibliotherapy, play therapy, fantasy, creativity* are some of the important therapeutic interventional strategies also used as and when required by the competent, professional social workers specially with children group to sustain their interest in learning and productive channelization of their respective potentialities.

Conclusion

As we have restricted our discussion only on educational activities, but the Mission has spread its activities in other fields also—spiritual and cultural development, rural welfare, tribal welfare, women's uplift, and relief and rehabilitation work done during disasters caused by famine, flood, plague, fire, earthquake and landslide, cyclone, drought and cholera. So Ramakrishna Mission as a faith based organization is tirelessly heading towards the nation's all-round development through preaching, practicing and upholding Ramakrishna's and Vivekananda's ideology, mission and vision of life.

SUGGESTED READINGS

1. Swami Gambhirananda; (1989); *Apostles of Sri Ramakrishna*, Advaita Ashrama, Kolkata.
2. Swami Budhananda; (1983); *The Ramakrishna Movement*, Advaita Ashrama, Kolkata.
3. *Four Decades of Literacy Efforts by Lokasiksha Parishad;* (2005); Ramakrishna Mission Ashram; Narendrapur, South 24-Parganas.
4. His Eastern and Western Disciples, (1989) *The Life of Swami Vivekananda;* Kolkata: Advaita Ashram.
5. *The Story of Ramakrishna Mission* (*Swami Vivekananda's Vision and Fulfillment*); (2006) Advaita Ashram, Kolkata.
6. Swami Gambhirananda; (1957); *History of Ramakrishna Math and Ramakrishna Mission*; Advaita Ashram, Kolkata.
7. Romain Rolland; (1984); *The Life of Ramakrishna*; Advaita Ashram, Kolkata.
8. Swami Saradananda; (1984); *Sri Ramakrishna: The Great Master;* Madras: Ramakrishna Math, Mylapore.
9. *The Gospel of Sri Ramakrishna* (1980); Madras: Ramakrishna Math, Mylapore.
10. Vide the Presidential Address of Swami Shivananda (1926); in the *Ramakrishna Math and Mission Convention*, Howrah: Ramakrishna Math.

28

Globalization and Social Work as a Profession
A Synergy and Implications

Social work as a profession

It includes a diverse, complex, multidimensional model of professional practice. It includes intervention models that deal with individuals and households, with communities, with organizations, and with social policy.

Social workers work in all types of communities, serving individuals and households from all economic levels, from all types of cultural and social backgrounds. One of the major changes from the society of 100 years ago is that the work settings of social workers are not limited primarily to non-profit agencies, as they were during the first two decades of this century. Social work includes practitioners in private practices and those providing professional services in for-profit firms. Social work practice is not limited to one type of community or one economic group of service users.

Social work professional practice does include the critical analysis of social policies that impact the lives of individuals, families, and communities. In order to increase the impact of such analyses by social workers, there must be such greater attention to the economic dimensions of such policies. But social work is not primarily a profession of policy analyses or a profession of full-time policy advocates (Abbott, 2002).

Social work shares the processes of policy analysis, and social action and advocacy, with many other groups in society.

Social workers are predominantly direct service practitioners who provide helping services directly to individuals and households, as well as to groups and communities.

Thematic introduction to the issue

Events of the latter half of the 20th century have demonstrated that, indeed, we do live in a global village where human needs and events cannot be viewed in national isolation. Therefore, in this global village we must begin the practice of **global social work** (Barclay, 2006).

As a social work educator, researcher and practitioner, I have seen tremendous impact of globalization in my fields of operation. Whether working in community organizing, child protection, HIV/AIDS advocacy, women empowerment, health, urban planning, disaster management or any other field of practice at the local, national or international level, the changing world economy has made its impact felt. At the same time, improved international communication and exchange as well as phenomenal development of information technology have given me an opportunity to meet many professional socials workers from South-East Asia, South Africa and Europe. These expensive and valuable experiences have opened the eyes of the author with the conviction that social work practice around the world will be forced to adjust to and sometimes resist changing socio-economic circumstances. It will be challenging to encounter with the forces of globalization and to developing models of practice that are able to address emerging social issues. Impacts and responses will differ according to cultural and political contexts but the fact of globalization is held in common. Opportunities are present but so are dangers.

In the context of globalization and social work, **International Federation of Social Workers** (IFSW) conducted a study (2000). The sample was selected to represent different regions of the world, fields of practice and gender. Replies were received from twenty-five of these practitioners. Among respondents were social workers practicing in a wide variety of fields such as:

- women's rights
- community development and empowerment
- social administration
- family, couple and individual counselling
- gerontology
- social work education and training
- urban planning
- environment
- health education
- community and international economics
- medical and hospital social work
- HIV/AIDS
- refugee issues
- domestic violence
- labour issues
- mental health
- cross-cultural perspectives

Replies of the respondents had opened up various issues circumscribing the advent of globalization and how social work as a profession reacting to this. The issues which were identified are the following and the discussion in the rest of the chapter is based on these reactive and emerging dimensions—(a) how social workers experience globalization and social work practice; (b) has this phenomenon affected the issues faced in practice; (c) have social workers' analyses of social issues been influenced; (d) have the strategies used by social workers to address social issues changed; and (e) whether the practitioners like my view of the role of social work itself.

Concept of social work and globalization: From practice based

It is important to understand that the definition of Social Work itself differs greatly across cultural contexts (Payne, 2001). The professionalized conception of the 'social worker'—especially the social worker who provides individual clinical services—originated in Western industrialized countries but most societies have always had a role for individuals who worked to improve conditions for their fellow community members. While clinical practice may be more characteristic of industrialized countries, community organizers in Western countries have learned many of their strategies and skills from their peers in developing countries.

Verscheden (2005) suggests the following as underlying social work values. Out of these last three values are held commonly by all cultures and societies. The first one makes a lot of differences across cultures.

1. Primary importance and dignity of the individual.
2. Respect and appreciation for differences.
3. Commitment to social justice and the well-being of all in society.
4. Willingness to persist despite frustration.

Another difference raised by Tsang (2007) is that while Western social workers have traditionally separated theory and practice, in South-East Asia and presumably many other cultures, the concept of **'praxis'** is a better fit. So it is not assumed that social work practice follows the same patterns in all parts of the world. There are a few thoughts of social work practitioners from different perspectives across the globe in terms of social work approaches and contexts of practice as well as the term globalization they have conceptualized, have been highlighted.

I am not an economist and I don't want to become an economist because they believe that development is economic growth, and I strongly disagree. I am a social worker and believe the success of development means their full participation of the people (Indonesia).

My theoretical and ideological orientation is for participation of the population in the decisions affecting their lives, for the achievement of full citizenship—something far from reality in countries with non-democratic governments (Brazil).

We believe in working with people to empower them to participate actively in defending their rights. We are working in an environment that is severely affected by a history of conflict and struggle for essential human rights. After years of living under occupations, we are stepping to a new period of peace and great hopes for better life (Palestine).

My ideological orientation is Marxist while assimilating useful ideas from other contemporary theories (Cuba).

In offering counselling services to families from immigrant and minority communities; the approaches used are: (a) the transcultural approach, sometimes using ethno-psychiatry, (b) the feminist approach. But the concept of family is always integrated in my interventions (Canada).

The above responses have clearly reflected that social work values and ethics holds true as social workers around the world deal with the impact of globalization. Respect and appreciation for differences, commitment to social justice and well-being of all in society, as well as evidence of a willingness to persist, despite the frustration that we are sure to encounter in trying to address globalization, were present in almost all the responses.

In terms of **globalization**, it is described as an economic, social, cultural, political and environmental issue of central importance to their practice of social work.

Globalization is a process of converting producers in Third World countries into consumers through a capitalist economic process (Sri Lanka).

Globalization is the process of 'worldwide unification' of economic, social, political and cultural orientation through a borderless society thereby losing the country's indigenous cultural orientation (Philippines).

Such perception clearly implies the growth of poverty—or at the least; inequality and social workers often find themselves addressing the consequences of such social conditions. There are other comments on globalization which all positively reflect the brighter aspects of globalization.

Through globalization the world has in fact become smaller, more accessible to us in many different areas. Opportunities to exchange, complete work together in partnership in various fields (Canada).

Globalization as a process in which geographic distances and borders are less and less important. Through new technologies, new relationships and networks are created leading to economic, political and social opportunities. Communications becomes easy, efficient and instantaneous (United States).

In the course of discussion, the following statements reflect that while there are serious threats involved in the current manifestation of globalization as dominated by multinational corporations and international investors, the idea of increased communication and cooperation between people and communities offers possibilities for social workers resisting the negative effects of globalization.

Globalization for me has two conflicting interests: easy communication and exchange of experiences and research findings in all professional fields on one side; and lack of balance when being exposed to the influences and interests of the super powers (Palestine).

In one context (globalization) can be described as a view of the world as one large village which provides remarkable opportunities to learn about the varying inhabitants and their social, economic and political issues and organizations. In another context it can be viewed as an imposition of values, ideologies and beliefs of larger stronger industrial nations on smaller, weaker and developing and underdeveloped nations (Jamica).

Social Workers' use of International Conventions on Social, Political and Economic Rights

United Nations (UN) and other international conventions are important advocacy tools for social workers around the world. Standards that come with globalization such as human rights protection and environmental concerns will definitely positively impact social work practice (Yan, 2001). These conventions represent the difficult efforts to find universal standards for social, political and economic while allowing for some cultural difference in interpretation.

Perhaps in response to the internationalization of economics and of social issues, there also seems to be a rising awareness of the possible applications of these conventions. A good number of social work practitioners from different parts of the world have expressed their views that such conventions are aiding them in their practice or at least contributed to a better practice environment.

International conventions can be used by social workers to add moral weight to their work, as well as to break down activist isolation in demanding change. Such conventions can prove useful in many number of fields. There are challenges of globalization such as pollution, disease, crime and terrorism brought on by expanded trade and investment. Social workers must strive to see that governments, businesses and organizations respond to global opportunities in an ethical manner (Nichols-Casebolts, 2004).

International standards are welcomed by all the social workers all-over the world and believe that the requirements of international funding agencies to address basic social problems (for example sanitation, education, public health) can have a positive effect on standards of living in countries where ideology, corruption, or conflicting external constraints might otherwise discourage action.

So, the author urges that the profession must address the issue of promoting equitable societies in the global economy of the 21st century and address their various forms of social injustices. The promotion of the implementation of measures in line with UN charters on rights would aid social workers in this pursuit.

International social work

Social work is a profession whose primary mandate is the development and delivery of a broad range of social welfare policy and human services in the public and private sectors. Midgley (2002) defines it simply as exchanges between social workers from different societies and cultures. Others refer to as a field of practice within the social work profession that is primarily concerned with social work practice between nations or cultural groups, as well as practice in international social service organizations. As such, it has explicit goals and objectives but can be expected to vary among nations and cultures because of their different histories, situations, and needs. Sanders (1999) suggests that social welfare and social work must be considered together because one implies the other. He defines international social welfare as the arena of activity for human resource development efforts, services, and activities of governments and private organizations that cut across national boundaries and are designed to control or contribute to the meeting of human needs and their resolutions of social problems.

There are a plethora of reasons why international social work is so important in today's context and especially when we refer social work as a practicing profession:

- An international cross-cultural social welfare education can broaden one's horizons about alternative economic, political, and social welfare systems.
- A cross-cultural emphasis helps one to understand and appreciate diverse cultures from other countries, but also to gain added insight about one's own values, ideologies, and cultural preferences.
- An international approach exposes one to divergent thinking so that one can view social policies and services more critically and in a comparative perspective because there usually are alternative options.
- Cross-national collaboration between social workers and other human service professionals opens up many possibilities for innovation and change. Given the many serious problems that face the world, international collaboration is essential if we are to have any possibility of success.

Programmes in international social work have potential to enhance the profession in a variety of ways. Briefly, let's have a glimpse over it.

Knowledge development

Development of knowledge is the primary goal of any profession. So, the disciplinary aspects of international social work address the development and testing of knowledge that is useful for policy and practice in the international arena. Innumerable possibilities for comparative research and theorizing seek to identify conceptual dimensions and relationships that cut across societies/nations, which vary in their economies, polities, cultures, demographic and geographic characteristics, histories, and forces that influence stabilization and destabilization (Estes, 2003). Comparative social welfare research to date has been wide ranging, covering various aspects of social policies and services, but the knowledge gained provides insight that is useful in education, policy development, and planning, as well as in programme evaluation (Balbo and Nowotny, 1990; Dixon and Macarov, 1992).

Education

The development of an international and comparative perspective is desirable for all BSW and MSW graduates, argues (Boehm, 2003) because most problems that social workers address can no longer be viewed exclusively in national terms. Such an approach would require that courses which focus on social welfare and the profession of social work must indicate commitment to international affairs. There also needs to be a focus on global and regional influences on social welfare and social work. Education can take place collaboratively among nations, including practical training, exchanges, and work in international agencies.

Research

Cross-national collaborations in applied research, development, consultation, and action are presently under way in many areas and are providing knowledge for application within and between countries. When such research recognizes and respects local needs, values, institutions, and practices, it has the potential for creating the foundations for more effective social institutions throughout the world.

Social problems of globalization

Globalization has given birth of unaccountable social problems along with plethora of opportunities. Although international events have always impinged on the lives of ordinary people, the process of globalization is now having a major impact around the world. Globalization has been appreciated by some; it has been condemned by others. Although some welcome the growing interdependence of economies, nations, and cultures, others reject the view that increased internationalization has positive implications for humanity. The trends towards globalization have been accompanied by new social problems that social work profession needs to address. The globalization has also opened up many avenues of opportunities for social work profession to expand its knowledge base, improve its practice skills, and enhance its development as a profession. Let us first deal with the *problems* and later to talk about the *opportunities*.

- As the global economy has expanded; the incidence of poverty and deprivation in many parts of the world has increased (World Bank, 2001). Whereas some nations, particularly in Eastern Asia, have benefited from the expansion of the global economy, many people in the world's poorest nations have been left behind, and the incidence of absolute poverty in many African, Asian, and Central and South American countries has increased.
- The expansion of global economy has been substantiated with the problem of structural adjustment (Watkins, 2005). It refers to the policies adopted at the prompting of the International Monetary Fund and World Bank by developing countries with seeking international credit to stabilize their economies.
- The concomitant effects of structural adjustment are trade liberalization, increased deregulation, and retrenchments in public expenditures. In addition,

many middle and low income families in the industrial countries have also suffered as a result of economic globalization.

- Unemployment has been another issue accompanied by family disintegration, poverty, despair, violence, and drug abuse. Whereas multinational firms and investors in the centres of global economic power have enjoyed unprecedented prosperity, incomes for many ordinary people have stagnated.
- Globalization has also fostered increased ethnic conflict and violence in many parts of the world. This problem is related to the growth of migration, but it is also a function of the tensions accompanying economic, political, and social integration. Entire nations are now experiencing massive suffering, and large numbers of families and even whole communities have been dislocated.
- Globalization has also created massive new population movements, which have resulted in dislocation and problems of cultural adaptation and acceptance. Problems such as the exploitation of women migrants (particularly in domestic service), the harsh treatment of illegal migrants, and the growing attachment of racist sentiments to social policy issues affecting migrants are also areas of concern (United Nations, 2001).
- The global refugee problem may not be a new one, but it now exists on a huge scale as an outcome of enormous globalization process (United Nations, 2001).

Opportunities of globalization

- Globalization offers new opportunities for social work to expand its knowledge base. By engaging more actively in international activities, social work educators can enhance their understanding of pressing contemporary social problems. Problems such as AIDS, homelessness, substance abuse, and child neglect have critical; international dimensions that, if properly understood, can provide deeper insights into etiological and related issues.

- Comparative research allows hypotheses to be tested more widely and promotes a more accurate conceptual knowledge base within the profession.
- Globalization can also facilitate social work's efforts to enhance its own professional development. Greater international contacts will contribute to a greater shared identity among social workers, improved opportunities for collaboration, and a greater commitment to respond collectively to the challenges of an independent world. The instruments like International Federation of Social Workers, Associations of Schools of Social Work, European Association of Social Workers need to be augmented (Healy, 1995).

Responding to the challenges

- Indeed, social work has benefited from international exchanges from its very beginning. The emergence of case work and settlement work as prime social work practice methods in the United States at the end of 19th century owed much to British innovations. Similarly, the writings of American social workers as well as Indian in the early 20th century were widely adopted in Britain and in other parts of the world where social work was emerging as a profession. By the 1980s, social work profession was well established internationally in both the Western industrial countries and the nations of the Third World. Following the collapse of Soviet communism, social work spread to regions where the profession was previously unknown.
- Despite these achievements, social work is not fully prepared to respond to the challenges and opportunities of globalization. Greater efforts are needed to ensure that the profession is able to address the pressing social problems associated with globalization. Similarly, much more needs to be done to ensure that social work fully exploits the

opportunities afforded by increased internationalization.

- It requires that social work enhance its efforts to inculcate an international outlook among its students and that practitioners become more aware of the way international events affect their daily practice. Steps need to be taken to improve international exchanges and encourage social workers to become more involved in the activities and programmes of international agencies. Only in this way social work will be able to respond to the demands of an emerging global society in the new century.
- Another way of internationalization of social work is through the engagement of social workers in international agencies. More needs to be done to increase the participation of professionals in these arenas. However, employment opportunities of this kind are only likely to become available when the profession has demonstrated it in personnel with the requisite knowledge and skills, and when the profession's commitment to internationalism is more widely recognized and appreciated.
- Promoting international professional cooperation plays an obvious role in fostering international awareness in social work, but care must be taken to ensure that international exchanges are truly reciprocal.
- Social workers in the industrial countries are able to benefit from the extensive experience of their Third World colleagues with developmental forms of social work. This approach offers an exciting opportunity for the profession to transcend conventional remedial and maintenance-based approaches and to engage in forms of practice that address pressing material needs by promoting economic growth.
- A good example of the positive exchange of international professional experience is provided in the account by Martinez-Brawley and Deleven (2000) of a project that involve the transfer of practice innovations

from England to the United States. The British "patch" model of social work practice was really helpful to the needs of rural social work in United States. It is basically decentralization of public social services to small, local, community-based teams of social work practitioners who become intimately familiar with the people and with the neighbourhoods in which they work.

- Efforts should be made to modify the social work course curriculum where international social work components are enormously emphasized. The Council of Social Work Education in United States, India and other countries are taking this initiative and recognize the importance of including appropriate content to increase students' awareness of international issues.
- Efforts are being made to enhance international awareness in the arena of professional practice. Although evidence shows that practitioners are more interested in international social work than before, few are able to link international events to their everyday practice. Many of the problems social workers deal with are directly related to the trend toward globalization.
- Greater effort is also needed to strengthen the activities of the international professional associations. There are a few international professional associations which are continuously trying their best to uphold the profession for promoting greater international awareness and engagement in the profession. The tragic part is that all these types of associations are suffering from financial and organizational support and as a result their activities are not widely published. These associations and organizations are to be strengthened if social work profession has to encounter the process of globalization.

Conclusion

Globalization is affecting social work practice around the world. It has increased social problems, but also increased opportunities for international cooperation.

If social workers do indeed accept the challenge to co-operate across national boundaries and build this solidarity, then we may be able to make visible the human effects of economic globalization and effectively resist its negative effects. Kaseke (2002) urges social workers to tackle economic problems and to work to create social safety nets that feature equitable redistribution of income on the national, as well as the international level. Casework addressing individual problems remains important to people's on-going well-being but ultimately, social workers must support social development in order to reduce poverty and inequality. Economic globalization internationalizes certain elements of intersocietal exchanges without addressing the consequences of imbalances in power, resources and quality of life (Mohan, 2005). As social workers, our mandate is to work to address these negative consequences and resist their imposition.

One thing is clear, in this context of rapid change; many practitioners agree that the traditional dichotomies of macro/micro social work or of international/domestic issues must be set aside. The various levels of social work intervention cannot be fully understood or addressed in isolation from each other. If we as social workers are to live up to our values of working in the interest of society's disadvantaged—or as is increasingly urged, working toward social development—then we must begin to cooperate in efforts to counteract the negative impacts of globalization and take full advantage of its opportunities.

SUGGESTED READINGS

1. Abbott, A. (2002). "Boundaries of social work or social work boundaries?"; *Social Service Review*, 69, 545-562.
2. Barclay, H.H. (2006). "Validating tortured refugees: reconnection in social work policy and practice"; *International Social Work*, 41 (2), 211-26.
3. Balbo, L., and Nowotny, H. (1990). *Time to care in tomorrow's welfare systems.* Vienna: European Centre for Social Welfare.
4. Boehm, W. (2003). International and comparative social work in the undergraduate and graduate curriculum. In D. Sanders and P.

Pedersor (Eds.), *Education for international social welfare*. Honolulu: University of Hawaii Press.

5. Dixon, J., Macarov, D. (1992). *Social Welfare in a Socialist Country*. London: Routledge.
6. Estes, R. (2003). *Trends in the world social development: The social progress of nation, 1970-1978*. New York: Praeger.
7. Healy, L. (1995). "International social welfare: Organizations and activities". In R. Edwards *et al.* (Eds.). *Encyclopaedia of social work*.19th edition (pp.1499-1510). Washington, DC: NASW Press.
8. Kaseke, A.S. (2002). *The work of nations*, New York: Alfred Knopf.
9. Midgley, J. (2002). "International social work: Learning from the Third World"; *Social Work*, 35:4, 295-306.
10. Mohan, B.S. (2005). *Social development: The developmental perspective in social work*. Thousand Oaks, CA: Sage.
11. Martinez-Brawley, E.E., and Delevan, S.M. (2000). *Transfering technology in the personal social services*. Washington, DC: NASW Press.
12. Nichols-Casebolt, A. (2004). "The povertization of women: A global phenomenon"; *Affilia*, 9 (1), 9-29.
13. Payne, M. (2001). "Why social work? Comparative perspectives on social issue and response formation"; *International Social Work*, 41 (4), 443-453.
14. Sanders, D. (1999). "Developing a graduate social work curriculum with an international cross-cultural perspective". In D. Sanders and P. Pederson (Eds.), *Education for International Social Welfare*, Hawaii: University of Hawaii Press, 10-20.
15. Tsang, N.M. (2007). "Beyond theory and practice integration in social work: lessons from the West"; *International Social Work*, 41 (2), 169-180.
16. United Nations (2001). *Report on the world social situation*, New York.
17. Verschelden, C. (2005). "Social work values and Pacificism: Opposition to war as a professional responsibility"; *Social Work*, 38 (6), 765-769.
18. Watkins, K. (2005). *The Oxfam poverty report*. Oxford: Oxfam.
19. World Bank (2001). *World development report*, Washington, DC.
20. Yan, M.C. (2001). "Social functioning discourse in a Chinese context: developing social work in mainland China"; *'nternational Social Work*, 41 (2), 181-194.

Index